Developing Distributed and E-commerce Applications

Pearson
Education

We work with leading authors to develop the
strongest educational materials in computing,
bringing cutting-edge thinking and best learning
practice to a global market.

Under a range of well-known imprints, including
Addison-Wesley, we craft high quality
print and electronic publications which help
readers to understand and apply their content,
whether studying or at work.

To find out more about the complete range of our
publishing please visit us on the World Wide Web at:
www.pearsoneduc.com

Developing Distributed and E-commerce Applications

Second edition

Darrel Ince

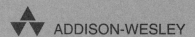

ADDISON-WESLEY

An imprint of **Pearson Education**

Harlow, England · London · New York · Boston · San Francisco · Toronto · Sydney · Singapore · Hong Kong
Tokyo · Seoul · Taipei · New Delhi · Cape Town · Madrid · Mexico City · Amsterdam · Munich · Paris · Milan

Pearson Education Limited
Edinburgh Gate
Harlow
Essex CM20 2JE

and Associated Companies throughout the world

Visit us on the World Wide Web at:
www.pearsoneduc.com

First published 2002
Second edition 2004

ISBN 0 321 15422 3

British Library Cataloguing-in-Publication Data
A catalogue record for this book is available from the British Library

Library of Congress Cataloging-in-Publication Data
Ince, D. (Darrel)
    Developing distributed and E-commerce applications / Darrel Ince.–2nd ed.
        p. cm.
    ISBN 0-321-15422-3 (pbk)
        1. Electronic data processing–Distributed processing.   2. Application software–Development.
    3. Electronic commerce–Computer programs.   I. Title.
    QA76.9.D5 I525 2003
    005.1–dc21   2002032966

10 9 8 7 6 5 4 3 2 1
06 05 04

Typeset by 35 in 10/12$\frac{1}{2}$ pt Minion
Printed and bound in the United States of America

Trademark notice

The following designations are trademarks or registered trademarks of the organisations whose
names follow in brackets:
Active Server Pages, Enterprise JavaBeans, Java, Javamail, JavaSpaces, Java Web Server
(Sun Microsystems Inc); Aelfred (Open Text Corp.); Amazon (Amazon.co.uk); Apache (Apache Foundation);
DCOM*, Internet Explorer, Microsoft Outlook, Windows (Microsoft®); Coca-Cola (The Coca-Cola Company);
Eudora* (QualComm Inc); Fujitsu Stylistic (Fujitsu); Linux (Linus Torvalds); Listerine (Warner Lambert);
Lotus Notes (Lotus Corporation), Maple (Adept Scientifica plc); Mathematica (Wolfram Research);
MQSeries (IBM); Netscape Navigator (AmericaOnline Time Warner); UNIX (AT & T); Symantec,
Visual Café Programming (Symantec).

Brief Contents

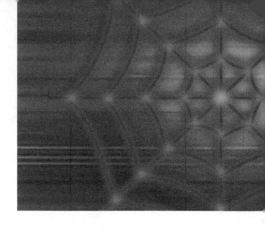

Contents

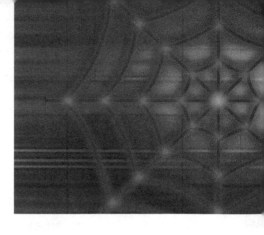

Preface

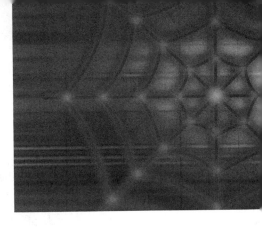

The first edition of this book had its genesis in a book I started writing in 1999 and never finished. The book was about distributed systems: their architectures, their components and how they are deployed. I decided to abandon the effort, although some of the original material can be found embedded within this book. My decision was made for two reasons: first, there are a number of good books on distributed systems, for example the book written by Coulouris *et al*. [1], and I felt that to better them would take me a considerable amount of time; and, second, and almost certainly the more important reason, that distributed applications – particularly those associated with e-business and e-commerce – were becoming increasingly important.

This book is about developing applications using the facilities provided by distributed system software; in particular those facilities offered by the Internet. The book is introductory. If you are looking for a broad overview of the subject then I would hope that you would consider this book. If you are looking for a detailed treatment of a particular topic, for example XML, then this is not the book for you; there are excellent books published by Wrox and O'Reilly and others, which run to many hundreds of pages.

I have targeted this book at two audiences. The first is undergraduates studying a computing or IT course at a university. There is a paucity of good texts which introduce distributed applications and I hope this one fills the gap. The second audience is that of staff in industry who are thinking of moving into the new areas described by this book, for example staff working in real-time computing who are increasingly required to interface their systems with Internet-based applications.

There are a number of features of the book (which comes with a CD that contains its text, the exercises and Web links) such as:

- There is a series of programming exercises dotted throughout the book. You will find a brief outline of these exercises in the margins of the appropriate page. The text of the exercises together with the supporting software can be found on the CD which comes with the book. Most of these exercises require a small amount of programming and provide a sort of proof of concept of the technologies detailed in the book.

- There is a series of Web links displayed in the margins of the book. These links will take you to a further collection of links on a particular topic, for example XML. I have carefully chosen these links so that, in the main, they point at introductory and tutorial material which the reader can use to supplement and extend the basic material found in the book. I estimate that there are something like 700 links associated with the book.

- There are also many tinted boxes and marginal notes and these act as a form of footnote where material not directly relevant to the text but of an interesting nature can be found.

- There is a major case study which appears as Chapter 17. This describes the use of the majority of technologies detailed in the book applied to an e-commerce application: that of a company selling an item of software. You can access this case study in two ways. You can either read through the first 16 chapters and then read the case study, doing the exercises associated with it, or you can access chunks of the case study after reading a particular chapter. A marginal note at the end of the chapter will direct you forward to the relevant section of Chapter 17.

- A set of Powerpoint slides are available to help the instructor to associate lectures and class discussions to material in the textbook. They can be found at *www.booksites.net*.

I have chosen the programming language Java as the medium for discussing many of the technologies. I make no apology for this: in a few years it has become the main Internet programming language and the language of choice as an introductory programming language within our universities. Anyone with a basic knowledge of Java picked up from an industrial training course or a first-year undergraduate course will gain maximum advantage from the book.

The second edition reflects the changes that have occurred in the short period since the first edition was printed. It also includes material suggested by the many lecturers who have adopted the book for their teaching.

Darrel Ince
Milton Keynes, 2002

Reference

[1] G. Coulouris, J. Dollimore and T. Kindberg, *Distributed Systems Concepts and Design*. Harlow: Addison-Wesley, 2001.

Acknowledgements

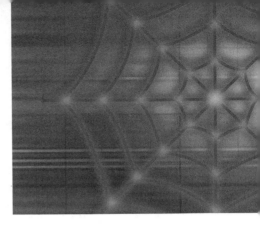

We are grateful to the following people for permission to reproduce copyright material:

Figure 1.2 reprinted with the permission of *Which?*, published by the COnsumers' Association, 2 Marylebone Road, London, NW1 4DF, for further information please phone 0800 252 100; Figure 1.3 request for permission approved by Google Marketing Department, USA; Figure 6.2 copyright granted on behalf of Delia Smith by Deborah Owen, 78 Narrow Street, London E14 8BP; Figure 6.9 http://www.useit.com this websit is copyright © by Jakob Nielsen. All rights reserved; Figure 9.1 from W. Emmerlich, *Engineering Distributed Objects*, © 2000 and reproduced by permission of John Wiley & Sons Limited; Figure 16.1 http://www.uk.research.att.com reprinted with the permission of Prof. Andrew Hopper, MD of AT & T Labs, University of Cambridge, Department of Engineering.

In some instances we have been unable to trace the owners of copyright material, and we would appreciate any information that would enable us to do so.

An Introduction to E-commerce and Distributed Applications

1

Chapter contents

This is an introductory chapter which examines the type of system which is described by the umbrella term 'e-commerce'. A number of typical application areas are examined including retailing using the Internet, supply chain management and online auctions. The chapter also looks at some of the underlying technologies used to implement e-commerce applications, for example Web technology. The final part of the chapter looks at some of the problems which are encountered when developing distributed e-commerce systems, for example problems in ensuring that a system is kept secure from criminal activity. This part of the book acts as an introduction to a number of the concepts that are described in detail in later chapters. It concludes with an examination of a typical retailing system, how some of the technologies described in the book fit together and business models used in the Internet.

Aims

1. To detail what is meant by the term 'e-commerce'.
2. To examine some typical distributed applications.
3. To detail some of the problems that are encountered when developing distributed applications.
4. To describe briefly some of the technologies that are used to support distributed applications.
5. To show how some of the technologies detailed in the book are used in concert to realise a typical commercial system.
6. To describe some of the business models used in the Internet.

Concepts

Anonymous remailer, B2B exchange, Browser, Checkout page, Common Gateway Interface, Cookie, Day trading, Denial of service attack, Design pattern, Disintermediation, Distributed objects, Dynamic pages, Dynamic pricing, E-auction, E-learning, E-mail server, E-mall, E-procurement, E-shop, E-tailing, File Transfer Protocol, Framework, Horizontal portal, Hyperlink, Hypertext Mailer, Hypertext Markup Language, Information brokerage, Java, Online trading, Portal, Posting, Procurement, Query, Rapid application development, Search engine, Secure Sockets Layers, Server Side Includes, Servlet, Shopping cart, Spam, Spider, Stateless server, Supply chain, Third party marketplace, Thread, Trust brokerage, Vertical portal, Virtual community, Web page, Web server, Web site, Webmaster.

1 Introduction

The past four years have seen an amazing growth of interest in distributed systems which address the business needs of companies and which use network technology – primarily the technology employed in the Internet. In that period newspapers, magazines and even government pronouncements have frequently mentioned the huge business prospects for companies who embrace Internet technologies. There is now a burgeoning literature on e-commerce aimed at the business person and the manager and a thriving industry of book publishing on specific technologies, for example [1]; however, there is little published on how to combine the various technologies that are available to *design* and *implement* e-commerce systems.

Internet jargon

Frankenedits

The Internet floats on a mountain of jargon and acronyms. Frankenedit is an example of jargon. It is used by writers on Internet topics and technologies who are often bullied or bribed by their publishers to write a book on specific technologies quickly in order to be the first to market. A frankenedit is what happens when such an author sends a book to a publisher for rapid editing and it returns in a worse condition than when it was sent.

1.1 What this book is about

This book is about the development of electronic commerce systems using the new technologies that have emerged or have matured over the last five years, technologies such as CORBA, Web servers, HTML, XML and Java.

Replicated databases are copies of the same database held in different parts of a distributed system. I shall be looking at this topic in more detail in Chapter 14

It is worth differentiating this book from others that have been published on distributed systems; this is a useful exercise since it puts into focus the agenda that I wish to develop. There are a number of books with the words *Distributed System* in their title. Most of these books deal with technologies which support the development of e-commerce systems. My favourite is [2] which deals with the technological infrastructure of distributed systems; this book contains an excellent description of how replicated databases are organised in a distributed system and how they are kept in step when transactions are applied to one of their number. Fortunately, for the developer, there are no requirements for an understanding of these techniques: there are many excellent products in the marketplace which administer replicated databases. There is, however, a requirement for the developer to use the products developed using the techniques and to design systems which take account of their characteristics.

My book is motivated by a distinction between what happens *under* the bonnet of the car and what happens in the car: it is not about how processes such as data replication work or how a distributed operating system is structured; it is about how to use such technologies to develop systems which are distributed over a number of computers and which are connected by means of the TCP/IP suite of protocols. This is the key to the title of the book and to what follows.

It is also worth differentiating this book from the small number of books which have been published on developing e-commerce applications. Such books deal with the technological skills required for relatively simple e-commerce applications such as those found in retailing where a Web server is placed in front of some collection of databases. This book looks at these applications, but also looks at many more challenging application areas, for example applications which involve the development of distributed systems which span continents and where major problems in performance and reliability need to be solved.

A typical example of such an application follows later in this chapter when supply chain processing is described

1.2 The audience for this book

The prime audience for this book is students in institutions of higher education – usually those studying for a degree which has a high computing content. Typically such students will have completed an initial year of basic computing which includes a high proportion of programming and are either studying distributed systems or are about to embark on a course which deals with the development of distributed systems. Usually these types of courses are offered in the second or third year of a computing or business studies degree.

I have deliberately written a book which is suitable for self-study. So, for example, if you are a developer who, perhaps, has been working with technology which is becoming dated and wish to transfer your skills to the distributed arena then I would hope that you would find this book an excellent introduction to the development of distributed systems. In writing this book I have drawn on many of the skills I have learned from working for the British Open University, the largest university in the United Kingdom and the largest distance education university in the world.

The Open University

One feature of the book is that it also exists in an electronic form: this can be found on the CD in the inside back cover. There are a number of motivations for this. The first is that the book contains a number of implementation exercises, for example you will be asked to develop a simple e-mail utility, a simple naming service and a small e-commerce system. By having the book in this form it enables you to download easily the program code required to carry out the exercises. A second motivation is that it will enable you to search the text more easily. A third arises from the fact that, increasingly, computing and business courses are being offered online or being planned to be offered online. For example, the British government recently announced an e-university initiative which will bring British quality higher education to a world audience via the World Wide Web.

The British e-university initiative

1.3 The features of the book

In the main this book is conventionally written; however, there are a number of features which are not normally found in educational texts:

■   There are a number of shaded text boxes which deal with material which is interesting, but not *directly* relevant to the aims of a chapter. You have already met one on page 2. For example, some of the boxes contain case studies, some contain large but interesting digressions and others contain descriptions of specific technology. I hope that you will read these as they break up the text into nicely digestible pieces and provide a form of pedagogic punctuation mark.

∎   In the margin you will find a number of occurrences of an icon showing a spider's Web adorned with some text. This is a reference to a Web page which contains further material that you might like to study. For example, in the next chapter I briefly describe the history of the Internet. Near this description you will find a spider's Web icon which directs you to a page which contains links to a number of documents that detail the history of the Internet and the World Wide Web. You can follow these links by browsing the electronic version of the book.

∎   You will find some commentary text in the margin of the pages. This text is similar to that found in the shaded boxes. However, it is much smaller and acts very much like a footnote.

∎   You will find references to programming exercises. There are quite a large number of these in the book. Each exercise is associated with a particular topic detailed in a chapter and will contain a lot of pre-written code; you will be asked to complete the implementation of the exercise. You can link to these exercises by browsing the electronic version of the text.

1.4 The technology used in the book

*Introductory material
on Java on the Web*

This book uses the **Java** programming language. There are two reasons for this. The first is that most students who study computing courses are taught Java, either as a first or second programming language. The second reason is that Java has the greatest number of clean hooks into a number of important distributed technologies, for example the CORBA distributed object technology and Web server technology. The exercises were all written using the JBuilder Programming environment; however, since Java is an excellent language for interoperability they can all be implemented on other platforms. Each programming exercise will consist of a little teaching of technology and will provide you with the data files and subsidiary source code required to carry out the exercise.

The book will not be teaching any of the basic facilities of Java; if you are hazy about the language or want to learn its elements then the best teaching book has been written by Ivor Horton [3].

1.5 Commerce and the Internet

There are a number of ways in which companies can make money from the Internet. Probably the best known way of making money is by selling some commodity; this could be a non-IT commodity such as a CD or item of clothing or it could be some piece of application software, a font, a browser plug-in or an operating system. Other forms of revenue raising are:

- *Auction sites* which auction items on the Internet and make profits by taking some commission from the sales.

- *Affiliate sites* which contain a link to a normal retailing site and are paid when a visitor from the affiliate site makes a visit to the retail site to make a purchase. The affiliate site will usually attract visitors by offering some information such as providing links to resources and tutorials on some specific topic or technology such as Java.

- *Banner adverts.* These adverts will contain links to the company doing the advertising; they will be displayed on a site and will result in some revenue being earned by the site owner when the banner advert is clicked.

- *Bulk-buying sites* where a site collects a number of users together all of whom want to buy some item; the site negotiates a discount with the supplier and takes a commission.

E-commerce

- *Shopping malls* where a number of e-commerce sellers congregate together on the same Web site; often these sellers will be related to each other, for example they may all sell luxury goods. The mall owner takes a percentage of their profit.

- *Portals* which contain massive amounts of material on a particular topic, for example a portal devoted to fishing. Such sites will contain thousands of resource links, tutorials and indexes. They will also contain links to merchants who sell goods associated with the portal topic. There may be a number of ways that the portal owner would make money, for example they could be paid by a merchant for each visit from the portal or the merchant may pay a flat fee for being included in the portal.

- *Digital publishing sites* which are effectively magazines on the Web. They make profits in a number of ways including advertising and charging vendors for references to their Web site.

- *Licensing sites* which make some software available to other sites, for example search engines which allow a visitor to the site to search for material more easily.

- *Community sites.* These are like portals but involve the visitors more, for example a community site devoted to nurses might include a number of chat rooms which allow nurses to talk together in real time and swap advice. Money is made from such sites in the same way as with portals.

This form of partially free charging has percolated down from the Internet to conventional software sales; for example, the company Qualcomm that markets the *Eudora* e-mail reader makes a version of the program available for

- *Name-your-price sites* are Web sites where the buyer haggles with the retailer and names what price they will pay for a particular product. Such sites make profits in the same way as normal retail sites.

Such applications have changed the face of retailing, for example the fast communication of the Internet has made bulk buying sites feasible and popular and has given rise to a number of novel commercial models. The most popular model is one which involves a pyramid of services, ranging from those that are free, to those which are charged at a premium rate. For example, a site which sells a piece of software might

no cost, but will charge for fully featured versions

give the basic software away for free and then offer increasingly more sophisticated versions of the software to buyers.

2 E-commerce applications

Before looking at the wide variety of e-commerce application areas that have flourished over the last decade in more detail, it is worth looking at one which may not be familiar to a reader, but which saves companies huge amounts of resources. The application involves a **supply chain**. A supply chain is a set of relationships between a number of companies who have a symbiotic relationship with each other in that one company supplies commodities or services to other companies which, in turn, supply commodities or services to other companies, and so on.

2.1 An example – supply chain management

The example was originally described by Kalakota and Robinson [4] in their excellent management introduction to e-commerce. It concerns the processes involved in getting a bottle of Listerine mouthwash to the shelves of a retail chemist. It consist of the following steps:

Supply chain management and the Internet

- In Australia a farmer sells his or her eucalyptus crop to a processing company that extracts the eucalyptus oil from the leaves.

- The oil is then sold to a distributor in New Jersey.

- At the same time as the eucalyptus oil is being extracted natural gas is being drilled in the Saudi Arabian desert in order to produce the alcohol that is added to the raw ingredients of the mouthwash.

- Union Carbide ships the alcohol to Texas City, Texas, where the company that manufactures the mouthwash (Warner Lambert) has its factory.

- Farmers in the mid-west of America grow corn which is used in the manufacture of Sorbitol which both sweetens and adds bulk to the mouthwash. This is harvested and sent to the factory in Texas City.

- The ingredients are mixed and the mouthwash manufactured.

An important point about an application such as this one is that information should be kept confidential as it flows across the Internet. This is a topic described in Chapter 11

- The final bottles of mouthwash are sent to wholesalers or to the warehouses of chains of chemists from where they are distributed to individual retail outlets.

Figure 1.1 shows the information flows in this supply chain. This is an example of a **supply chain**. It represents a typical e-business application. There are a number of commercial imperatives for Warner Lambert: first, it should not overstock bottles of Listerine and incur costs because its resources are tied up in unsold goods; on the other hand, it should always stock enough bottles to satisfy demand in the time that

Figure 1.1
A typical supply chain

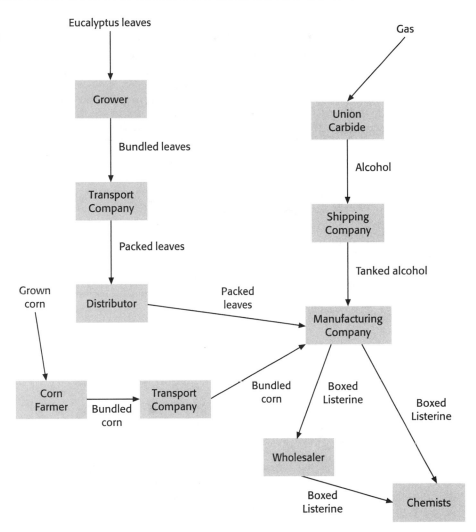

the reordering and replenishing processes can take place. Second it should be able to get as quick a response to an order for raw materials as possible. This requires every company in the supply chain to move quickly to process an order from a company which follows it in the chain. An empty warehouse would be a disaster for Warner Lambert. A third commercial imperative is for the elimination of waste bureaucracy and indirect connections between companies from the supply chain. This is again connected with responsiveness: the more paper that is used and the more companies have to communicate using devices such as e-mail the slower the process of reorder and replenishment will be. The ideal here is for a company higher up in the supply chain to share its data with companies further down the chain. For example, Warner Lambert should ideally be able to look at the stocks of the wholesalers and initiate a replenishment of those stocks when it discerns that they are becoming low – provided, of course, that some pre-agreement has been made about the quantities involved.

The mouthwash example is an e-business application

E-commerce and e-business

Internet terminology is still in a state of flux; nowhere is this more evident than in the past use of the terms *e-commerce* and *e-business*. Both have been used to describe any business activity which uses the Internet. However, some consensus is emerging in that the terms are gradually being employed in a more focused way. The term e-commerce is increasingly being used to describe online retailing, for example the use of the Web to sell books. The term e-business is increasingly being used to describe all business activities using the Internet, not just online retailing.

All these imperatives lead to one conclusion: the fact that each of the entities involved in the process of manufacturing the mouthwash should be connected together. Even the farmer should be able to communicate with the buyer of eucalyptus leaves by typing in crop yields using, say, wireless technology.

Connecting companies together using network technology is not new: companies such as Procter & Gamble have been leaders in this for years. However, the Internet provides an infrastructure which enables individuals and companies to connect using a technology whose details are open to all and which can be easily implemented on virtually every computer in existence. The Internet also provides a common interface to computing resources via a browser: everyone from the farmer in Australia to the manager of a retail chemist will be familiar with such technology and use it well.

A myth about e-commerce

One of the myths about e-commerce is that it is a comparatively recent phenomenon. Even in the early days of the Internet when connections between individual computers were achieved by hand dialling using a telephone, there were a number of Internet companies which had been set up to sell photographs and other graphic images of naked ladies and gentlemen. The earliest e-commerce applications were those associated with pornographers; indeed, a number of commentators have opined that the demands made upon the Internet by pornographers have speeded the development of a number of technologies such as streaming video and the deployment of new business models.

2.2 E-tailing

Amazon: the archetypal e-commerce company

The next example is probably the one that you expected me to introduce first: that of selling goods over the Internet. However, I deliberately introduced supply chain management first since it is an area where companies are making huge savings in their investment in Internet technology. The investments in retailing using the Internet (**e-tailing**) are only gradually being realised.

The archetypal e-tailing application is that of a bookseller such as Amazon. This company is renowned for the fact that it only sells books over the Internet and doesn't even take telephone orders. It has one of the best organised Web sites and is continually referred to by journalists as an e-commerce success story.

Customers of Amazon interact with its Web site and carry out a number of functions including:

- browsing readers' reviews of books;

- reading feature articles about books and authors similar to those found in magazines and newspapers;

- searching for details of a book based on information such as the author's name or the title of the book;

- browsing the books which are the Amazon bestsellers;

- ordering books using credit cards or some other similar payment method;

- tracking the progress of an order.

Behind the scenes of the Amazon site are a number of conventional functions which are found in all retailing applications, these include:

- *stock management*: keeping track of what books are in stock and ordering titles when stocks become low;

- *payment management*: paying suppliers of books for those that have been delivered;

- *customer payment management*: keeping track of payments made by customers and of payments made by credit card companies and banks which correspond to the customer payments;

- *delivery*: the process of sending books to customers;

- *market analysis*: the process of analysing sales in order to determine what books to order and which to discount in the future. This analysis occurs at both the customer level and at a temporal level in that customer preferences are processed and the times and dates when they express these preferences are analysed; for example, in order to answer questions such as what books sell well at Christmas or at Easter?

Retailing and the Internet

Most of these functions would be associated with any bookseller, irrespective of whether they use the Internet or not.

Another myth about e-commerce

One of the myths about e-commerce is that the development of e-commerce systems is radically different from other commercial systems. I would say that it is *somewhat* different in that you have to worry about many of the problems that occur with distributing processing in a network; however, many of the functions required in the majority of e-commerce systems can be found in their conventional counterparts. Indeed,

> many e-commerce systems which are fronted by Web servers still contain computers which were common ten years ago and are programmed in languages such as COBOL and C – languages which are not automatically associated with Internet software development. Much of the analyses required for an e-commerce system are the same that you would carry out for a conventional system and also quite a lot of the design; however, they do differ in that the design of such systems is a lot trickier, for example to guarantee response times from a collection of computers communicating over the Internet is a tough task.

2.3 Procurement

The term **procurement** is used to describe the purchase of goods and services which are not *directly* used in the main business of a company. For example, a car manufacturer will procure stationery for its employees or procure training courses for them to attend in order to improve their skills.

A typical conventional procurement process consists of a number of steps:

■ the person making the procurement expresses their need by typing in details of a requisition using either a computer-based or paper-based form;

■ the form is then dispatched to a member of staff who checks that it has been filled in correctly, that the amount is no larger than the amount that they are able to authorise and that there are sufficient funds available for purchase;

■ if the form is authorised then it is sent on to a member of staff who is concerned with the purchasing of the good or service that is required; they then fill in a purchase requisition and send it off to the company who supplies the item that is to be purchased. If the item is over the limit for authorisation, then it is sent to someone who can authorise greater amounts.

This is in contrast to an e-procurement system which would automatically take the form produced by the person making the procurement, check that it satisfies all the company rules for procuring the item that is required, carry out authorisation if it is below a certain limit or send the form to someone who can carry out authorisation and then log the purchaser into the site of the supplier. He or she is then able to use this site to make the purchase, quoting an automatically generated procurement requisition number.

Again this is not hugely different to a conventional automated procurement system; however, it does cut out a number of inefficiencies at the purchase requisition end by virtue of the fact that the purchaser of a good or service is able to interact directly via the Internet with the supplier. With procurement consuming as much as 10 per cent of a company's resources some large savings can be made by such an utilisation of e-commerce-based technology.

Another example of the myth detailed on the previous page

Microsoft and MSMarket

Microsoft discovered that 70 per cent of its purchases were for relatively small items which took up something of the order of 3 per cent of its purchase volume. The company discovered that a large amount of employee time was spent on the procurement process and hence invested $1.1m on a system known as *MSMarket*. When a Microsoft employee wishes to buy some item such as stationery they log into *MSMarket*, the system identifies them from their login identity and consults its database to discern what rules should be applied to purchases from that employee. The employee informs the system that they require some stationery and a screen of items and prices negotiated with a supplier are displayed. The employee purchases what is required and the order is sent over the Internet; an e-mail is then sent to their manager to inform them of this and a tracking number generated which can be used to query the supplier if the item has not been delivered by a certain time. The use of *MSMarket* has increased exponentially since it was deployed and it now handles more than $3 billion of orders.

2.4 Auction sites

Auctions on the Internet

These are sites on the Web which run conventional auctions. There are two types of auction: those that are carried out in real time, where participants log in to an auction site using a browser at a specified time and bid for an article until the highest price is reached and no other bids are forthcoming. The other type of site – and the most common – is where an item is offered for sale and a date advertised after which no more bids are accepted. Such sites make a profit from two sources: first they usually charge a commission on the items that are sold and, second, they display adverts which are viewed by visitors to the site. The auction site will then receive some fee for displaying the advert, a further fee if a visitor clicks on an advert and it takes them to the advertiser's Web site and another fee if they purchase something from this site. Again, this is just an online analogue of a conventional business.

Banner advertising and the Internet

2.5 Other commercial Web sites

So far I have detailed e-commerce applications which are connected with very large organisations; to conclude this section it is worth looking at a number of smaller applications, many of which are distinguished by the fact that they are novel. They are in contrast to the applications discussed in previous subsections which mainly consist of standard functions such as order processing.

eCoverage

eCoverage and disintermediation

An increasingly popular e-commerce enterprise which does not involve e-tailing is that of quote finding. For example, a number of companies have set up Web sites which enable you to get quotes on various types of insurance policies including those for car, property and life insurance. One of the pioneers in this area is *eCoverage* who provide online car insurance quotes and who boast that it can insure you in minutes. This is an example of a growing trend in e-commerce applications: the cutting out of intermediaries; in the case of insurance this is the insurance broker. This is a process known as **disintermediation**.

2.5.1 Anonymous remailers

*Spam, the curse
of the Internet*

An **anonymous remailer** is a Web site which enables you to send an e-mail anonymously to some recipient. The main reason for this is to do with something known as **spam**. This term describes unsolicited e-mail which tries to sell the recipient something.

If you have not met the
terms **Internet service
provider** and **news-
group** before do not
worry: they are
introduced later
in the chapter

Spam

Throughout the Internet you can find e-mail addresses. They can be found embedded in Web pages in the member's directories of Internet service providers and in newsgroups. There are a number of companies who use programs known as **spiders** or **address harvesters** to search the Internet for such addresses. These are then written to a file and sold to individuals and companies who then send bulk e-mails to the unlucky recipients. Often these e-mails are part of some crime such as selling bogus insurance policies. Spam is universally detested by Internet users. Its name is derived from the Monty Python sketch which takes place in a café where a number of Vikings rampage round the café repeatedly shouting out the words spam, spam, spam.

You log into the site and type any message that you want to send; it will then forward the message on to its recipient with a dummy e-mail address for the sender.

2.5.2 Link checking sites

Error 404 is a standard
message returned by
Web servers when a
non-existent page is
accessed. It is also
the telephone area
code for Atlanta in the
United States; you
will occasionally hear
technical staff referring
to non-existent Web
documents as having
'gone to Atlanta'

The World Wide Web contains millions of Web pages. Many of these pages are impossible to read, even though many existing Web pages will reference them: your browser will usually return with some message such as 'Error 404 Page not Found' when you try to access them. There are two main reasons why a Web document disappears from the World Wide Web: the first is that the developer or company might have deleted it, for example the company associated with the site has filed for bankruptcy or the individual who developed the site has moved it to another computer. The second reason is that the computer holding the Web document is currently malfunctioning or has been switched off.

A link checking site is one to which you submit the address of a Web page; it will store this address in a database and will then periodically check that the document is still accessible. If it discovers that a document is no longer available then it will e-mail the customer who asked for the site to keep an eye on the document.

This is the type of service that technical staff who look after a collection of Web documents find valuable; such staff, often known as **webmasters**, need to know very

*Some examples of
link checking sites*

The term webmaster is applied to both male and female staff, although the equivalent female term **webmistress** is very occasionally used

quickly when this happens. For example, the page that is no longer accessible could be the home page for a company that sells some goods through the Internet: having Web documents unavailable means that it effectively shuts the front door of the store to customers. Because speed in this case is essential a number of link checking sites offer webmasters a notification service via a customer's portable phone or pager.

2.5.3 Archive sites

These are Web sites which offer customers a facility for storing their files at a safe location. This guards against anything disastrous happening to the customer's computer and their losing valuable data. Often the files will be duplicated at a number of computers at different locations in order to guard against the possibility of one of the locations being affected by a natural disaster such as an earthquake, or a computer being affected by a catastrophic failure which results in its stored data being destroyed.

The user of such a site usually registers with it using a name and a password; they are then presented with a set of instructions which take them through the process of collecting their files together to send to the remote location.

2.5.4 Change notification sites

These sites are a variation on link checking sites. Here, the customer is notified not when a Web document becomes unavailable, but when the document is changed. For example, the customer might be interested in a particular page which advertises some holiday package offers to a particular destination and wants to keep abreast of any changes to the page which might signal the fact that a new improved offer has been added.

2.5.5 E-mail providers

These are sites which provide free e-mail facilities; often they provide other facilities such as sending anonymous mail and constructing mailing lists. Such sites are valuable to users who are too impecunious to be able to afford conventional mailing software and to frequent travellers who can access such sites anywhere in the world. Their main disadvantage is that they tend to be slow compared with conventional mailing utilities such as *Microsoft Outlook* and *Eudora*.

> ## B2B and B2C
>
> The Internet is awash with acronyms. Two acronyms used within e-commerce are B2B and B2C. The former stands for Business to (2) Business while the latter stands for Business to (2) Consumer. B2C is used to describe those business ventures which use Internet technology to sell goods and services to Internet users, for example the online selling of insurance policies is an example of B2C. B2B describes the use of the Internet for business transactions between companies, for example the holding of online auctions of bulk commodities such as crude oil. Current business thinking is that although B2C applications receive the most publicity it is the B2B applications which will have the biggest financial impact. There is also C2C (Company to

Company) which is business between companies, for example the use of a network when two companies join together in some commercial activity such as building a shopping complex. The acronym C2C is occasionally used to describe ventures where consumers interact together, for example bulk buying sites; in this case it stands for Consumer to (2) Consumer.

2.6 Search engines

Search engines and the Internet

The Web contains a huge amount of material. Finding specific information is a huge problem; even in the early days of the Internet this was a problem which threatened to slow the growth of the net. Fortunately a partial solution to this problem emerged: the **search engine**. This is a program which accesses a huge database of information about the World Wide Web; it contains individual words in Web documents and the location of the documents containing the words. When the user of a search engine wants to find any document they type a **query**: a series of keywords joined by Boolean connectives such as 'and' and 'or' or, in some cases, a natural language sentence. For example, the query

Java & compiler

would return with the addresses of all those Web documents which contain the words 'Java' and 'compiler'.

This is a description of those search engines which carry out automatic indexing. There are a few general search engines where the indexing is done manually by trained indexers. Two examples of this type of search engine are Yahoo and Ask Jeeves

In order to build up a search database the search engine will employ a program known as a **spider**. This will visit a Web site and access the Web documents stored there, keep track of the address of the documents and the words that are stored in them and update the search engine's database. Spiders will not visit Web sites randomly: they will only visit those sites whose developers inform the search engine they want them linked to the engine's database. A developer will interact with the search engine site by requesting and filling in a form; this form will normally just ask for the address of the document to be indexed and a contact e-mail address. After a few seconds the spider will visit the Web site and start the indexing process; usually, after a week or two, details of the Web site are added to the search engine's database.

Spamdexing

One of the tricks used by companies to make sure that their Web site is placed first when a search engine retrieves the results of a query is to include certain key words a large number of times in the Web documents in the site. For example, the word 'Java' repeated a large number of times will ensure that the site is displayed prominently when any search using this word takes place. This technique is known as spamdexing. Companies go to huge lengths to disguise spamdexing as search engine companies look upon the practice with huge disdain and will de-list any spamdexed pages. One technique that is used is to have a Web page displayed with a graphic that has a coloured background and write the repeated words in the same layer and in the same font as the background.

Search engines are big business on the Internet. They mainly make money by displaying banner adverts or sponsored links. There are a wide variety of search engines on the Internet ranging from those which catalogue any Web site to specialised search engines which catalogue Web sites which address a single area such as Shakespearean studies or the LINUX operating system.

3 The facilities of the Internet

Look at the topics in this section, you may be familiar with them; if so, then it is worth moving to the next section which describes problems with Internet-based software development

The aim of this section is to describe briefly the main facilities of the Internet that are used to support e-commerce and e-business systems.

3.1 The World Wide Web

The Web is nothing more than a collection of files stored at locations throughout the world. These files are written using a special language known as the **Hypertext Markup Language** (HTML). A file written using this language will contain text which forms the information content of the file, together with instructions which define how the text is to be displayed; for example, HTML contains a facility whereby blocks of text are specified to be displayed as bullet points.

In Chapter 6 you will learn more about HTML; in Chapter 7 you will develop some Web server programs

The user of the World Wide Web employs a program known as a **browser**. When the user wishes to read a file on the World Wide Web they will inform the browser of its address on the Web and the browser will fetch the file. The browser will then examine the contents of the page and will determine from the HTML in the file how it is to be displayed; for example, it might meet some HTML which switches the display of the material from one font to another font.

A file which is downloaded into a browser is known as a **Web page**. The computer that holds Web pages is known as a **Web server**. The collection of pages which are linked by some theme – for example, they may be pages which all belong to the same retail company – is known as a **Web site**.

Each page that is downloaded into a browser will have references to other pages expressed as **hyperlinks**. For example, a page belonging to a book retailer will have hyperlinks to the various sections of the site which deal with different types of books. Hyperlinks can refer to pages within the same site or can refer to pages within another site; for example, an online magazine might refer to other online magazines which are part of the same publisher's stable. Figure 1.2 shows a typical display from a browser. It represents a page from a site run by a British consumer organisation. There are hyperlinks embedded in the site in the main parts of the text (these are underlined) and hyperlinks in the left-hand side of the page in the shaded square.

History of the World Wide Web

The description above of the World Wide Web is a bare bones one which was true about eight years ago: Web pages can now contain a wide variety of media including audio files, video files, graphics and even programs which can execute while the browser is being viewed. Without the World Wide Web e-commerce would be barely

Figure 1.2
A typical Web page

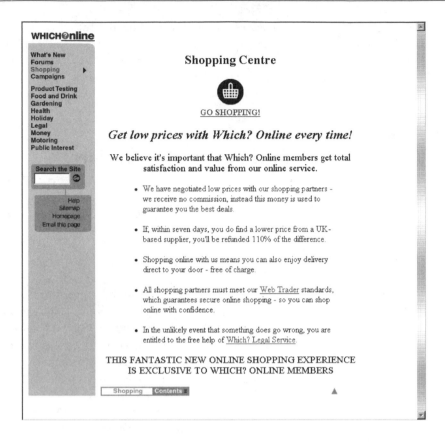

possible: it provides a standard interface to a variety of documents, products, services and software.

3.2 FTP

The acronym FTP stands for the **File Transfer Protocol**. It provides the facility whereby files can be downloaded into a computer from another computer in the Internet.

Although there are a number of utilities for file transfer most users now employ browsers for this via FTP links

There are a number of utilities which enable you to load anything from clip art to the latest updates for operating systems. Many of these utilities are very primitive: they use a simple command line interface which lets you log in to the computer which holds the files, and then enables you to use simple textual commands to identify the files to be downloaded. However, there are now a large number of sophisticated FTP programs which, for example, allow you graphically to show the structure of the file system on the remote computer, use drag and drop to download files and resume processing when transfer is interrupted by a network hang-up. Web documents can also contain FTP links which also enable the downloading of files.

FTP and the Internet

FTP is the mainstay of commercial companies who sell electronic products; it is a simple facility which has been found on the Internet since its inception in the 1980s.

Mailers are sometimes known as mail user agents while mail servers are sometimes known as mail transfer agents

E-mail and the Internet

3.3 E-mail

This is one of the most ubiquitous technologies on the Internet and, along with the World Wide Web, is the most used. When you write an e-mail you use a program known as a **mailer**. When the e-mail is completed it is sent via a number of computers known as **e-mail servers** and via a number of other intermediate computers before it reaches its destination where it is read. In e-commerce applications e-mail is a subsidiary, but important technology. It is used as the transport medium for mailing lists, for enabling customers to communicate with a company, for sending documents and data to customers and for keeping customers up to date about current products and services.

3.4 Newsgroups

Newsgroups and the Internet

A **newsgroup** is a collection of Internet users who are interested in a particular topic. The topic may be a technical one, for example the LINUX operating system, or a recreational one such as fly fishing. Members of a newsgroup send messages associated with a particular issue such as the date of release of the next version of LINUX or the efficacy of using certain flies on certain rivers. Each message – known as a **posting** – will contain the user's thoughts on the topic. Once posted these thoughts are responded to by other users. For example, one user may say that they have got solid information that the next version of LINUX will be released next week. The collection of responses to a posting and the original posting is known as a **thread**.

Newsgroups can be moderated or unmoderated. If a newsgroup is moderated a member will examine each posting and determine whether it should be posted. There are a number of reasons why postings are rejected: one major reason is that it is not relevant to the area that a newsgroup covers; another reason is that the posting is abusive to another user. There are no restrictions on posting to unmoderated newsgroups.

Newsgroups are accessed by using a special purpose software utility known as a newsreader; although there is an excellent search site known as *Deja.com* which allows access to newsgroups. Figure 1.3 shows a particular posting displayed by *Deja.com*.

The September that never ended

In the early days of the Internet newsgroups suffered a major drop in the quality of contributions every September. This was due to the fact that many students who commenced university at that time, were given their first Internet accounts and started using newsgroups. After a comparatively short time, the standard of discussion rose as the students realised what was a valid and what was an invalid posting to a newsgroup. However, one September, according to Internet veterans, the standard of contributions fell even further and never really regained its previous standard. This was the September when the large American Internet provider America Online allowed its members access to newsgroups. This September was known as the September that never ended.

Figure 1.3
A typical posting
displayed by
Deja.com

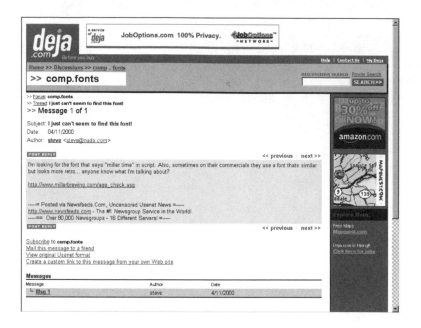

Many newsgroups form part of the collection known as Usenet. This consists of a large number (30 000+) of newsgroups which are organised hierarchically and rooted in a number of categories such as `rec` which designates newsgroups that deal with recreational topics and `comp` which deals with computing topics. The newsgroup designated as `comp.fonts`, shown in Figure 1.3, is an example of a technical newsgroup which forms part of the `comp` hierarchy.

Newsgroups are normally employed by ordinary users of the Internet and have not really been associated with e-commerce. However, a number of companies are beginning to wake up to their potential. For example, a number of software companies assign staff to read the postings in newsgroups which are devoted to one of their products in order to field any questions which might arise about them: it provides a good impression to future and present customers if a company will provide help about a product without, for example, users having to ring a high-tariff phone line.

Other companies are also beginning to embed newsgroup technology into their Web pages in order to create customer feedback groups which enable them to decide on future upgrades and new products.

3.5 Mailing lists

Mailing lists are groups of users who have some interest in common, for example they may all be network professionals. Such a list is used by organisations or individuals to inform the members of topics of interest to them. For example, my local cinema has a mailing list of cinema goers who have bought season tickets. It e-mails everyone on the list with the titles of those films which are to be shown in the coming week and notifies them of any special ticket offers. While there are many uses for mailing lists *within* companies there are also plenty of uses in e-commerce. For example, a mailing list can be used to inform current customers of any new products or services that are being offered. Most mailing lists are automatically maintained by specialised software. Such software allows someone to subscribe to a mailing list or drop out of a mailing list by just sending a simple e-mail message to the software; for example, often all that is needed to subscribe to a mailing list is a single line e-mail containing the message

```
Subscribe
```

This will result in the user who sent the e-mail being added to the list of users associated with the mailing list.

Kevin Kelly and Wired *magazine*

Kelly's Rules

This book is about the technical processes that are involved in the development of e-commerce and e-business systems. However, it is worth saying in passing that e-commerce and e-business applications seem to be radically changing the face of business. Probably the best chronicler of these changes is Kevin Kelly, one of the founders of *Wired* magazine. His most influential work is *New Rules for the New Economy* published by Fourth Estate. In this book he shows how e-commerce and e-business have overturned many of the conventional laws and rules about business. For example, he shows how companies can make huge profits by giving away free products, such as operating systems and browsers, with the profit being made from hardware, support software and services.

4   Issues and problems in e-commerce development

The aim of this section is to examine some of the issues and problems which affect the development of Internet, e-commerce and e-business applications. The rationale behind my including this section is that it provides a nice hook for me to detail the contents of the book and place them in context.

4.1 Legacy technology

CERN and the World Wide Web

The World Wide Web was developed as a way of dispensing documentation within the large research laboratory at CERN in Geneva. I am sure that the originator of the technology, Tim Berners-Lee, did not realise at that stage how it would expand and become a major component of our economic infrastructure. Because many of the developers of the technology were unaware of its potential there are a number of problems associated with its huge expansion. Three of these are discussed in the following subsections.

4.1.1 Space problems

Probably the best known of these is the fact that the Internet is running out of space for identifying computers. In Chapter 2 you will read about the detailed working of the Internet and be told that each computer in a network needs to be identified by a unique data pattern known as an IP address. The current technology used to transport data around the Internet is such that in the comparatively near future we shall run out of space to hold these unique addresses. Happily this is a problem that has been identified and groups of researchers around the globe have developed new technologies which will eventually overcome this problem, one of these technologies being a new version of the protocol used to transfer data over the Internet.

New protocols and the growth of the Internet

It is tempting to describe this in more detail; however, remember that this book is about developing applications for the Internet: I shall confidently assume that all the work that has been carried out to cope with the explosive growth of the Internet will be implemented 'under the bonnet' and developers will not need to know the details of this. I have, however, inserted a Web reference which you can chase up.

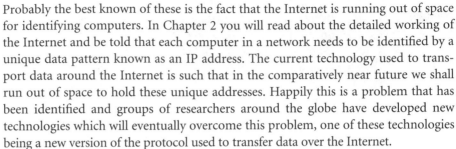

The great renaming

Periodically parts of the Internet have to be reorganised. In the late 1980s the administrators of the newsgroups within Usenet decided to reorganise the naming conventions used for the newsgroups. They adopted a hierarchic convention so that topics would include sub-topics which, in turn, contained sub-sub-topics and so on. This was known as the great renaming.

Having again made the point about what is not relevant to this book it is worth looking at something that is: Web servers, and the fact that what they were designed for is not what they are now being expected to do.

4.1.2 Stateless servers

This is not the full story: there is some indirect knowledge. Web servers will keep details of the accesses to their stored pages in a simple sequential file known as a **log file** which is used for marketing purposes and for optimising the Web server. This is discussed in more detail in Chapter 6

Web servers are what are known as **stateless servers**. What this means is that in their pure form they keep no memory of what has previously happened to them between requests; for example, when a request is processed by a Web server for a page they have no direct knowledge about whether the page request was made by the same browser that asked for a previous page to be returned.

While this was not serious when Web servers were being mainly used for dispensing documentation (their original use) it is a serious problem in e-commerce. One example of this is the **shopping cart**, or as it is known in the United Kingdom, the **shopping trolley**. When you visit an e-tailer and purchase goods you interact with a simulation of a shopping cart which keeps details of the goods that you have purchased. At the end of your interaction a Web page, often known as a **checkout page,** will display the contents of the shopping cart and present you with the monetary total of your purchases. Web servers as originally envisaged are unable to do this as they have no knowledge of any previous visit: they would not be able to remember the previous purchase.

In the comparatively early days of the Web this was seen to be a problem and a form of programming known as **Common Gateway Interface** programming was developed which enabled a Web server to have a memory. There are a number of other, more recent technologies which have been developed to cope with this problem. The first is **cookies**; these are chunks of data which are stored on the computer running the Web browser and which can be accessed by the browser throughout their interaction with a particular Web site. Such cookies can, for example, store the data associated with a shopping cart. Another technology used to store state is **servlets**; this is a technology, which employs cookies, and which is associated with Java; it enables the programmer to develop reusable code that can be plugged into a server and which keeps data persistently in the Web server. Chapter 6 looks at Web servers in detail. Chapter 7 describes how Web servers are programmed and looks at how servlets are used and how they can be employed in developing Web interactions which are allowed to access the results of previous interactions.

4.1.3 No dynamic Web pages

Another example of a problem with Web servers which arises from their original functionality is the fact that Web pages were designed to be static: they were files which were stored on a computer and delivered in their stored form to anyone using a browser to access them. Many e-commerce and e-business applications require something much more dynamic, for example there are a number of financial service sites on the Web which provide customers with up-to-date stock and share prices. These prices are stored on Web pages and need to change very frequently – often every few seconds. There have been a number of add-on technologies that have been developed in order to cope with this problem.

Saloman Smith Barney

Saloman Smith Barney and paying for education

Saloman Smith Barney is one of the largest and innovative financial companies in the United States. Its Web site is an excellent example of a feature-packed site. One part of the site which requires dynamic pages allows the visitor to plan the funding of their son or daughter's education; it prompts the visitor with a number of financial questions and constructs Web pages which provide details of the investment needed to pay college fees.

There is also a Microsoft implementation of dynamic pages known as **active server pages**. There are a number of other technolgies such as *mod_perl* and *php*

One early solution is something known as a **Server Side Include** in which parts of a Web page are marked as being dynamic and, prior to their being sent to the browser, they are updated with data that has changed. Servlets are also used to produce dynamic pages, for example they can be programmed to return specific Web pages to a browser containing content loaded in from a database. Another technology which has become very prominent over the last two years is known generically as **dynamic pages**. This is a more flexible version of Server Side Includes which allows the Java programmer to insert data into a Web page at specified points on a real-time basis. I shall be looking at the technology associated with dynamic pages in Chapter 7.

4.2 Security and privacy

I shall be discussing open systems in more detail in Chapter 2

The Internet is not a particularly secure place. There are two aspects to this: the first is that information is widely published throughout the Internet which can be used for criminal and near-criminal activities. The second aspect is that since the Internet is an open system, details of its underlying technologies are freely available to anybody. This means that the way data passes through the Internet is in the public domain; the consequence of this is that, theoretically, anyone with the right tools can eavesdrop on data passing from one computer on the Internet to another.

Share ramping, book ramping and painting the tape

Later in this book you will learn about the security problems that face Internet application developers. This is not the only problem that faces Internet users. The Internet, and in particular the World Wide Web, has provided such a fast and anonymous means of communication that old forms of criminal activity have had a second breath of life. Share ramping is the process whereby rumours are started about a company which would result in its shares either rising or falling, for example a rumour about it being taken over. The criminals who started the rumour will then either buy the shares if they have fallen and make a profit when they rise or sell shares they had bought previously when the price rises. The Internet makes communication so fast and anonymous that share ramping has become a major financial phenomenon during the last five years. Share ramping was once known as painting the tape; it is derived from the ticker tape machines which were used to communicate share prices to dealers before the 1960s. A less serious form of ramping has occurred on online book retailing sites which publish readers' reviews of books, where authors and the staff at publishers submit reviews under an assumed name and which greatly praise a book. This is known as book ramping.

Cyberstalking and privacy

It is worth examining the first problem. Already you have met one of the consequences of data being readily published on the Internet: the fact that spammers can use programs known as address harvesters to send large quantities of unsolicited e-mail to users. There are much more serious manifestations of this problem, for example a phenomenon that has occurred in the last three years is cyberstalking. This is where a user of the Internet finds the details of another user's e-mail account and harasses them electronically, sending them e-mails, contacting them via newsgroups and intruding into the chat rooms that they use.

An example of this occurred when Serbian nationalists flooded the main Nato e-mail server during the attack on Serbia in 1999

The possession of an e-mail address can even provide the means whereby someone can bring down part of a networked system. It is relatively easy to program a computer to send many thousands of e-mails to a computer which is handling e-mail communication for a company or organisation; the volume of e-mails can be so high that the computer is unable to carry out its main function: that of enabling staff of the company or organisation to send and receive e-mails. This is a form of attack known as a **denial of service attack** or **degradation of service attack**; this, and a number of other attacks on networks, are discussed in Chapter 11.

List linking

This is a recent form of harassment where someone discovers your e-mail address(es) and subscribes you to a large number of mailing lists. Often these lists generate as many as a hundred e-mails a day and some also send e-mails with large file attachments associated with them. A malicious user who wishes to disable another user's e-mail processing can easily do this by subscribing them to hundreds of mailing lists; this is a process that is quite easy to automate. An attacker who wants to disable the communications of a large company can, if they have access to the internal e-mail directory of the company, disable its e-mail system completely.

Security and the Internet

The second aspect of security is that data flow across the World Wide Web and the protocols used to communicate with computers in the Internet are public. This means that anyone who wishes to enter a computer system which has a connection to the Internet or anyone who wishes to read the data passing through it has a major advantage. There is, however, a contrary point of view which states that by keeping security details open any security breaches can be plugged easily by patches generated from a knowledgeable community of developers.

There are major gains for the criminal in being able to access a 'secure' system, for example a criminal who can read the details of a credit card passing along a transmission line from a browser to a Web server, can use that data to order goods over the net and remain undetected until the next time the credit card statement is delivered to the card holder; in this respect they have a major advantage over the criminal who just steals the card. A criminal who wishes to sabotage a network – perhaps they are a disgruntled former employee of the company – can send a program over the Internet which is then executed on the internal network of the company and deletes key files. A commercial spy can monitor the data being sent down a communication line and discover that it is from a company to a well-known research and development organisation which specialises in certain niche products. This information, even just the name of the R&D company, is valuable to any competitor.

How secure is the Internet?

In 1996 Dan Farmer, one of the leading members of the Internet security community, analysed a number of Internet sites using a tool known as SATAN which reports on security vulnerabilities. He discovered that out of the 2200 sites he accessed, 1700 were relatively easy to attack (77 per cent of the sites). This is a staggering figure; however, what makes it more staggering is the fact that Farmer chose sites which should have been neurotic about security, for example sites owned by banks, government agencies, insurance companies and credit card companies.

When the Internet and the World Wide Web were developed security was not high on the agenda. There were two reasons for this: the first is that the developers of the embryonic Internet were tussling with what was then novel technology and most of their focus was on basic aims such as establishing and maintaining reliable communications; the second reason is that very few people realised then that the Internet was going to be used for commercial purposes – a theme which the previous section detailed.

Happily there has been a huge increase in technologies used to secure the Internet; these are described in detail in Chapter 11 together with descriptions of the many threats that occur. For example, I shall describe a technology known as **Secure Sockets Layer** which uses cryptography to encode the data passing between a Web browser and a Web server so that anyone eavesdropping is unable to read it.

4.3 Programming and abstraction

In the early 1990s programming an application for the Internet was a tough proposition. I remember that I once had an application which required a very simple form of communication with another application located at a remote computer. I used a technology known as Winsocks which required me to carry out some pretty arcane code development just to send a simple test message to another computer and to receive a reply from that computer.

Java, when it appeared in 1996, enabled developers to treat another computer on a network essentially as if it was an input or output device; the programming code required to send data or receive data from another computer differed only slightly from that required to send and receive data from files.

However, even the programming facilities provided in the initial releases of the Java system are in opposition to a principle which I shall return to time and again in this book: this is that both the developer and the user of a networked system should be unaware of the fact that they are accessing a networked system. This principle has been enshrined in a sales statement from Sun Systems, the original developer of the Java language, that the 'network is the computer'. What this means is that the developer should be designing and programming in such a way that much of the detail of the Internet is hidden away under a number of levels of abstraction.

This is best exemplified by the idea of **distributed objects**. Many of you reading this book will have used Java: you will have developed a number of classes which describe objects whose methods were executed in order to achieve some processing aim. The objects that you employed were all created and stored in the main memory of the computer which you were using to carry out the programming. I would hope that you found that the object-oriented paradigm was a useful one which allowed you to think of a system in an easily approachable way: as a collection of objects interacting with each other in order to implement some functionality.

Distributed objects are objects which are stored on computers in a network, and to which messages can be sent as if they were objects residing on the computer which is sending the messages. In this way a programmer develops software for a distributed system in the same way that they would for a single computer: by defining classes and by executing code containing objects defined by the classes, with the code sending messages to the objects; the actual details of how the transport of messages occurs would be hidden from the programmer.

In Chapter 2 you will see some examples of Java code for network programming; the chapter also includes a number of programming exercises

This is not the full truth, somewhere someone still has to distribute the objects to the computers in which they are stored

In Chapters 9 and 10 I shall be looking at two distributed object technologies: RMI, which is a pure Java technology, and CORBA, which enables distributed objects programmed in different languages to interact with each other.

The theme of greater levels of abstraction does not stop there, however. In Chapter 4 I shall be briefly looking at a form of distributed development which is as far from the physical details of the Internet as you could possibly get. I shall be describing a form of distributed programming known as tuple space development. Here the underlying model is that of a large shared data space to which computers on a network can read and write data. In Java this is implemented using a specific technology known as *JavaSpaces*.

4.4 The speed of development

E-commerce consultants speak of a Web year. This is the time which it takes to bring to implementation a conventional system that would normally take a calendar year to develop. Current estimates are that one calendar year is equivalent to seven Web years. Nowhere is there more of an imperative for companies to develop products and services quickly, together with the computing infrastructure required to support them, than in e-commerce. In software engineering terms this has given rise to a number of software development methods which are loosely described by the term **rapid application development**. In technology terms it has given rise to a number of ideas which go some way along the path which ends with providing facilities that enable companies to develop systems by just bolting components together, with many of the components being specified using design templates.

The rapid development of object-oriented programming languages such as C++ and Java has meant that the last five years have seen a growth of technologies that enable a developer to program software components that can be reused time and time again in applications other than those which they were originally developed for.

It is worth pointing out that the ideas detailed here are not just confined to the Java programming language components; patterns and frameworks could, for example, be equally applied to C++

Over the last five years there has also been a major increase in interest in reusable design. In 1995 Erich Gamma, Richard Helm, Ralph Johnson and John Vlissides published a book which has become a major bestseller [5]. This book describes how many software systems contain commonly occurring **design patterns** and that these patterns could be catalogued and reused time and time again in the design process.

4.5 Structure and data

A problem that is being increasingly experienced by Internet companies is the fact that they have to interchange a large amount of data and that such data inherently lacks structure. For example, HTML has proved to be an enduring markup language for developing Web pages; however, there are no facilities within the language, for example, to indicate whether an item of data, say a three-digit number, represents the price of a commodity or some hourly rate charged by a company employee.

There are also problems with browsers. There are two main browsers employed by users of the World Wide Web: Internet Explorer and Netscape Navigator. Each of these browsers can display the browser pages they process in different ways, especially if they contain advanced facilities of HTML.

The WML markup language

There is also a further problem with browsers which is even more serious than the one detailed in the previous paragraph. Networking technologies are now being used in conjunction with other technologies such as those associated with mobile phone technology and television. This has led to the emergence of a number of different markup languages which are focused on particular devices, for example there is a markup language known as WML (Wireless Markup Language) which is used to display documents on Internet mobile phones. The diversity of such languages means that the overhead in maintaining a number of versions of a document for different media can be very large.

I shall be looking in more detail at WML in Chapter 16

XML and the Internet

Happily a technology has been developed known as XML which can be used to indicate structure in a document. There are also a number of tools available which allow the developer to maintain a single version of a document expressed in a language defined by XML and easily convert it into a form that can be displayed on a variety of media including television sets, Internet phones and a variety of World Wide Web browsers. Chapter 8 looks at markup languages in general and focuses on XML as a structuring technology.

4.6 Problems with transactions

A distributed transaction is a sequence of operations applied to a number of distributed databases which form a single functional step. For example, a transaction which moves an amount of money from a customer's account to an account owned by the same customer is an example of a transaction. It consists of two operations: the operation of debiting one account and the operation of crediting another account. There are a number of problems associated with distributed transactions. This section will briefly concentrate on one. This is the problem of deadlock: the fact that a transaction applied at one server might be waiting for data which is currently contained on another server, with the other server awaiting some resource that is held on the first server. For example, the first server might contain the account data that the second server needs to complete a transaction, while the second server might require other account data for it to proceed. There are a number of solutions to this problem and these will be discussed in Chapter 13. The chapter also discusses a technology known as *Enterprise JavaBeans* which removes from the programmer the need to worry about many of the problems detailed in that chapter. *Enterprise JavaBeans* is a distributed component technology which allows developers to develop reusable components which can be used in transactions.

4.7 Design

Designing a distributed system can also be a problem, for example the fact that computers in a distributed system are joined by communication media which can stretch over thousands of miles provides an added dimension to the design process in that response time can be a problem. Another, equally serious problem is that of reliability, for example the fact that a hardware malfunction can bring down a poorly-designed distributed system.

Replicating data is such a common technique that there are a large number of products available that allow you to implement it without very much programming

As an example of one design problem that a distributed systems developer has to face consider that of replicated data. A replicated database is a database which exists in the same form at a number of points in a distributed system. There are two reasons for having replicated databases: the first is reliability. When a system contains a number of replicated databases and one of them becomes unavailable – perhaps because of a hardware fault – another database can take over its role. The second reason is to improve response time. A designer of a distributed system will try and place a database close to its users, usually connected via a fast local area network. Often the original database that is used is a long distance away and can only be accessed via slow Internet connections; hence replicating the database and placing it close to the users usually results in a large reduction in response time.

However, using replication comes at a cost: each replicated database needs to keep up-to-date data and will need to coordinate with other databases in order to do this; this gives rise to synchronisation traffic over the network which supports the databases, and can result in a very slow response time. Designing for data replication, where the amount of replication and the location of the replicated data is such that response time is lowered, and yet traffic is not increased to the point where all the gains are nullified, is an art. In Chapter 14 I describe some of the main design principles for distributed systems.

5   A distributed system

The description here is closely modelled on the Amazon site

Before finishing this chapter it is worth looking at the architecture of a typical e-commerce system in order to see some of the technologies that will be detailed in this book used in anger. This is followed by details of a real application which I shall use to discuss some of the issues involved in distributed system development.

5.1 The application

The first application I shall describe is that of an online bookseller. Such a book sales system would carry out a number of functions:

- It would allow the user to browse through a catalogue of books.

- It would allow the user to browse through a list of the most popular books, with the list being updated every hour.

- It would provide the facility whereby a user can buy books and add them to a notional shopping basket.

- It would inform the user when the books ordered have been sent.

- It would provide customers with the facility to contribute reviews of the books that they have bought.

- It would send regular e-mails to users who have subscribed to an e-mail list informing them of any recently published books and any special offers.

5.2 The architecture

The architecture of the system is shown in Figure 1.4. It consists of a number of components. The most important of these is the Web server. This communicates with browsers used by customers.

There are two other computers that are used in the system which are directly connected to the Web server: a mail server which sends and receives mail from customers and a mailing list server which administers the mailing lists of customers and their interests. Both these servers communicate with the Web server, for example the mailing list server is periodically sent the e-mail addresses of users who wish to be added to a mailing list. The system will have a number of backup servers, for example the Web server will have a backup which is brought in if hardware problems affect the main Web server.

The main data store for the system is a series of databases which contain details such as customer payments and the number of books on stock and on order. These databases are replicated and are stored on a separate computer which is a very powerful server. The package which maintains stock details and customer financial details is a specialised one which has been developed for booksellers; unfortunately it is not well suited for Internet use since it was developed some time ago. In order for it to connect with the front end of the system – the part that is implemented via the Web server – a number of distributed objects are stored on the server that holds the databases. The Web server communicates its requirements by means of sending

This, again, is an example of the second myth I detailed earlier: that e-commerce systems are totally new. Often such systems will contain quite old technology which is hidden behind Internet-based technology

Figure 1.4
A simple e-commerce system

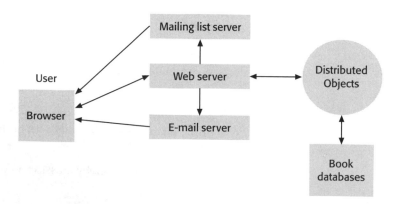

messages to these objects which then interact with the database software. The distributed objects act as a form of interface which hides the details of the databases and provides an object-based interface to the Web server.

This, then, is a typical retail system that would use a number of the technologies and techniques detailed in this book: Web servers, browsers, distributed objects, mail servers, replication and persistent state Web server technologies; all these will be described in varying detail in the remainder of the book.

Sydney Olympic Games

5.3 The Sydney Olympic Games system

IBM was responsible for the computer systems which were used in the 2000 Sydney Olympic Games. There were a number of components to the system, these included:

- A Web site which was publicly accessible and which contained features on the Games, the competitors and the results.

- A Games management system which administered the logistics of the Games, for example arranging transportation, accreditation and accommodation for athletes.

- A Games results system which captured input from all the events in the Games and distributed them to judges, scoreboards, competitors, commentators and the Web site detailed in the first bullet point above.

- A commentator information system which provided real-time information to journalists and broadcasters, for example this system would flash up on a commentator's PC the times achieved by the runners in a race, only a few seconds after the race was completed.

The statistics associated with the development were staggering:

- 7300 PCs were used as clients.

- 2000 information workstations and kiosks were spread around the Olympic site.

- 1500 IBM staff worked on the system.

- 10 km of cable were laid.

- 815 network switches were employed to transport and send data.

- 600 servers were used to store data and provide other services.

- 13 million lines of code were written.

- During the 16 days of the Olympics the Web site had 230 million page views, 8.7 million unique visitors and 11.3 billion hits.

- The highest number of hits in a day for the Web site was 874.5 million.

- 371 654 e-mail messages were sent to competitors from fans.

- The system achieved 100 per cent availability.

Many of the issues detailed here are dealt with in Chapters 12, 13 and 14

Clearly the project was a major challenge in software engineering, project management and logistics terms. It was also a major problem in terms of distributed systems development. The problems that the developers had to solve were the sort of problems whose solutions will be described in this book.

First, very high reliability was required. If a computer malfunctioned then it should not affect the functioning of the system, for example if the computer tracking athletes' timings in a race malfunctioned then the system should substitute another computer for it on-the-fly with no discernible difference to the users of the timing data.

Second, a large number of disparate pieces of hardware were used – both computers and output devices such as scoreboards. The system was developed as a classical client–server system in such a way that new hardware could be easily added. This was achieved via the use of standard protocols.

Third, high performance was required, for example results from the sailing events should have been sent to officials, journalists and competitors a few seconds after a race was completed. IBM carried out a large number of performance studies to ensure this was achieved and used techniques such as adaptive switching and data fragmentation to achieve this.

Fourth, scalability needed to be built into the system. IBM had made major investments in its Olympics system and a main aim was that it should be capable of being reused time and time again, even if the number of sports, number of competitors and duration of the games get larger. Using a client–server system ensured that there is a high probability of this happening in the future.

6   Internet business models

6.1 What is a business model?

The aim of this section is to look at some of the business models which have been used to drive Internet applications. A **business model** is a high-level description of an application type which contains all the common features which can be found in specific examples of the model. For example, one of the most popular business models is the e-shop which describes a Web site that sells products. The model is general in that it does not describe the item that is sold or the mechanisms that are used to carry out the sales process. The remainder of the chapter describes a series of e-commerce and e-business models.

Business models and the Internet

6.2 Business models

6.2.1 E-shop

This model is
sometimes
known as the
storefront model

This is the most ubiquitous form of commerce on the World Wide Web. It involves a company presenting a catalogue of its wares to Internet users and providing facilities whereby such customers can purchase these products. Almost invariably such a site will contain facilities for ordering and paying for products by means of credit cards. The sophistication of sites described by this business model range from just the simple presentation of a static catalogue to the presentation of an interactive catalogue, the display of samples of products – for example the use of sound clips in a site selling CDs – the maintenance of mailing lists and the ability for customers to post reviews or customer reactions to specific products.

Sites described by the e-shop model provide global presence, a cheap way to place products in front of an audience and decrease marketing and promotion costs.

6.2.2 E-auction

Auctions on the Web

This model describes sites which electronically simulate the bidding process in a conventional physical auction. Such sites can range in sophistication from those which present a simple catalogue of items to those which offer multimedia presentations. Most sites which are described by this business model are concerned with selling items to individual consumers. However, there are an increasing number of sites which provide facilities for businesses to auction products to other businesses.

Revenues are raised by this form of site by charging for a transaction and for advertising. Some sites also sell the technology they use to other sites.

6.2.3 E-procurement

*Procurement
on the Web*

'Procurement' is the term used to describe the tendering of goods and services: a company decides that it requires some goods, say a fleet of cars for its salesforce. It would then announce this publicly and invite a number of auto companies to bid for the business.

Many companies are now switching to the Web for the procurement process. A Web site devoted to procurement will normally advertise current procurement opportunities, provide forms facilities for companies interested in tendering and provide facilities whereby the progress of a tender can be tracked.

There are a number of advantages in carrying out the procurement process electronically. For suppliers it means that there are often more tendering opportunities, lowered cost of tender submission and collaborative tendering with other companies. For the company offering tenders there is a major reduction in costs.

6.2.4 E-mall

An electronic mall or e-mall is a collection of e-shops which are often devoted to a specific service or product, for example an e-mall might be devoted to selling goods associated with a leisure activity such as fishing. Usually e-malls are organised by a company which charges the e-shops for administering their presence: maintaining the Web site, hosting the e-mall, and providing payment and transaction facilities and marketing.

The e-mall operator gains revenue for charging the e-shops; the individual e-shops have the benefits normally associated with e-shops, plus the fact that they are clustered together with other shops which operate in the same market segment and hence attract customers who might be browsing from shop to shop.

6.2.5 Virtual communities

Virtual communities

A virtual community is a Web site which sells some product or service. In this respect there is no difference from an e-shop. The feature which distinguishes a virtual community is that the operator of the Web site provides facilities whereby the customers for a product or a service interact with each other, for example by pointing out ways a product can be improved. Technologies used for this interaction include mailing lists, bulletin boards and FAQ lists. The theory behind virtual communities is that they build customer loyalty and enable the company running the Web site to receive large amounts of feedback on the product or service they sell. A typical company that might run a virtual community would be a software supplier. Customers for software products manufactured by the company might post bug reports, bug fixes and work-arounds on a set of FAQ pages. Staff from the company would participate in the bulletin boards and also organise the FAQ lists.

Customers are often attracted to companies associated with virtual communities, particularly those that are maintained by companies that sell complex products, in that they see them as readily accessible stores of experience and unbiased advice.

A company can make profits from virtual communities in a number of ways. They can charge for participation in the community, and they can benefit from increased sales to customers attracted by the knowledge base held by the company and from a reduction in support costs.

The virtual community model is usually associated with another Internet business model, for example the Amazon Web site is primarily an e-shop; however, the fact that it contains facilities for users to submit reviews and questions to authors and artists gives it the flavour of a virtual community.

6.2.6 Third party marketplaces

A third party marketplace is characterised by Web sites which offer access to a number of related companies, for example companies that are wholesalers of office stationery. A distinguishing feature of this model is that the companies delegate the marketing and sales of their products to the company that administers the marketplace. Typically a Web site which operates as a third party marketplace would provide a common interface to the products or services which are being sold, together with facilities for payment and delivery.

A third party marketplace is similar in some ways to the e-mall. The main difference is the fact that the product or service providers within the marketplace are more closely integrated, for example by virtue of the fact that there is a common catalogue interface to the products or services offered.

6.2.7 Information brokerage

Information brokerage on the Web

Web sites described by this business model offer access to information – usually business information. For example, a Web site which offers the results of surveys of customer satisfaction for a product such as a car would be used by car hire companies, auto companies and consumer organisations. Major providers in this area provide information derived from financial data such as company performance figures, pension fund performance figures and financial market trends such as the growth of different types of mortgage. Companies whose Internet presence can be described by this business model usually raise revenues by subscription or by a per-transaction charge.

6.2.8 Trust brokerage

Chapter 11 describes the role of these companies in more detail

This business model describes those companies or organisations who provide some service connected with security or trust. For example, as you will see later in the book, copyright is a major issue for the Internet. A company might develop a sophisticated graphic which could easily be copied by another company that would then claim that they developed the graphic. A trust company might offer the facility for companies to register their work with them and then be able to testify to the date that the work was registered. Other trust brokers are associated with computer security and, for example, certify that a particular Web site run by a company is in fact associated with that company.

6.2.9 Collaboration platforms

Companies whose Internet offerings can be described by this business model provide sites which enable companies to collaborate with each other, usually when the companies are spread over large distances. For example, a company which runs a collaboration platform might provide facilities for companies who wish to come together in order to tender for a complex project in a particular market sector such as aerospace.

6.2.10 Portals

Portals on the Internet

A portal is a Web site which collects catalogues and characterises a huge amount of information. By displaying a large number of hyperlinks such sites provide an entrance (or portal) to the World Wide Web. Search engines originally provided fairly basic searching facilities; however, the past two years has seen them evolve into portals. Portals are categorised as either horizontal portals or vertical portals. A

vertical portal offers an entrance to large amount of information into a particular topic area, for example American football. A **horizontal portal** offers information over a large area.

6.2.11 Dynamic pricing

The dynamic pricing model is one which has a number of different instantiations. Basically, such models treat the price of a product or service (primarily a product) as variable and open to negotiation.

Name-your-price on the Web

The **name-your-price** instantiation of this model is where the customer of a site offers the price that he or she thinks is reasonable for a product or service. The administrator of the Web site will pass on this bid to the provider of the product or service who will decide whether to accept it.

Comparison pricing on the Web

The **comparison pricing** sub-model encompasses Web sites which provide an interface to e-shops that sell a specific product. The model provides the facility for the customer to interrogate a database of product catalogues to look for the cheapest price for a particular product such as book or a CD.

The **demand sensitive pricing** sub-model is based on the fact that suppliers of a product will lower the price of a product if a number of units of that product are included in a single sale. Web sites which employ this model provide facilities whereby consumers can notify each other of their interest in buying a particular product such as a freezer. The site keeps a database of current products that have attracted a number of buyers with a predicted price and allow users to join the database of buyers who are committed to a sale.

The **bartering** sub-model allows consumers to barter services or products for other services or products. A site devoted to this form of economic activity will keep a structured database of items for sale and allows a buyer to barter with a seller.

6.2.12 B2B exchanges

A B2B exchange is a Web site or collection of Web sites which make the process of carrying out business to business transactions much easier. Under this banner comes sites which enable multiple companies to procure services and products from each other; help businesses form temporary alliances to carry out activities such as joint marketing or project bidding, and enable a marketplace in raw materials to function.

6.2.13 Online trading

Online trading on the Web

This business model encompasses the trading of financial instruments such as bonds and stocks via the Internet. Online trading has been a feature of the financial industry for some time. However, it was carried out using internal networks. The Internet has enabled the individual user to trade stocks and shares from home and has given rise to the term **day trading**.

6.2.14 E-learning

E-learning on the Web

This term is used to describe companies or organisations who offer educational courses via the Web. The quality and features found in sites which can be described by this business model can vary. At its simplest such sites offer students the ability to download conventional texts. More complex instantiations of the model offer the students facilities to read individual lessons, try out online multiple choice questions and experience simulations relevant to the topic being taught.

6.2.15 Free products and services

It might seem paradoxical to include sites which provide free products or services under the category of business models. Typical sites which come under this category include gaming sites where users can play computer games using their browser, sites which run free raffles and sites which offer free software.

Such sites do not earn any revenues from the products or services they offer; revenue is earned indirectly, for example by means of banner adverts or by receiving revenue from sites which you have to visit before experiencing a service or buying a product.

One of the largest free product areas is that of free software. Organisations in this area include those who raise revenues and those who do not. An example of a company in the former category is Red Hat. This is a company that provides free versions of the LINUX operating system. You can download LINUX from the Red Hat Web site and install it on your computer without paying a penny to the company. Red Hat raise their revenues through support, packaging distributions onto CDs and providing services to companies who employ LINUX for application development. Companies such as Red Hat are the analogue of those companies who sell a razor for little or no cost but make their profit from selling the razor blades.

LINUX is a free variant of the venerable UNIX operating system

There are a number of sites in the Internet which do not make any money from issuing software. These are sites associated with Open Source development.

The Open Source movement

In Chapter 6 I shall be using Apache as a case study

The Open Source movement

The Open Source movement is a phenomenon of the 1990s. It is truly a child of the Internet because it is only the Net that provides the communicational infrastructure to enable it to succeed. A typical Open Source project involves a number of programmers deciding to collaborate on the development of a useful piece of software. Initially the software might have been developed by one of them with some minimal set of functions. Over time the software is enhanced and undergoes a series of builds. The software is made available to the general programming community at no charge, including its source code. Other developers are free to modify the source code and release it. The Open Source movement has generated some very popular software systems which have gained a large number of adherents. The two most popular are LINUX and the Apache Web server.

7　Further reading

There are a large number of books that have been written on e-commerce, many of which are of varying quality. I have found three useful. The first is by Kalakota and Whinstone [6]. It is an excellent introduction to both the technologies and applications involved in electronic commerce. Kalakota has also written a book [7] on electronic commerce which avoids many of the clichés and which concentrates on unglamorous areas such as supply chain automation. If you ignore the jargon and the management speak in this book, you will find it a useful introduction to the way in which computers will affect major economies in the next decade. If you are interested in the economics of e-commerce then a good treatment is a book written by Choi, Stahl and Whinstone [8]. If you wish to delve further into the underpinning technologies of distributed systems then [2] is the best introduction and is an excellent complement to this book. A good introduction to e-business has been written by Timmers [9].

The e-commerce gold rush

During the publication of the first edition of this book the e-commerce boom came to an end. Companies which were funded on the basis of a good idea and nothing else came quickly to grief, and the whole area of distributed applications became tainted with the fallout. However, writing in 2002 it is clear that distributed applications are still being deployed at a fast rate and that those e-commerce companies who still survive are making quite healthy profits. Surveys of e-commerce applications and e-business applications predict a steady growth in the use of technology mainly in the e-business arena and in the development of systems for individual companies.

References

Internet book links

[1] M. Brown and J. Honeycutt, *Using HTML 4.* Indianapolis, IN: QUE, 1998.

[2] G. Coulouris, J. Dollimore and T. Kindberg, *Distributed Systems Concepts and Design.* Harlow: Addison-Wesley, 2001.

[3] I. Horton, *Beginning Java 2.* Birmingham: Wrox, 1999.

[4] R. Kalakota and M. Robinson, *e-Business, Roadmap for Success.* Reading, MA: Addison-Wesley, 1999.

[5] E. Gamma, R. Helm, R. Johnson and J. Vlissides, *Design Patterns.* Reading, MA: Addison-Wesley, 1995.

[6] R. Kalakota and A.B. Whinstone, *Electronic Commerce.* Reading, MA: Addison-Wesley, 1997.

[7] R. Kalakota, *E-Business.* Reading, MA: Addison-Wesley, 1999.

[8] S. Choi, D.O. Stahl and A.B. Whinstone, *The Economics of Electronic Commerce.* Indianapolis, IN: Macmillan, 1997.

[9] P. Timmers, *Electronic Commerce.* Chichester: John Wiley, 2000.

The Internet and TCP/IP

2

Chapter contents

This chapter is introductory. It looks at the infrastructure used to support the Internet and how the layers of the Internet compare to the standard OSI reference model. The TCP/IP protocols which are used to support the Internet and intranets are described and a number of the more important facilities which are supported by these protocols are outlined. The chapter describes how computers are addressed on a TCP/IP-based network and how symbolic names can be associated with the addresses. The chapter concludes with a description of the low-level programming facilities in Java which enable a programmer to develop distributed systems using ports and sockets.

Aims

1. To introduce the idea of a layered architecture.
2. To detail a number of network topologies.
3. To outline the history of the Internet.
4. To describe the main layers of the Internet and the facilities it offers.
5. To describe the naming and addressing facilities found on TCP/IP-based networks.
6. To show how Java can be used for simple Internet programming using ports and sockets.

Concepts

Backplane, Browser, Bus network, Client, Distributed system, Dotted quad notation, FTP, Gateway, HTTP, Hub network, Internet, Internet Domain Name System, IP, IP address, Java, Loopback address, Multicast address, Multicasting, Name server, Open system, OSI reference model, Port, Ring network, Server, SMTP, SNMP, Socket, TCP, TCP/IP, TFTP, UDP, Web server, World Wide Web.

1   Introduction

This book is about the development of applications which exist on computer networks. More specifically it is about applications which are supported by a set of technologies which are used on a massive computer network known as the **Internet**. This chapter is introductory: it describes all the hardware and network technology that is required to build such systems. First and foremost it is about using **open systems**.

2   Open systems

There are many definitions about what is meant by the term *open system*. Probably the best is that it is a system whose architecture is not a secret; that the developers or sponsors of an open system have publicised its structure in such detail that developers can interface their software easily with it.

Probably the best example of an open system is the **UNIX** operating system. This has been in existence for over 30 years. The source code of a number of versions of UNIX is available to anyone who wishes to implement it on a new computer and develop tools and applications which can run on UNIX. The fact that UNIX is an open system has meant that:

- There are a wide variety of implementations running on a large number of hardware bases.

- The cost of UNIX implementations is considerably less than that of non-open operating systems. There is even one version of UNIX, LINUX, which is free.

- There is a very high level of compatibility between different applications running on different variants of UNIX: for example, source code can be easily ported between versions of the operating system.

- There are a wide variety of developers selling UNIX products.

In this book we shall be looking at the use of a technology which supports the idea behind an open system: the Internet. This is a massive collection of computers networked together which can communicate with each other using technologies and standards which are open. For example, the Internet relies on something known as a protocol; this is a convention which allows computers on the Internet to talk to each other and coordinate their actions. The set of protocols used in the Internet is known as **TCP/IP**; it is public and its details are freely available: any computer manufacturer or software developer is totally free to produce software which takes advantage of or uses the protocol.

Another example of an Internet protocol which adheres to broad open system principles is **HTTP**. This is a protocol which is used to define the traffic between Web **browsers** and the computers which hold **World Wide Web** documents. This protocol

We shall be looking at protocols in much more detail in Chapter 3

We will be looking at this protocol in more detail in Chapters 3 and 6

enables the user of a browser to specify which Web document they wish to read and carry out actions such as filling in a form.

Another example of a technology which is inspired by the open system idea is the programming language **Java** – the language used in this book. Java has been developed in such a way that its object code (byte code) can be moved from one operating system to another operating system without modification. How it does this is unimportant in the context of this book; in the context of this section of the book Java is important in that all the details of the language, its syntax and the details of the byte code are freely available and can be used by anyone interested in developing a version of the language for a specific operating system.

This book concentrates on the development of distributed systems and applications using the open system technology associated with the Internet. A **distributed system** is one in which the computer power in the system is distributed geographically around a number of computers which share the processing load of the system. A typical distributed system is a banking system which administers the accounts held by customers in the bank. A typical banking system would contain large minicomputers or mainframe computers usually situated in some head office which store account details for all customers, local computers – usually large microcomputers – which store local customer data at each bank branch and small microcomputers which control ATM machines and local teller machines in each branch. Each of these computers would be connected to other computers and carry out some set of functions in the system, for example the mainframe computers would be responsible for the storage and archiving of customer records and the computers associated with ATM machines would be responsible for functions such as debiting an account when a withdrawal occurred or notifying a mainframe computer when a customer asked for a statement.

3 Network concepts

The aim of this section is to look at some of the hardware concepts associated with network technology. The section does not go into too much detail – just enough to understand the software concepts which will be detailed in the book.

3.1 Network topologies

A computer network will consist of a number of computers which are either standalone or are embedded into some other device such as an ATM machine; it will also include peripherals such as printers and bulk storage devices. There are three popular ways of connecting up the components in a network. These are known as a bus network, a ring network and a hub network.

Figure 2.1 shows an example of a **bus network**. This is the simplest form of network in which a single main communication pathway is used and is connected to each of the components of the network. Every component on the network is assigned

Figure 2.1
A bus network

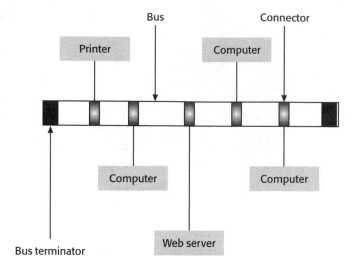

Networking and networking architectures

Figure 2.2
A schematic of a ring network

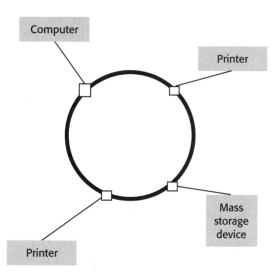

a unique address. When a message is sent to a device the address is embedded in the message; any device which is not the intended recipient of the message ignores it, while the recipient of the message reads it and interprets the data in the message and carries out some function such as processing the data.

The second type of network is a **ring network**. Often a ring network is shown displayed as a ring, as in the schematic shown in Figure 2.2. However, there is no physical ring in existence. The term *ring* is actually given to the design of the central unit which carries out the process of sending and forwarding messages in the network.

The final type of network is known as a **hub network**. Such a network uses a main cable like the bus network. This cable is often referred to as the **backplane**. From this backplane a series of connections lead to ports into which devices can be plugged. Hub networks have, over the last five years, become very popular; this is due to the fact that

Figure 2.3
A schematic view of
a hub network

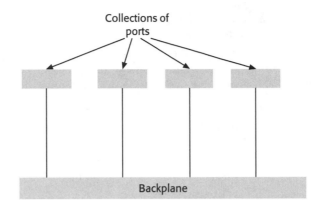

Collections of
ports

Backplane

Figure 2.4
The OSI seven layers

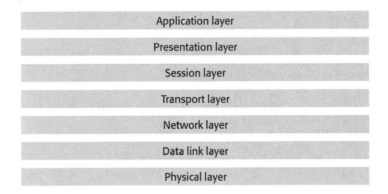

Application layer

Presentation layer

Session layer

Transport layer

Network layer

Data link layer

Physical layer

they are easy to set up, very easy to maintain and are cheap. Figure 2.3 shows a schematic of a hub network.

3.2 Layered models

Network protocols are partitioned into layers corresponding to the type and level of functionality that each layer carries out. The classical layered architecture is known as the **OSI reference model**. This has seven layers each corresponding to a well-defined set of functions. Each layer is described below and shown in Figure 2.4.

■   *The application layer* is a layer where applications such as electronic mailers reside. This is the layer that is responsible for displaying data. It also communicates with the other layers in the model via the presentation layer.

■   *The presentation layer* acts as a buffer between the application layer and the remaining layers of the model. It converts data in the application layer which might be in a variety of forms used by computers, such as ASCII, into some internal form that the network understands. It also carries out the reverse process of converting data in an internal form into a form that the application layer can understand.

*Network standards
and OSI*

- *The session layer* synchronises the exchange of data between applications. It allows each application to know about the state of another application so, for example, if one application program was expecting data from another application program and the second program went into an error state, then it would be the responsibility of the session layer to inform the first program of this fact.

- *The transport layer* is responsible for the transfer of data through a network. The transport layer has the important function of checking that the data that was sent from one part of the network to another part has been correctly received; if it has not, then it has the responsibility of informing the process that originated the data that an error has occurred. Normally, in this case, the sending process will resend the data.

- *The network layer* carries out the physical routing of data from one computer to another. It carries out functions such as determining the route an item of data is to take through a network.

- *The data link layer* carries out the process of managing the transmission of low-level items of data such as bytes. It does this in conjunction with the final layer: the physical layer. This layer is responsible for the monitoring and recovery from low-level transmission errors, for example errors caused by malfunctioning hardware.

- *The physical layer* is responsible for the low-level process of sending the electrical signals which correspond to low-level entities such as bytes.

During the development of the OSI model there was a lot of controversy over the final two layers: many researchers and developers felt that they were inseparable. In most systems these layers are in fact combined

3.3 The Internet

The Internet is an open system which is implemented as a layered architecture. This means that the functions of the system are embedded within layers which communicate with lower layers in order to carry out their functionality. Before looking at these layers and comparing them with the OSI model presented in the previous section it is worth recounting some history.

3.3.1 The history of the Internet

The Internet was originally proposed by an American body known as ARPA (Advanced Research Projects Agency). It was originally conceived as a way of testing the viability of networking. During the later stages of its life ARPA became more defence-oriented and was renamed DARPA (Defense Advanced Research Projects Agency) and oversaw the first implementation of a network originally known as ARPAnet. The network was commissioned in 1971. In the early days of the network there was a perceived need for users at one computer to log into another computer. The protocol that was used in the original ARPAnet, the 1822 protocol, was inadequate for this and another protocol, NCP, was devised and implemented. By 1973 it became clear that NCP was inadequate to handle the volume of data that was being generated. In 1974 two researchers, Vincent Cerf and Robert Kahn, suggested that

Internet history and anecdotes

At this stage of the book do not worry too much about what a protocol is. Effectively it is a procedure whereby one entity (usually a computer) on a network can send messages to another entity. More details on protocols can be found in Chapter 3

because of the growing use of networking and the inadequacy of current protocols a new set of protocols needed to be devised. The radical suggestion that they made was that the protocols should be independent of any hardware. This set of protocols that was developed was known as TCP/IP (Transmission Control Protocol and Internet Transmission Protocol) and, by the early 1980s, had supplanted NCP as the protocol set of choice for American networking. As networking spread in the USA more and more non-military organisations joined the ARPAnet; in the initial stages these were mainly universities. This led to the splitting of the ARPAnet into two networks: MILnet which was devoted to military networking and ARPAnet which became a civilian network. As ARPAnet was transformed into a civilian network it was renamed the Internet. ARPAnet went into decline when the United States Government Office of Advanced Scientific Computing instigated a high-speed network of supercomputers known as NSFNET; it was eventually retired in 1990.

3.3.2 Internet structure

Sometimes a gateway is known as a router

The Internet is not a network of computers but, rather, it is a network which consists of a number of other sub-networks. A computer in one network communicates with a computer in another network using a **gateway**. Each network in the Internet will contain a gateway; its function is to provide communication facilities between its own network and other networks. Each gateway communicates with other gateways using TCP/IP facilities. In very simple terms the role of the gateway is to monitor the data that it processes and check whether the data is intended for a computer on its sub-network. If the data is intended for the computer on the sub-network then the gateway forwards it to that computer: if not, the gateway tries to determine the location of the gateway that connects to the network with the destination computer. It will then pass the data to that gateway. Often this will be the gateway that acts as a front end to the network with the destination computer and the data can then be forwarded to the computer; sometimes this will not be the network and the data is then forwarded on to another gateway with the data eventually being delivered.

The size of the Internet

The size of the Internet

One of the most difficult tasks in computing is discovering how big the Internet is. Some organisations do monitor network growth. One of these is Network Wizards who, in July 1998, estimated that 36.7 million host computers were connected. This means that there are many more since a host can be connected to many other computers which are not hosts. The company has a Web site you can access for more up-to-date statistics. For more recent statistics access the sites detailed in the Web link above.

Figure 2.5, which shows the relationship between the Internet layers and the OSI model, details some of the protocols associated with the Internet. It is worth pointing out that some of the names below are also used to describe a service provided by the Internet, for example FTP. The protocols are:

Figure 2.5
Internet layered
architecture
compared with OSI

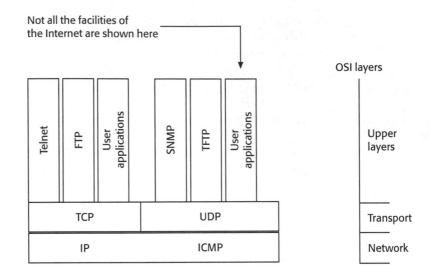

■ *Telnet.* This is a protocol which allows users on one computer to access and log in to other computers on the Internet provided, of course, that the user has permission to do so.

■ *File Transfer Protocol.* This is commonly known as **FTP**; it allows a user to transfer files from one computer to another computer.

A description of name services can be found at the end of this chapter; there is also a Java exercise in which you will be asked to develop a simple name server

■ *Simple Mail Transfer Protocol.* This is a protocol which enables electronic mail to be transferred from one computer to another. It is often referred to as **SMTP**.

■ *Kerberos.* This is a security protocol which allows highly confidential data to be transferred from one computer to another.

■ *Domain Name System.* This is a service which enables computers to be referred to by a symbolic name rather than a numeric address.

■ *Simple Network Management Protocol.* This uses the User Datagram Protocol (UDP) described below. It is used to monitor a network for problems such as a malfunctioning computer issuing spurious data onto the network. It is often referred to as **SNMP**.

■ *Network File System.* This is a collection of protocols developed by Sun Microsystems which enable computers on a network to transparently access files and file directories on other computers in a network. A user who employs this protocol is usually unaware of the location of a particular file; the only item of information that the user normally requires is the name of the file.

■ *Trivial File Transfer Protocol.* This is usually referred to by the acronym **TFTP**. This is a very simple protocol used for the fast transmission of files in a network. It lacks security.

- *Transmission Control Protocol.* This is a protocol which enables data to be reliably passed through a network. A higher level such as an application program will collect transmission data together and pass it to this layer which then carries out the function of sending the data to its destination. This protocol has the facility to retransmit data, for example if an error prevented an original collection of data arriving at its destination. This protocol is usually referred to by the acronym **TCP**.

This does not mean that UDP is unusable; there are some applications where speed is of the essence but where some data loss is acceptable, for example sending audio data over a network

- *User Datagram Protocol.* This fulfils the same function as TCP. However, unlike TCP, it does not have the facility to retransmit data; because of this data can be lost using this protocol. This protocol, usually known by the acronym **UDP**, enables fast transmission of data; however, there is no error checking so, for example, under certain network conditions such as heavy traffic, data sent using the protocol can be lost.

- *Internet Protocol.* This is usually referred to by its acronym **IP**. This has the basic function of moving data which has been created by either TCP or UDP across a network of networks.

- *Internet Control Message Protocol.* This is responsible for checking the status of computers and other devices attached to a network.

Figure 2.5 shows the basic layered architecture of TCP/IP compared with some of the layers of the OSI model; not all the facilities described below are shown. In Figure 2.5 the transport level of the OSI model is equivalent to TCP and UDP, while the network layer corresponds to IP and ICMP.

3.4 Internet addresses

A network is a mechanism for sending data from one computer to another computer. The key question which this statement raises is: given that a computer wants to send data to another computer how does it specify the destination computer?

The answer is that each computer on the Internet is assigned a unique address known as its **IP address**. This unique address is expressed in a notation known as the **dotted quad notation**. It consists of four integers separated by dots. The address 137.9.12.20 is an example of an address expressed as a dotted quad.

The address of a computer on a TCP/IP network is stored in 32 bits. There are four formats for these addresses known as class A, class B, class C and class D formats. Figure 2.6 shows the partitioning of the 32 bits for each of these formats.

Addressing and naming on the Internet

Telnet

Telnet is one of the most useful tools for checking out a network and for accessing facilities in a primitive way. Virtually every operating system has a version of Telnet which can be used to connect into another remote computer as if you were a local user. There are a number of uses of Telnet; one of the most valuable is for debugging remote servers.

Figure 2.6
IP addresses

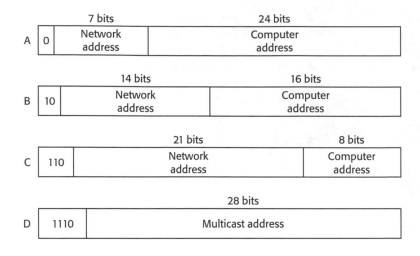

Class A addresses are used for large networks that contain many computers; 7 bits are used to identify the network while 24 bits are used to identify the computers on the network. Class B addresses are used for medium-sized networks; 14 bits are used to identify the network and 16 bits are used to identify the computers on the network. Class C addresses are used for small networks where 21 bits are allocated to the network address, while 8 bits are used to identify computers on the network.

Multicasting will be described in more detail in Chapter 4

Class D addresses are used for a technique known as **multicasting** where a message is simultaneously sent to a number of computers. Here the bulk of the address (28 bits) is made up of what is known as a **multicast address**.

Each IP address is unique and can be used to identify a computer on a TCP/IP network. However, the dotted quad notation is somewhat cumbersome: trying to remember four digits in order to access a computer is difficult. Ideally what is required is some form of symbolic naming so that we can refer to computers using some easily remembered name. Happily there is a service that provides this facility. You have already briefly met it in the previous section; it is known as the domain name system.

The loopback address

The address 127.0.01 is known as the **loopback address**. Any data which is sent to this address from a computer will return straight to the computer. This might seem odd. Why should you need to send data back to the computer which has originated it? The answer is that it is used for local debugging: instead of using two computers to test a distributed program you can use just one. Many of the exercises associated with this book use this address.

3.5 Domain names and naming

The domain name system is a hierarchic way of naming a computer on a TCP/IP network. An example of a name which uses this hierarchic description is

Exercise 2.1

Developing a simple tool to discover computer names from IP addresses

```
smtpmail.open.ac.uk
```

This is a computer which is used by members of my department to send mail. Each suffixed element of the name (apart from the first) is known as a domain. In the example above the domains are `open.ac.uk`, `ac.uk`, `uk`. Each represents an increasingly larger collection of computers, for example `open.ac.uk` represents those computers at the Open University and `ac.uk` represents those within the ac.uk domain of which the Open University computers are a subset. In this address the computer `smtpmail` precedes the domains. There is a domain `uk` associated with organisations within the United Kingdom. The string `ac.uk` is another domain which is a sub-domain of `uk`, where `ac` indicates an academic institution. The string `open.ac.uk` identifies my organisation (the Open University) and is a sub-domain of `ac.uk`. Thus the symbolic address has identified the country (United Kingdom), the type of organisation (an academic institution) and the name of the organisation (the Open University). Finally the string `smtpmail` identifies the computer which is used for mailing.

A common mistake to make is to assume that if a computer is associated with a country domain you will find that computer in the country. All it means is that some organisation associated with the country uses the computer; it may be located elsewhere

In the Internet there are currently a number of top-level domains. Some of them are listed in Table 2.1.

As well as these top-level domains there are domains for countries, for example the domain `uk` is associated with the United Kingdom and `fr` is associated with France. Some examples of symbolic addresses are shown below, some of these do not contain country names; if a country name is not used then the domain is associated with the United States.

Table 2.1
Top-level domains

In 2000 seven new domains were added to the DNS; they include aero and biz

Top-level domain name	Organisation
`com`	Commercial company
`edu` *or* `ac`	Educational institution
`gov`	Governmental organisation
`mil`	Military organisation
`biz`	Show business
`org`	Organisations not catered for above
`aero`	Aeronautics industries

Figure 2.7
The hierarchic
structure of the
Internet domain
name system

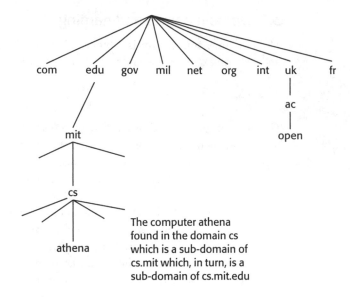

```
mit.edu

java.sun.com

time-A.timefreq.bldrdoc.gov
```

The first identifies a university domain (at the Massachusetts Institute of Technology), the second a commercial organisation domain belonging to Sun Microsystems and the final address identifies a computer at a US government organisation which provides an ultra accurate time reading. Figure 2.7 shows the general structure of the domain naming service of the Internet; not all the domains are shown.

Electronic mail

Many of you will have seen mail addresses such as

A.N.Other@Univ.edu

which consist of a recipient (A.N.Other) and a symbolic name Univ.edu. This latter name is the same one which we have been describing above. The lookup process which is involved when a mailing is sent is a little more complex than suggested in the main text above. First the domain is looked up; then the name server which is consulted will return with the address of computers which can receive the mail and the mailing software at the domain will search for the computer that can accept mail for the recipient.

When a computer wishes to contact another computer given its symbolic name the following actions take place. It first checks that the computer is on its local domain. This may be a domain associated with a particular company or university. If it is then it establishes a connection with the computer. If not it searches for a computer known as a **name server** which will contain the correct address. This may necessitate the search of a number of name servers. How it does this is beyond the scope of this book

The collection of name servers is known as the **Internet Domain Name System** or DNS. It is probably the most used part of the Internet: for example, every time someone sends e-mail or consults a Web document then the service is consulted.

3.6 Clients and servers

The term *server* was used in the previous section. At this point in the book it is worth briefly describing what a server is and also introducing the associated concept of a client. A **server** is a computer on a network which carries out some service for another computer known as a **client**. The terms can also be used to describe running programs on a computer so, for example, someone talking about a Web server might be referring to a computer or a running program.

One of the simplest examples of servers is the name server detailed in the previous section. This provides the service of translating a symbolic name into some address. Its clients are those computers which require this service, for example a computer which is being used to send emails or a computer which is being used to browse Web documents.

Another example of a server is the computer which is used to hold Web documents and which sends pages of these documents to computers which are running browsers that are accessing the Web documents. The server is acting as a **Web server** while the computers running the browsers are acting as clients to the Web server.

> ### Intranets
>
> This chapter has concentrated on the Internet. You may also have come across the term **intranet**. This usually describes some internal, closed network which is used by an organisation and which uses Internet technology. Intranets are becoming increasingly popular for a number of reasons: first, much of the software technology associated with TCP/IP is either free or inexpensive; second, TCP/IP is universal and open, which means that widely disparate networks employing hardware from different manufacturers can be easily connected together; third, intranets, since they use Internet technology, can be easily connected to the Internet.

3.7 Ports and sockets

So far this book has described how computers are uniquely identified on a TCP/IP-based network. What it hasn't discussed is, given a destination computer address, how it is transferred via a protocol suite such as TCP/IP over a network. In order to understand this I need to introduce the concept of a port.

It is important that you do not gain the impression that the only naming service that you will encounter in your study of distributed systems is DNS. There are a large number of naming services which can be found in distributed systems

Chapter 3, which is devoted to introducing client–server software development, describes types of servers

Chapter 6 looks at Web technology in much more detail; in particular it will look at the programming of Web servers

Table 2.2
Some popular ports
and their use

Port number	Facility	Description
7	ECHO	Echoes back anything sent to it
13	DAYTIME	Gives the time of day
21	FTP	File Transfer Protocol
23	TELNET	Remote use of computer
80	HTTP	Web server access
25	SMTP	Simple Mail Transfer Protocol
110	POP3	Post Office Protocol version 3
150	SQL-NET	Database access protocol
443	SHTTP	Secure Web server access

Dedicated ports

A port is a conduit into a computer through which data flows. A **port** on a computer is identified by a unique number. By convention the port numbers from 0 to 1023 are reserved for special services. Some of these services and the corresponding port numbers are shown in Table 2.2. For example, port 110 is used for mail being sent using a protocol known as POP3 (Post Ofice Protocol version 3). This is a very simple protocol which is used to send electronic mail. Ports above 1023 can be used for any user application.

It is worth stressing at this point that a port is not a hardware concept. It is a network abstraction which enables programmers to easily develop programs which read data from and write data to a network.

Each communication channel into and out of a TCP/IP-based computer is identified by the unique pair of numbers consisting of the IP address and the port number. This combination is a programming abstraction known as a **socket**. In the next section of this book I shall be describing how to write Java programs to read and write data from a TCP/IP-based network. The main way that you do this in Java is via sockets.

4 Network programming in Java

The facilities for simple network programming in Java can be found in the `java.net` package. This package allows the programmer to set up sockets and connect up streams so that data can be read from and written to these streams.

Different classes are used for datagrams

The two main classes which are used for TCP/IP socket-based programming are `Socket` and `ServerSocket`.

4.1 The Socket class

Tutorial on socket programming in Java

The Socket class has a number of constructors which enable the programmer to create a socket to a remote computer. The simplest of these has two arguments. The first is a string which is the name of the computer using the DNS convention explained in the previous section; the second argument is a port number. The code

```
Socket oldSock = new Socket("penny.open.ac.uk", 1048);
```

will set up a socket connected to the remote computer penny in the domain open.ac.uk with communication occurring via port 1048. The socket is attached to the computer communicating with penny.

The method getInputStream will obtain an InputStream object attached to the socket which can then be used to read data. For example, as in the code

In this code the BufferedReader requires an InputStreamReader object as its argument. This object is obtained by creating one based on the input stream associated with the socket; for this the method getInputStream is used

```
Socket ss = new Socket("archer.open.ac.uk", 2048);
InputStream is = ss.getInputStream();
BufferedReader bf =
        new BufferedReader(new InputStreamReader(is));
```

The first line establishes a socket connected to the computer archer.open.ac.uk on port 2048. The next line gets an InputStream object which can be used to read data from the socket. Finally, the last two lines set up a BufferedReader object. This is an object which has methods that read character data and which uses an area of memory known as a buffer which accumulates data until enough can be sent in an efficient way. For example, the code

```
String lineRead = bf.readLine();
```

reads a string terminated by a new line from bf. This string is a copy of one created by the remote computer to which the socket ss is connected.

This, then, is the way that a socket can be set up by a client which connects into some computer acting as a server. Once a stream has been attached to a socket, data can be read from and written to that socket. As a further example consider the code for writing data to a socket.

The constructor for the PrintWriter object has a second Boolean argument which, if true, will automatically flush data from the buffer used by the PrintWriter object, when enough has been accumulated for transfer

```
Socket ss = new Socket("archer.open.ac.uk", 2048);
OutputStream os = ss.getOutputStream();
PrintWriter pw = new PrintWriter(os, true);
```

This code uses the method getOutputStream to obtain an OutputStream object attached to the socket ss. The next line sets up a PrintWriter object based on the OutputStream object associated with the socket. If you are unfamiliar with the PrintWriter then all you need to know is that it is used for character output. It has a number of print methods which write basic Java data to a stream. For example the code

```
pw.println("Hello  there");
```

will write the string "Hello there" to the stream associated with pw.

OutputStream and InputStream objects can be associated with the same socket; as a consequence of this a client can establish two-way communication with a server. For example, the code below sends the message "Hello" to a server penny.open.ac.uk and receives a reply from that server. The code uses the port 2500.

Remember that ports less than 1024 have specialised uses so pick a high-number port

```
// Set up the socket to the remote computer penny
Socket pSock = new Socket("penny.open.ac.uk", 2500);
//Obtain the streams
InputStream is = pSock.getInputStream();
OutputStream os = pSock.getOutputStream();
//Set up the BufferedReader which is
//associated with the socket
BufferedReader bf =
     new BufferedReader(new InputStreamReader(is));
PrintWriter pw = new PrintWriter(os);
//Send message to server
pw.println("Hello");
//Get reply from server
String reply = bf.readLine();
if(reply.equals("Hello"))
   //Process the reply
else
   //Carry out some error process
```

Exercise 2.2

Developing a simple client that accesses the echo port of a server

In a number of the exercises associated with this book you will find yourself using code similar to that above, so it is well worth spending a little time understanding it.

4.2 The ServerSocket class

In the previous section I described the Socket class. This class is associated with clients. The ServerSocket class is the other side of the story in that it is associated with servers. It is used to establish a socket on a server. This class is associated with three constructors. The simplest of these is

```
ServerSocket(int  port)
```

This creates a server socket associated with the port given by its single argument. The most important method within this class is accept; this method suspends the server until a client attempts to connect to it. The server effectively waits until it receives a message from a client. When a client sends a message to the server the execution proceeds. The method `accept` returns the `Socket` object which can be used to establish a connection with the client that has connected in. The code below shows this in action.

The code here represents something called a handshake: two entities on a network start a conversation by issuing a simple message to each other. In practice the messages exchanged will contain much more data and will provide information about the entities

```
ServerSocket ss = new ServerSocket(3412);
//Wait for a connection
Socket sockS = ss.accept();
Set up the streams and BufferedReader
InputStream is = sockS.getInputStream();
OutputStream os = sockS.getOutputStream();
BufferedReader bf =
    new BufferedReader(new InputStreamReader(is));
//Send data
PrintWriter pw = new PrintWriter(os, true);
//code for sending data not shown
String readString = bf.readLine();
if(readString.equals("Hello"))
    pw.println("Connection established");
//Remaining processing
```

It first sets up a server on port 3412. It then suspends processing waiting for a client to connect into this port. When a client connects into this port execution resumes and the input and output streams used by the server are established. Next the server reads a message from the client; if the message was the string "Hello" then the server sends a message back which tells the client that a connection has been established. The remaining code will carry out the service that the server provides.

It is worth pointing out that programming servers so that a client gains exclusive access is very inefficient. In Chapter 12, which discusses concurrency, a much better solution is presented

Often a server will have a large number of clients trying to make a connection. What happens in the simple case above is that if a client and a server are communicating with each other and another client tries to establish a connection, then that client is put on hold until the current client relinquishes its conversation with the server. It is effectively queued up waiting for its turn. The single argument constructor which I have described will queue clients up to a default maximum of 50. If a client attempts to connect when this queue has 50 clients attached to it then the connection will be refused. A second constructor

```
ServerSocket(int port, int backlog)
```

allows a queue of waiting clients of maximum length `backlog`.

Exercise 2.3

Developing a client which accesses a simple name server

This section has described the basics of communication using sockets in Java. This form of communication is reliable since it uses TCP/IP: any errors in the transmission of data will result in the data being re-sent. However, since there is an overhead in using the TCP/IP protocol it is not a fast transmission process. Datagrams are a faster medium for this.

5   Summary

This chapter has introduced you to the main network concepts associated with the Internet. In particular we have looked at how the TCP/IP protocol suite supports communication and how Java enables us to easily develop simple programs which enable communication between computers on a TCP/IP-based net.

6   Further reading

If you are doing the case study as you progress through the book, read Sections 1 to 4 of Chapter 17

This book is really about using the facilities of the Internet and, as you will discover later, you do not need to know much about the workings of the Internet to develop distributed applications. If you wish to know more, however, then there are two books that I would recommend. The first is an excellent book written by Tanenbaum [1] which has become a classic and is on the reading list of every electronic engineering and computer science student. Although it deals with networks in general – not just the Internet – it is a terrific book. A gentler approach to the Internet is taken by Martin [2] who has written a slightly less technical book.

References

Internet book links

[1] A.S. Tanenbaum, *Computer Networks*. Old Tappan, NJ: Prentice Hall, 1998.
[2] M. Martin, *Understanding the Network: a Practical Guide to Internet Working*. Harlow: Longman Higher Education, 2000.

Clients and Servers

3

Chapter contents

A distributed system will consist of clients and servers. The latter provide some service such as sending Web pages to a browser. The former requires a service from a server. This chapter looks at how clients and servers interact and the way that a protocol embodies this interaction. Some of the more common servers are described together with some of the more common protocols such as POP3. The chapter also looks at software known as middleware which is interposed between clients and servers and one specific example – message-oriented middleware – is described. The chapter concludes by detailing the rationale for client–server computing and describing the difference between internal and external services.

Aims

1. To describe how distributed systems consist of clients and servers.
2. To outline the function of a client.
3. To outline the function of a server.
4. To introduce a number of different categories of server.
5. To show how a protocol is used to coordinate the processing between clients and servers.
6. To outline some common protocols used in a TCP/IP network.
7. To describe how middleware mediates between clients and servers.
8. To describe the concept of an internal and external service.

Concepts

Access transparency, Application server, Client, Concurrency control service, Concurrency transparency, Database server, Data layer, Directory service, Enterprise framework, External service, Failure transparency, Fat client, Fat server, File service, Groupware, Host processing, HTTP, ICMP, Internal service, Location transparency, Mail server, Middleware, Naming service, Object server, Performance transparency, POP3, Presentation and logic layer, Processing layer, Protocol stack, Replication transparency, Replication service, Security service, Server, SQL, Thin client, Three-tier architecture, Time service, Transaction service, Two-tier architecture, Web server.

1   Introduction

This is not a hard and fast distinction: a client may act as a client to a server but may then act as a server to another client. Also I am still using client and server to describe hardware entities, remember these terms can also be used to describe programs

The aim of this chapter is to describe in detail the concept of a client and the idea of a server already outlined in Chapter 2. These are the two main components of a distributed system: a **server** is a computer which carries out a service such as printing out a file or responding to a Web page request and a **client** is some computer which requires the service.

Client–server computing is an attempt to balance the processing in a network to the point where specialised services are provided by servers which can be tuned to the specific task that they carry out. Later in the chapter I shall describe a fuller rationale for client–server computing.

Enerva *and the oil industry*

The *Enerva* system relies on the use of data expressed in a language known as XML; later in this book (in Chapter 8) I shall look at XML in more detail

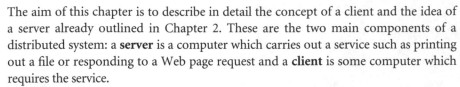

Enerva and client–server computing

Enerva is an organisation sponsored by a number of companies who are associated with the petroleum and petro-chemical industries. It was set up in order to provide an electronic marketplace for transactions for these industries, ranging from the supply of chemicals to the provision of tanker transport. A typical user of the *Enerva* computer system might be an oil company who would, for example, use the system to look for financial backing, the supply of crude oil, refining capacity and shipping capacity. This application is an excellent example of an application which requires a client–server solution: high reliability is required since, if a supplier goes offline, it can cost millions of dollars in lost business; scalability is important – as the application becomes more and more successful more and more companies will want to join *Enerva*; and openness is important, since the companies that use the facilities of *Enerva* will have a variety of computing systems which will need to communicate with the *Enerva* servers.

2   Servers

There are a large number of types of server which can be found in a distributed system. This section details the main ones. It is based on lists presented in [1, 2].

2.1 Types of server

Servers

2.1.1 File servers

A **file server** provides files for the clients that ask for its service. A typical example of this type of server is one which maintains a database of scientific data, for example files containing a description of bimolecular data used in the Human Genome Project. They act as a central repository of data and dispense files when a client asks for them.

Computing and the
Human Genome
Project

The Human Genome Project

The last 20 years have seen a huge expansion in what we know about the genetic makeup of human beings. The project which has enabled this to happen is the Human Genome Project. The project, which has involved thousands of researchers throughout the world, had as its main aim the plotting of the genetic structure of mankind. This major scientific achievement was completed in 2000; however, it is not the end of the story. A huge mass of data has been created by the project which requires computer processing to discover, for example, the function of parts of our genetic structure; research which the American computer scientist Donald Knuth has stated will keep computer scientists busy for the next 500 years. There are a number of file servers and database servers located throughout the Internet which provide facilities for geneticists, molecular biologists and computer scientists to download the data prior to analysis.

2.1.2 Database servers

Chapter 5 will look at database servers in more detail

Database servers are computers which store large collections of data which are structured, for example the data on the stock in a warehouse which relates products to the number in stock. The main use of such servers is to support queries made upon the database by clients.

The query is normally framed using a special language known as SQL (**Structured Query Language**) with the database server carrying out most, if not all, of the processing, and with the client carrying out the display of the query result.

2.1.3 Groupware servers

Groupware

Groupware is software which organises the work of a number of staff in some enterprise – often these staff are collected together into teams or some other functional grouping. A groupware system typically implements the following functions:

- Managing the time of individuals and teams, for example maintaining a chart of tasks and the dates that they should be completed by.

- Providing reports for billing of the time spent on particular tasks.

- E-mail list management, for example adding members to a list, deleting members and sending messages to members.

Lotus Notes

Lotus Notes: an example of groupware

Without a doubt one of the most popular groupware products is *Lotus Notes* developed and marketed by the Lotus Corporation. It contains a large amount of functionality including that of administering personal diaries, administering the diary for a particular project, filing and archiving personal and project e-mail and searching for company information such as the e-mail address of a particular employee. A typical task that *Notes* carries out almost automatically is that of cancelling and rearranging meetings. When a user wants to cancel a meeting they will inform *Notes* which meeting is to be cancelled; it will then e-mail all the participants with this information and check their diaries for a spare slot into which the rearranged meeting can be scheduled. It will then inform the person that cancelled the meeting the details of the slot; they will then confirm that it is acceptable. *Notes* will then e-mail all the participants with details of the new meeting and update their diaries.

2.1.4 Web servers

Web servers and their programming will be examined in a lot more detail in Chapters 6 and 7

A **Web server** is a special type of file server. It contains files which store the various components of a Web site: pages of text, video clips, audio clips, animations and graphics. When a file is required, say when the user of a browser clicks on a hyperlink referencing a Web page, then the server will send the page to the client. The client will then process the page and then display it.

2.1.5 Mail servers

Later in this chapter I shall look at one example of a mail protocol, POP3

A mail server is a computer which has the task of receiving, storing and sending e-mail. Such servers do not require a massive amount of processor power and are often implemented on small to medium PCs.

Mail servers

Eudora Internet Mail Server: an example of a server

This is an archetypal mail server program which is intended for the Macintosh series of operating systems. It is a typical example of a server in that it provides a wide variety of services connected with one particular functional area: that of e-mail processing. It provides facilities for sending mail using any of the standard Internet protocols, allows spam blocking and implements a number of security controls. The server also provides facilities for the mail administrator to tune it in order to adjust mail message queue parameters to optimise the speed with which users can send and receive e-mail.

2.1.6 Object servers

Distributed objects will be described in a lot more detail in Chapters 9 and 10. As part of Chapter 9 you will be provided with an exercise which asks you to implement a simple object server

One area of distributed computing which has made great strides over the past five years has been that of distributed objects. This technology has enabled developers to create objects on one computer and provide facilities for programs executing on a client computer to send messages to them. A server holding distributed objects is known as an object server.

2.1.7 Print servers

A **print server** is a computer which receives requests from clients for printing. Typically such a server will:

- Queue up requests for a printing facility.

- Schedule requests for a printing facility.

- Instruct a printer to carry out some printing process.

- Inform a requesting client that a printing request has completed successfully.

2.1.8 Application servers

Later in this chapter I shall be describing tiered architectures. Application servers provide an intermediate tier in such architectures

An **application server** is a server which is dedicated to one or more particular applications and contains special-purpose programming code that is specific to that application. A server which implements functions associated with air-traffic control is a good example of an application server.

SETI and mass computing

The search for extra terrestrial intelligence

The World Wide Web is an example of a client–server system, albeit a conceptually very simple one. One of the most remarkable popular developments that the Web has enabled is that of mass computing, or as it is more commonly known, meta computing. Here, users of the Web employ slack time on their computer to carry out some computationally heavy task as part of a larger project. Probably the best known mass computing project is SETI (Search for Extra Terrestrial Intelligence). Web users register with the SETI site and download a program which analyses radio telescope data to look for regularities which might indicate life outside our solar system. The program is executed in slack periods, for example when a participant is sitting at a computer reading a Web page. The calculations produced are periodically uploaded to the SETI site for further analysis. SETI is not the only mass computing project: currently projects exist which are attempting to find large prime numbers, calculate pi and crack cryptographic codes. They represent examples of an unusual client–server system which we can all participate in!

2.2 Tiered architectures

The aim of this section is to look at two popular architectures used in distributed systems, architectures which are made up of clients, servers and a software layer known as middleware. Middleware is discussed in more detail in the next section.

In Chapter 7 there is a programming exercise which gets you to develop a very simple Web server. Also the case study in Chapter 17 is designed as a three-tier architecture. Exercise 3.1 below asks you to develop a simple three-tier system

The first is a **two-tier architecture**. It consists of a presentation and logic layer and a database layer. The **presentation and logic layer** has the function of displaying some set of visual widgets to the user (buttons, text fields etc.) and carrying out the processing on any data returned by a server, for example displaying it on some text widget.

The **data layer** or database layer which resides on a server is used for the storage of any application data such as bank accounts in a banking application or invoices in a sales application. This data is usually stored in some permanent medium such as a relational database.

Figure 3.1
A three-tier
architecture

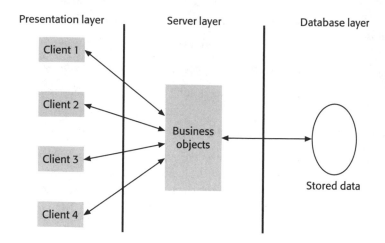

Presentation layer   Server layer   Database layer

Two-tier architectures are used when there is little or no processing required of data. A good example of this is the Web server. The browser represents the presentation and logic layer and the Web server data (Web pages, audio clips, animations etc.) is stored in the data layer. There is little processing required of the data (a Web page), just its display.

When applications involve considerable processing and experience changes in functionality during their lifetime problems start to emerge. For example, software used by clients has to be kept up to date and versions of client code have to be distributed to what could be a very large number of clients. Figure 3.1 shows the solution adopted by the vast majority of developers to overcome these problems: the three-tier architecture. It consists of a **presentation layer**, a **processing layer** (or **application server layer**) and a **data layer**. This architecture turns up time and time again in this book.

The presentation layer is responsible for the human–computer interface, the database layer holds the permanent data and the processing layer is responsible for the processing associated with the application, for example it will interpret requests from a client and route them to a suitable server.

This middle layer enables the developer to isolate the main part of an application that can change over time: the data and the relationships inherent in the data. In this layer can be found objects known as **business object**s. These correspond to entities in the application domain, for example in a sales application, objects such as invoices, products and sales notes and in an online auction application entities such as buyers and bids. The presentation layer will communicate with the objects in this layer; these will then communicate with the database layer in order to retrieve data that the user has requested.

The middle layer could be placed on the same server which holds the application data or it could be placed on a separate server. There are a whole series of application factors and design criteria which guide this decision, for example whether the server is required to be physically located near to the clients that use it.

Exercise 3.1

Developing a
simple three-tier
application for an
e-commerce
application

The topic of distributed
system design is
described later in
Chapter 14

There are a number of advantages to using three-tier architectures [1]:

Servers which contain a lot of code are also known as **fat servers**. If the client does not contain much code then it known as a **thin client**

- It isolates the database technology used to implement the final layer. For example, upgrading to another SQL-compliant database should only require small changes to the server layer.

- It removes a large amount of code from the clients and places it on the server.

- It fits in with modern object-oriented ideas as the processing code is associated with objects.

Network computers

An extreme view of a client–server system where nearly all the functionality of a system is embedded within a server, with the client acting virtually as a dumb terminal, is the network computer idea which Sun Microsystems tried to popularise in the late 1990s. Here the idea was that virtually all the software in a client–server system was embedded in the server, with clients having minimal hardware. Such clients, known as network computers, contained only input/output devices and memory, not mass storage. They would access software such as word processors and spreadsheets from the server. Network computing has a number of advantages. The two main ones were the fact that software version control was easy: since software was executed on a server there would be no problems with ensuring that every client had the same version of software. It also meant that administration of a system containing network computers was easy. The idea of the network computer has not taken off; the fact that it looked very much like a return to the days of mainframe computers and dumb terminals put very many potential customers off.

---

3 Middleware

Communication between a client and server is not direct. Often when a client demands a service of a server the request proceeds through a number of intermediate layers of software which interpose themselves between clients and servers. This intermediate software is known as **middleware**. It forms a vital part of any client–server system. Happily, for most of the time, the programmer and designer do not have to worry about how it works; they just have to use it via method invocations. The concept of middleware is somewhat nebulous; the best definition is from Orfali, Harkey and Edwards [2]:

> Middleware is a vague term that covers all the distributed software needed to support interactions between clients and server. . . . Where does the middleware start and where does it end? It starts with the API set on the client side that is used to invoke a service, and it covers the transmission of the request over the network and the resulting response.

It is worth pointing out that there are many types of middleware that you will meet and this is only one example

The best example of middleware is the software that interfaces a browser and the World Wide Web. When a Web page is requested, say when a user clicks a hyperlink in a page, a text message which forms part of a protocol is sent to the middleware asking for this page. The middleware will then locate the page, retrieve it and send it back to the browser. As part of the middleware there is code which is concerned with finding pages, monitoring errors, reporting errors, transporting data and communicating with the low-level software which forms part of the TCP/IP suite discussed in the previous chapter.

There are two categories of middleware [1]: general middleware and service middleware. General middleware is software which is associated with services required by *all* clients and servers; normally much of this middleware is associated with an operating system. Typical software that comes under this banner includes:

■ Software for carrying out processes such as transporting raw character data around the Internet.

Database processing is described in Chapter 5

■ Software which keeps a number of replicated files in synchronisation.

■ Software which administers a distributed collection of files.

Service middleware is associated with a specific service such as printing a file on a remote printer. Typical examples include:

■ Software which allows a client to query a database, for example software which interprets and executes a query made by the user of some client computer and processes the results of the query sending back the results to a client.

RMI is described in more detail in Chapter 9

■ Software associated with distributed object schemes such as RMI. Such software enables a user to create an object and allows clients to send messages to that object. It will implement functions associated with security, locating an object, transporting data associated with method arguments to a distributed object and transporting the result of a message being sent to a distributed object.

■ Middleware associated with newsgroups which allows the user to read and post to the newsgroups.

Before moving on it is worth looking in a bit more detail at a general form of technology known as message-oriented middleware. It provides a simple example of general middleware.

3.1 Message-oriented middleware

Message-oriented middleware

Message-oriented middleware (MOM) is software which manages the transactions that pass from a client to a server and vice versa. A typical piece of MOM will contain a number of queues which contain messages and data originated by either a server or a client. Clients – for example, a salesman using a portable computer – will continually deposit requests into the MOM and a server will take those requests, respond to them and deposit any data that should be sent back into the MOM. The middleware mediates between the clients and any servers. Such software has a number of advantages: clients do not need to be connected all the time – they can just place data in the middleware and disconnect, picking up any responses at a later time. Also, the model of interaction is simple: all it consists of is the client placing data on a queue maintained by the middleware and the server removing the data, processing it and placing some response back on a queue. Because of this simplicity MOM is often used to connect software to legacy systems.

An example of MOM being used for integration is detailed in the second shaded box below

MQSeries

The *MQSeries* of middleware products was extensively used in the Sydney Olympics system described in Chapter 1

MQSeries

Without a doubt the leading message-oriented middleware product is *MQSeries* which has been developed by IBM. It processes four types of messages: Datagrams are one-way messages with no associated reply message to be returned, for example a signal that a client is online; Request Messages are used when the sender expects to get a reply, for example when sending a query to a database; Reply Messages are the messages that are sent in response to request messages; and, finally, Report Messages are used to signal to a client that some unexpected event has occurred. For example, a server has malfunctioned. The API for *MQSeries* is exceptionally simple and consists of just 11 program calls.

The VF Corporation

System Integration, MOM and the VF Corporation

The VF Corporation is one of the largest clothing manufacturers in the United States. Like many companies it has grown partly through acquiring other companies that complemented its core business. This meant that in the late 1990s the corporation was running a large number of heterogeneous systems. As part of a business re-engineering process the corporation decided to integrate all its systems so that data from one system, for example a materials ordering system, could properly communicate with another system, for example an accounting system. The company chose as the software glue the MOM product *MQSeries*. This software has an exceptionally simple programming interface. Rather than change the large amount of software which their current systems contained so that they communicated with other software, the MIS department decided on using MOM since it has a simple interface and could be managed centrally; for example, *MQSeries* enables staff to tune the algorithms that it uses in order to respond to changes in transaction rates. Carrying out such an optimisation locally on the various systems used by the VF Corporation would have been a nightmare.

4   Protocols

The aim of this section is to look at the concept of a protocol and describe a small number of popular protocols. A protocol is a set of rules governing message interchanges which occur between a number of computers in a distributed system; each of

In Chapter 11 I look in great detail at the protocol used by the secure sockets layer to implement secure transaction processing across the Internet

these messages implement functions of the system. A protocol is also used to establish a connection and allow entities to exchange data about themselves, for example the operating system they are using and the format of the data that they intend passing; this is known as a **handshake**.

4.1 A simple application protocol

In order to describe the concept of a protocol I shall use a small example: that of a client that is used to interrogate a database of clothing products in an e-tailing application, where the client and the server communicate using a series of messages which embed some indication of the functionality required and the data associated with the function that is to be carried out. This is an example of an **application protocol**; later in this section I shall look at some protocols associated with middleware.

For example, the customer may exercise the function of asking for details of all the shirts stocked by the clothing company.

```
Det  Shirts
```

where `Det` specifies the fact that the user wishes details of a certain category of clothing to be returned. The server will then process this message and return the details; the message that is returned might look like

```
DetList

Shirt Blue 1999 ..
Shirt White 2199 ..

..
```

Where the string `DetList` indicates that a list of product details is being sent, with each product being identified by its name, price in pence or cents and other data. The client will then process this message and display the details of each product on some output widget.

If the client wanted to know the specific price of a certain product such as a red jumper then a message such as

```
ProdPrice   Red1001
```

would be sent, where the string `ProdPrice` indicates that a price is required and the string `Red1001` is some catalogue number that identifies the product involved in the query. The server might then respond with the message

```
Price  2499
```

which indicates a price of £24.99.

An important point to make about protocols is that whatever mechanism is used to communicate between clients and servers at the lowest level a protocol will be involved. For example, later in this book you will learn about distributed objects – objects which can be placed on a remote computer and to which messages can be sent. All the distributed object schemes that are used in the computer industry employ some low-level protocol to implement the process of sending messages and transferring data.

The RMI distributed object model in Java, detailed in Chapter 9, employs TCP/IP

The protocol that I have described is an application protocol; it is now worth looking at some more protocols which are associated with middleware.

4.2 The POP3 protocol

The POP3 (Post Office Protocol version 3) is a widely used mailing protocol that is used for the processing of electronic mail.

The IMAP protocol

There are a number of mail protocols used in the Internet. They range from simple ones such as POP3 to more complicated ones such as IMAP. The POP3 protocol enables users to send and retrieve e-mail from a special mail server known as a POP server.

Table 3.1 taken from [1] shows a small subset of the POP3 protocol in terms of the messages that can be sent.

A mail server using POP3 as its protocol will use the dedicated port 110. The Java code below shows how you can interact with a POP3 server using the protocol.

```
String userIdentity = "D.C.Ince";
String passWord = "Cludge4";
Socket popSock = new Socket(110, "e-mailR.open.ac.uk");
OutputStream os = popSock.getOutputStream();
InputStream is = popSock.getInputStream();
PrintStream inPop = new PrintStream(os, true);
// Here we would set up a BufferedReader br to
// read responses, it would be based on the InputStream is
ps.println("USER "+ userIdentity);
. .
ps.println("PASS "+ passWord);
```

Table 3.1
A subset of the POP3 protocol

Message	Meaning
USER	The user is going to retrieve mail
PASS	Here is my e-mail password
STAT	How many messages are there waiting to be read?
DELE	I want to delete an e-mail message
RETR	I want to retrieve some e-mail messages

POP3

```
String response = br.readLine();
//If the mail server does not respond with a line with a first
//character '+' then an error has occurred, since the
//command communicated a password there must be a problem
//with it
if(response.charAt(0) != '+')
{
    System.out.println("Password not recognised");
    ..
}
else
{
    ps.println("STAT");
    //Processing of email statistics follows from here
    ..
}
```

Exercise 3.2

Developing a
simple mail client

The processing shown in the code above is straightforward. First a socket is established to the POP mail server emailR.open.ac.uk. This is followed by the establishment of an input and output stream to the server using this socket. The input stream is then used to send messages to the mail server using the POP3 protocol. The first message informs the server of the name of the user, the second message informs the server of the user's password. After the password has been communicated to the mail server the server responds with some indication of whether it has recognised the user. The normal rule with the POP3 protocol is that if a response line starts with the character '+' then everything is proceeding normally; if not an error has occurred. This means that an explicit check needs to be carried out for this after the client has communicated the password to the server. Finally, the client asks the server for the number of mail messages waiting to be read by sending a STAT message to it.

JavaMail

Mail APIs and JavaMail

The example above represents a form of raw low-level programming which is gradually declining. Increasingly, collections of classes and associated methods for mail protocols have become available. Such collections, known as Application Programming Interfaces (APIs), provide high-level interfaces to mail protocols. Almost certainly the best known of these is *JavaMail*. This enables the programmer to very quickly develop e-mail applications for all the popular e-mail protocols without knowing very much about the low-level details of individual protocols.

4.3 The Secure Sockets Layer

Chapter 11 describes
this protocol in much
more detail

In Chapter 11 you will learn about security in distributed applications. It is vitally important that sensitive applications such as those used in e-tailing which use credit card details send data in such a way that an intruder cannot read it. One way of doing this is to use a technique known as cryptography which transforms any transmitted data into a form which cannot be deciphered. The Secure Sockets Layer is a middleware technology which is used to send this data. It uses a protocol to negotiate a specific algorithm used to carry out the transmission and a key which is used to transform the data.

4.4 Stacks and hierarchy

Exercise 3.3

Sending an HTP message to a Web server

In Chapter 2 I described the concept of a layered architecture which consists of a number of layers which draw services from lower layers. Protocols fit nicely into this model; for example, the HTTP protocol uses and depends on protocols which are embedded within the TCP/IP suite of protocols. The hierarchical collection of protocols which are related to lower level protocols by virtue of the fact that they employ them to carry out their functions is known as a **protocol stack**. It is worth pointing out that this bears no relation to the data structure known as a stack.

5   Internal and external services

5.1 Introduction

The aim of this section is to describe the panoply of services that are provided as part of the infrastructure of a distributed system. In order to do this I will need first to distinguish between an external service and an internal service.

An **external service** is one which is provided to a user, the best example of this is a Web service. This is a form of file service which dispenses HTML and associated files to a user who employs a browser. It is the service that the user *directly* experiences when interacting with a distributed system.

Internal services are sometimes known as operating system services

An **internal service** is a service which supports an external service and which forms part of the infrastructure of a distributed system. An example of such a service is a file service which maintains files within the system and enables programmers to access these files without worrying about where they are located. Usually, internal services are provided as part of the system software that is used to support distributed applications.

The remaining part of this section looks broadly at the services that a distributed application can call on. The middle of the book will look at external services and application topics, finally returning to topics such as concurrency which, although they are associated with internal services, are an important consideration when designing a distributed application.

5.2 File services

File services are one of the most heavily used parts of a distributed system. They should have the following properties [4]:

Many of these transparencies are reflected in Date's rules for distributed databases detailed in Chapter 5

In Chapter 12 I look at concurrency in more detail with a view to seeing how it affects the design processes involved in developing distributed systems

■ *Access transparency*. The software facilities for accessing (reading, writing, modifying and deleting) a file should not be different depending on whether the file is held on a local or a remote computer.

■ *Location transparency*. This means that whenever a program refers to a file that file can be moved to another location without changing the file reference. That means, for example, program code referring to a file should just refer to its symbolic name without specifying where on a network the file is held.

■ *Concurrency transparency*. This means that when a number of concurrently executing programs access a file they should not interfere with each other, for example erroneously overwriting data which has been written to the file. This is a major problem which has bedevilled programmers for many years and has not been confined to distributed systems. The internal service which implements the control of concurrency should take all the complexity away from the programmer. It should provide a layer of software access that hides the concurrency control processes.

■ *Failure transparency*. This means that when a failure occurs, whether it is a software or hardware failure, then it should not affect the file system; it should not, for example, corrupt the data held in a file. Again the details whereby this is implemented should be totally hidden from the programmer and is normally implemented as part of the operating system.

■ *Performance transparency*. This means that programs which access a distributed file system should perform within a specified performance limit during what is regarded as the normal loading of the system.

■ *Hardware and operating system heterogeneity*. This means that when a distributed system consists of a number of different hardware and software components, perhaps spread over a number of different operating systems, then the access to files within the system is uniform.

■ *Scalability*. This means that a file service should be able to cope with the growth of a system: as more and more computers hosting more and more files are added, the system should cope with this in terms of performance.

■ *Replication transparency*. One common technique for providing reliability, and also increasing performance, is that of data replication. Here copies or partial copies of files are maintained across a distributed system so that, for example, the user of a file has a local copy stored at their computer or at the local area network to which their computer is connected, rather than having to access the file across a slow wide area network connection. Replication transparency ensures that when a program accesses a file there is no extra code at the application level that is needed in order to cope with the fact that the file is a replica.

■ *Migration transparency*. This means that when a file is physically moved from one computer to another, or even from one folder to another on the same computer, the programs that access it do not need to be modified.

5.3 Naming services

In a distributed system there will be a large number of entities such as computers, files, printers and networks which require to be accessed by programs. Such entities often have physical addresses. For example, on the Internet, computers are uniquely identified using dotted quad notation, for example 104.55.66.90.

A naming service is a way of associating entities in a distributed system with some symbolic name. Already you have seen one example of such a service: the Internet Domain Naming Service which associates the name of a host on the Internet with some hierarchically qualified name such as www.open.ac.uk.

The association between a name and the physical resource that it refers to is known as a **binding**. The process of discovering the physical identity of a resource given its name is known as **resolving**.

Name services are usually implemented in a distributed system in a highly reliable way. A naming service is continually being consulted by programs in the system, and if it malfunctioned the system would be seriously compromised. A typical way of implementing a naming service is to have it run concurrently on a number of servers each running the same service.

5.4 Directory services

A directory service is similar in many respects to a naming service; indeed, many developers regard it as synonymous. However, there is an important difference. A naming service associates a name with some object such as a printer or a computer; a directory service associates a name with a set of attributes and resources. When you use a naming service you ask for the object associated with a single name; when you use a directory service you can specify a general set of search criteria such as 'find me all the printers in the system which deliver a speed of 10 pages or more and which are connected to the local area networks LAN1 and LAN2'. Such directory services are also used to store non-computer data such as companies, staff and departments.

LDAP

Almost certainly the most popular directory service is LDAP. This is a practical version of the service specified by the X.500 standard for directory services. It organises itself into a tree similar to that found in the Internet Domain Name Service. There are a number of programming interfaces to LDAP. In Java the interface is via a set of components known as JNDI (Java Naming and Directory Interface).

5.5 Time services

Computers in a distributed system will have their own clocks. These clocks are accurate for tasks such as displaying the current time to the user. However, when transactions that are time-sensitive are involved these clocks can be unreliable if, for example, certain operations depend on accurate timing. Computer clocks suffer from time drift, for example the crystal oscillators in the computer are sensitive to heat and their frequency will vary with temperature; and, in order to provide time data, a distributed system will often have a time service implemented. Such time services rely on sampling time from highly accurate clocks that use atomic oscillators whose accuracy can be as small as 1 part in 10^{13}. Time services rely on sophisticated algorithms and employ a number of replicated servers, each of which takes over the time service if a time server fails.

5.6 Replication services

Chapter 14 describes this and similar design techniques

A distributed system will contain replicated data. There are a number of reasons for this: having copies of data on a number of servers means that if one fails then another can be used by the system. There is also a performance reason in that replicated data can be held physically close to a user and reduces the transmission time which might occur if the data were held on a wide area network.

A replication service carries out a number of functions:

- It keeps track of the physical locations of the replicated data.

- It monitors changes to a database and then applies the same change to other replicas.

- It holds back transactions on a replicated database until that database comes back into synchronisation with the most recent copy.

5.7 Transaction services

Chapter 13 describes problems with transactions and some solutions

A transaction is a series of operations on stored data in which all the operations either succeed or fail. For example, a transaction which created a new customer record, set up an empty account and wrote data to a journal file, is an example of a transaction. Because the three operations are related they all have to fully complete or not complete at all if, for example, an error occurred.

A major component of a distributed system is a transaction service which monitors the transactions that are occurring and ensure that the above property together with a series of other properties are maintained. Such services are implemented by servers sometimes known as **transaction monitors**. Such servers are highly complex pieces of software and are a major source of business for large system suppliers.

5.8 Concurrency control services

Distributed systems operate concurrently, for example a database server will execute at the same time as a Web server which will operate at the same time as an application program. Such concurrency is used for performance reasons: it makes no sense for a program executing on one computer to wait for another program on another

Chapters 12, 13 and 14 look at the problems of concurrency, the solutions and how the solutions affect the distributed application design process

computer to complete if the first program does not require to communicate with it. Sometimes, however, programs need to communicate, for example when exchanging data or when they read or write to the same area of memory or a file.

When this happens the data that they access can be corrupted. In order to ensure that this does not happen, a distributed system will provide a concurrency control service. In essence this service makes sure that any sensitive operations are completed by one program before another program accesses the data that was the subject of the operations.

5.9 Security services

As you will see later in this book, the Internet is something of an insecure network. The major reasons for this are that it is pervasive and its protocols and software specifications are public. This means that intruders could enter a computer which is connected to the network and carry out acts such as destroying files, reading sensitive information and using sensitive information for criminal intent such as masquerading as the owner of a credit card.

Chapter 11 describes these services in more detail

Security services pervade a network; they range from providing cryptographic facilities whereby traffic across a network is coded so that it cannot be read, to providing certification of users so that they can be authenticated when they carry out a potentially sensitive task such as reading a file or instigating a credit card transaction.

5.10 External services

The previous sections have described the infrastructural services that are provided within a distributed system. How these services are provided depends on the service; for example, a distributed file system often forms part of an operating system, and security services are often supplied by special-purpose software which acts as an add-on to an operating system. What is clear, however, is that for most of the time the developer should be unaware of the mechanisms used to implement the services: the designer or programmer should just assume that an application programmer's interface exists that calls on this interface. The remainder of the book will concentrate on external services at the application level; whenever an internal service is described it will be done only in order to illustrate some teaching point about an external service.

6   Enterprise frameworks

6.1 Introduction

An enterprise framework, sometimes known as an application framework, is the term given to a collection of software which enables a programmer to access the facilities that implement distributed applications. The term **enterprise application** is beginning to take over from more venerable terms such as management information application (American) and data processing application (British).

In effect, an enterprise framework provides a set of application programmer's interfaces (APIs) which shield the programmer from the details of protocols and transport mechanisms.

Application programmer's interface

Such an interface provides methods and constants which enable a programmer to rapidly develop software, not just for the Internet but for any application. In the context of this book the APIs that are described will all be Internet-related. As an example of the facilities offered by an API and how it shields the programmer from messy detail, consider the Java mail API. Within this API are two methods – `setText` and `send` – which create the text for an e-mail message and then send it. For example:

```
. .
emailMessage.setText("Hello  there");
transportMechanism.send(emailMessage);
```

will set the text of an e-mail message to a simple greeting and send it. The object `transportMechanism` is set to whatever mail protocol is being used, for example SMTP or POP3. The code assumes that other parts of the e-mail message have been set, for example the destination and the header.

6.2 Features

An enterprise framework should ideally have the following features:

- *Multi-language support.* Ideally the framework should be capable of being programmed in a number of programming languages, with these languages compiling to object code which has a common format. This would enable compiled code from a number of sources to be integrated.

- *Support for legacy code.* It should provide interfaces to code written by older programming languages so that Internet-based systems can be easily integrated with that code.

- *Support for high-volume transactions.* The framework should be capable of supporting code which can be used in an application server; the code should be capable of being efficiently executed – even when the volume of transactions is high.

- *Messaging support.* Much of the communication between entities in a distributed application is done via messages. Already you have seen how POP3 does this. An enterprise framework should support this communication paradigm.

- *Web server programming.* When a Web server receives a request for a Web page, such as a form, there is a need for a program to be executed, for example to

An example of an application server can be found in Chapter 13

retrieve data from a database. A good framework should provide the programmer with the facilities that enable browser requests to be parsed, unbundled and the processing associated with the request to be carried out, with some response being sent back to the browser.

- *XML facilities.* As you will see later in this book, XML is a major Internet technology which is beginning to control the textual chaos of the Internet. It is a technology which allows developers to define special-purpose languages, for example to describe the wares of an e-shop; such languages can then be processed by anyone with XML software. An enterprise framework which does not provide facilities for XML processing is severely limited.

XML is described in Chapter 8

- *Interface to standard protocols.* An enterprise framework should enable a programmer to access the individual commands that make up a protocol such as HTTP. While, increasingly, this is not required for many applications, there are some applications (usually those that require runtime efficiency) where access to low-level details of an Internet technology is required.

- *Database connectivity.* The vast majority of enterprise applications require databases to function. An enterprise framework must be capable of interfacing with the main database types.

Chapter 5 describes how Java interfaces with relational databases

- *Naming services.* An enterprise framework should provide facilities whereby the programmer can write code that consults a naming or directory service such as LDAP.

- *Security services.* As you will see later in this book, security is a major problem in distributed systems. An enterprise framework should provide facilities whereby the programmer can send secure data across a network, authorise access and check that an entity that is accessing an application is allowed to do so.

6.3 The J2EE framework

One of the best-known enterprise frameworks is the J2EE (Java 2 Enterprise Edition) framework. The aim of this section is to briefly describe its main features. Many of the components of this framework will be described in detail in later parts of this book.

6.3.1 Java Database Connectivity (JDBC)

The JDBC API contains facilities whereby a relational database can be written to and read from. It allows the programmer to:

- connect up to a database on a local or remote computer;

- send programming statements in a language known as SQL to the database. Such statements will either retrieve data from the database or update it;

- interpret and process the results of any queries that have been sent in SQL, for example the names of staff in a personnel system.

The JDBC API enables the Java programmer to interface with any standard relational database.

6.3.2 Remote object access

Increasingly, the object-oriented paradigm is being used to develop systems, and languages such as C++, C# and Java are beginning to predominate over non-object-oriented languages such as C. There is hence a need for distributed systems to be viewed and developed as a collection of objects to which messages can be sent. Distributed object schemes implement objects on remote computers and allow other computers to send messages to them. The J2EE framework contains two such schemes: CORBA, a multi-language approach which allows communication between objects written in a number of languages, and RMI, a Java only solution.

Chapter 9 describes RMI and Chapter 10 describes CORBA

6.3.3 Enterprise JavaBeans

J2EE contains a facility whereby Enterprise JavaBeans can be developed. These are chunks of code which handle transactions and have the property that they can be moved easily from one Enterprise-JavaBean-compliant transaction server to another. Enterprise JavaBeans solve many of the transaction problems associated with the high-volume transaction rates found in modern distributed applications.

6.3.4 The Java Message Service

Much of the communication in a distributed system is carried out by computers sending messages to each other: a client will send a message to a server asking for a service and the server will satisfy the service by sending data to the client, encapsulated in a message.

J2EE contains a set of facilities known as the Java Message Service which allows a form of message processing similar to that found in message-oriented middleware. It enables the client-side programmer to establish a connection to a queue and then send messages to that queue. These messages can then be read by a server which might then add further messages to the queue for the client to process.

6.3.5 Java Naming and Directory Interface (JNDI)

JNDI is an API that enables the programmer to write program code to interface to an existing naming or directory service. For example, using JNDI it is easy to interface to LDAP and query an LDAP server for directory information.

6.3.6 Legacy interfacing

When you want to connect to another system from a Java-developed system then the facility that you use is called the J2EE Connector. The program code required is similar to that used for the JDBC: a connection is established to the foreign code and data is sent using that connection.

6.3.7 XML processing

In Chapter 8 you will meet two of these models: DOM and SAX

The J2EE framework contains facilities whereby languages which are defined by XML are processed and, for example, converted into source expressed in another language such as HTML. There are a large number of APIs available to the Java programmer based on a number of processing models which enable lines of XML-defined source to be read, elements of the source recognised and code executed based on what has been recognised.

6.3.8 Web server programming

In Chapter 7 you will meet both servlets and JSP

J2EE contains extensive facilities for augmenting the actions of a Web server with programmer-defined code. The two main components of J2EE that do this are servlets and Java Server Pages (JSP). A servlet is a snippet of code that is executed whenever a request is processed by a Web server. For example, the Web server associated with a stockbroking firm may receive a request for a stock quote from a user employing a browser who has just filled in a Web form. The browser communicates with the Web server, the server recognises the form that has been filled in, executes the servlet associated with the form which retrieves some stock data from a database and then sends back a Web page with the required data. Java Server Pages are similar to servlets, the major difference being that the processing code is intermingled with the HTML code within the page.

6.3.9 Security in J2EE

Security is discussed at great length in Chapter 11

Security is a major worry in any distributed system, in particular Internet systems because they are so pervasive and are implemented over publicly accessible communication media which require very high levels of security. Java contains a sophisticated security framework which enables a high degree of security to be achieved. For example, the main technology that is used to enforce security is cryptography. This involves changing data in a message by modifying the individual characters in the message so that it could not be read by an electronic eavesdropper. J2EE contains a security known as the Java Cryptography Extension (JCE) which contains facilities for using a wide variety of secure algorithms for cryptography together with allied facilities which verify digital signatures and check that users are authorised.

6.3.10 Access to standard protocols

In this chapter you have seen how sockets and server sockets can be used to send messages to and from a server. One of the examples I used was sending POP3 messages to a POP mail server. This type of processing can be carried out with any of the protocols that are employed on the Internet, including HTTP, IMAP4 and SMTP. Although many of the APIs – for example the Java mail API – in the J2EE framework abstract away from this level of processing, it is still available for the Java programmer who wishes to achieve an extra level of efficiency.

.Net

6.4 The .Net framework

In 2000, Microsoft announced what is probably its largest software development programme. It was known as .Net and involved configuring many of its products such as Excel, Word, MS Access together with its supported programming languages such as Visual Basic and C++ so that they are seamlessly integrated with the Internet and with each other.

The .Net framework provides similar facilities to the J2EE framework detailed above:

- Access to relational database products such as Access and SQL Server.

- Access to the remote object technology DCOM.

- The ability to send messages using the messaging technology known as SOAP.

- The ability to access directory and naming services.

- Facilities for Web server programming.

- The ability to interface with legacy applications, both those developed using Microsoft products and those which have been developed using other platforms such as LINUX. The latter would be integrated into .Net systems using SOAP and standard Internet protocols.

- Access to standard protocols such as HTTP and FTP via programming languages such as Visual Basic and C++.

These technologies are detailed in Chapter 11

- Security implemented using cryptography, digital certificates and other security technologies.

- Access to a sophisticated range of XML facilities.

There are a number of differences between J2EE and the .Net framework. First, J2EE is platform independent. Although it is possible to integrate legacy software from other platforms with .Net code, currently the main thrust of the framework is development using Microsoft proprietary products. However, Microsoft has published details of the framework so that other vendors can implement it on other platforms.

Another important difference is that .Net is a multi-language approach. A large number of programming languages are able to be used with the framework and modules from each of these languages integrated together. This is achieved by having a common compiled language known as MSIL (Microsoft Simple Intermediate Language) which is similar in concept to Java byte code.

Another important difference is that the XML technology is placed more centrally in .Net than in J2EE. The key idea behind .Net is that of a Web service: a service which is provided over the Internet using standard Internet protocols. The .Net technology uses XML to implement these services.

XML is discussed in detail in Chapter 8 and the concept of a Web service is detailed at the end of Chapter 7

At the time of writing, .Net is still in its infancy and no predictions can really be made about its uptake. However, it is certain that the size of Microsoft's customer base is such that it will be extensively used.

7 Why client–server?

A question which was probably on your mind when you started this chapter was: what is the point in organising a computer system as a set of servers with clients accessing the services provided by them? Some of the advantages of client–server computing were alluded to in this chapter and it is now worth collecting them together with some of the advantages which were not described.

It is worth pointing out that as computers are added the performance of a system does not increase linearly, communication processing reduces the gain; however, careful design usually means that most client–server systems can be fairly easily upgraded to cope with increased demand

- *Openness.* Connecting computers together using a protocol that they all understand means that a wide variety of computers running different operating systems can be employed in a network: all that is needed is for there to be code within each computer that understands the protocols that are employed.

- *Scalability.* Many systems have to grow: for example, a computing system used by a successful company has to cope with larger and larger volumes of transactions. Client–server computing allows servers to be easily added incrementally to cope with any increase in processor, memory and file requirements.

- *Specialisation.* By designing a system containing a large number of relatively small computers acting as servers a designer can ensure that a particular computer is optimised for a particular task such as dispensing files, carrying out processor-intensive calculations or printing files. If many services were centralised on a single computer there would be little chance of such optimisations being carried out.

- *Reliability.* By duplicating data and hardware a high degree of reliability can be achieved. For example, running a server in such a way that its service is taken over by an identical server when it malfunctions means that client–server systems are now being used in the most demanding applications.

Chapter 14 looks at distributed system design in more detail

- *Design flexibility.* Because the hardware elements of a system are fragmented into a number of computers it means that the distributed system designer is faced with a much richer space of design options. For example, one technique used to speed up access in a distributed system is to keep databases close to the computers that use them. Often this is achieved by replicating databases and storing them on the same local area network containing the clients that require the data. This sort of design decision could not be taken with a system where hardware is centralised.

8 Summary

This chapter has examined the basic building blocks of a modern distributed system: servers which provide some service and clients which demand that service. It has looked at a number of servers ranging from a simple name server to very complicated database servers. It has also detailed the way that clients and servers communicate using messages which form part of a protocol. A number of protocols have been described in outline and the fact that they often have a hierarchic relationship with each other explained.

In Chapters 5 and 6 I shall look at two of the most important types of server, Web servers and SQL servers, and show how they can be programmed and how clients interact with them.

9   Further reading

One of the best books that has been written on client–server computing is by Orfali, Harkey and Edwards [2]. It is mainly intended for a professional audience and can be faulted for the large amount of descriptive material on products; however, it is panoramic in its coverage of client–server computing. You do need a little knowledge about TCP/IP to develop distributed applications using the Internet; the book by Parker [3] is a good, gentle introduction. The best book written on the internals of distributed systems is by Coulouris, Dollimore and Kindberg [4].

References

Internet book links

[1] R. Pressman and D.C. Ince, *Software Engineering*, 5th edn. Maidenhead, Berks: McGraw-Hill, 2000.
[2] R. Orfali, D. Harkey and J. Edwards, *The Essential Client/Server Survival Guide*. New York, NY: John Wiley, 1998.
[3] T. Parker, *Teach yourself TCP/IP in 14 Days*. Indianapolis, IN: SAMS Publishing, 1997.
[4] G. Coulouris, J. Dollimore and T. Kindberg, *Distributed Systems Concepts and Design*. Harlow: Addison-Wesley, 2001.

Distributed Paradigms

4

Chapter contents

In this chapter I look at a number of different programming and design styles associated with distributed system development. The chapter first examines message passing and the role of protocols – both fixed and adaptive protocols. Two styles of message passing are also examined: synchronous and asynchronous message passing. The next part of the chapter introduces distributed object technology and acts as a curtain raiser to later chapters which look at specific distributed object technologies in some detail. Event-based development relies on listener objects listening to events which are propagated along a bus; the chapter looks at this form of implementation and details its relationship to multicasting. A commercial implementation of event-based technology is presented. The chapter also includes a description of the oldest paradigm: remote procedure call. The chapter concludes with a description of the most abstract model we have available for distributed system development: that of tuple architectures. A Java implementation known as *JavaSpaces* concludes the chapter.

Aims

1. To describe some of the architectural and programming paradigms used in distributed system development.
2. To describe message passing and the role of protocols within a message passing paradigm.
3. To introduce the concept of a distributed object.
4. To describe how event-based architectures are used within distributed system development.
5. To introduce one implementation of an event-based architecture.
6. To outline the concept of tuple-based development.
7. To introduce the main ideas behind remote procedure call.
8. To introduce one commercial example of a tuple-based technology.

Concepts

Adaptive protocol, API, Asynchronous message passing, Distributed event, Distributed object, Fixed protocol, Hub and spoke architecture, Interface Definition Language, Message passing, Multicast bus architecture, Multicasting, Protocol, Pull technology, Push technology, Remote procedure call, RPC-XML, Space, Synchronous message passing, Tuple.

1   Introduction

So far I have just looked at some general issues concerning distributed systems made up of clients and servers. Before looking in detail at some of the technologies it is worth examining some of the implementation and design models that can be used for distributed system development ranging from the familiar, message passing, to the unfamiliar, tuple-based technology. In describing these I have two aims: first, to detail the variety of methods and architectures that are available and the degree of closeness they have to Internet technologies such as TCP/IP, for example message passing is close in concept to the idea of data flowing down a transmission line, while tuple-based development views a distributed system as just a big, persistent store of objects. The second aim is to examine two different categories of architecture and development: those that are associated with the client initiating a data transfer and those associated with the server carrying out the initiation.

The distributed models that I shall look at in this comparatively brief chapter are: message passing, distributed objects, remote procedure call, event-based technology and tuple-based technology.

2   Message passing

Message passing is the simplest form of development paradigm. In the following chapters you will meet it in a number of forms. For example, in Chapter 7, which deals with programming Web servers, you will see that the way that a client running a browser communicates with a Web server is via message passing.

2.1 Protocols

Protocols have already been introduced in Chapter 3

Message passing is based on the idea of a **protocol**: a language which embodies the functions required by one entity in a distributed system (usually a client) which another entity provides (usually a server). As an example of a protocol consider Table 4.1. It shows the protocol associated with a naming service. This is a service in a

Table 4.1
An example of a simple protocol for a client of a naming service

Function	Meaning
Find *Name*	Finds the resource identified by *Name*
Delete *Name*	Deletes the resource identified by *Name*
Add *Name, Resource*	Adds a new resource identified by *Name*
Modify *Name, Resource*	Changes the resource identified by *Name*

Table 4.2
An example of a
simple protocol
for a server which
implements a
naming service

Function	Meaning
DeleteOK	Deletion of a resource has been carried out successfully
AddOK	Addition of a resource has been carried out successfully
ModifyOK	Modification of a resource has been carried out successfully
Error *Errorcode*	An error has occurred, the nature of the error can be found within the error code value
Resource *Resourcedetails*	A find has been carried out successfully and the resource returned by the client and associated with the name provided

distributed system which associates a name with some resource in the system. For example, it might associate the location of a file within the distributed system with some symbolic name.

Effectively a naming service provides a lookup service for a distributed system. A client using the naming service detailed in Table 4.1 would communicate with the server implementing the naming service using sockets. It would send messages such as

```
Delete  DepartmentX
```

to delete a name/resource pair identified by the string *DepartmentX* and

```
Find  DepartmentY
```

to find details of the resource(s) identified by the string *DepartmentY*.

Table 4.1 shows only one half of a protocol: that associated with client messages; most protocols will also contain the messages sent by a server. For example, Table 4.2 shows a selection of messages which could be sent by the server implementing the name service.

For example, if a client asked for a resource associated with a name using a `Find` message and that resource was successfully identified by the server implementing the name service, then the server would return with the string

```
Resource  Details
```

where `Details` was the details of the resource associated with the name provided by the `Find` message that was issued.

The best known naming service is the domain naming system in the Internet which associates domain names with IP addresses. However, many distributed systems contain their own naming service for resources such as files and collections of data. Such a service provides a simple way of insulating a distributed system from changes in physical details, for example when a file is moved from one computer to another.

*The Internet Domain
Naming system*

For example, a naming service might provide lookup for the symbolic names of files which are stored at a server in a distributed system. Every program which accessed files would consult the naming service before carrying out any processing. If a file location changed then all that would change would be the data held by the naming service, the programs which accessed the files would not need to be changed.

Directory services and JNDI

Naming and directory services

You will often come across the term 'directory service' in the literature. Such a service is a type of very flexible, naming service which contains data about the resources and users of a distributed system. For example, if you want to write a program which discovers what the fastest printer is in a distributed system then the program will consult a directory service. Almost certainly one of the most popular directory services is LDAP (Lightweight Directory Access Protocol). Its roots lie in the development of the OSI Reference Model when a standard called X500 was developed as a part of the OSI effort. Unfortunately X500 was far too complicated and heavy in terms of facilities, even for large distributed systems, and a number of much lighter directory services have emerged over the last decade and become popular. These include LDAP, Novell Directory Services (NDS), Sun's Network Information Services (NIS and NIS+) and the Windows NT Domains from Microsoft. Java has a standard API known as JNDI (Java Naming and Directory Interface) which is able to interface with all these directory services.

2.2 Fixed and adaptive protocols

A fixed protocol could change over a period of time because the functionality provided by a server changes. However, this change will be over months or years rather than over seconds

The protocol described above for a simple naming service is an example of a **fixed protocol**. This is a protocol whose vocabulary is fixed: it is embedded in the client and server's code and data and does not change. An adaptive protocol is one where the protocol changes.

There are some instances where a strictly fixed protocol is not adequate. The most common reason for this is where an application supports variable numbers of arguments. For example, a protocol for a server which supports the functions of reporting on system usage might consist of a command which asks for the identities of the current users of the system. The reply to this service request might consist of anything from zero to thousands of user identities. Another example is where the types of the entities in a protocol command might vary, for example a banking application might require the balance of an account to be returned for either the name of an account holder or the unique integer key which identifies the account.

Another example where an adaptive protocol might be used is when a client and a server have to negotiate some subset of a protocol which they both understand: for example, the client may only understand an early subset of a protocol while the server understands the full up-to-date version of the protocol. This type of negotiation occurs in client–server systems which form part of multimedia applications.

A further example of a need to make protocols adaptive is where a highly reliable service is required and where circumstances such as functional changes necessitate a protocol being modified without a server being taken out of service for a significant time or, ideally, not taken out of service at all.

There are a number of techniques used for implementing adaptable protocols; these range from simple ones such as adding extra arguments to a protocol command to indicate the number of arguments that have been provided or an argument which identifies the type of the argument, to the use of serialisable objects which embed the functionality of a command within the protocol.

<table>
<tr><td>

Exercise 4.1

Implementing an adaptable protocol using serialisable objects

</td><td>

Serialisable objects

Serialisation is the process whereby objects are turned into raw data so that they can be sent over a transmission medium. Many Java distributed technologies such as the RMI distributed object technology need to send such objects over a network and hence they need to be able to be converted into their raw data. In Java this is done very simply by specifying that a class implements the `Serializable` interface. Exercise 4.1 shows you how this done.

</td></tr>
</table>

2.3 Synchronous and asynchronous message passing

Synchronous message passing involves one entity (usually a client) in the message passing process sending a message and a second entity (usually a server) receiving it, carrying out some processing and then sending back some response which the first entity processes in some way. While the second entity is carrying out the processing the first entity pauses waiting for the response.

In asynchronous message passing each entity in the process does not have to wait for the next part of the dialogue they are engaged in and can carry out some other task. For example, the server could be carrying out some processor-intensive task for another service which it provides. This form of message passing, where there is no close coordination between message passing entities, is known as **asynchronous message passing**.

This is the idea behind message-oriented middleware discussed in the previous chapter

One way of implementing this would be to place protocol messages on some intermediate queue middleware which would be periodically interrogated by a client; in between interrogating the middleware the client would carry out useful work.

2.4 The message passing idea

Figure 4.1 shows the central idea behind the message passing paradigm. It involves an architecture in which clients and servers communicate using communication lines. In this model, in contrast with the others that are to be presented in this chapter, the underlying structure of the network is visible via the communication media used to connect servers and clients and devices such as sockets, ports and server sockets which are involved in the transfer of a message from one computer to another.

In general message passing is used in applications which satisfy one or more of a number of criteria:

Figure 4.1
A message passing
architecture

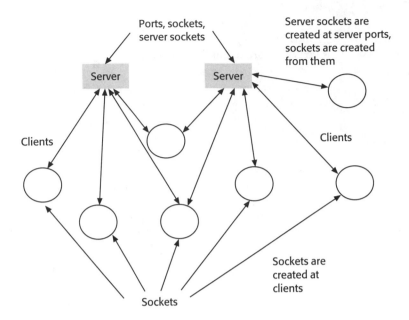

It is worth saying at this point that the message passing architecture detailed here is an abstraction of what really happens, with many communication lines and hardware carrying the messages. Ports, sockets and server sockets are abstractions of some rather nasty low-level entities

■   Communication needs are very simple.

■   High performance is required; message passing is a much more efficient mechanism than those technologies detailed later in this chapter. However, you pay for this in terms of programming complexity.

■   Rapid implementation is required, for example an e-commerce application may be required quickly in order to react to a competitor's new Web site; if there is no time to carry out sophisticated design and you are prepared to countenance the inevitable errors that this brings, then a message passing solution might be chosen.

■   The system uses a technology that no existing protocols will communicate with.

This, then, is an introduction to message passing. In the remainder of this book you will see plenty of examples of this type of development style in action. In particular Chapter 7 details how to program Web servers using HTTP, a protocol which is firmly based on message passing.

3   Distributed objects technology

This technology virtually hides the network from the designer and programmer. A distributed object is an object which is resident on one computer and for which methods can be invoked associated with code resident on other computers. A good

Figure 4.2
A distributed objects
architecture

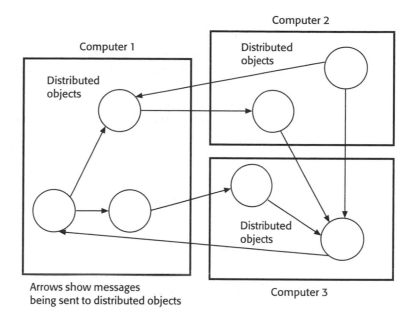

Arrows show messages
being sent to distributed objects

distributed objects technology should totally hide the underlying communication details from the programmer, for example when a programmer wants to invoke the method `update` to an object called `monitor` on a server, then the programmer should produce the code

```
monitor.update()
```

in the same form as if the object was contained in the computer in which the code is resident. There should be no references to ports, sockets and server sockets.

The vast majority of distributed objects schemes involve the generation of 'under the bonnet' code which carries out the actual processes of sending messages to objects and transmitting the data associated with such messages.

In this book I shall describe two distributed objects technologies: CORBA, which is a multi-language technology, and RMI, which is a Java-based technology.

Distributed objects technology works by intercepting calls to distributed objects and executing system code which carries out the process of locating objects and sending data and execution instructions. All this is carried out 'under the bonnet' with the programmer not being forced to include communication code. The architecture of a distributed objects system is shown in Figure 4.2. Here, a number of objects spread around a collection of computers communicate by invoking methods, all data transfer being carried out by means of arguments to the method calls which correspond to the messages.

The main advantage of using a distributed objects scheme lies in the fact that it has a 100 per cent fit with object-oriented technology: that classes identified during the analysis and design phases can be immediately implemented in terms of classes in

CORBA will be
described in detail in
Chapter 10 and RMI in
Chapter 9

some programming language, deposited on some remote computer which forms a component of a distributed system and reused without any modification.

The main disadvantage with distributed objects currently being experienced by developers is that their performance, certainly compared with message passing technologies, is inferior.

The mechanisms for developing distributed objects are straightforward and involve either processing source code or an intermediate language. Much more detail of the mechanisms involved can be found in Chapters 9 and 10.

4   Event-based bus architectures

Object bus technologies

4.1 Introduction

Many of you will already be familiar with event processing if you have developed visual interfaces with the later versions of Java. Developing such an interface consists of a number of steps:

- A visual object such as a button is placed in a container such as an applet or a `Frame` object.

- An object such as a container implements a listener interface.

- Methods in the interface which the container implements will react to events such as a button being clicked or a pull-down menu being activated and an item selected. The code for these methods is provided within the container class.

- Finally, code is placed either in the constructor for the container or in the `init` method for an applet, which registers the container as a listener to certain events such as a button being clicked.

This model of processing is based on code being written which responds to events such as a button being clicked, a window being closed and text being deleted from a text box.

The same model of processing is used in bus architectures. An example of such an architecture is shown in Figure 4.3. Here a bus connects a number of listener objects to a transmitter object which sends data along the bus. When data appears on the bus each listener object is executed to read and process the data.

In order to listen to data which is being transferred across a bus the listener objects have to be registered with the bus in the same way that event handlers need to be registered when developing visual interfaces.

An object bus is very much like a radio transmitter in that listeners to a radio station tune into a channel and receive data (sound) transmitted by the radio transmitter. In the bus architecture listener objects tune into a channel (subscribe) and receive objects which are dispatched along the bus.

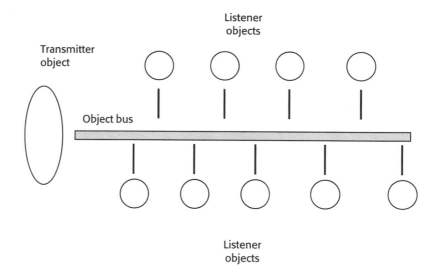

Figure 4.3
The object bus
architecture

In this figure only one
channel is shown,
there may be many
more

The model here is somewhat different to that of the distributed object model. In that model, objects communicate with other objects via method calls; invariably the client initiates the processing with the server being a passive entity until it receives some request for a service. This is an example of **pull technology** where clients *pull* data from servers. The object bus model is an example of **push technology** where the server is *pushing* data out to the clients which, when they receive it, carry out some processing action.

The object bus architecture is particularly well suited to applications where real-time events are being generated and have to be processed by a dynamically changing collection of listener objects. Typical applications include:

- The delivery of stock market data to financial subscribers on a real-time basis.

- Teleconferencing applications where messages from conference participants have to be broadcast in real-time to other participants.

- Distributed multimedia applications such as video on demand where large chunks of data have to be delivered to subscribers on a real-time basis.

Chat rooms

- Conversational applications such as chat rooms where a number of participants communicate with each other in real-time.

4.2 Architectures

4.2.1 Hub and spoke architectures

There are two main types of bus architectures. These are **hub and spoke architectures** and **multicast bus architectures**. Figure 4.4 shows a typical hub and spoke architecture.

Figure 4.4
A hub and spoke
architecture

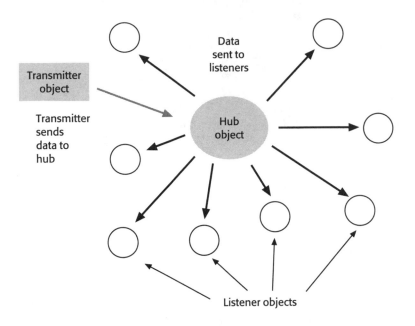

It consists of a central hub object which carries out the transmission of data to listener objects. Each listener responds to the event of objects being dispatched to the hub object from a transmitter object which produces the objects to be broadcast. In such an architecture there might be one hub object per channel or a single master object serving all the channels.

This type of architecture is one of the easiest to implement since it can be developed using base technologies such as RMI or `Socket` and `ServerSocket` objects. It also has the advantage that since all objects pass through the hub object, accounting and management functions can be centralised on this object. The main disadvantage of this approach, as compared with the multicast bus architecture approach, is that it can generate large amounts of traffic. There is also a reliability problem in that when the server containing the hub malfunctions the whole system goes down.

Exercise 4.2

Implementing a
simple hub and
spoke architecture

4.2.2 Multicast bus architectures

This form of technology, like the hub and spoke approach, allows the broadcasting of messages to a number of receivers. Some of the implementations of bus architectures are rooted in multicasting, a technique which allows data to be broadcast to a number of clients. However, some, like the industrial example *iBus* detailed later in this chapter, are a sort of software implementation of an Ethernet, where objects are sent down a bus and only processed by any receiver that requires the object; if it isn't required it is passed on to the next receiver.

Figure 4.5
The multicast bus
architecture

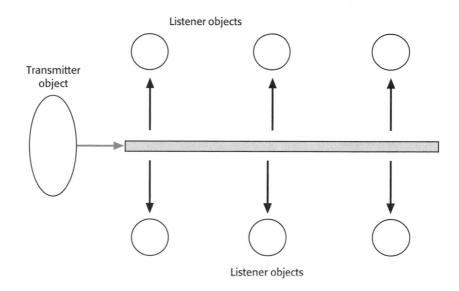

The architecture of a simple multicast bus architecture is shown in Figure 4.5. It consists of a transmitter object which sends objects along a multicast bus; attached to the bus are a number of listener objects which are activated when the event corresponding to the dispatch of the object occurs.

> **Multicasting**
>
> Multicasting can be thought of as a primitive form of broadcasting of packets. It is carried out using Unreliable Datagram packets (UDP) that are broadcast out on a multicast IP address. Because it is based on UDP, multicasting will suffer from loss of packets when a network is congested. In Java multicasting is based on the `java.net.MulticastSocket` class which is an extension of the `DatagramSocket` class.

---

iBus

4.3 A commercial implementation

In order to conclude this section I shall describe a commercial implementation of an object bus. It has been developed by a company known as *SoftWired Ltd* and is known as *iBus*. It is based on TCP/IP rather than UDP. The facilities offered by the *iBus* API provide developers with the facilities to construct objects which can subscribe to channels and to transmit any Java object to a channel. The code for a transmitter is shown below; the import statements are not shown. In the code for the transmitter and the receiver an object which is sent along the bus is known as a `Posting` object.

```
class Transmitter
{

public static void main(String[] args)
{
    String message;
    //Create a protocol stack, note that
    //this is not a java.util.Stack, the stack
    //should be reliable and, not say UDP
    Stack st = new Stack("Reliable");
    //Open the bus ready for objects to be sent along
    //it, it is situated on the computer Venus, note the
    //use of the string ibus in the URL
    iBusURL url =
        new  iBusURL("ibus://Venus/Generator/Text");
    st.registerTalker(url);
    //Construct a posting using the zero argument
    //constructor
    Posting pst = new Posting();
    //There will only be one object in the posting
    pst.setLength(1);
    //Put the string object to be sent in the 0th position
    //in the posting
    message = "Hello there";
    pst.setObject(0,message);
    //Further code here
    ..
    //Now push the posting out on the bus
    st.push(url, pst);
}

}
```

This example is based on one used in a Sun Java training course *SL301 Distributed Programming with Java*

Distributed systems training

This is simple code: all that it does is to send the string `message` out on the bus. The bus is identified by a special type of URL which starts with the protocol identifier `"ibus"`. The variable `st` is a protocol stack; the constructor uses the string `"Reliable"` to indicate that it wants the data sent using a reliable protocol where data is guaranteed to arrive at its destination – not, for example, UDP.

The code for a very simple listener object is shown below; it just receives an object, displays it and exits.

```
public class Listener
{

public static void main (String[] args)
{
    //Use a reliable protocol stack, not for example UDP
    Stack st =
```

```
                         new Stack ("Reliable");
            //Set up an object that will receive messages
            ReceiverObject ro=
                    new ReceiverObject();
            //Create a new bus object, it should match the
            //one that has been set up by the transmitter
            iBusURL url =
                    new iBusURL("ibus://Venus/Generator/Text");
            //Tell the bus that the receiver is now attached to it
            //waiting for messages
            st.subscribe(url, ro);
            ..
            //Suspend the program and wait for an object,
            //if this wasn't done then
            //the program would exit immediately
            st.waitTillExit();
    }


    }
```

The interface
Receiver acts very
much like a listener
interface found in the
Java AWT

```
class ReceiverObject implements Receiver
{
//This is the listener class, the iBus
//interface Receiver contains three methods
//dispatchPush, dispatchPull and error. This
//example only uses the first, blank or null code
//is provided for the other two.

public void dispatchPush(iBusURL srce, Posting post)
{
    //The first argument which represents the address
    //of the bus on which the object was dispatched is
    //not used
    System.out.println("The message that was sent was:"+
                    post.getObject(0));
}

public Posting dispatchPull(iBusURL iURL, Posting post)
{
    return null;
}

public void error(iBusURL iURL, String errorDetails)
{
    //No code required here for such a simple example
    //Normally it is used for error monitoring
}

}
```

The code is relatively straightforward. The class `Listener` acts as the driver class. The method `main` inside this class sets up a receiver object which is defined by the class `ReceiverObject` and attaches it to the bus. The class `ReceiverObject` implements the interface `Receiver` which has three methods whose code has to be provided. The only processing code for a method in this example is needed in `dispatchPush` which is executed when an object is sent down the bus.

5   Remote procedure call

5.1 Introduction

Remote procedure call (RPC) is a technology that has been around since the early 1980s. In essence it allows a program or subroutine on one computer to execute a program or subroutine on another computer to which it is attached on a network. For example, a query program on one computer would be able to execute a program on another computer which searched a database using remote procedure call. Remote procedure schemes have been designed so that the programmer should be unaware that when a program is executed it might be on a separate computer.

5.2 Features of RPC

There are a number of features associated with remote procedure call [2]:

Remote procedure call

- When remote code executes other remote code the execution is associated with input and output parameters. For example, the execution of some query code which processes a remote personnel database might be associated with input parameters which designate the employee whose staff details need to be retrieved and output parameters which hold the details of the staff which are returned when the remote code is executed.

- The code that is remotely executed cannot access and modify global data stored on the computer that carries out the remote call. So, for example, if the calling code has access to a global variable which contains company information the called code cannot access this data.

- It is not possible to use memory addresses or pointers to memory locations as input or output arguments.

Usually the programmer accesses programs on a remote computer using an API (application programmer's interface).

APIs

You will come across the acronym API many times in software development, in particular in Internet software development. In object-oriented terms, what it refers to is a collection of classes which contain methods that allow the programmer to access some collection of related facilities. For example Java has a mail API which enables programmers to develop software which processes and sends e-mails without knowing anything of the details underlying the mail protocol that is used.

5.3 RPC systems

There are two types of RPC system [2], those which are implemented using a programming language that have facilities for defining the interface to remote code and those systems which rely on an interface definition language.

An interface definition language is a special-purpose language which describes the facilities that are implemented by remote procedure code; typically such a language will describe the names of the code chunks which are to be executed and the number, names and types of input and output arguments which are used in RPC.

You will see an interface language being used in Chapter 10 which describes the distributed object technology CORBA

When a system is developed using RPCs, code files containing an interface definition language are processed, these files generate code which carries out the communication between a client computer and the server running the remote code.

RPC middleware has to carry out a number of functions:

■ It has to locate the computer containing the remote code. For this it uses a naming service.

■ It has to convert input arguments to a form which can be transmitted to the remote code.

■ It has to send the input arguments to the remote code that is to be executed. These arguments are transmitted via some hardware medium.

■ It has to execute the remote code.

■ It then has to convert output arguments to a form which can be transmitted to the local code which made the remote call.

■ It then has to send the output arguments back to the code which called the remote code.

■ It then has to process the output arguments so that they are in a form that can be interpreted by the calling computer.

XML-RPC

XML-RPC

Industry pundits have been predicting the death of RPC now that there are a number of distributed object technologies such as CORBA, available to the programmer. However, RPC lives on. Its latest instantiation is XML-RPC. This allows the Internet programmer to send client messages to code running on a server which results in the execution of code on the server. XML-RPC has been implemented for a variety of Internet programming languages including Java, Perl and Python. In a sense it also lives on in the SOAP technology which is being championed by Microsoft as part of its .Net programme.

XML-RPC is based on the XML technology which is described in Chapter 8

6 Tuple architecture

6.1 Introduction

JINI

I look at JINI in more detail in Chapter 16

The final approach to developing distributed systems is based on a radical view of such systems. The approach is based on work carried out by two American academics, Nicolas Carriero and David Gelerntner. These two academics developed a language known as Linda in the 1980s. The language, and its associated technology, has always been thought of highly by other academics within the distributed systems area, but has never taken off in terms of commercial use. However, in the late 1990s Sun developed a version of the Linda technology as part of its JINI programme. This programme has, as its main aim, the interfacing of disparate technologies into a distributed system: JINI envisages hardware such as burglar alarms, coffee machines, refrigerators, video recorders and mobile phones being seamlessly integrated into distributed systems using uniform interfaces.

The part of JINI which has been inspired by Linda is known as *JavaSpaces*. It views a distributed system as consisting of one or more spaces each of which contains objects that can be read from or written to. This is shown in Figure 4.6.

A distributed system can consist of a number of spaces which do not have to be allocated individually to each computer on a network: the spaces could be shared by a number of computers.

Linda, JavaSpaces and tuple-based development

In Figure 4.6 the distributed system is split up into three areas; each of these is known as a **space**. A space is a persistent object store in which objects exist; theoretically they can exist forever. Clients can access these spaces using three operations. They are:

■　*Write*. Clients can write new objects to a space.

■　*Read*. Clients can read an object's contents from a space.

■　*Take*. Clients can read an object from a space and remove it completely from the space.

Figure 4.6
The JavaSpaces
architecture

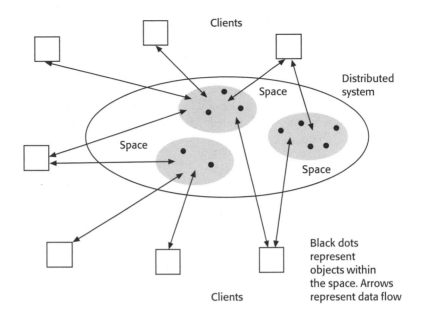

There are a number of important points to make about *JavaSpaces* technology. The first is that data can be held in a space permanently; in effect this makes *JavaSpaces* a rudimentary implementation of a distributed persistent object store.

Chapter 12 deals
with the topic of
concurrency

The second point is that spaces are shared: client objects can access the same space concurrently. As you will see later in this book concurrent access to shared objects brings with it a number of advantages, but also some rather tricky programming problems. A major advantage of *JavaSpaces* technology is that many of these programming problems are hidden under the bonnet and the programmer does not have to worry about them.

The third point that is worth making about *JavaSpaces* is that the objects stored in a space are associative. This means that they are retrieved using some unique attribute or sets of attributes. For example, if the objects were credit cards then they would be retrieved using the unique credit card number associated with each card. Programming using *JavaSpaces* involves using associative lookup, where a key is used to read, take or write to an object stored in a space. The effect of this is that the *JavaSpaces* API is very simple consisting of a very small number of methods. The consequence of this is that using a *JavaSpaces* system, while still challenging, tends to be a lot easier than developing a system using more complicated technologies.

Transactions are
described in more
detail in Chapter 13

A fourth point to make about this technology is that it is transactionally secure. Later in the book you will learn a lot more about transactions. All that is necessary to say here is that a transaction is a set of operations which are applied to a state (usually some data stored in a database). For example, a transaction in a retail e-commerce system might consist of changes to a sales database, stock database and a credit card transaction database. The key idea about a transaction is that it either succeeds, or totally fails in that none of its operations will succeed if a problem occurs during its execution. When a technology enforces this property then it is known as **transactionally secure**. The implication here is that the programmer does not have to write complicated code to ensure this property every time a transaction is executed. In *JavaSpaces* transactions are supported on a single space or over a number of spaces.

The main disadvantage of a tuple-space-based approach is that it is somewhat inefficient compared, for example, with a message passing architecture. In gaining conceptual simplicity it has lost performance.

6.2 An example

In order to complete this section I shall present a simple example. This is loosely based on one described in [1], currently one of the very few books written on *JavaSpaces* technology.

An object that can be stored in a space has to implement an interface `Entry`. The objects that form part of the example will just be strings which will be concatenated by characters fed to them by client objects. The code for an entry is shown below:

You will probably have noticed that the instance variable in the code is public; this goes against a main principle of object-oriented design. However, the designers of the JavaSpaces technology have implemented the technology in such a way that all instance variables have to be declared public. Another restriction is that all instance variables must be objects not scalars such as `int`. If you want to use scalars you need to use their corresponding wrapper class

```
public class StringMessage implements Entry
{
//Unfortunately, the developers of JavaSpaces insist that
//instance variables should be public, however, the
//programmer should treat them as private
public String content;

public StringMessage()
{
    content = null;
}

public StringMessage(String content)
{
    this.content = content;
}

public void addTo(char ch)
{
    //Just concatenates the character to the string
    content+=ch;
}

public String toString()
{
    //Developed in order to display values of strings
    return "current value of content is "+content;
}

}
```

In this respect it is similar to interfaces such as `Serializable`

`Entry` is an interface with no methods; it acts as a tag which informs the *JavaSpaces* run-time system that the class which implements it will generate objects that can be stored within a space.

This, then, is the code for the objects contained in a space. The code for placing them in a space and reading their contents is shown below; it places one object in a single space:

```
public class TesterReaderServer
{

public static void main(String[] args)
{
    try
    {
        StringMessage sm = new
                        StringMessage("Start");
        //Create a new space
        JavaSpace sp = SpaceAccessor.getSpace();
        //Place sm in the space forever
        sp.write(sm, null, Lease.FOREVER);
        //The object has been placed in the space
        //Now keep reading it back and displaying it
        StringMessage retTemplate = new StringMessage();
        while(true)
        {
            //Retrieve the object and display it
            StringMessage result = (StringMessage)sp.read
                        (retTemplate, null, Long.MAX_VALUE);
            System.out.println(result);
        }
    }
    catch(Exception e)
        {System.out.println("Problem accessing object");}
    }

}
```

Note the exception handling. An exception will be thrown if a problem occurs such as a faulty connection between the computer implementing the spaces

What this code does is first to create a new space using the code

```
JavaSpace sp = SpaceAccessor.getSpace();
```

and then writes a `StringMessage` object `sm` to the space using the code

```
sp.write(sm, null Lease.FOREVER);
```

The method `write` has three arguments, the first is the object that is to be written, the second is a transaction associated with the object and the third argument specifies

For the time being don't worry about transactions, they will be described in Chapter 13

how long the object is to be resident in the space; in the example the constant `Lease.FOREVER` specifies that it will effectively be resident forever.

The remaining part of the code will loop forever retrieving the object from the space displaying its current value. The core part of this code is the statement

```
StringMessage result = (StringMessage)sp.read
                       (retTemplate, null, Long.MAX_VALUE);
```

This uses the method `read` which reads an object from a space. This method has three arguments. The first argument is a `StringMessage` object which acts as a template for retrieving objects from a space. What `read` does is to find an object which has its instance variables equal to the instance variables found in the first argument. Since these variables are set to `null` for `retTemplate` the `read` method will retrieve any object – since there has been only one object deposited in the space it will be this object that is retrieved. The second argument is the transaction associated with the `read` used – since there is no transaction this is `null`. The final argument to the method specifies a time-out period; if the `read` has not retrieved the object by the time that the period has been completed, the method will return `null`. Normally an object might be timed out if other client objects are currently accessing the object for longish periods. In the example I have specified a very long time-out period (`Long.MAX_VALUE`) so that the operation will always complete even if other objects were accessing the object for some time.

The code above is for a simple server which places an object in a space and continually retrieves its value and displays it. The remaining client code will modify objects in a space so that the server code above will display different results. The code is shown below:

```
public class TesterClient
{

public static void main(String[] args)
{
    try
    {
        //Get a space
        JavaSpace sp = SpaceAccessor.getSpace();
        //Set up a template
        StringMessage template = new StringMessage();
        //Repeatedly take the object from the space
        //and modify it. Pause every .5 secs
        while(true)
        {
            //Take the object from the space, this
            //removes the object completely
            StringMessage res = (StringMessage)
                sp.take(template, null, Long.MAX_VALUE);
```

```
            //Modify it
            res.addTo('*');
            //Write the object back to the space; it
            //stays there forever
            sp.write(res, null, Lease.FOREVER);
            //Pause for half a second (500 ms)
            Thread.sleep(500);
        }
        catch(Exception  e)
            {System.out.println("Problem with accessing object");}
    }

    }
```

The code reflects the structure of the code of the class `TesterReaderServer`. The main work is carried out in the endless loop which extracts the object stored in the space, concatenates it with a single character and then writes it back to the space. When the server and client is executed what will be displayed by the server will be lines such as

```
Start*
Start*****
Start*********
```

where the number of asterisks following the string "`Start`" will depend on factors such as the latency of the network in which the spaces are implemented and the loading of the computer in which the code is placed and its power.

There are three components to the simple distributed system that I have presented: the class which implements the objects stored in a space, the class which represents a simple server that deposits an object in a space and continually monitors the state of the object and a client class which retrieves and updates the state of an object in the space.

The tuple model is a little more complicated than the example above has, perhaps, suggested. However, it is not very much more complicated and compared with, say, message passing techniques it has a breathtaking simplicity.

7   Further reading

There is not a lot published on distributed development paradigms. The book by Coulouris *et al.* [2] indirectly introduces some of the paradigms introduced in this chapter. Lynch's book [3] on distributed algorithms is full of algorithms which are message passing based. The book by Patzer and 14 others [4] is a good practical introduction to many of the technologies detailed in this chapter. One of the few current books on *JavaSpaces* has been written by Freeman *et al.* [1].

References

Internet book links

[1] E. Freeman, S. Hupfer and A.K. Arnald, *JavaSpaces Principles, Patterns and Practice*. Reading, MA: Addison-Wesley, 1999.

[2] G. Coulouris, J. Dollimore and T. Kindberg, *Distributed Systems Concepts and Design*. Harlow: Addison-Wesley, 2001.

[3] N. Lynch, *Distributed Algorithms*. New York: Morgan Kauffman, 1996.

[4] A. Patzer *et al.*, *Professional Java Server Programming: with Servlets, JavaServer Pages (JSP), XML, Enterprise JavaBeans (EJB), JNDI, Corba, Jini and Javaspaces*. Birmingham: Wrox, 1999.

Database Servers

5

Chapter contents

This chapter looks at one of the most important servers that can be found in a distributed system: an SQL server. Such a server services requests which are expressed in a programming language known as SQL. The chapter first describes some very simple database concepts and introduces the SQL language and then describes the main functions of a database server. A major part of the chapter is devoted to distributed databases: collections of data spread around a number of computers in a network. The chapter includes a description of the programming facilities of the JDBC (Java Database Connectivity) facility. It shows how to use simple SQL queries, prepared statements and stored procedures, concluding with a description of how metadata can be obtained from a database. The chapter concludes with a brief look at a popular database server product MySQL.

Aims

1. To describe some simple database concepts.
2. To describe some simple components of the SQL programming language.
3. To introduce the main functions of a database server.
4. To describe the main ideas behind distributed databases.
5. To introduce the main programming facilities in Java that are used for accessing relational databases.

Concepts

Autocommit state, Callable statement, Database server, Declarative referential integrity, Distributed database, Downloading Horizontal fragmentation, Key, Metadata classes, Prepared statement, Referential integrity, Relational database, Stored procedure, Trigger, Uniform Resource Locator, Vertical fragmentation.

1   Introduction

Relational databases

This chapter examines database servers in more detail. In particular it looks at the topic of SQL-based relational databases which are the overwhelming data technology used in commercial database systems. Towards the end of the chapter I shall introduce the topic of distributed databases and some of the problems that occur with them.

There will be some programming associated with this chapter and so a major part of the chapter is concerned with the SQL language used for accessing relational databases. It is worth stressing at this point that this chapter is not a programming primer for relational database programming; all I aim to do is to teach you enough Java and SQL to enable you to gain a flavour of what programming a distributed application based on relational technology is all about.

2   Relational databases

If you are familiar with relational technology and SQL then you can skip the next two sections

A **relational database** consists of a series of tables and is normally accessed using a special programming language known as SQL (Structured Query Language) often embedded within another language such as C++ or Java. With the exception of a few object-oriented database products released in the late 1980s and the 1990s relational database technology has been the overwhelmingly dominant database technology for the last 20 years. Table 5.1 shows a typical table that might be found in a warehouse application.

This consists of a number of rows each of which contain data about a particular part stocked in a warehouse: the name of the item, a unique identity and the quantity of the item held in stock. Each of the items in a row are known as fields. If a field contains a unique identifier then it is known as a **key**; for example, the *ItemId* field in Table 5.1 is an example of a key since the contents of this field will not be duplicated in a column of the table.

Normally a relational database will contain a number of tables. Such a collection of tables become a powerful means of storing relationships between data and accessing

Table 5.1
A relational table

ItemId	Item	NoInStock
Aw222	Washer A	300089
Ntr444	Nut A	2009
Wdt675	Widget Q	300001
Bt56ww	Bolt A	200
Bt5556q	Bolt B	200009

Table 5.2
A relational table
associated with
the one shown in
Table 5.1

Supplier	PostCode	PhoneNumber
Timms	NN12 8BA	0771 348890
Feters	NM8 7UU	0197 889765
Rowlands	BA33 6YT	0123 889765
Thomas	TG55 8UU	01908 88769
Terry	UX76 9OI	01488 904322

information. For example, the warehouse application which is supported by Table 5.1 might also contain the table shown in Table 5.2.

Here the table contains details of the suppliers who provide products which are stored in the warehouse and contains details about the suppliers' phone numbers and postal (Zip) codes. Normally such a table would contain much more information such as address, discount terms for purchases etc. Another table might relate items such as Washer A to suppliers via their name and would have a column which had supplier names (*Supplier*) and a column which had item identities (*ItemId*).

Tables are linked together by virtue of the fact that the key for a table (e.g. the supplier name) is stored in them; consequently, queries such as the one below can be easily answered.

Find all the suppliers who have a phone code which starts with 01234 and supply Bolt A.

3   SQL

SQL is a simple language for accessing and updating relational tables. The aim of this section is to provide *enough* details for you to gain an impression of its facilities and enough expertise to attempt the exercises associated with this chapter. A selection of SQL statements is shown in Table 5.3.

An example of an SQL statement using SELECT is shown here:

```
SELECT EmployeeName, Salary FROM Employees WHERE Salary>35000
```

This creates a table which is formed by selecting two columns from certain rows from a table called Employees. Inside the Employees table are two columns labelled Salary and EmployeeName and the query forms a table which contains these two columns from Employees solely consisting of those employees whose salary is greater than £35 000.

An important use of SQL SELECT statements is when two or more tables are joined. What this does is to form a table which is constructed by taking two existing

Table 5.3
A selection of SQL
statements

Statement	Purpose
SELECT	Selects rows from a table
INSERT	Inserts rows into a table
DELETE	Deletes rows from a table
UPDATE	Updates rows in a table
COMMIT	Commits a transaction
ROLLBACK	Rolls back a transaction
GRANT	Grants security rights
REVOKE	Revokes security rights

Table 5.4
A relational table
holding borrowing
details

BookId	Title	BorrowerName
ui345699	Jane Eyre	Ince
uk776598	Cranford	Roberts
ul974399	Snow Times	Timms
yt441297	American Tabloid	Ince
tt660198	August 1914	Davies

Table 5.5
A relational table
holding borrowers
with special
privileges

BorrowerName	TelNo	Location
Ince	x65543	Maths
Roberts	x55789	Science
Timms	x77889	Library
Duval	x88654	Arts

tables and forming a new table based on criteria which reference common data in each table. An example will make this clear. Table 5.4 shows data for the books borrowed in a library. This is held in a table called Borrowings.

Table 5.5 shows a table called Privileged containing those borrowers who are allowed special borrowing privileges, for example they may be staff in a university using the university library.

Table 5.6
The result of a
`SELECT` over two
tables

BookId	Title	BorrowerName
ui345699	Jane Eyre	Ince
uk776598	Cranford	Roberts
ul974399	Snow Times	Timms
yt441297	American Tabloid	Ince

An SQL `SELECT` statement which lists the books and titles borrowed by privileged users is shown below. It also lists the name of the borrower.

```
SELECT BookId, Title, Borrowings.BorrowerName FROM Borrowings,
Privileged
WHERE  Borrowings.BorrowerName = Privileged.BorrowerName
```

This forms a table with three columns: the book identifier, title and the borrower. The result is shown as Table 5.6.

In the `SELECT` statement above the column references to `BorrowerName` are preceded by the name of the table in which they are found. This form of qualification is needed since the two tables contain duplicate names and we need to have a convention which allows us to distinguish between them.

The history of SQL and relational databases

SQL was based on ideas propounded in the early 1970s from the ideas of the research scientist Ted Codd at the IBM San José Research Laboratories. It was originally developed in order to provide a semi-natural language interface to the IBM System R relational database system. Originally relational databases had a number of competitors which were much more efficient in terms of performance, for example database management systems which were based on a network model of data. However, more and more efficient implementations emerged in the late 1980s and this has led to the situation where relational databases and SQL now dominate the software industry.

In the context of this chapter a transaction is a series of operations which transform a database from one consistent state to another

Before leaving this section it is worth just describing the `ROLLBACK` and `COMMIT` statements. These are vitally important statements which are used in error processing, in particular when the databases which are being accessed are distributed.

A database which will be the target of a number of transactions that will update it can be in two states. The first is the **autocommit state**. In this state any change that is required to the database occurs automatically. The second state is often referred to as the **manual commit** state. Here changes occur when the programmer explicitly issues a commit command. What this does is to apply all those changes to a database which have been saved up from the last commit command or a command known as a rollback command.

Chapter 13 describes the use of commits within transactions in much more detail

The aim of the rollback command is to roll back the state of the database to the point where it was at the last commit. As I have already stated these commands are invaluable within a distributed database environment. As an example of this consider a transaction which affects two databases; for a successful transaction to occur both these databases have to be correctly updated. Assume a commit has been issued before each of the databases is updated; the part of the transaction that is associated with the first database is then applied followed by the second. If an error occurred in applying a transaction, for example there may have been a communication problem with the database server, then program code would pick this up and issue a rollback to the point where the commit occurred using the rollback command and some further action takes place, for example both transactions could be retried.

Exercise 5.1

Issuing some queries against a relational database

SQL

Dialects of SQL

There are, unfortunately, many dialects of SQL which differ slightly from one implementation to another. The main ones are:

■ *ANSI/ISO SQL*. This is the standard version of the language defined by two standards organisations. There are two standards: SQL-89 or SQL1 and SQL-92 or SQL2. Most implementations try to remain true to SQL-92.

■ *IBM DB2*. A sort of *de facto* standard associated with the dialect used within DB2, the IBM relational product.

■ *Server-specific variants*. There are a number of variants which correspond to the major servers, for example an Ingres variant, a Microsoft SQL server variant and an Oracle variant.

4   Database servers

Commercial database servers

4.1 Functions

There are a number of **database server**s on the market; however, the vast majority of servers are centred on a small number of very popular products such as the Microsoft DBMS: SQL Server; others can be found in the Web link to the left. The main functions of a database server are:

■ To interpret SQL statements sent to it by a client, execute them and send back the results.

■ To optimise queries. An SQL query can be executed in a number of ways and the difference in response time can be very large. A good database server will examine an SQL query, look at how tables are stored and work out an execution plan which minimises execution time.

I will be looking at the topic of concurrency in general, and locking specifically, in Chapter 12

- To prevent the errors that occur when one user concurrently accesses data which is being accessed by another user. Concurrent access, particularly updates, can give rise to errors in a database and a database server will lock areas of the database so that access is only allowed to one user at a time.

- To detect and act upon deadlock. Deadlock occurs when one user transaction has got exclusive access to a resource such as an SQL table and is waiting for a resource which is held exclusively by another user transaction; however, this second transaction is unable to proceed because the first transaction has exclusive use of another resource that the second transaction needs to proceed. A database server will detect such serious conditions and remedy them in a drastic way, often by terminating one of the user transactions; happily the termination is normally followed by the re-execution of the transaction by the server, when usually the first transaction has proceeded and has released the resource that the second transaction was blocked on.

- To administer security. A good database server will ensure that no user is allowed access to a database who has not been authorised.

- To administer backup and recovery. There are two aspects to this. A database server will keep a log of transactions which is used to recover a database when some large problem occurs such as a gross system failure. This log keeps details of the transactions against tables and which parts of them were affected. When a problem occurs the recovery facility of the server will find a copy of the last saved version of the database and then reapply all the transactions held in the backup log.

4.2 Stored procedures

Not all database products or drivers support stored procedures

Stored procedures are snippets of code which are equivalent to subroutines. They can be written in a variety of languages including SQL, C, C++ and Java. They reside on the server and are executed by calling them programmatically. Stored procedures represent an attempt to overcome efficiency problems in that all that is required to trigger a stored procedure is a short textual call to a stored procedure which can be sent over a communication medium very quickly. Such stored procedures can also be optimised. The alternative is for the client to send the SQL query which corresponds to the stored procedure direct to the server. Since stored procedures often represent major processing comparable to that achieved by tens, if not hundreds, of SQL statements, major performance savings can be achieved.

Stored procedures are very much like subroutine calls or method invocations in that they can contain arguments so that clients can use them with a variety of actual arguments, for example a stored procedure might carry out the processing of a request for a sequence of account transactions on a bank account owned by a particular customer, with the customer's name being used as an argument to the stored procedure.

Stored procedures can emanate from two sources. They can be part of general service functions supplied by a database or server vendor or they can be application-oriented as in the account query example I used above. Stored procedures represent a solution which:

- is more efficient in terms of processing time;

- reduces network traffic;

- keeps code for accessing and updating a database close to the database because it is held on the server. This means that software maintenance becomes easier since you do not have to download updates to clients.

There are, however, some problems with stored procedures. First, they are non-standard: implementations differ from vendor to vendor, which leads to a lack of portability across servers. The second problem – a lesser problem than the first one – is that optimisation needs to be repeated as access strategies to a database change. A stored procedure is associated with some plan of execution which will minimise processing and the degree of database access. This plan will have been set up when the stored procedure is first compiled. If the access to the database changes as an application changes then the plan has to be modified by the database administrator.

Chapters 9 and 10 describe distributed objects in more detail; stored procedures can be seen as a primitive precursor to this technology

4.3 Referential integrity

The term **referential integrity** refers to the fact that tables in a relational database are consistent with each other. The following examples are of databases whose tables do not have referential integrity:

- A customer is associated with a transaction which does not occur in a table.

- A part stored in a warehouse that has no suppliers associated with it.

- A supplier has been given a new reference number, yet the old reference number of that supplier can still be found in other tables.

Business objects are objects that reside in the middle layer of a three-tier client–server architecture. They were described in Chapter 3

Referential integrity is often associated with business rules that are associated with business objects. Typical business rules are:

- No account holder is allowed to hold more than 10 accounts.

- An order for a product which is more than £400 must be accompanied by an official order form.

- No student can borrow more than five books from the university library.

- When a salesperson achieves more than £10 000 of sales in a year they will start earning commission.

- An employee on salary scale C will be allowed 25 paid holidays in a year.

A typical three-tier implementation of an e-commerce application will involve visual objects stored on the client, business objects stored in the middle tier with these objects being associated with classes containing code to retrieve data from a relational database held in the final tier. For example, a method `getSalaryDetails()` which might be associated with a class `Employee` in a personnel application would contain SQL statements that retrieve details of past salaries from a relational database and return that data as objects defined by the class `SalaryDetail`.

There are two methods which are used to impose referential integrity on a database. The first is achieved by the use of **declarative referential integrity**, the second by means of a **trigger**.

The former involves the designer of the database writing the rules into the SQL which define the database. The latter involves specific code to check that each time an operation occurs, for example a row being added to a table, then referential integrity is not compromised.

In general, declarative referential integrity is preferable to trigger-based referential integrity. There are a number of reasons for this:

- Declarative referential integrity is self-documenting as it forms part of the SQL code which defines a database.

- Triggers, on the other hand, will be found scattered over the code of a system and hence will be something of a maintenance headache.

- Triggers are non-standard.

- Some trigger implementations have an upper limit to the number of triggers which can be supported per relational table. These may not be sufficient to impose enough referential integrity.

- The implementation of triggers is often non-standard and leads to a lack of portability.

4.4 Relational middleware

There is a wide variety of middleware available which fits between clients and database servers and Figure 5.1 shows some of these. The first component is an SQL

Figure 5.1
Database server
middleware

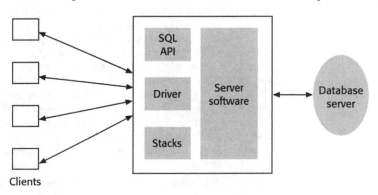

Clients

API (Application Programmer's Interface). This provides programming facilities for developers who wish, for example, to embed SQL code within procedural languages. The API is also used by SQL programs which make internal calls to the facilities offered by the API.

The second is a database driver. This is usually a small piece of software which takes SQL statements, formats them and then sends them over to the server.

The third is the protocol stack which is used for communicating between the client and the server. The fourth is server software. This includes conversion software. Such software is used to make other database products look like the product supported by a database vendor. Also included in this category is bridge software which converts SQL code into a standard form supported by a number of database products.

A fifth category of software is that associated with remote administration of a database. Most database products allow you to administer a database, for example setting and removing security permissions from a remote client, and it is this software that enables you to do it.

> A good example of bridge software is the JDBC/ODBC bridge used to convert between SQL calls embedded in Java code and databases which support the Microsoft ODBC standard. You will be using this bridge in the exercises associated with this chapter

5 Distributed databases

5.1 Introduction

A **distributed database** is one whose tables are distributed among a number of networked computers. There are two reasons why data is distributed. The first is for performance reasons: often clients will access a small subset of the data in an application, for example a bank branch will normally only access customer details for its own customers. By taking frequently accessed data and placing it close to a client, for example by copying it to a server on a local area network, then major performance increases can be obtained.

CORIS and WebDIRECT

CORIS and WebDIRECT

CORIS is a subsidiary of one of the largest printing companies in the world: R.R. Donnelly and Sons. It specialises in online delivery of content, for example product catalogues, libraries of marketing literature and editorial content such as product reviews. One of the major products developed by CORIS is WebDIRECT. This is a system which allows a user to access one of a large number of content databases via any Web browser. Users interact with such data via simple queries similar to those used in search engines. The vast amount of data handled and stored by WebDIRECT is distributed across a large number of computers and usually held in a number of relational databases which are spread across a CORIS customer's networked system. There are a number of reasons why this distribution occurs; a major one is that many customers consist of separate divisions which require access only to subsets of the content and which require fast local access to this data. Another reason is reliability where the use of a set of duplicated databases ensures continuous access to stored data.

The second reason for distribution occurs because many systems have evolved from separate systems. In this age of integrated management information many companies have created databases which are distributed and are made up of separate databases which used to exist in isolation.

5.2 Problems with distributed data

There are a number of problems with distributed data which a server and the host operating system need to sort out. These problems are all specific instantiations of problems which generally need to be solved in any distributed environment.

■   If data is replicated then there is the problem of making sure that all the replicated data is up to date without compromising performance: you do not want clients waiting for some time for a database to be synchronised with all its copies.

Concurrency is the subject of Chapter 12

■   Ensuring that concurrent access to a database which is distributed does not result in the database holding erroneous data. For example, a user may hold some data in memory from a database but, at the same time, another user may read and write to the data before the first user has had the opportunity to write back their results to the database. This will corrupt the database. There are a number of techniques which can be employed in a single computer user environment to get over this. Applying them in a distributed environment is a little trickier.

■   In a distributed environment where there are a large number of computers, security is a much bigger headache than with say a single, mainframe computer.

■   Reliability is a problem in a distributed environment. For example, distributed transactions are chunks of processing which result in the state of a system being changed and where a number of distributed databases are affected. If there is a failure in a transaction which accesses a number of distributed databases the process of reacting to this can be very complex, particularly if each distributed transaction is split into a further number of distributed transactions.

■   One of the problems in a distributed system is that clocks in the computers connected to the system may be out of synchronisation with each other. In a distributed system where the order of transactions applied to a database is irrelevant this is not a problem. However, if certain transactions have to be applied in some temporal order then the timing problem has to be solved.

These are all quite different and difficult problems to solve; however, the good news is that if you are a programmer then you should be immune to many of these problems in that the server and operating system that you use will usually sort them out for you. If you are a designer then you will have problems in developing distributed designs which use current server and database technology and which conform to what can often be harsh time–performance and reliability constraints.

Date's rules

Chris Date, who was one of the pioneers of relational technology, has devised 12 rules which should be used to judge the effectiveness of a distributed database technology. I have reproduced below the six which I regard as the most important:

1. *Continuous operation*. A distributed database system should run continuously; all maintenance operations should be applied to it while it is running.

2. *Transparency*. The programmer or user should not be aware that a particular database is distributed. The use and programming of a distributed database application should be the same as if the database was stored on a single computer.

3. *Replication independence*. The programmer or user should not be aware of the fact that a database has been replicated.

4. *Mixing servers*. It should make no difference to the development of a system that a number of disparate servers are used. You should be able to freely use and interchange database servers.

5. *Operating system independence*. The operating system used in a server should make no difference to the system, for example a server running one operating system, say Windows NT, should be easily replaced with a server running another operating system such as UNIX.

6. *Optimisation of queries*. A database server's query engine should be aware of the distribution of data and be able to make decisions about the way data is to be retrieved based on the location of the data.

5.3 Types of distribution

There are three ways of distributing data. They are downloading, replication and fragmentation.

Downloading is the simplest form of data distribution. It involves periodically copying data from some central repository to a client or to a computer connected to a client by some form of fast transmission medium such as a local area network. This is a very simple form of distribution: the programming is very straightforward; however, it is only viable in applications where the fact that the data is a little out of date is not important. An example of this is the data in a banking application which updates accounts overnight. This data can be copied to bank branches at the start of each business day.

These techniques are further discussed in Chapter 14

The second mechanism for distribution is **data replication** where copies of a database or part of a database are kept at specific points in a network close to the users that require the data. This solution increases performance and is used in applications where users require up-to-date data.

The third form of distribution is fragmentation where tables are split across a number of computers. The term **horizontal fragmentation** is used to describe the process of splitting a table into two subtables where each subtable contains the original columns that were part of the original table. An example of this type of fragmentation is where a subset of a database is frequently used by a particular client, for example local suppliers in a materials purchasing system, and where this subset can be copied to a computer close to the client in order to obtain a performance gain.

The term **vertical fragmentation** refers to the process of splitting a table so that each subtable consists of two tables with smaller numbers of columns in each table than in the original table.

This form of fragmentation is used when a subset of the data in a table is required which is specific to a particular application. For example, a table might store details on the employees in a company with some columns storing data used for salary calculations and other columns used to keep track of the qualifications and training of employees. A training department might hold a table containing basic employee details such as the employee name and phone number, together with the training and qualification data, while the payroll department might hold a table which is constrained to contain basic employee data plus payroll data such as the number of hours worked.

6   Programming databases

Java and the JDBC

6.1 The basic classes

The aim of this section is to describe the facilities available in Java for accessing SQL databases. Figure 5.2 shows the main classes which are involved in this process. In the remainder of this chapter you will see most of these in action. The vast majority of the classes used for accessing SQL databases can be found in the `java.sql` package.

The functions of these classes are:

■   `Driver`. This is a class associated with the database driver that is used to communicate with a database. This class is not usually accessed by the programmer.

■   `Statement`. This class is used to create and execute SQL statements.

■   `PreparedStatement`. This class – a subclass of `Statement` – is used to develop SQL statements which have an increased efficiency when executed a number of times with different arguments.

Figure 5.2
The main Java SQL
database classes

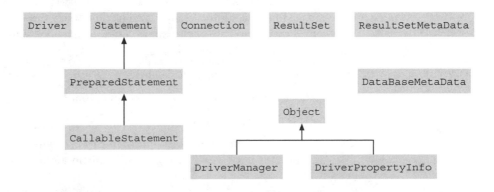

- **CallableStatement.** This is a subclass of **Statement** which provides the programmer with the facilities for calling stored procedures.

- **Connection.** This is the class which contains facilities for connecting to a database. Execution of SQL statements is associated with a database connected to a **Connection** object.

- **ResultSet.** When an SQL statement is executed a result set is usually returned. This result set will contain objects which are rows of the table which has been created by the query. In order to access the data in a **ResultSet** object the programmer has to loop around it extracting each row.

ResultSetMetaData is an example of a class which accesses meta-data; this is data about data, for example the name of a database product expressed as a string is an example of metadata

- **ResultSetMetaData.** There are a collection of classes in **java.sql** which provide data about the main entities that this package manipulates. This class provides data about result sets extracted as a result of queries. For example, this class enables the programmer to find out whether a column represents a currency, what the name of a column is and how many columns there are in the rows of a **ResultSet** object. This class is one of a set of classes known as **metadata classes**.

- **DatabaseMetaData.** This is another metadata class. In this case it provides information about a database. For example, it enables the programmer to discover whether the database supports stored procedures, whether the database supports ANSI92 SQL and what the product version of the database is.

- **DriverManager.** This is a class that manages the drivers that are available for connecting to a database. For example, if a programmer attempts to connect into a database the driver manager will find a suitable database driver to use.

JDBC tutorials

- **DriverPropertyInfo.** This class is not used by application programmers. It contains a number of instance variables which are used by drivers in order to connect into a relational database.

6.2 Processing steps

There are a number of steps that need to be programmed when developing code which accesses a relational database using Java.

The **Properties** class defines a sort of persistent **Hashtable** which can be used to associate keys with some data, for example a key associated with a driver name and the associated data being the name of the driver

1. Load a driver which is compatible with the database that is to be processed. This can be done programmatically or can be done via a **Properties** object which is set up by the user. In the examples used in this book and the accompanying exercises the former course is taken.

2. Establish a connection to the database.

3. Associate an SQL statement with this connection.

4. Execute the SQL statement.

5. The SQL statement which has been executed will produce a table which is stored in a **ResultSet** object. This object will contain a reference to the rows of the

table that has been formed by the execution of the SQL statement. The rows are traversed and some processing applied.

6.   Execute further SQL statements as above.

7.   When the processing associated with the database is complete the database is closed and the connection to the database is also closed.

The code which results in the execution of a simple SELECT statement on a table Employees is shown below. The statement selects all those employees who have a salary greater than £35 000 per year. The table that is formed as a result of the query is processed row by row with the employee name and employee salary displayed on System.out.

```java
import java.sql.*;
public class JDBCCode{

public static void main(String args[])
{
    //Set the name of the file that is to be accessed
    //and the name of the driver
    String fileURL = "...";
    String driverName = "...";
    try
    {
        // Load in the driver programmatically
        Class.forName(driverName);
    }
    catch (ClassNotFoundException cfn)
    {
        //Problem with driver, display error message and
        //return to operating system with status value 1
        System.out.println("Problem loading driver");
        System.exit(1);
    }
    try
    {
        //Establish a connection to the database, second
        //argument is the name of the user and the third
        //argument is a password (blank)
        Connection con =
            DriverManager.getConnection(fileURL, "Darrel", "");
        // Create a statement object
        Statement selectStatement =
                con.createStatement();
        // Execute the SQL select statement
        ResultSet rs =
            selectStatement.executeQuery
```

The database administrator will have set this database up without passwords

You can use upper and lower case in an SQL statement

```
                      ("SELECT name, salary FROM
                           employees WHERE salary >35000");
          String employeeName;
          int employeeSalary;
          while(rs.next())
          {
              employeeName = rs.getString(1);
              employeeSalary = rs.getInt(2);
              System.out.println
                  ("Name = "+ employeeName +
                  "Salary = "+ employeeSalary);
          }
          //Close down the database connection, result set
          //and the SELECT statement
          selectStatement.close();
          con.close();
          rs.close();
      }
      catch(Exception e)
      {
          System.out.println
              ("Problems with access to database");
          e.printStackTrace();
          System.exit(2);
      }
   }
}
```

printStackTrace provides a set of diagnostic information about the throwing of exceptions

The static method `Class.forName` is used to load a driver as a class. This class name will usually consist of symbolic names separated by full stops, for example `my.SQL.Driver`. If the class is not found then a `ClassNotFoundException` is thrown and the corresponding catch clause results in an error message being displayed and the program exiting to the operating system.

If the driver was successfully loaded then a connection is formed to the database. In the example above this is achieved by means of the statement:

```
Connection con =
    DriverManager.getConnection(fileURL, "Darrel", "");
```

Chapter 6 looks at URLs in more detail

The method `getConnection` has three arguments. The second is the name of the user registered with the database and the third is a password which again has been registered with the database (in this case there is no password). The first argument is something known as a **Uniform Resource Locator** (URL): a URL represents a form of addressing of resources on the World Wide Web. A typical URL for a database is shown below:

ODBC is a Microsoft standard which allows a number of disparate databases to be accessed

```
jdbc:odbc://open.ac.uk/myFile
```

It consists of a substring which identifies the resource (jdbc identifies a relational database); a substring which indicates what type of database is being referred to, in the case of the URL above the database is an ODBC-compliant database; a string which identifies the computer using the domain notation introduced in Chapter 2, in the string above this is open.ac.uk; and the name of the database, which in the example above is myFile.

In the next section of code the createStatement method creates a statement which can be used to send SQL statements to the database and the method executeQuery executes the SQL statement which is its argument.

The next part of the processing accesses the table that is formed by the query that has been executed. This table will have two columns: the first column will be the names of those employees with a salary greater than £35 000, the second column will be the salary of the employee. This table is stored in a ResultSet object. The method next will return true as long as a row of the result set is available for processing; thus, the processing loop will continue until the last row has been processed. Inside this loop can be found the use of two methods, getInt and getString. Each of these takes an int argument which represents the column number of the table that is stored in the resultSet object to which the message is sent. Thus, the message getString(1) will return the string which is in the first column in the row that is currently being processed. Similarly getInt(2) will return with the int in the second (last) column of the row that is being processed.

The methods getInt and getString also have corresponding methods which take a string argument that represents the name of a column. For readability they should be used although they do slow down performance a little

Finally the connection and the result set are closed down and the program exits.

The fragment below is part of another Java program which updates a database by inserting a single row:

```
String fileURL = "...";
String driverName = "...";
try
{
    //Load in the driver programmatically
    Class.forName(driverName);
}
catch (ClassNotFoundException cfn)
{
    //Problem with driver, error message and return
    //to operating system with status value 1
    System.out.println("Problem loading driver");
    System.exit(1);
}
try
{
    //Establish a connection to the database, second
    //argument is the name of the user and the third
    //argument is a password (blank)
```

```
Connection con =
    DriverManager.getConnection(fileURL, "Darrel","");
Statement updateStatement =
            con.createStatement();
String employeeName ="...",
    employeeSalary = "...",
    employeeDepartment = "...";
//Execute the SQL insert statement
int noOfRows =
    updateStatement.executeUpdate
    ("INSERT INTO employees (name, salary, department)"+
    "VALUES(" +"'"+ employeeName + "','" +
    employeeSalary+"','"+employeeDepartment +"')");
}
catch(SQLException sqe)
{
System.out.println("Problem updating database");
}
```

The value of
noOfRows is not
used in this program

The int which
is returned that
represents the number
of rows affected can
be ignored; if it is not
needed then there is
no need to write the
method call within
an assignment
statement, it appears
in the fragment for
the sake of
completeness

Much of the code is similar in this fragment to the program shown before it. The major difference lies in the way that the insertion is handled. First, the method executeUpdate carries out the insertion. This method will return an int rather than a result set. This int represents the number of rows affected by the insertion. The next difference lies in the fact that a different SQL statement is used. The one used is the INSERT INTO statement. In the example above this would be executed as

```
INSERT INTO employees(name, salary, department)
VALUES(name of the employee, salary of the employee,
    department of the employee)
```

This inserts a row with the values specified by the string within the single quotes.

The final example shows the use of the commit and rollback facilities within Java when a database is updated.

```
try
{
    //Establish a connection to the database, second
    //argument is the name of the user and the third
    //argument is a password (blank)
    Connection con =
        DriverManager.getConnection(fileURL, "Darrel","");
    //We have to program the commits, the statement below
    //means that commits are not automatically applied
    con.setAutoCommit(false);
    updateStatement =
                con.createStatement();
```

```
            //Carry out some update operation on the database
            //described by fileURL
            //...
            updateStatement.close();
            //If this point is reached then the update on
            // the database has been successful, commit by
            // sending the commit message to con.
            con.commit();
    }
    catch(SQLException sqe1)
    {
        //There was a problem, for example no database was
        //found, insert recovery code or error code here
    }
```

Remember, the `commit` message will inform a database that all transactions on that database are to be applied from the last commit.

Exercise 5.2

Developing a three-tier application involving a relational database

In the code above the database is placed in manual commit mode where the programmer has to explicitly program the commit process. If the code in the `try-catch` clause executed correctly then the commit is applied; however, if it has not then an `SQLException` is generated and caught. How this is then processed is determined by the application.

6.3 Some support classes

There are a number of support classes which are used within more complex JDBC programs. This section briefly describes them.

6.3.1 The `java.sql.Types` class

This class contains constants which map onto SQL data types. Each SQL data type is represented by one of these constants. Section 6.4 shows these constants in action.

6.3.2 The `java.sql.SQLException` class

This is a subclass of the Java `Exception` class. It provides a lot of useful information about the specific error which caused the exception to be thrown:

■ It describes the error that has occurred.

■ It provides some information specific to the database vendor about the error that has occurred. In order to interpret this error you will need to consult the vendor's manuals.

■ It contains a sequence of exceptions which lead up to the one being caught. Thus if one exception created another which, in turn, created a further exception this chain can be accessed via an `SQLException`.

The code for processing chains of SQLException objects is shown below:

```
try
{
    // Code which accesses some database(s)
}
catch(SQLException  sqe)
{
    do
        sqe.printStackTrace();
    while((sqe  =  sqe.getNextException())!=null);
}
```

Note that the method printStackTrace produces a trace of the execution of each exception; this is a very useful method to use when debugging

Here the catch code prints out the chain of exceptions which lead to the original exception that caused the execution of the catch. The method getNextException delivers the exception previous to the current SQLException object.

6.4 Prepared statements

When an SQL statement is executed by a server a number of processes are applied to it. First its syntax is analysed, second the mechanism used for execution discovers what processing is required and finally the statement is optimised so that the time taken to retrieve the data required by the statement is minimised. This process can take some time, particularly if the statement is to be executed a large number of times.

One way of eliminating much of this processing is to use a device known as a **prepared statement**. Using a prepared statement only requires an SQL statement to be created once; the statement can then be executed repeatedly without the processes described in the previous chapter being applied. The code below shows prepared statements being employed. The code uses the class PreparedStatement which is a subclass of Statement.

```
Connection  connection;
int  salValue;
. . .
PreparedStatement  ps  =  connection.prepareStatement
                        ("SELECT  employeeId, salary FROM
                        EMPLOYEES  where  salary>?");
do
{
    //Processing  which  gives  the  int  variable  salValue  a
    //value.  To  terminate  the  loop  salValue  is  given  a
    //value  zero
    ps.setInt(1,  salValue);
    if(salValue  !=0)
        ps.execute();
```

```
            //Code which displays the results of the query
            //It would need to extract out the result set
        }
        while(salValue !=0);
```

There are a whole range of set methods including setInt which set various data types, for example setString would set a string value

The second line sets up the PreparedStatement object based on an SQL SELECT statement. The ? in the string which defines the SQL statement is a placeholder for an argument.

The loop which follows the declaration and creation of the PreparedStatement object ps sets the argument of the SQL statement to the value of the int variable salValue. This is achieved via the method setInt which has, as its first argument, the argument position within the SQL statement and the second argument the value of the argument in the SQL statement. So, for example, if salValue was 23 500 then the SQL SELECT statement would extract a two-column table containing the names and salaries of employees who earn more than £23 500.

The prepared statement is then executed. Each time the loop is traversed the prepared statement is executed without any costly syntax checking, semantic checking and optimisation.

6.5 Callable statements

As you will remember from Section 4.2 a stored procedure statement is one which is held on the server and called by a client; in Java callable statements communicate with stored procedures. The JDBC contains facilities for such statements to be executed. The code for the execution of a callable statement java_count which returns with the number of staff who have been trained in Java in a software company is shown below; the object conn is a Connection object.

```
CallableStatement  csta;
csta = conn.prepareCall("{call  java_count[(?)]}");
csta.registerParameter(1,java.sql.Types.INTEGER);
csta.execute();
System.out.println("Number of staff trained in Java is "
                + csta.getInt(1));
```

Some primitive database systems and drivers do not support stored procedures

Here a CallableStatement object csta is declared. The second line then registers the callable statement. The curly brackets within the string that is the argument to prepareCall represent what is known as an escape convention. This is used when there are major differences between the way that SQL implementations handle certain facilities of the language. In this case different implementations have different syntaxes for callable statements. The curly bracket followed by call informs the JDBC that the string inside is a callable statement which needs to be converted into a form recognised by the particular database that is being processed. There are other examples of this convention which are not detailed in this book, for example dates are handled in slightly different ways by different database systems and so an escape is used when communicating them.

The callable statement has a single argument (designated by a question mark) which is an output argument; in order to execute the callable statement this output argument has to have its type registered. This is achieved by means of the registerParameter method which has an int constant as its second argument and the number of the argument reading from left to right in the SQL callable statement as its first argument. The second argument identifies the type of the argument.

The next line executes the callable statement and then the final line displays the result from the callable statement using the method getInt.

6.6 Metadata

Metadata, as the name suggests, is data which describes other data. The Java JDBC contains a number of classes which can be used to extract metadata about database entities including result sets, tables, databases and drivers. The aim of this section is to describe those facilities which allow the programmer to extract such data.

You would be forgiven for asking why do we need metadata? There are a number of reasons: the first is the fact that some databases do not support certain facilities and metadata allows the programmer to check on this before carrying out what might be error-prone programming. A good example of this concerns stored procedures. Not all database management systems support this type of access. If you are writing an application which is to access a wide variety of database products and you want to use stored procedures then you will need to check whether they are supported. There is a method supportsStoredProcedures within the class DatabaseMetaData which returns true if they are supported and false otherwise. A programmer writing code which wants to take advantage of stored procedures would first use this method; if the result was true then a stored procedure would be executed; if it was false then a normal query equivalent to the SQL code contained in the stored procedure would be executed.

Exercise 5.3

Finding out about a database and a database product

A second important use of this type of data occurs when you have an application which uses a database whose structure you do not know. There are many facilities in the DatabaseMetaData class which enable information such as column identifiers and column types to be determined at run time.

6.6.1 Database metadata

This is metadata which describes a database. It is a very large class containing over 140 methods and can be found in java.sql.DatabaseMetaData. Typical facilities it offers include the ability:

■   To find the name of the driver that is used.

■   To find the version number of the driver that is used.

Some databases do not support some types of metadata. If a Java program attempts to access metadata which is not supported then an `SQLException` is created

- To check whether ANSI92 SQL is supported.

- To check whether certain esoteric facilities of SQL such as outer joins are supported.

- To check whether mixed case identifiers are allowed.

This is just a small selection of the methods that can be accessed in this class. The vast majority are only really useful to the hardcore SQL programmer.

6.6.2 `ResultSet` metadata

This metadata describes the structure of result sets. It allows the programmer to interrogate a result set returned from an SQL query and find out information such as:

- The number of columns in the result set.

- The database name for a column.

- The display name of a column – this is the name that will be displayed in reports and printed output.

- The name of a table from which a column came from.

- The precision of numbers in a particular column.

- Whether a column represents a currency value such as dollars or pounds.

6.6.3 Obtaining metadata

The previous two sections have broadly described the two important metadata classes in the JDBC. So far I have not described how to obtain metadata objects. To obtain a `DatabaseMetaData` object you use the method `getMetaData` found in the `Connection` class. The code below shows a simple example of this:

```
Connection  c;
// Code to establish a connection
DatabaseMetaData  dmd  =  c.getMetaData();
System.out.println("Driver  is  "+ dmd.getDriverName()  +
        " Version  number  = "+dmd.getDriverVersion());
```

The code uses the methods `getDriverName` and `getDriverVersion` to return a string which represents the name and version of the database driver which is being used for access to the database which is connected to the `Connection` object c.

There is also a similar method `getMetaData` found in the class `ResultSet` which can then be used to obtain information about a result set which has been formed by an SQL query. The code below will obtain a count of the number of columns within the `ResultSet` object rs.

```
ResultSet  rs;
// Code which executes an SQL query and sets rs
ResultSetMetaData  rsmd  =  rs.getMetaData();
System.out("The result set contains " +
            rsmd.getColumnCount()+  " columns");
```

This code uses the method `getColumnCount` which is found in the class `ResultSetMetaData` and which returns with an `int` value that is the number of columns in the result set.

7 Object to database mapping

In Chapter 3 I introduced you to the idea of a three-tier architecture. This is, without a doubt, the most popular way of organising an e-commerce application: using a presentation layer, a business object layer and a data layer which stores data associated with business objects in some permanent medium such as a relational database system. When you use such an architecture one of the programming tasks that you will need to carry out is mapping the business objects that form the core of the application into relational tables. For example, a customer for an e-tailing application might be associated with the class shown below:

```
class  Customer
{
private  String  customerName;
private  int  customerId;
private  String  address;

..

public  String  getAddress()
{
..
}

public  String  getCustomerName()
{
..
}

public  OrderList  getOrderList()
{

}
..

}
```

where `customerId` is some unique key. Within the code for the class you will have to develop SQL code which maps the data associated with the methods into the relational tables used to store application data. For example, the method `getOrderList` which retrieves the list of orders made by a customer would be associated with the execution of SQL statements which retrieved data from a customer table and an order table and selected those orders corresponding to a particular customer. This is a mapping process which is often hand crafted; however, there are a number of tools which enable the program to automatically produce SQL code. Exercise 5.4 shows you how to develop a simple mapping from a class to a table of a relational database.

8 The anatomy of a database server

To complete this chapter I shall describe in outline a typical database server. The server that I will describe is *MySQL*. This is a freely available server which arose from a previous project known as *mSQL*. It is a concurrent server which launches a thread whenever a new connection is received from a client. In this it differs from *mSQL* which was single threaded. *MySQL* runs on a wide variety of UNIX- and Windows-based platforms.

A thread is a
concurrently executing
piece of code

8.1 Setting up the server

The installation of the server is easy: all it requires is the execution of a simple installation script. Once the server has been installed, the database administrator is able to carry out a number of tasks using utilities which come with the *MySQL* software, some of these are shown below:

■ *Setting up a password for the database administrator.* The server comes with a default password which is commonly known by the *MySQL* user community so it has to be changed.

■ *Creating any relational tables.* This is carried out by a utility known as *mysqladmin*. This creates empty databases. Programs written in a variety of languages, including Java, can then be used to write to these with any data that is required to be stored. There are also a number of utilities which can carry out bulk conversions of tables.

■ *Creating user tables.* A number of users are allowed to concurrently access a *MySQL* database. Details of each user and their privileges are held in a relational table. Each user is given a name, a password and is allowed certain access privileges, for example a user might only be allowed to select items and not write or delete items.

MySQL

- *Creating the database table.* This table refers to individual relational tables and relates users to the access privileges that each user has with respect to that table, for example for a specific table a user may be allowed to insert and retrieve rows from that table.

- *Creating the host table.* This table relates access from a particular computer on the Internet. For example it allows access to be denied to users from a particular address.

- *Setting performance parameters.* There are a number of performance parameters that can be adjusted for *MySQL*. For example, an area of memory known as a cache is used to store frequently accessed tables. Such tables can be accessed quickly without reading data from some slow file-based memory. There are a number of these parameters which can be set based on the anticipated traffic on the server. Normally these are adjusted when greater information about use of the server is obtained after a period of use.

8.2 Monitoring the server

A utility *mysqladmin* provides a rich set of information on the server which enables the database administrator to monitor its efficiency. The information provided includes: the current number of threads accessing the database; the number of queries sent to a database since the server started; the number of queries that have taken an excessive time to execute (the upper limit to the time is set by the database administrator when setting up the server); and the number of queries that have been sent to the database since it was last started.

Database administrator resources

8.3 Programming

Programming a *MySQL* database is just the same process that I have described previously. The only real difference is that a *MySQL* driver needs to be loaded. In the exercises that are associated with this chapter the driver was for a Microsoft Access database, the line that refers to the driver in such programs is:

```
String driverName="...";
```

where the name of the driver is inserted into the double quotes. To modify the program all that is needed is to insert the name of a *MySQL* driver, for example:

```
String   driverName="com.imaginary.sql.mysql.MySqlDriver";
```

All the remaining code in the program remains the same.

9   Summary

This chapter introduces database servers and database programming; you will see them used in anger in the final chapter which describes a large-scale case study

This chapter has described an important class of server: the SQL server. It is important because the main way that the vast majority of distributed applications access stored data is via relational database technology. The chapter has introduced relational technology, provided a short tutorial on SQL, the language used to access relational databases, and has looked at database servers and some of the middleware that sits between such servers and clients. The last half of the chapter has looked at some of the detailed programming that is required when accessing a relational database using the JDBC facilities of Java.

10   Further reading

Reese has written an excellent book [1] which describes the minutiae of database programming in Java. Almost certainly one of the best general books on databases has been written by Elmasri and Navathe [2]; it is both comprehensive and authoritative. Ozsu and Valduriez have written an excellent introduction to distributed database technology [3]. Yarger, Reese and King [4] have written a good introduction to *MySQL* and *mSQL*.

References

Internet book links

[1] G. Reese, *Database Programming with JDBC and Java*. Sebastopol, CA: O'Reilly, 1997.

[2] R.E. Elmasri and S.B. Navathe, *Fundamentals of Database Systems*. Harlow: Longman, 1999.

[3] M.T. Ozsu and P. Valduriez, *Principles of Distributed Database Systems*. Old Tappan, NJ: Prentice Hall, 1997.

[4] R.J. Yarger, G. Reese and T. King, *MySQL and mSQL*. Sebastopol, CA: O'Reilly, 1999.

6

Web Servers and the World Wide Web

Chapter contents

This chapter describes the architecture of Web servers and how they function. It describes the language HTML which is used to develop Web pages and how pages expressed in the language are processed by a server and a browser. The protocol that mediates between a Web server and a Web browser is known as HTTP; the chapter describes this in some detail. The chapter also contains a description of the Common Gateway Interface, the part of the Web server which is used to communicate with other application programs, and a description of client side programming using applets and JavaScript. The chapter concludes with a description of the most popular Web server Apache. The chapter acts as an introduction to the next one which describes ways of programming a Web server so that it can be used in an e-commerce environment.

Aims

1. To detail the relationship between a Web browser and a Web server.
2. To outline some of the features of the HTML markup language.
3. To describe the main features of the HTTP protocol.
4. To show how HTML forms communicate data to a Web server.
5. To describe the main functions of the Common Gateway Interface.

Concepts

Anchor, Applet, Cascading Style Sheets, Common Gateway Interface, Environment variable, Form, HTML, Hypertext Transfer Protocol, JavaScript, Lifecycle methods, Markup language, Page cache, Status line, Table, Tag, Web browser, Web server, Wide Area Information System.

1   Introduction

Web servers

The use of HTTP is an example of the message passing paradigm detailed in Chapter 4

A **Web server** is a server which dispenses documents that reside on the World Wide Web. There are hundreds of thousands of these servers in existence and they rank in importance with database servers. Figure 6.1 shows the relationship between Web servers and the clients that make use of their services.

Clients use a program known as a **Web browser** to communicate with a Web server. Stored on the Web server are the many pages which make up a Web document. When a client wishes to view a Web page it instructs the browser which page is required. The browser will then send a message using a protocol known as HTTP which identifies the page to be accessed and its location. The Web server will then recover the page and send it back to the browser executing on the client. The Web server, in effect, acts as a file server. The aim of this chapter and the next is to look at both sides of the client–server equation. In particular it will look at how Web servers are programmed, how Web documents are constructed and the numerous technologies which are used on the Web. First it is worth looking at the client side of the equation.

2   Browsers and HTML

2.1 Markup languages

Figure 6.2 shows a typical Web page displayed on a browser. It is formatted in such a way that it is pleasant to read. The aim of this section is to outline how a Web page, when it is returned from a Web server to a client running a browser, is displayed on

Figure 6.1
Web browsers and a Web server

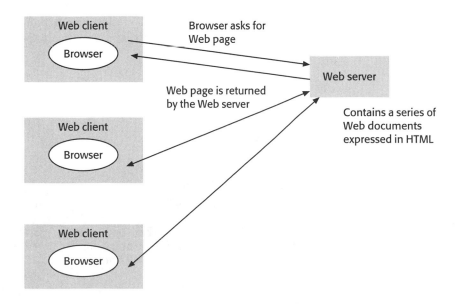

Figure 6.2
A sample Web page taken from a Web document devoted to Delia Smith, the greatest cook in the world

the browser, for example how pictures are displayed and how text is formatted in relation to the pictures. The way that a browser lays out a Web page is determined by instructions embedded in the Web page.

These instructions are expressed in a language known as **HTML**. HTML is an example of a **markup language**. There are many of these languages in existence. They include SGML which is a huge markup language used for normal document processing and which is the parent of HTML, XML, a new markup language which promises to revolutionise the Web, and LaTeX which is a markup language used to lay out mathematical documents such as research papers.

I will be looking at XML in more detail in Chapter 8

A markup language consists of a number of elements identified by **tag**s; these elements contain text. The tags are interpreted by some document processing software and the content between the tags is displayed in a way that the tags determine. In the case of a Web document written in HTML the software that carries out the processing and layout is the browser.

HTML tutorials

Dynamic and static pages

In the early days of the World Wide Web the pages which form part of a Web site were copied to the browser in exactly the form that they were stored. However, as e-commerce applications became more and more common there was an increasing demand for pages to be modified in some way before being downloaded, for example a site which published up-to-date stock and share prices would want a page to include the current price of the stocks and shares which it reported on. A number

Dynamic page technology

of technologies emerged which enabled this form of dynamic loading. The first was called Server Side Includes; this has now been superseded by a number of other technologies, for example Active Server Pages, developed by Microsoft, and Java Server Pages, developed by Sun. The following chapter will describe Java Server Pages in outline.

2.2 An example

In order to gain an idea of what this means for a Web document I have reproduced the text of a very simple Web document below:

```
<HTML>
<HEAD>
    <TITLE> Darrel's Rudimentary Home Page </TITLE>
</HEAD>
<BODY>
<H1> Darrel Ince </H1>
Hi I am Darrel Ince. I am a Professor at the Open University.
There are a number of things worth knowing about me:
<UL>
    <LI> I own a psychotic cat. </LI>
    <LI> My youngest daughter is named after Dylan Thomas's
        late wife. </LI>
    <LI> I am a fanatical Welsh rugby supporter. </LI>
    <LI> I am very tall. </LI>
    <LI> I am a proficient Java programmer. </LI>
</UL>
</BODY>
</HTML>
```

Exercise 6.1

Building a simple
Web page

Figure 6.3 shows how this page was displayed on Internet Explorer, the Microsoft Web browser.

The various elements of the HTML are described below; the tags used by HTML are enclosed in angle brackets.

Figure 6.3
A browser display of
some HTML

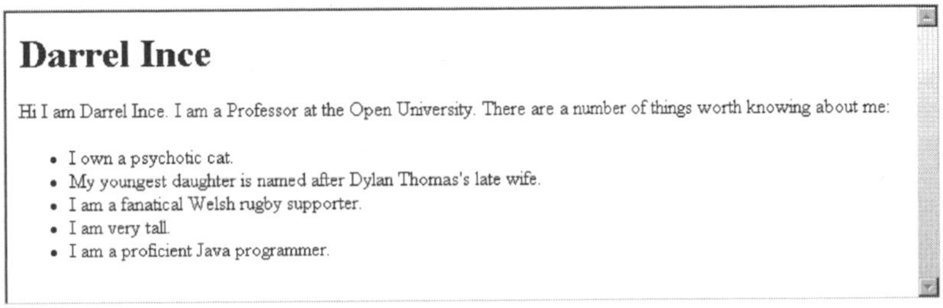

Darrel Ince

Hi I am Darrel Ince. I am a Professor at the Open University. There are a number of things worth knowing about me:

- I own a psychotic cat.
- My youngest daughter is named after Dylan Thomas's late wife.
- I am a fanatical Welsh rugby supporter.
- I am very tall.
- I am a proficient Java programmer.

- The `<HEAD>` and `</HEAD>` tags enclose information for the header of the Web page. The only information enclosed is the title of the Web page.

- The `<TITLE>` and `</TITLE>` tags enclose the title of the Web page. This title is displayed on the title bar of the Web browser.

- The `<BODY>` and `</BODY>` tags delineate the main text of the document. Enclosed within these tags is the text of the Web page.

- The tags `<H1>` and `</H1>` enclose a major heading. A heading is text which is usually in bold and in a large typeface. The largest is delineated by `<H1>` `</H1>` the smallest by `<H6></H6>`.

- Most of the text contained in the Web page follows the major heading.

- The next tag pair is `<UL></UL>`. This introduces a bulleted list. Each element of the bulleted list is preceded by the tag `<LI>` and terminated by the tag `</LI>`.

2.3 Components of HTML

When talking about HTML we refer to three components of an HTML document. An **element** is the name given to a markup instruction such as UL, and a **tag** is the name of the element enclosed within angle brackets. The final vocabulary term is **attribute**. So far I have not introduced attributes. An example of one is shown below:

```
<FONT COLOR ="blue">
This text will be displayed in blue.
</FONT>
```

Here the FONT element enables the HTML coder to designate the colour, size and font used for some text. The attribute COLOR is written within the tag `<FONT>` and is set to the value blue. Many HTML elements have a number of options which correspond to attributes with defaults which allow some or all of the attributes to be omitted, for example the COLOR element has a FACE attribute which displays text in a specific font. For example, the HTML

```
< FONT COLOR ="blue" FACE = "Helvetica">
This text will be displayed in blue and in the Helvetica font.
</FONT>
```

At this stage you may not see what the need for ID is; in the latter stages of this chapter in which I look at the programming language JavaScript you will see it enables programs written in that language to access and change the properties of an HTML page

will display the text between the `<FONT>` and `</FONT>` tags in blue using the Helvetica font.

Another example of an attribute occurs with the P element. This has two tags `<P>` and `</P>` which delineate a paragraph of text. You can give this paragraph a unique identity using the ID attribute as in

```
<P ID = "HeaderPara">
This is text in a paragraph.
</P>
```

Table 6.1
HTML tags

Tag	Meaning
`<P>..</P>`	Delineates a paragraph
`<FONT>..</FONT>`	Specifies a font for some text
`<IMG>.. </IMG>`	Introduces a graphic image into a page
`<EM>..</EM>`	Emphasises text
`<SUP>..</SUP>`	Makes text superscripted
`<SUB>..</SUB>`	Makes text subscripted
`<DEL>..</DEL>`	Strikes out text with a horizontal line
Tags `<H1>..</H1>`, `<H2>..</H2>` **through to** `<H6>..</H6>`	Produces headings of various sizes and emphases
`<HR>`	Produces a horizontal rule
` `	Produces a line break
`<CENTER>..</CENTER>`	Centres some text

A selection of HTML editors

A list of some of the common HTML tags with their meaning is shown in Table 6.1.

This is just a small sample of the facilities offered by HTML. Later in this section I shall describe some further facilities. However, before doing this it is worth saying something about the preparation of HTML documents. The document on page 131 was produced using a very unsophisticated text editor. However, there is now a wide range of very powerful editors which virtually take away from you the need to know the detailed syntax of HTML.

2.4 Anchors and links

The example in the previous section has not really conveyed the power of the World Wide Web; it was merely used to show you some of the major facilities of HTML. The power of the Web comes from the fact that you can connect a document to many other documents on the Web, many of which will be thousands of miles away. How is this achieved in HTML? It is achieved by means of linking using a concept known as a Universal Resource Locator (URL) which I very briefly touched on in the previous chapter.

Web pages will often contain elements known as **anchors**, more usually known as **links**. These are areas of a Web page which, when clicked, will transfer the page they reference to the Web browser's window. A link can be textual or graphical; if the link is graphical then it is embedded inside some picture. The HTML below contains a link which transfers to another document on the World Wide Web.

```
<HTML>
<HEAD>
<TITLE> Links Page </TITLE>
</HEAD>
<BODY>
<H1> Darrel Ince's links </H1>
You really ought to look at these sites:
<UL>
    <LI> <A HREF = "http://www.WelshRugby.com/home"> The
    home of Welsh rugby </A> </LI>
    <LI> <A HREF = "http://www.open.ac.uk/staff/Darrel"> My
    home  page</A></LI>
    <LI> <A  HREF  =  "http://www.open.ac.uk/Faculty/Computing">
    My  department's  page</A></LI>
</UL>
</BODY>
</HTML>
```

The URLs in the example consist of http then the name of a Web server (usually www) followed by a domain name and then concluded by the path to be followed to find the Web document

Most of the elements of this text you have met previously. The one element you have not met is the anchor tag. There are three of these tags in the text. They have the form

```
<A HREF = "URL"> Text </A>
```

The URL part represents a Uniform Resource Locator which points at a file stored at an address on the World Wide Web or to a local file. The text is the text that will be displayed associated with the link. This will be highlighted in such a way that it is obvious to the user of the browser that it is a link, for example the text may be displayed in some bright colour and underlined.

The colour can also be set by the HTML code

Figure 6.4 shows how this HTML is displayed by the browser. The links appear in a different colour and are underlined, with the text within the <A> </A> tags being the part of the document that will be clicked in order to transfer to the address specified by the URL. Normally these textual links are displayed in blue; after they have been

Figure 6.4
A browser display of some HTML

Darrel Ince's links

You really ought to look at these sites:

- The home of Welsh rugby
- My home page
- My department's page

Notice that the `<A>` tag contains information (the URL) over and above that found between `<A>` and `</A>`. Many HTML tags have this property

clicked they are displayed in a sort of light purple colour for a time determined by the settings of your browser. Such links give the Web its full power enabling users to seamlessly move from one Web site to another.

You can also move from one part of a Web document to another. For example, the line

```
<A HREF = "Example1.html"> Example 1: The AWT </A>
```

will display the text *Example 1: The AWT*, which when clicked will transfer the reader to the page held in the file `Example1.html` within a set of Web pages.

Jargon and the Web

There is a host of jargon which is used to describe Web sites and Web pages. A poorly designed page full of intrusive media such as video clips is known as a jello page and is said to be full of dancing baloney or angry fruit salad. A link which leads to a site that no longer exists is known as an Annie or orphan Annie. A site which has just been constructed by cutting and pasting from existing non-Web documents is described as being full of shovelware. A site which has not been updated for some time is known as a cobweb site.

The main component of a link is the URL. So far you have only seen URLs which refer to files, either within a Web document or held on a remote Web server. A URL can refer to more than files. The URLs that you have seen have all been preceded by the string `http`; this indicates that the URL refers to a Web document. There are a number of other strings that can be used to vary the URL. These are shown in Table 6.2.

The second row shows how you can embed a mail address in an HTML document. Clicking on this link will transfer you to a mailing program that you have set up for your browser and will normally start up a blank e-mail for you to fill in details such as the message, subject and recipient.

Table 6.2
Some options for URLs

Gopher, WAIS and Telnet links are now only of historical interest

Link	Form	Example
Web page	http://Web site	http://www.Ans42.com/
Mail	mailto:mail address	mailto:d.s.ince@open.ac.uk
Newsgroup	news:newsgroup	news:news.weird.questions
FTP	ftp://FTP site	ftp://ftp.ous.com/
Gopher	gopher://Gopher site	gopher://gopher2.jj.co/
WAIS	wais://WAIS site	wais://ince.ac.uk/
Telnet	telnet://Telenet site	telnet://bujsite.ddu.org/

Dead link services

Dead link services

One of the problems facing a webmaster is the fact that a link in a Web page may no longer exist. There are a number of reasons for this ranging from the server hosting the page malfunctioning to the fact that a page may have been deleted. There are a number of Web sites which provide a monitoring service whereby a user specifies a series of links and the site periodically checks them to see whether they are still live. If a link is dead then the user is contacted, usually by sending an e-mail.

A newsgroup is a collection of Internet users who are interested in a specific topic such as chess or the LINUX operating system. They communicate using a form of bulletin board system

The third line shows that you can embed newsgroups into your HTML page. By clicking on a news link a newsreader program is normally started and you can participate in the discussions which are specific to the newsgroup.

The fourth line in the table describes the fact that you can embed FTP links into an HTML page. When such a link is clicked the FTP site which it is linked to will start a process which will eventually lead to the downloading of some file.

A gopher link is a link to a site which dispenses a large amount of automated information such as stock price histories or past weather conditions.

The WAIS link detailed in the sixth row of the table is a link to a **Wide Area Information System** site. These are sites which allow you to search through huge volumes of information.

Telnet was described in more detail in Chapter 1

The final link is a Telnet link. This allows the user of a browser to connect into a computer and send text messages to it.

This, then, is a brief introduction to basic HTML; later I shall look at how forms are embedded in HTML documents. It is worth stressing that this section has been the briefest of introductions. HTML is a pretty big markup language and to do justice to it would require a much larger book; indeed books of over 500 pages have been written on HTML, although there are many good tutorials and resources available on the World Wide Web. I shall return to one aspect of HTML, forms, in the next section.

HTML resources

The Third Voice *tool and its impact*

Web graffiti

The description of the role of the Web server and browser has detailed the fact that pages are totally under the control of whoever is in charge of the server, for example users cannot change stored pages. A tool was released in 1999 which changed this relationship and which led to huge controversy. The *Third Voice* tool enabled users to add text and graphics to a Web page. These adornments, together with the address of the page, were stored on a database separate from the server containing the pages. If a user wanted to view the adornments then they would need to use a piece of software known as a 'plug in' which would retrieve both the modified Web page and the adornments. The *Third Voice* tool was very controversial because it was used to express users' views about companies and personalities on the Web, for example the Microsoft site was particularly badly affected.

2.5 Forms

In the next chapter I shall be looking at the various ways you can develop Web server programs which access such forms

HTML also contains facilities for displaying **forms** into which a user can place data. Forms are used to communicate data to programs running on a Web server. There are a number of ways that these programs are developed using languages such as C, Perl and Java.

A form is introduced via the FORM tag. An example is shown below:

```
<FORM METHOD = "POST" ACTION = "cgi-bin/tracker">

. .

</FORM>
```

Forms processing in HTML

Later in the chapter and in Chapter 7 I shall look at the HTTP protocol in more detail

The FORM tag encloses the elements of the form: for example, buttons, text boxes and radio buttons; it also defines which program is to be executed when the form contents are transferred to the Web server, in this case the program is called tracker which is stored in a directory cgi-bin. The keyword POST indicates that a POST command is sent to the server. This command informs the server that forms data is to be communicated which needs some form of processing. POST is a part of the HTTP protocol which is used by both a browser and a Web server to communicate with each other.

There are a number of individual widgets that can be placed in a form. The remainder of this section will describe them.

The first is the text area. This is an area of a Web page which can contain free flowing text. This is introduced using the TEXTAREA tag which has three options: NAME is mandatory and gives a name to the text area, ROWS specifies the number of rows in the text area and COLS gives the number of columns. For example, the HTML

```
<TEXTAREA NAME = "User reply" ROWS = "12" COLS = "40">
This is where you should place your input
</TEXTAREA>
```

I shall only be looking at some of the forms elements in HTML in this section – just enough to support the programming that will be described in Chapter 7

sets up a text area which has 12 rows and 40 columns and in which the text starting 'This is where . . .' is placed.

The SELECT tag shows a list of choices. It has a number of different options. NAME gives the name of the select box, SIZE designates the number of choices to show and the MULTIPLE tag allows multiple selections. Within the SELECT tag the various choices are designated by OPTION tags. This tag has a number of options: the first is VALUE which gives the value assigned to the choice and SELECTED which nominates which choice is the one to be initially selected.

The HTML code shown below displays a form based on SELECT.

Other visual elements such as buttons are not shown here

```
<FORM   METHOD="POST"
ACTION="cgi-bin/FprmProc">
<SELECT  NAME="select"  SIZE="5">
    <OPTION>Computer1</OPTION>
    <OPTION>Computer2</OPTION>
    <OPTION  SELECTED>Computer3</OPTION>
```

```
        <OPTION>Computer4</OPTION>
        <OPTION>Computer 5</OPTION>
          ..
  </SELECT>
  </FORM>
```

The CHECKBOX tag displays a simple checkbox which can be checked or left empty. It has a number of options. The CHECKED option ensures that the checkbox is checked, the VALUE option gives the checkbox an initial value which can be used by Web server programs and the NAME option names the checkbox.

The INPUT tag is a general tag which defines simple text fields, password fields, radio buttons, checkboxes and buttons used to submit a form and reset a form. It is associated with a number of options:

- NAME defines the name for the object. This is mandatory.

- TYPE sets the type of visual object. This can have the value TEXT to indicate a simple text field; PASSWORD to denote a text field where, when the user types in data, bullets appear to disguise what has been typed in; CHECKBOX to designate a checkbox; RADIO which designates a radio button; RESET which is a button that resets the data submitted to its original displayed value; and SUBMIT which is a button that sends the data in the form to be processed by some Web program. SIZE is the size in terms of the number of characters it can hold.

- VALUE for a text field or a password field defines the default text that is to be displayed. For a checkbox or a radio button it specifies the value that is returned to the server when it is selected. For buttons it defines the text inside the button.

- MAXLENGTH is the maximum number of characters allowed.

- CHECKED sets a checkbox or radio button to on.

An example of a form is shown below. It contains two fields, one for a name and one for an address and two radio buttons. It also contains a button which submits the form to a Web server.

```
<FORM  METHOD="POST"  ACTION="/cgi-bin/Form1process">
<P>
    Please type your name below
</P>
<P>
    <INPUT  TYPE="TEXT"  NAME="nameField"  MAXLENGTH="30">
</P>
<P>
    Please type your address below
</P>
<P>
    <TEXTAREA NAME="addField" ROWS="5" COLS="40">
    </TEXTAREA>
</P>
```

```
<P>
    Male<INPUT  TYPE="RADIO"
    NAME="maleButton"
    VALUE="mButt">
</P>
<P>
    Female<INPUT  TYPE="RADIO"
    NAME="femaleButton"
    VALUE="fButt">
</P>
<P>
  <INPUT  TYPE="SUBMIT"
  VALUE="Submit">
</P>
</FORM>
```

A SUBMIT element is a button which when clicked will result in the form details which it is associated with being sent to a Web server

The form is shown in Figure 6.5. The only thing to say about this code is that the tags and options can be expressed in upper or lower case; in the code above they are in upper case.

These, then, are the elements of HTML. There are many more facilities in the language than there is space to describe them in this chapter, but there are also a number of Web sites which are dedicated to presenting tutorials on the language.

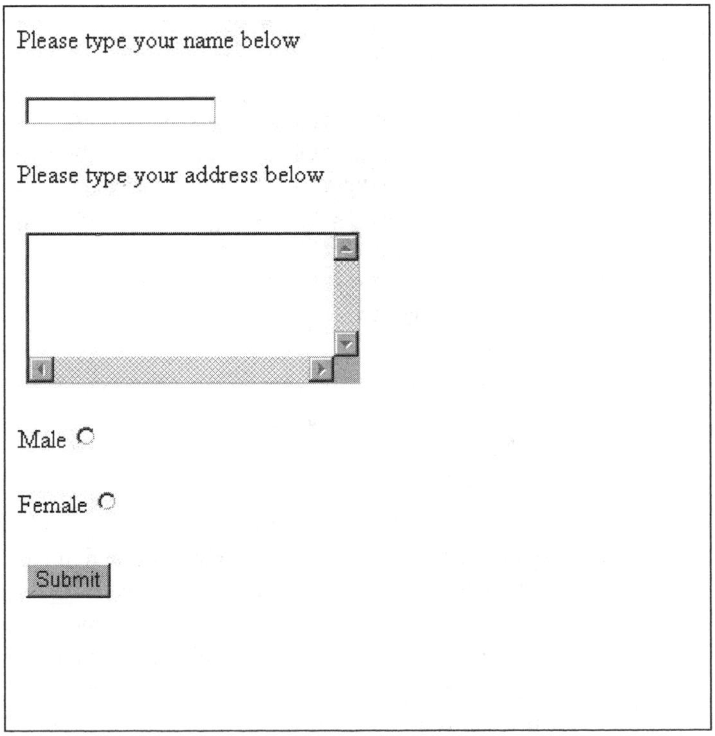

Figure 6.5
A form displayed by a browser

Exercise 6.2

Developing a
more complicated
Web page

2.6 Tables

HTML has features which allow the designer to define tables. These are delineated by the `<TABLE>..</TABLE>` tags.

A table consists of two types of element: table headings and table rows. The table heading is delineated by the `<THEAD>..</THEAD>` tags with individual cells introduced using `<TH></TH>` and rows delineated by `<TR></TR>`. The body is delineated by the `<TBODY> </TBODY>` tags with the rows being delineated by the `<TR></TR>` tags. Within a row, cells are delineated by the `<TD></TD>` tags. An example of a table with six rows is shown below:

```
<HTML>
<HEAD>
<TITLE>
    Table example for book
</TITLE>
</HEAD>
<BODY>
    <H1> Table shown below</H1>
    <CAPTION> This is the table</CAPTION>
    <HR>
    <TABLE>
        <THEAD>
            <TR><TH>  Name  </TH><TH>Age</TH></TR>
        </THEAD>
        <TBODY>
            <TR><TD> Arthur Davies</TD> <TD> 45</TD> </TR>
            <TR><TD> Anne Davies</TD> <TD> 42</TD> </TR>
            <TR><TD> William Rees</TD> <TD> 17</TD> </TR>
            <TR><TD> Mary Bignall</TD> <TD> 22</TD> </TR>
            <TR><TD> Li Yeng</TD> <TD> 19</TD> </TR>
            <TR><TD> Rowan Rees</TD> <TD> 34</TD> </TR>
        </TBODY>
    </TABLE>
    <HR>
</BODY>
</HTML>
```

This uses the `<CAPTION></CAPTION>` tags to produce a caption and two `<HR>` tags to produce horizontal lines. The table is shown in Figure 6.6.

The table in Figure 6.6 is quite primitive. The elements that make up a table have a number of attributes that provide for improvement: for example, they allow the designer to specify borders, place elements at a particular position in a cell, specify a width and have cells spanning a number of columns. An example of the use of some of these attributes is shown below:

Figure 6.6
The display of a
simple table

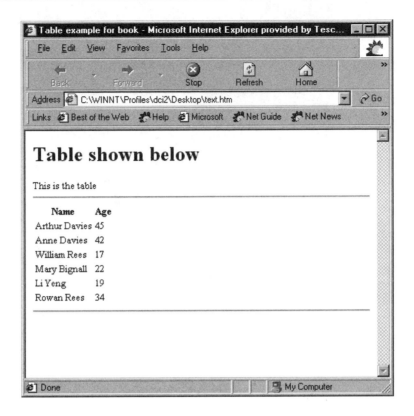

```
<HTML>
<HEAD>
<TITLE>
    Table example for book
</TITLE>
</HEAD>
<BODY>
    <H1> Table shown below</H1>
    <Caption> This is the table</CAPTION>
    <HR>
    <TABLE BORDER = "2" ALIGN = "center" WIDTH = "60%">
        <THEAD ALIGN= "Center">
            <TR><TH>  Name   </TH><TH>Age</TH></TR>
        </THEAD>
        <TBODY ALIGN = "Center">
            <TR><TD> Arthur Davies</TD> <TD> 45</TD> </TR>
            <TR><TD> Anne Davies</TD> <TD> 42</TD> </TR>
            <TR><TD> William Rees</TD> <TD> 17</TD> </TR>
            <TR><TD> Mary Bignall</TD> <TD> 22</TD> </TR>
            <TR><TD> Li Yeng</TD> <TD> 19</TD> </TR>
            <TR><TD> Rowan Rees</TD> <TD> 34</TD> </TR>
```

Figure 6.7
A more complicated table

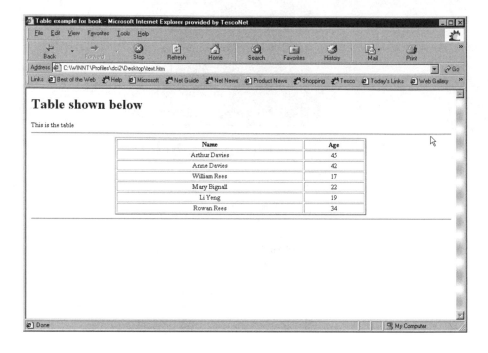

```
        </TBODY>
        </TABLE>
<HR>
</BODY>
</HTML>
```

Here, the attribute BORDER associated with the TABLE element specifies that a border is to be drawn of width 2, the ALIGN attribute specifies that the table is to be centred and the WIDTH attribute specifies that the table should occupy 60 per cent of the length of the browser page.

The ALIGN attribute for the THEAD and TBODY elements specifies that the cells are to be centred. The display of the table defined by the HTML above is shown as Figure 6.7.

It is important to point out that this section is just an *introduction* to HTML tables, enough to enable you to access the remainder of the book.

2.7 Cascading Style Sheets

One of the most important design directives for the Web page designer is to ensure that the pages in a Web site have the same look and feel. This is an important design principle not just for the Web designer, but for all staff involved in the development of documents. The conventional document designer usually employs a word processor or a desktop publishing (DTP) package which allows a consistent style to be applied to all the elements of a document; for example the designer may decide that all major headings are to be displayed in 20 pt type using the Arial font. Word processors and DTP packages allow the designer to specify a style for an element of a document and consistently apply that style to all the occurrences of that element.

HTML has a similar facility: it is known as **Cascading Style Sheets**, usually abbreviated to CSS. An example of such a style sheet is shown below:

```
<HTML>
<HEAD>
<TITLE>
    CSS example for book
</TITLE>
<STYLE TYPE = "text/css">
    I {background-color: #32CD32; color: white}
    H1{color: cyan}
    P {font-size: large}
</STYLE>
</HEAD>
<BODY>
    <H1>The   heading</H1>
    <P>
        The body text is <I>displayed</I> here
    </P>
</BODY>
</HTML>
```

Colours can be specified by hexadecimal or by their names

This shows a style sheet introduced by the tag STYLE which specifies that it is to be a CSS style. Within the body of the style sheet there are three redefinitions of HTML elements. The I element which provides italics will be displayed with a background colour of lime green (specified by hexadecimal 32CD32) and a colour of white for the type. The H1 text will be displayed using the cyan colour and the text within a paragraph will be displayed in a larger font size (HTML has a number of identifiers which specify font size). The display of the HTML is shown as Figure 6.8.

CSS allows the designer a huge amount of flexibility:

■ It enables the look and feel of individual elements of an HTML document such as H1, P and I to be consistent throughout a document.

■ It allows text to be precisely positioned on a page.

■ It allows the definitions of styles to be stored in a file and applied to pages in different Web sites.

■ It allows *users* to define their own style sheets to display a Web page in the way that they require, for example visually impaired users might use a style sheet which displays text in a much larger font size than is normal.

CSS and style sheets

This, then, is just an introduction to CSS. The Web references associated with the book will point you at a number of sites which contain tutorial material.

Figure 6.8
The display of a
browser page
defined by a CSS

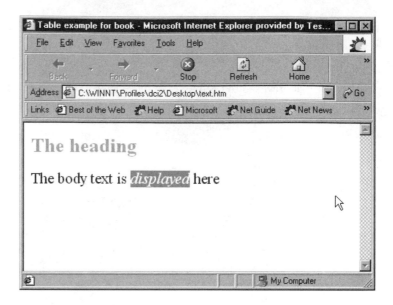

2.8 Web site design

This is a book about the technology which is used to develop large, distributed
Internet-based applications and so a section – albeit a small one – might seem out
of place. However, a poor design of the front-end to a system can sink even a well-
designed software architecture.

Jakob Nielsen

The principles outlined in this section were, in the main, taken from [6]; this is
an excellent book, written by Jakob Nielsen, one of the few Web designers who use
research into the human–computer interface to inform Web design.

The major principles that you should bear in mind when designing a Web site are:

- *Design so that consistency is achieved.* This does not mean that Web pages in the
  same site should look the same. What it means is that certain elements should be
  implemented in the same way, for example the way that links to other pages in
  the Web site are displayed should be consistent across the site. Also, pages which
  carry out the same function should look the same, for example pages which
  contain forms should have the same look and feel, and pages which provide
  information about products that are to be sold should also look the same.

- *Concentrate on user content.* Do not use lots of space on a page for navigation.

- *Make sure that different browsers display pages in similar ways.* Even today, different browsers will display a page in quite different ways. If you expect users of the
  site to use a variety of browsers, check how the pages look and be prepared to
  design two or more different pages which can be read by different browsers.

- *Be sparing with colour.* One of the major errors made by the designers of the
  early Web sites was to employ too much colour in a page, particularly in the text

where words were displayed in different colours. In deciding to use a colour, ask yourself why you want to use the colour. For example, you may want to use red to highlight a very important point. A warning though: overuse of a colour such as red can lead to readers ignoring the text.

- *Do not design pages that take a long time to download.* Although this issue will decrease over the next five to ten years with broadband connections becoming cheaper, it is a vital issue now. Research has shown that users are not prepared to wait for a long time for a page containing animations and fancy graphics to download. Keep the bulk of a page devoted to text. If you think that a user wants to look at a specific graphic then display a small, memory-spare version of the graphic (known as a thumbnail) with a link to the large version of the graphic.

- *Make full use of linking.* If a page consists of three sections which are notionally separate, for example a description of the teaching of a university department, the research and a list of the staff in the department, do not place all the text for these sections on the same page; place each in a separate page and link to them from a summary page.

- *Make hyperlinks small.* If you link large amounts of text in a Web page the text will become very difficult to read. If the link is short, say no more than four words, it might not fully describe what is being linked to. If so, place some text close to the link (say, in brackets) which describes what resources the link points at.

- *Use familiar conventions for links.* The default within browsers for displaying links is to underline them in blue. Most users are culturally used to this; designing a Web site with non-standard ways of implementing links, for example as orange links against a black background will confuse users.

- *Use style sheets throughout your site.* This means that they will have a uniform appearance and when you decide to change some aspect of the look and feel of your site the change will be reflected throughout the site.

- *Provide printed versions of pages.* If you think that a certain page, or collections of pages are going to be frequently printed then provide downloadable versions of the pages in some word processing or document display format. Browsers are still quite poor at displaying pages and often crop them.

- *Keep the text on a screen short.* Users feel uncomfortable reading text from a screen. Use hyperlinks to reference other pages which might have been physically included in the text.

- *Make your text readable.* For example use colours which contrast highly with the background of a page, use a plain background, use big enough fonts and do not use moving effects such as flashing text: they make a page quite unreadable.

- *Signal the use of multimedia.* If you are going you use a multimedia presentation with all its attendant download problems, reference the page containing the material from another page and warn the user what they will be getting in terms of download and in terms of what the multimedia do.

- *Design the home page in a different way from other pages*, albeit using the same style. The aim of a home page is to encourage users to enter the Web site so it should succinctly describe what lies in the site and hence should contain a map of the site. A search form which enables the user to search the site should also be provided. You should also place recent news or offers on the page.

- *Make sure the user knows where they are.* The user should be aware of where they are both in terms of the World Wide Web and in terms of the site they are visiting, where they have been and where they could go. Where the user is relative to the World Wide Web can be catered for by having some graphic or noticeable text which tells the visitor what company or organisation the site is associated with. In terms of where they have been, adopt the practice of displaying past page titles when the user is traversing a set of linked pages, for example when registering for an ISP. These titles, together with the titles of future pages, can be displayed prominently at the top of the page with the current page being highlighted in a different colour. In terms of where a user can go, place a navigation map in the page which shows the map of the site with the current page highlighted in a prominent colour. If a user is traversing a series of pages then do not forget to include a link backwards in the page as well as the link forwards.

These are just a selection of hints and tips. If you are interested in more detail I would heartily recommend [6] to you. An example of a well-designed Web page is shown as Figure 6.9 which is taken from Nielsen's site. It demonstrates many of the principles

Figure 6.9
Design by Jakob Nielsen

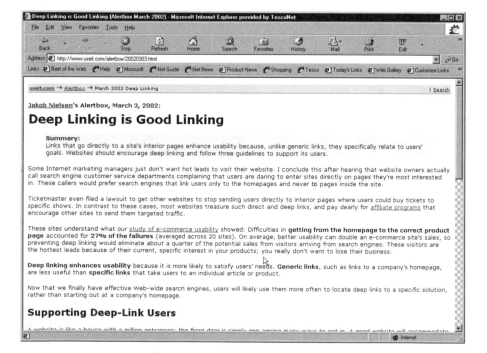

that I have detailed above, including the restrained use of colour, conventional linking and the use of a navigation bar.

2.9 The evolution of the Web

The last decade has seen a huge advance in the breadth of facilities that have been made available to Web developers and designers. The aim of this section is to briefly describe this evolution.

When the Web emerged at CERN it was developed as a form of distribution mechanism for documents. As such it was just capable of displaying simple pages. Web sites which used such simple facilities are often referred to as first-generation sites. However, as the Web emerged into the outside world further facilities were added to HTML and to browsers to enable the development of more interesting pages. The first of these was the ability to process forms and display images. Web sites which used these facilities are often known as second-generation sites.

As Web technology started being used by commercial companies more and more design elements became available to Web designers and developers. These included animations, video clips and sound clips. Sites which freely used such technologies are known as third-generation sites. Around the time that this richer form of content was becoming available, computer scientists started developing the technologies which enabled more dynamic pages to be built. Foremost among these was the programming language Java. One of the major features of this language was its ability to provide programming facilities that enabled chunks of code known as applets to be embedded within a Web page. Other technologies which were developed in order to provide what is known as executable content were the programming language JavaScript and dynamic page technology.

3   How Web servers work

A Web server is effectively a very sophisticated file server which dispenses files that contain Web pages, graphic images, sound clips, video clips and other media. When a user carries out some action such as clicking a link or submitting a form, a message is sent to the server which communicates the action that has taken place, together with the data associated with the action, for example a name in a text field that has been typed in by a user.

HTTP is an example of a protocol known as a request/reply protocol

The message that is sent by the browser is read by the Web server which decides what is required: whether, for example, a Web page is to be returned to the user or whether some program needs to be executed. In the latter case this might involve the modification of a stored Web page before it is sent to the browser; such processing is dealt with in the next chapter. The request is carried out and the server makes itself ready for the next request which may, or may not, come from the same browser that issued the previous request. The requests made of a Web server and the replies that emanate from the server are expressed in a protocol known as the **Hypertext Transfer Protocol**, more usually known as HTTP.

3.1 HTTP

Exercise 6.3

Examining the HTTP protocol using Telnet

HTTP

There are two aspects to the HTTP protocol. The first is the set of messages that are sent from the Web client running a browser and the second is the set of replies from the Web server. I shall look at the former first.

As an example of the client side of the protocol consider the GET message. What this does is to request some resource from the Web server. An example of this is shown below:

```
GET /index.html HTTP/1.1
User-Agent: Lynx/2.4
Connection: Keep-Alive
Host: www.openaccess.com
Accept: text/html
```

Lynx is a text-only browser which enables Web pages to be displayed very quickly

The first line specifies that the browser wants to retrieve the file *index.html* and that the browser is currently using version 1.1 of the HTTP protocol.

The next line states that the user is running version 2.4 of the Lynx browser. The next line states that the browser wishes the connection to the Web browser to be kept alive, for example to load images that are contained on a page that has been downloaded. The next line identifies the computer on which the resource requested is held. Finally the last line informs the Web server that it can accept only text files which contain HTML code. When the request involves a form being processed the data communicated by the form will follow the last line of the header lines.

The first line is known as the **request line** and the subsequent lines are known as **header lines**; each header line consists of some keyword followed by a colon and an argument which corresponds to a value for the keyword.

Currently there are three versions of HTTP: 0.9, 1.0 and 1.1. Nobody now uses 0.9

When the server receives this message it carries out the response that the browser has asked for. So, for example, if the request was for an HTML file which could be found in the Web server's file store then the following response would occur:

```
HTTP/1.1 200 OK
Date: Thu, 22 July 1998 18:40:55 GMT
Server: Apache 1.3.5 (Unix) PHP/3.0.6
Last-Modified: Mon, 19 July 1997 16:03:22 GMT
Content-Type: text/html
Content-Length: 12987

. . .
```

The response consists of three parts. The first part is the first line which states that the server is using version 1.1 of the HTTP protocol and that the request by the browser has not generated an error (the 200 stands for a status code which indicates this). This is known as the **status line**.

Apache is currently the most popular Web server. It is freely available and was used in the next chapter for Web programming. It gained its name from the fact that it was associated with a large number of software patches during its early life

The next set of lines are known as header information. It has the same format as the header information found in a client request. The first line identifies the time at which the request was processed, the next line identifies the server (Apache) that is responding to the request, the next line specifies when the resource that was requested was last updated, the penultimate line specifies that the file is a text file containing HTML markup code (this is known as the MIME type) and the final line gives the length of the file in characters.

MIME types

When a browser sends a file back to a client it has to tell the client what is in that file as it can contain anything from plain HTML to an executable program. The text that describes the content is known as a MIME type (short for Multipurpose Internet Mail Extensions). In the example above text/html is the MIME type that is associated with HTML expressed as plain text. Other MIME types include image/gif which describes an image expressed in the gif graphic format, video/quicktime which describes an animation expressed in the QuickTime format and text/plain which is unadorned plain text. The general form of a MIME type is Content category/Content type where content category defines what type of media are being described, for example text, and content type defines what *specific* media are being described, for example HTML text or ASCII text. MIME types were originally used to tag non-text content in e-mail messages.

The header information is followed by the lines of HTML markup and content from the file that has been requested. This is preceded by a blank line.

When the browser receives the status line, the header lines and the HTML code it will then display the content formatted on the user's screen after interpreting the markup instructions detailed by the HTML tags.

There are a number of different request types that can be issued by a browser. Table 6.3 summarises them. There are a number of things which are worth saying about this table and its contents. First, not all the commands are shown, just a selection. Second the HEAD command is similar to the GET command; however, it does not return any content, just the HTTP header. It is used when the browser just wants to obtain some information about a particular resource such as when it was last modified. The PUT command will only work if the user is allowed to place resources

Exercise 6.4

Installing and running the Apache Web server

Table 6.3
A selection of HTTP commands

Command	Meaning
GET	Get a file from the server
HEAD	Like GET but no content returned
POST	Invokes a program on a form
PUT	Store some resource
OPTIONS	Find out about communications options

on the Web server. Finally the OPTIONS command will result in data about the server or a particular resource on the server being sent back to the requester, for example it would result in the list of HTTP requests that are available being sent.

Before moving on it is worth describing how forms data is handled. When a submit button is clicked in a Web page this will result in a POST or GET line being generated together with some associated content. For example, the lines

The blank line here is significant

```
POST /cgi-bin/searcher/ HTTP/1.1
Content-Length: 46

userName=Darrel+Ince&email=d.r.ince@fizzer.com
```

cgi-bin is the normal directory where cgi programs are placed

The first line informs the Web server that a form has been submitted and the program that is to be executed to process the forms data resides in the server directory cgi-bin with the name searcher.

The next line states that the content associated with the command is 46 characters long. The third line is the content. It describes the fact that the visual widget named userName has generated a string 'Darrel Ince' (the space is represented by +) and the visual widget email has generated the string 'd.r.ince@fizzer.com'. This is known as the **query string**. This data is then processed by the program.

3.2 Status codes

When a Web server responds to a request originated by a browser it will respond with a three-digit status code and text which indicates what has happened to the request. Already you have seen one example of the use of a status code where the code 200 indicated that a successful GET had been carried out. These status codes are partitioned into a number of categories.

Status codes which start with a 1 will provide information to the client; for example, as a response which indicates that a change in protocol requested by the client will be acceded to.

Status codes starting with a 2 indicate that a correct response has occurred. For example, the code 202 indicates that the request has been successful but has not been acted upon yet, but will eventually be carried out.

Status codes starting with a 3 indicate that the browser must carry out some further action in order for the request to be successful. For example, the code 301 indicates that the resource that was requested has been permanently moved to another location.

Status codes starting with a 4 indicate that something has gone wrong; for example, the most frequent status code that is returned is 404 which indicates that the resource that has been requested cannot be found.

Status codes starting with a 5 indicate that the server has experienced a problem. For example, the status code 503 indicates that the service requested has not been able to be carried out; this is usually because of routine maintenance of the server, or the server has become overloaded and refused any connections.

3.3 The Common Gateway Interface

The Common Gateway Interface

In some of the fragments of HTTP that I presented in the previous sections you will have seen programs stored in a directory called cgi-bin. You may have wondered what the cgi stands for. The aim of this section is to detail a component of a Web server known as the **Common Gateway Interface**. This interface enables other programs and applications to interact with clients, for example when a client in an e-commerce application sends a request to look up some data in a relational database it is the Common Gateway Interface that provides the facilities whereby a database management system can be instructed to send this information back to the client.

> ### Programming and the Web
>
> Until fairly recently the only type of programming that could be carried out with a Web server was CGI programming. Such programming suffers from a number of disadvantages. The main one is that since a CGI program has to be loaded into memory and then unloaded each time a request is made this provides a large degree of inefficiency. However, a number of different technologies have now been developed which alleviate the problems with CGI programming: Java servlets are memory-resident Java programs which carry out an equivalent type of programming and Java Server Pages allow Java code to be embedded into Web pages to carry out the display of information as and when it is needed on-the-fly.

When a browser initiates some request which requires interaction with non-Web server software the following processes occur:

- First the browser issues some command in the HTTP protocol which informs the Web server that some response is to occur. For example, the command may be a POST command which sends data that has been entered in a form.

- The Web server interprets the command. It discovers the name of the program that is to be executed from the command; this program will usually be in a directory known as cgi-bin or servlet.

- The program is loaded and executed.

- The program will carry out the processing that is needed, say consulting a database and retrieving some data.

- The data will be returned to the client embedded in a Web page.

- The program will finish executing and be unloaded.

CGI environment variables

In order to function the Common Gateway Interface provides a number of what are called **environment variables** which are available to the programmer. These variables contain information pertinent to the request that has been made to the server, information which is associated with the client that made the request and information associated with the Web server. A selection of some of these variables is shown in Table 6.4.

Table 6.4
Some CGI
environment
variables

CGI variable	Purpose
SERVER_SOFTWARE	Describes the Web server software and its version number
GATEWAY_INTERFACE	The name of the gateway interface and its version number
REMOTE_ADDR	The address of the client
SERVER_PROTOCOL	The protocol used by the server and its version number
REQUEST_METHOD	The method used for the request, for example GET
SERVER_ADMIN	The e-mail of the person who administers the Web server
SERVER_PORT	This is the dedicated port that the Web server will use to listen to incoming requests; normally this is port 80
QUERY_STRING	The query string containing visual object identities and values passed when a form is submitted

Query string was
introduced on
page 150

3.4 Logging

One feature of Web servers which I have not described is that of logging. When a request is processed by a Web server it writes the details of that request to a logging file which will contain details such as the date and the time of the request and the identity of the resource that was requested. This can generate a lot of data and the vast majority of Web servers will provide facilities that enable a webmaster to cut down on the information that is written. For example, it is fairly easy to restrict the logging to the retrieval of the Web pages and omit logging details of the graphical files associated with a page.

*Common log file
formats*

There are two uses for logging. The first is connected with marketing. Log files are a useful medium for determining who is visiting a Web site and what they are doing when they visit. For example, a log may show that certain pages, such as the home page of the site, are getting a very large number of accesses, but many of the pages connected to these popular pages are not being frequently accessed. This information might lead to the Web designer responsible for the pages looking at the popular ones and discovering that the links to the least used pages were not prominent and required redesigning.

Another use for log files is in speeding up the performance of a Web server. For example, the webmaster – the person who administers a Web server – may discover that 5 per cent of the pages stored in the Web server are requested 95 per cent of the time. Many Web servers contain areas of memory which can store Web pages and whose access time is fast compared with normal files. This area is known as a **page cache**; a webmaster who discovers popular pages from a log file can ensure that these pages are permanently stored in the cache.

*Log file analysis
software*

Log files are huge and they require special-purpose software packages to analyse them. This software ranges from shareware to sophisticated $2000 packages. Typical information that such packages generate includes the path taken by users through a Web site, the most popular page visited in a site, the least popular page and the time spent on a page.

4 Administering a Web server

*Webmaster
resources*

The webmaster has a number of tasks that need carrying out:

- Optimising the performance of the server. For example, a major decision that a webmaster has to make is what pages should be cached (held in some fast memory store). To do this the webmaster needs to examine the log files which are generated when browsers access the server in order to determine what are the popular pages.

- Setting the initial configuration of the server. This involves everything from small tasks such as setting the e-mail address of the webmaster to selecting which software modules to load.

Robot exclusion

Robot information

When search engines index a Web site they send an agent known as a robot (or bot) to examine the pages of the site. An important task for a webmaster is to provide helpful information for a robot, either as part of the HTML of the site or in a special file which, in Apache, is known as `robots.txt`. In the early days of search engines robots tended to slow down the performance of a Web site and so robot information was used to minimise the time that they spent at the site, for example by informing them which pages to visit. A warning though: not all robots take notice of robot information provided by the webmaster; however, the robots associated with the main commercial search engines do.

- Setting up the initial directories and files which will form part of the Web site(s) administered by the server. These files will normally be produced by designers, although in very small organisations the webmaster often doubles as the Web site developer.

- Setting up security policies which enable or disable access to users. For example, some pages in a Web site may only be accessed by subscribers who have paid for the privilege. A webmaster will normally set up some form of password protection to ensure that this happens.

Exercise 6.5

Developing a very
simple Web server

- Monitoring security logs for potential intrusions which could compromise the security of the server.

5   Client-side Web programming

There are two types of programming associated with the World Wide Web: client-side programming and server-side programming. The former involves associating program code with Web pages that are downloaded into a client running a browser with the code being executed on the client computer; the latter involves code being stored on the server and being executed when a particular event such as a page being demanded occurs. In this chapter client-side programming will be described and in the following chapter I shall look at servlets – snippets of Java code that can be executed by a server – and an associated technology known as Java Server Pages. The two technologies I shall look at briefly are applets and a scripting language known as JavaScript.

5.1 Applets

Applets

The main mechanism for client side programming in Java is the **applet**. Applets are found embedded within Web pages and contain visual widgets and `Panel` objects. Applets enable the developer to embed functionality within a Web page. Typical examples of the use of applets include:

It is worth pointing out that applets are not the only technology that can be used for the applications bullet-pointed here, for example HTML can be used for forms

■   Providing forms in which the user can put information, for example a form which collects comments about a Web page.

■   Providing simple animations on a Web page; an applet will implement such functionality by repeatedly displaying a series of graphics which differ in only small respects from each other.

■   Displaying data from a database, for example returning with the products from an e-commerce site which have been requested by a user.

■   Implementing graphical devices such as image maps: graphics in which hyperlinks are embedded.

There are other facilities in HTML for applet specification, for example for communicating parameters to an applet

An applet is embedded into a Web page by writing some very simple statements in HTML, the *lingua franca* of the World Wide Web.

The simplest form for this HTML is

```
<OBJECT code = "java:name" WIDTH = n HEIGHT = n>
</OBJECT>
```

Here *name* is the name of the file which contains the generated class code for the applet, *width* is the width of the applet in pixels and *height* is the height in pixels. Thus, the HTML

```
<OBJECT code = "java:MyAp.class" WIDTH = "200" HEIGHT = "300">
</OBJECT>
```

specifies that the applet contained in the file *MyAp.class* must run in a container of size 200 pixels by 300 pixels and will appear at the point at which the code above appears in the HTML source of a Web document.

As well as enhancing the functionality of Web pages, applets are useful because they transfer some of the processing load from a server to a client; rather than overload a server with the processing required for an applet's functionality it is shared round all the clients accessing the server. In order to move this processing load an applet is transferred to the client computer when the page in which it is contained is first accessed. This means that the applet executes on the client computer.

JavaScript and VBScript

> ## JavaScript, JScript and VBScript
>
> One of the aims of this book is to describe e-commerce and distributed application topics within the context of the Java programming language; this is why applets are used as an example of client side Web programming. There are, however, other technologies for this form of programming. One of the most popular is JavaScript; this is a scripting language which looks like a loose amalgam of C, Java and Basic and which implements much of the functionality of applets. The language was initially developed by the Netscape Corporation and a version (JScript) has also been developed by Microsoft. JavaScript source code can be directly placed into Web pages, rather than be referenced by a file name as with applets. JavaScript has evolved into a very sophisticated technology. There are also other scripting languages available including VBScript, a variant of the Visual Basic language. More material on JavaScript is given in Section 5.5.

A simple programming language which is used in connection with a browser is often known as a scripting language

5.2 Applets and security

Applets can connect to the host on which they reside

Plain applets are very limited as to what they can do. An applet residing on a client running a browser cannot, for example, access local files, run another program, delete a local file or connect to another host. This is because they could potentially cause havoc on the computer system that they are downloaded onto. For example, if the restrictions above were relaxed it would be quite possible for someone to write an applet which would delete all the files on the client running the browser which is accessing the applet. When applets were first announced they were referred to by detractors as the best way to create and spread viruses that had yet been invented.

You will meet digital signatures later in Chapter 11

In later versions of the Java system there is a facility which uses a technology known as a digital signature which enables applets to be built that can, for example, access a file on a client computer. Such applets are normally built for closed networks, for example the local area network used by a company.

5.3 Developing applets

Developing applets is rather different from developing code which implements other containers such as frames. The main difference is that applets do not have constructors: an applet is created by the browser and not by constructors found in program code.

Table 6.5
Applet lifecycle
methods

Method	Action
init()	Executed when the applet is created by the browser
start()	Executed when the browser displays a page containing the applet
stop()	Executed when the browser displays another page
destroy()	Executed when an applet is finished with, for example when the user exits a browser or when the page containing the applet is decached

In order to develop an applet you will need to extend the class Applet and override a number of methods which are known as **lifecycle method**s. These are methods that are called when some browser activity occurs. Table 6.5 describes these methods.

All these methods have default code which does very little; if functionality associated with any of them needs to be implemented then they should be overridden. Normally the only method which is overridden is init.

An example of applet code is shown below. It displays a button and every time the button is clicked it will display a count of the number of clicks on the browser's status bar; for the display on the status bar it uses the method showStatus.

The header code for the applet is shown below:

```
public class ButtonApplet extends Applet
    implements ActionListener
{
private Button clickButton;
private int buttonCount;
```

All it does is to extend the class Applet which contains the methods init, start, stop and destroy and implements the interface necessary to listen to button events.

The code for init is shown below:

```
public void init()
{
    clickButton = new Button("Click here");
    add(clickButton);
    buttonCount = 0;
    clickButton.addActionListener(this);
}
```

Exercise 6.6

Developing a
simple image map
applet

You can see it contains the sort of code that is normally found in the constructor of a container. All the code does is to deposit a button into the applet, set a count of the number of clicks to zero and ensure that the applet is registered as a listener to button events.

The only remaining code is the method actionPerformed associated with the interface ActionListener; this is shown below:

```
public void actionPerformed(ActionEvent ae)
{
   buttonCount++;
   showStatus("Click total = "+buttonCount);
}
```

This code increments the count of clicks whenever a button event occurs and then displays the count on the status bar of the browser; this is achieved via the method showStatus which is found in the class Applet.

DHTML

Dynamic HTML

This is a technology implemented by Microsoft which provides an object interface to the elements of a Web page, elements such as tables, forms, frames and headings. Effectively it provides an API which enables the JavaScript or VBScript programmer to access these elements and either retrieve information about them or change their properties, for example the contents of a displayed page can be changed just by clicking a mouse using this technology. It is often abbreviated to DHTML.

5.4 The differences between applets and applications

There are a number of differences between applets and Java applications. These are:

- Applets do not use constructors; they use the overridden init method to carry out tasks such as initialising instance variables.

- They are not allowed to use System.exit() to terminate. It is the browser which terminates the execution of applets.

- All output is to visual widgets which reside on the Web page rather than to objects such as System.out.

- Applets are always developed by extending the Applet class. Applications usually extend the Frame class.

6 JavaScript

6.1 Introduction

JavaScript is also known as JScript

Another approach to client-side programming is exemplified by JavaScript. This is a programming language which can be integrated with the HTML that describes a Web page. Later in this section I shall describe how JavaScript is able to interact with a Web page, but for now I shall describe the basic programming facilities of the language.

A simple JavaScript program is shown below:

```
<HTML>
<HEAD>
<TITLE>
    First program for book
</TITLE>
<SCRIPT LANGUAGE = "JavaScript">
    document.writeln
        ("<H2> Hello there, this is the first JavaScript"+
        "program</H2>");
</SCRIPT>
</HEAD>

<BODY>
        Some text
</BODY>

</HTML>
```

Note that I have indented the code for readability

Here the code within the page is introduced by the `<SCRIPT>` tag. The program consists of a single line which displays the text

```
Hello there, this is the first JavaScript program
```

using the `H2` heading format.

The code sends a message `writeln` to the object `document` which represents the page being browsed. This results in the argument of the message being displayed on the page. This is shown as Figure 6.10. Notice that the text produced by `writeln` is displayed before the body text.

Figure 6.10
Output from the simple JavaScript program

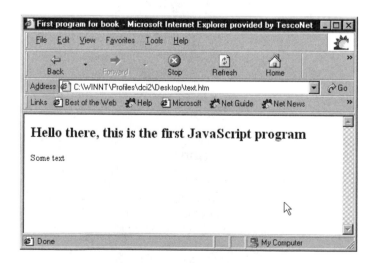

Another JavaScript program is shown below. This time it reads some data and then displays it on the Web page.

```
<HTML>
<HEAD>
<TITLE>
    Second program for book
</TITLE>

<SCRIPT LANGUAGE = "JavaScript">
    var no,      //Number to be input
        double; //Double the number
    no=window.prompt
        ("Give me a number and I will double it", "0");
    double = 2*parseInt(no);
    document.writeln
        ("<H2> Hello there, this is the number " + no +
        " and the double is " + double + "</H2>");
</SCRIPT>
</HEAD>

<BODY>
    Some further text
</BODY>

</HTML>
```

This JavaScript program declares two variables: no and double. The variable no represents an integer read into the program and double is double that integer. The next line displays a prompt box. This box will show a text field and two buttons, with the initial value of zero in the text field. This is shown as Figure 6.11.

When the user has entered a value into the textbox and clicked the OK button the page will display the number and its double. Notice the use of the method parseInt which converts a string to an integer. This is because the window.prompt code delivers a string. Also note that variables are not typed in JavaScript: there is, for example, no notion of an int or a real. Everything is a variable defined by var.

Figure 6.11
A window prompt

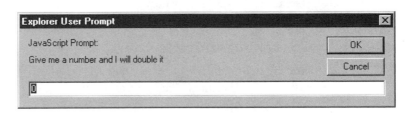

6.2 Operators

The modulus operator delivers the remainder when its first argument is divided by its second argument

JavaScript contains all the standard arithmetic operators you would expect in a modern programming language: + (addition), – (subtraction), * (multiplication), / (division) and % (modulus). As well as these it contains the standard incrementing and decrementing operators ++ (increase by one) and –– (decrease by 1). It also contains the standard assign and apply operators: += (add and assign), –= (subtract and assign), *= (multiply and assign), /= (divide and assign) and %= (modulus and assign).

JavaScript also contains all the standard logical operators that you would expect: == (equality), != (non-equality), > (greater than), < (less than), <= (less than or equal to) and >= (greater than or equal to).

A program that uses some of these operators is shown below. All it does is to read in an integer from a prompt window and display whether it is negative or not. It uses a JavaScript if statement.

Exercise 6.7

Preparing and running a simple JavaScript program

```
<HTML>
<HEAD>
<TITLE>
    Third program for book
</TITLE>
<SCRIPT LANGUAGE = "JavaScript">

    var no; //Number to be input

    no=window.prompt
        ("Give me a number and I will check it", "0");
    if(parseInt(no)<0)
        document.writeln
          ("<H2> The number is negative</H2>");
    else
        document.writeln
          ("<H2> The number is either positive or zero</H2>");
</SCRIPT>
</HEAD>

<BODY>
    Some text
</BODY>

</HTML>
```

JavaScript teaching resources

Here the code is self explanatory.

6.3 Control structures

JavaScript contains the standard repertoire of control structures found in languages such as C++, Java and C. The control structures generally mirror those found in Java. A list is given below:

In the text to the left the the word 'statement' means either a single statement or a series of statements (a compound statement) enclosed in curly brackets

```
if  (condition)
    statement
else
    statement

while(condition)
    statement

do
    statement
while(condition)

for(initialisation,  condition,  variable  change)
    statement

switch(value){

case   "constant1":
    statement;
    break;

case   "constant2":
    statement;
    break;

. .

case   "constantn":
    statement;
    break;

default:
    statement;
}
```

Before seeing these control structures in action it is worth looking at arrays.

6.4 Arrays

This has a different format to the new used in Java

JavaScript contains facilities for declaring arrays, both single-dimensional and multi-dimensional. In the book I will concentrate on single-dimensional arrays. An array is created by using the new facility. An example of this is shown below:

```
var n1 = new Array (5);
```

This declares an array n1 which has five elements, currently the array is empty.
Arrays can be initialised in two ways. The first is via the use of new. The code

```
var arrn = new Array(12, 23, 45, 66);
```

Arrays start in JavaScript at zero

creates a single-dimensional array arrn which contains the four integer values specified within the round brackets.

An alternative way of initialising arrays is to use square brackets, as in

```
var arrn = [12, 34, 45, 66];
```

which is the equivalent of the previous declaration.

6.5 Some larger JavaScript programs

Before looking at JavaScript objects in detail it is worth looking at some slightly more complicated programs involving both arrays and control structures.

The program below sums up the values within the array container and displays the result in the Web page in which it is contained.

JavaScript allows you to initialise variables as they are declared

```
<HTML>
<HEAD>
<TITLE>
    Fourth program for book
</TITLE>

<SCRIPT LANGUAGE = "JavaScript">
    var sum=0; //Running sum
    var arr = [22, 33, 9, 8, 7];

    for(var i = 0; i<arr.length;i++)
        sum+=arr[i];
    document.writeln
        ("<H2> The sum of the values in the array is "
        +sum  +"</H2>");
</SCRIPT>
</HEAD>

<BODY>
    Some further text
</BODY>

</HTML>
```

The code is self-explanatory and differs very little from the equivalent Java code. JavaScript also contains a facility which enables a more succinct form of iteration over an array. An example of this is shown below for a program equivalent to the one above.

```
<HTML>
<HEAD>
<TITLE>
    Fifth program for book
</TITLE>
```

```
<SCRIPT LANGUAGE = "JavaScript">
var sum=0; //Running sum
var arr = [22, 33, 9, 8, 7];
for(var i in arr)
    sum+=arr[i];
document.writeln
    ("<H2> The sum of the values in the array is " +sum
    +"</H2>");
</SCRIPT>
</HEAD>

<BODY>
    Some further text
</BODY>
</HTML>
```

Another example of a program which uses a `while` structure is shown below. It is equivalent to the two programs previously detailed.

```
<HTML>
<HEAD>
<TITLE>
    Sixth program for book
</TITLE>

<SCRIPT LANGUAGE = "JavaScript">
    var sum=0,    //Running sum
        count=0; //Loop count
    var arr = [22, 33, 9, 8, 7];
    while(count<5){
        sum+=arr[count];
        count++;
    }
    document.writeln
        ("<H2> The sum of the values in the array is "
        +sum  +"</H2>");
</SCRIPT>
</HEAD>

<BODY>
    Some further text
</BODY>

</HTML>
```

Exercise 6.8

Developing a doubly nested JavaScript program

By now you will have gained the impression that JavaScript is very much like Java in terms of control structures, arithmetic operators and logical operators. Indeed this is true: the only major difference that you have met is the fact that JavaScript is untyped; that when you declare a variable it is done via `var` and can stand for any type of data.

Because of its similarity to Java I shall not detail any more programs containing other control structures. The next section details a way in which JavaScript differs from Java.

6.6 JavaScript objects

A major difference between Java and JavaScript is that you cannot define classes. However, there are a number of classes that are built into JavaScript. These are there for two reasons: to provide methods which process basic data such as numbers and strings and to provide an interface to the Web page in which the JavaScript code is embedded.

6.6.1 The Math class

The Math class contains facilities for mathematical functions, for example the function abs which forms the absolute value of a number, the function power which raises a number to a power, the function max which finds the maximum value of two numbers and the function min which finds the minimum value of two numbers are all contained in this class. The program below applies some of these functions. The result of its execution is shown in Figure 6.12.

```
<HTML>
<HEAD>
<TITLE>
    Seventh program for book
</TITLE>

<SCRIPT LANGUAGE = "JavaScript">
var first=7,
    second=2;
```

Figure 6.12
The result of applying some mathematical methods

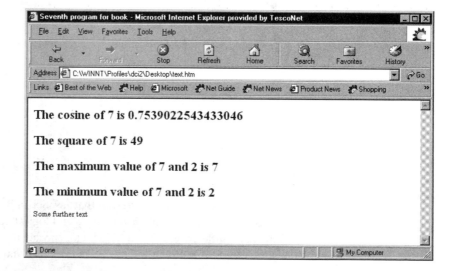

```
document.writeln
   ("<H2> The cosine of "+ first+ " is "
   + Math.cos(first) + "</H2>");
document.writeln
   ("<H2> The square of " + first + " is "
   + Math.pow(first, second) +"</H2>");
document.writeln
   ("<H2> The maximum value of " + first + " and "+
   second + " is "+ Math.max(first, second) +"</H2>");
document.writeln
   ("<H2> The minimum value of " + first + " and "+
   second + " is "+ Math.min(first, second) +"</H2>");
</SCRIPT>
</HEAD>

<BODY>
   Some further text
</BODY>

</HTML>
```

6.6.2 The `String` class

JavaScript also has access to a string class. Table 6.6 shows a selection of methods which form part of the class.

Table 6.6
String methods in JavaScript

split treats strings very much like the `StringTokenizer` class does in Java

Method	Description
`charAt(int)`	Returns the character that is indexed by the argument. Characters start at position 0
`concat(string)`	Joins two strings together. For example `s1.concat(s2)` joins the strings `s1` and `s2` together with `s1` being the leading string
`slice(int, int)`	Forms a string from another string from the first `int` position to the next `int` position
`toLowerCase()`	Converts a string to lower case
`toUpperCase()`	Converts a string to upper case
`split(string)`	Converts a string into an array of substrings. Each substring is the substring in the destination object which is terminated by the argument to be split
`indexOf(string, index)`	Searches for the first occurrence of its string argument in the destination object, starting at the position designated by its second argument

Because JavaScript integrates with Web pages there are also a number of methods which generate HTML tags. For example, the method `anchor(string)` wraps the string argument between the tags `<A></A>` and the method `italics(string)` wraps the argument in the italics tags `<I></I>`.

The JavaScript program below shows some of the string methods in action.

```
<HTML>
<HEAD>
<TITLE>
    Eighth program for book
</TITLE>

<SCRIPT LANGUAGE = "JavaScript">

    var first="Hello there",
        second=" My friend";

    document.writeln
       ("<H2> The catenation of '"+ first + "' and '" +
       second + "' is '" + first.concat(second) +
       "'</H2>");
    document.writeln
       ("<H2> The substring of '"+ first +
       "' from zero to 3 is '" +
       first.slice(0,3)  +  "'</H2>");
    document.writeln
       ("<H2> The upper case version of '"+
       second+ "' is '" + second.toUpperCase()
       +  "'</H2>");
</SCRIPT>
</HEAD>

<BODY>
    Some further text
</BODY>

</HTML>
```

Exercise 6.9

Developing a string manipulation program

The display from this program is shown as Figure 6.13.

6.7 Functions

JavaScript also allows the programmer declare chunks of code known as functions which can be programmatically referred to time and again.

An example of such a simple function and its use is shown below. It takes two `int` values and finds their sum.

Figure 6.13
The display from the
string program

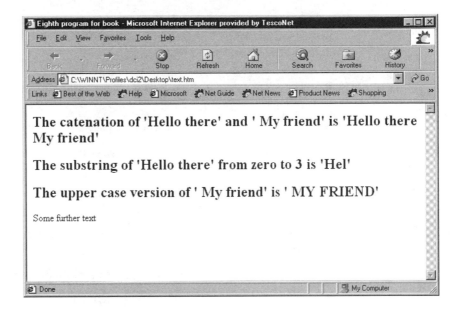

```
<HTML>
<HEAD>
<TITLE>
    Ninth program for book
</TITLE>

<SCRIPT LANGUAGE = "JavaScript">
    function  addUp(a,b){
        return a+b;
    }

    document.writeln("<H2> The sum of 3 and 4 is " +
                        addUp(3,4)   +"</H2>");
</SCRIPT>
</HEAD>

<BODY>
    Some further text
</BODY>

</HTML>
```

This will just display the line that the sum of 3 and 4 is 7.

6.8 Access to Web documents

So far there has not been much that is remarkable about JavaScript. The aim of this section is to briefly show the power of JavaScript as a medium for manipulating Web pages.

HTML which contains facilities for reacting to events and modifying page properties is often known as Dynamic HTML or DHTML

Before doing this it is worth looking at the event mechanism in HTML. When a user interacts with a Web page a number of events can occur. Some of the more important ones are detailed below:

■   The event ONCLICK occurs when a user clicks a mouse on an element of a Web page.

■   The event ONLOAD occurs whenever a page is loaded into a browser.

■   The event ONMOUSEMOVE occurs whenever the mouse is moved by the user when it is over an element of the page.

Events and JavaScript

■   The event ONMOUSEOUT occurs whenever a mouse leaves an element of a Web page.

■   The forms event ONSUBMIT occurs whenever a user submits a Web form for processing by a Web server.

■   The event ONHELP occurs whenever the user asks for help.

■   The event ONCUT occurs whenever an item is cut.

■   The ONSCROLL event occurs whenever a user scrolls an element of a Web page.

These are just a very small selection of events which occur when a user interacts with a Web page. JavaScript enables code to be written which allows the action of the user to be monitored and acted upon.

Some examples of the sort of processing that is programmed in JavaScript are:

■   An image changing when a mouse moves over it, for example a graphic changing to show the user that the mouse is over it. This technique is known as a rollover and is very commonly used on Web pages.

■   A window being launched when a page is loaded.

This is not far-fetched: different browsers can display the same page in different ways

■   Code checking what browser the user is employing to load the page and then transferring to a page that has been designed for that particular browser.

■   A Web page with help information being displayed when the user presses the F1 key (the key used to indicate that help is required).

The simple JavaScript program below displays the window shown in Figure 6.14 when the text in the paragraph identified by "onlypara" is clicked.

Figure 6.14
An alert window

```
<HTML>
<HEAD>
<TITLE>
    Tenth program for book
</TITLE>
```

Notice that onclick
is in lower case

```
<SCRIPT LANGUAGE = "JavaScript" FOR = "onlypara"
    EVENT = "onclick">
    alert("You have clicked the text");
</SCRIPT>
</HEAD>

<BODY>
    <P ID = "onlypara">
        Some text
    </P>
</BODY>

</HTML>
```

Here the paragraph is associated with a label onlypara which is then referred to in the code that is executed when the paragraph is clicked.

Another example of code responding to events is shown below. This time an alert window is generated welcoming the user when a page is loaded. For this the code responds to the ONLOAD event.

```
<HTML>
<HEAD>
<TITLE>
    Eleventh program for book
</TITLE>

<SCRIPT LANGUAGE = "JavaScript">
function   launchAlert(){
    alert("Hello  there  welcome");
}
</SCRIPT>
</HEAD>

<BODY ONLOAD = "launchAlert()">
    Just some text here
</BODY>

</HTML>
```

Here, the body of the page is associated with the ONLOAD event which executes the simple function launchAlert. This just displays a window which welcomes the user to the page. The window will contain a button which, when clicked, will get rid of the window.

So far I have shown how events are generated and how they are reacted to. The final part of this brief introduction to JavaScript looks at how elements which make up a Web page can be accessed and changed. Usually this change will be at the behest of the user in that an event will be monitored and some code that carries out the change executed.

Elements in an HTML page are normally addressed using their ID attribute. The following example gives a flavour of the sort of processing that JavaScript is capable of. It launches a window with a text field when the page is loaded, the user provides some text and this is written to the page after the text which is already displayed on the page.

```
<HTML>
<HEAD>
<TITLE>
    Twelfth program for book
</TITLE>

<SCRIPT LANGUAGE = "JavaScript">
function loadup(){
    var reply;
    reply = window.prompt ("Hi type some text in", "");
    singlepara.innerText = (singlepara.innerText)
                                    .concat(reply);
}
</SCRIPT>
</HEAD>

<BODY ONLOAD = "loadup()">
    <P ID = "singlepara">
        This is the original text
    </P>
</BODY>

</HTML>
```

Here the function `loadup` displays the window and then updates the property `innerText` of the page. This property holds the text found on the page. It is updated by forming the concatenation of the old text and the text found in the text field of the window that has been launched.

There are a number of features here worth noting:

■ The use of the ONLOAD event to start the processing off.

■ The access to the paragraph object named `singlepara`.

■ The use of a property of the paragraph (`innerText`) with it being read and then updated.

The next example is the processing of button being clicked. When the button is clicked the background colour of the page in which it is embedded changes from white to red. The code for this program is shown below:

```
<HTML>
<HEAD>
<TITLE>
    Thirteenth program for book
</TITLE>

<SCRIPT LANGUAGE = "JavaScript">

    function changeColour(){
        document.body.style.backgroundColor = "red";
    }

</SCRIPT>
</HEAD>

<BODY>
    <P> The button is below </P>
    <INPUT TYPE = "button" VALUE = "Click here"
      ONCLICK = "changeColour()">
</BODY>
</HTML>
```

Here the action of changing the background is delegated to the function changeColour. In order to do this it has to access the property backgroundColor associated with the property style which is associated with the body property of the current document. Again, the pattern of processing is the same as in the previous example.

A program which switches between white and red for each click is shown below. It uses the % operator to determine the state of the background of the Web page.

% is the operator which delivers the remainder when its first argument is divided by its second argument

```
<HTML>
<HEAD>
<TITLE>
    Fourteenth program for book
</TITLE>

<SCRIPT LANGUAGE = "JavaScript">

    var count =0;

    function changeColour(){
        count++;
        if(count%2==0)
            document.body.style.backgroundColor = "white"
        else
            document.body.style.backgroundColor = "red"
    }
```

```
</SCRIPT>
</HEAD>

<BODY>
    <P> The button is below </P>
    <INPUT TYPE = "button" VALUE = "Click here"
     ONCLICK = "changeColour()">
</BODY>

</HTML>
```

As well as accessing individual objects, JavaScript can access collections of objects. The code below displays all the elements on the page in which it is embedded.

```
<HTML>
<HEAD>
<TITLE>
    Fifteenth program for book
</TITLE>

<SCRIPT LANGUAGE = "JavaScript">

    var collectedElements ="";

    function gather(){
        for (var i =0; i<document.all.length;i++)
            collectedElements +=(document.all[i].tagName +
                                  " ");
        para.innerText = para.innerText+collectedElements;
    }
</SCRIPT>
</HEAD>

<BODY>
    <P ID = "para"> The elements will follow here </P>
     <INPUT TYPE = "button" VALUE = "Click here"
     ONCLICK = "gather()">

    <UL>
        <LI> First </LI>
        <LI> Second </LI>
        <LI> Third</LI>
    <UL>
</BODY>

</HTML>
```

The bulleted list is in the page just to show the action of the processing. When the button is clicked the text on the page is updated to show the elements contained on

Figure 6.15
Display of HTML
elements on a page

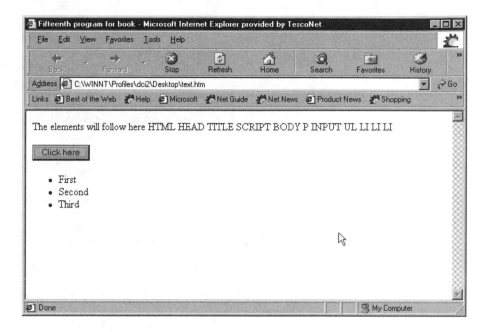

the page. The browser display is shown as Figure 6.15. It shows the HTML elements that are contained on the page. The code that you need to concentrate on is:

```
collectedElements +=(document.all[i].tagName +  "  ");
```

This retrieves the collection of HTML elements in the property `all` (an array) and then sequentially retrieves each of the names of the tags associated with the elements. Each tag is then concatenated to the string which is the text in the paragraph which has the name `para`.

Some of the more important objects which JavaScript can access are shown in Table 6.7.

Each of the objects in the JavaScript object model is associated with a collection of properties. For example, `window` is associated with a property known as `navigator`. This in turn is associated with another set of properties:

- `appName`, which is the simple name of the browser;

- `appVersion`, which is the version number of the browser;

- `userAgent`, the string which is used by the browser to send to a Web server to identify itself;

- `appCodeName`, the code name of the browser, for example Netscape Navigator is known as Mozilla.

- `platform`, the name of the operating system on which the browser is executing;

- `language`, the language which the browser supports, for example English or French.

Table 6.7
Objects in JavaScript

Object	Description
window	This represents the browser window and enables the programmer to access the HTML document object that is in the window
document	The HTML document that is in the window described above
body	The body part of an HTML document, this is the part delineated by `<BODY></BODY>`
history	An object that keeps track of the Web sites that have been visited by the browser
event	An object that can be interrogated to discover what type of event has occurred
location	The URL of the document that is currently being browsed
anchors	The collection of anchors which are in the document
applets	The collection of applets contained in the document
forms	The collection of all the forms contained in the document
scripts	The collection of all the scripts in the document
images	A collection of all the images in the document

As you will have seen in some of the JavaScript programs that I have presented, such properties are accessed by means of a dotted convention, for example the platform on which a browser is executing is written as `window.navigator.platform`. You have seen other examples of properties in action including `innerText`, `all` and `tagName`.

This, then, is an introduction to JavaScript. It has shown you the main features of the language, including data and control structures, detailed how functions are written, and shown how events are processed and the elements in a Web page (document) are accessed and changed. It has not been an in-depth description but has given you enough information to continue your study using a book dedicated to the language, for example the excellent book written by David Flanagan [5].

Exercise 6.10

Accessing some properties of a Web page

7   Accessing Web sites

The previous section has described how JavaScript code is able to be included in a Web page and can access and modify the properties of that page. This is not the only model of access that is available to the developer. Many programming languages allow the programmer to connect to a Web page and then read the HTML lines that make up the page. The code below shows how this can be done in Java.

```
import java.net.*; //Contains the URL class
import  java.io.*;

public class WebReader {
public static void main(String[] args){
    try{
        String address = "http://www.open.ac.uk";
        System.out.println("Trying to contact "+address);
        URL selectedURL = new URL(address);
        BufferedReader br = new BufferedReader
            (new InputStreamReader
                (selectedURL.openStream()));
        String lineRead ="";
        //Loop, reading reply lines from host
        while(true){
            lineRead = br.readLine();
            if(lineRead ==null) //End of host resource
                break;
            //Display the line, any other processing
            //can be inserted here
            System.out.println(lineRead);
        }
    }
    catch(MalformedURLException me){
        System.out.println("Malformed URL encountered");
    }
    catch(IOException io){
        System.out.println("Problems connecting");
    }
}
}
```

Exercise 6.11

Accessing a
Web site

An object defined by the class URL is first created; an input stream is then attached to the Web document described by the URL and a BufferedReader is used to read each line until the end of the file (a null is encountered).

This is a simple program; however, its core can be used to develop sophisticated systems such as search engines and address harvesters.

8   The Apache Web server

The aim of this section is to describe an example Web server. The one which I shall describe is Apache. This is certainly the most popular Web server being used on the Internet at the time of writing.

There are a number of reasons why Apache is popular. The main one is that it is free. It is the product of an open source project that distributes a number of Internet related products to anyone that has the facility to download them.

The Apache project

The Apache project

It is a commonly held belief that the Apache project just deals with the Apache Web server. While this is its main product there are a host of software products which can be downloaded from the Apache Web site. These include Xerces, a parser for the XML metalanguage; Tomcat, a server which processes Java servlets; Cocoon, a Web publishing system; PHP, a dynamic page technology; processors which enable the Apache server to integrate with programs written in the Perl programming language; processors for the XSLT transformation language, and Xang a rapid development environment for implementing dynamic pages in JavaScript.

Apache can be installed on UNIX, LINUX or Windows-based computers although the Apache Web site recommends UNIX or LINUX.

The installation of Apache is relatively easy. An installation script takes the user through the basic installation. After this has completed, the user can change a number of basic items of information that can be found in a configuration file. These include: the server name, for example www.open.ac.uk; the IP address that the server is mounted at; the port or ports that the server listens to (usually 80); whether the server is to stand alone (the most common configuration) or whether other software should handle connections into the server; the e-mail address of the administrator who is associated with the server; where the essential files for Apache are to be stored; where server logs will be found; and finally the location of the pages that the server is to dispense.

Once the basic features of the server have been configured it can be started. This is straightforward; on Windows-based computers it involves double clicking an executable file; on a UNIX system all that is required is to enter the command line

If you are unfamiliar with UNIX the list of words leading to `httpd` *and separated by a forward slash are file directories (or folders)*

```
$  /usr/  local/apache/bin/httpd
```

This will start the server and it can tested by placing a simple HTML file in the directory nominated as holding Web pages, starting a browser and selecting the address of the page.

Once a basic configuration has been set up there is a host of modifications that can be carried out; these include the following:

SOAP is a messaging technology which is described in the next chapter

■ Adding third party modules, for example adding modules which deal with new technologies such as SOAP.

■ Configuring Apache so that it is capable of hosting a number of Web sites.

■ Restricting access to the server so that certain HTTP commands are not allowed to access resources stored at the server.

■ Restricting access from certain computers identified by their IP address.

- Setting up a file known as `robots.txt` which describes the wishes of the Web administrator concerning external indexing of the site. Web sites are continually visited by software agents known as robots which carry out indexing, usually for a search engine. The `robots.txt` file specifies what should be indexed; for example those documents which are in the course of construction can be specified as not being indexable.

- Enabling the Web server to deliver dynamic content. The next chapter details how Web pages can be modified before they are sent back to a browser, for example a page updating the current shopping cart for an e-commerce application. The Apache Web server can be configured to handle a number of these so-called dynamic page technologies, including PHP and JSP.

Chapter 7 describes JSP in more detail

- Loading and storing any programs (or scripts) which need to be executed when a Web page is processed. Typically these programs are associated with Web forms and reside in a directory known as `cgi-bin`. When a form is processed by a browser the script is executed and processing associated with the form carried out, for example retrieving stored data from a relational database.

- Improving the performance of the server, for example by specifying cache sizes and what pages should be loaded into a cache. The cache in a Web server is fast memory into which popular HTML pages are loaded. When a user requests such a cached page it is returned immediately without the attendant delay of retrieving it from file-based memory.

The Apache server

- Configuring the various log files used by Apache which store data about its running, for example data that specify which pages were retrieved.

- Carrying out a security configuration. This involves a host of modifications to the server; the more secure that the server and its contents are required to be, the more modifications that are needed. These include ensuring that users and other Web sites are authenticated and that transfer of data to and from the server is secure.

This, then, is a brief introduction to the Apache Web server. If you are interested in looking at this software product in more detail, the Web links provide information from simple tutorials to complex articles on how to use the more esoteric features of Apache.

9 An example of a rich type of Web site

Many of the technologies described in this chapter can be found in Web sites which host electronic magazines or e-zines. E-zine sites will contain:

e-zines

- Large amounts of content: articles, tutorials, product reviews etc.

- Animations, usually associated with banner advertisements, but also video clips associated with the topic of the e-zine, for example a video clip of one of the highlights of a sporting game featured in a sports e-zine.

- Chat rooms or bulletin boards whose participants discuss some aspect of the topics covered by the e-zine. For example, I regularly visit an e-zine devoted to rugby where a chat room often discusses the rugby games played over the previous weekend.

- An alerting service to which the e-zine users subscribe and which sends the subscribers e-mails when some breaking news occurs. For example, a Java e-zine may provide facilities where you can subscribe to e-mail alerts about topics such as Java and XML, JavaBeans, the JDBC or object-oriented databases and Java.

- A searchable archive of back issues. Such an archive would be searched in the same way that a search engine's database would be searched.

- Mailing lists on a particular topic to which the e-zine readers can subscribe.

- A bulletin board or series of bulletin boards that users can participate in, for example a bulletin board devoted to a particular operating system associated with an e-zine devoted to operating systems.

- Dynamic content, for example a quiz game on topics covered by the e-zine for which prizes are awarded or a page which allows visitors to vote on a particular topic.

Such dynamic content is often referred to as 'fish food' since it is used to attract visitors to a Web site

Slashdot and Java World

Two of the most popular computing e-zines are *Slashdot* and *Java World*; both contain many of the elements detailed above. *Slashdot* is devoted to computing issues and features news, product reviews and content which has both a hardware and software focus. *Java World* is the premier Java site on the Web and contains company news, product news, excellent tutorials and book reviews. *Slashdot* is a hugely popular site and has given rise to the term 'Slashdot effect'. This is where the Web server of a software or hardware company becomes overwhelmed with visitors from the *Slashdot* site or a similar site because a particular product has been mentioned favourably.

Slashdot *and*
Java World

10   # Further reading

If you are doing the case study as you progress through the book, read Chapters 5 and 6 and Sections 1 and 2 of Chapter 17

There has been very little published on Web server technology over and above books which are simply glorified manuals for particular Web servers. If you are interested in the programming required for access to the CGI then a book by Brown, Livingston and Bellew [1] is a good introduction. A good book on Web server administration has been written by Larson and Stephens [2]; while it concentrates on security there is quite a lot of general information. A good introduction to Web servers for beginners has been written by Collin [3]; while it is short on technical details it does provide information for the complete beginner. A good solid introduction to many of the topics detailed in this chapter has been written by Ford [4]. An excellent introduction to JavaScript has been written by David Flanagan [5].

References

Internet book links

[1] M. Brown, D. Livingston and C. Bellew, *Essential Perl5 for Web Professionals*. Old Tappan, NJ: Prentice Hall, 1999.

[2] R. Larson and B. Stephens, *Administering Web Servers, Security and Maintenance*. Old Tappan, NJ: Prentice Hall, 2000.

[3] S. Collin, *Setting Up a Web Server*. Oxford: Butterworth–Heinemann, 1997.

[4] A. Ford, *Spinning the Web*. Chichester: John Wiley, 1994.

[5] D. Flanagan, *JavaScript, The Definitive Guide*. Sebastopol, CA: O'Reilly, 2000.

[6] J. Nielsen, *Designing Web Usability*. Indianapolis, IN: New Riders, 2001.

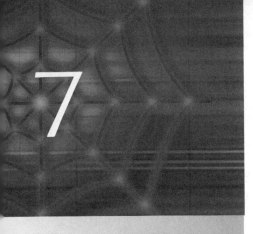

7

Programming
Web Servers

Chapter contents

The previous chapter has looked at the architecture of Web servers. This chapter details how such servers can be programmed and the Common Gateway Interface accessed. The stress in this chapter is on the programming of servlets: small snippets of memory-resident Java code which can process commands expressed in the HTTP protocol. The lifecycle of a servlet is described and a number of important methods corresponding to HTTP commands such as PUT and GET are detailed. The use of Perl as a server programming language is outlined. The chapter includes a description of the persistence problem as it affects Web servers and how session management overcomes this problem. The chapter concludes with a description of the concept of a Web service.

Aims

1. To detail the main components of servlets.
2. To show how methods associated with servlets can be programmed to respond to HTTP commands.
3. To detail how servlets can be connected to HTML forms.
4. To describe the problem of persistence that has dogged the HTTP protocol.
5. To outline how session management is able to overcome many of the persistence problems with HTTP.
6. To describe the use of Perl in server programming.
7. To describe JSP as an example of a dynamic page technology.
8. To outline the concept of a Web service.

Concepts

ASP, Hack, Hidden field, Hit counter, JSP, Perl, Persistence, Servlet, Session, Session tracking, Shim, SOAP, URL rewriting, Web service.

1 Introduction

This section introduces Web server programming; larger examples of its use can be found in the case study in Chapter 17

The previous chapter described the main features of Web servers and showed how they communicate with browsers using the HTTP protocol. The aim of this chapter is to describe how to program both clients and servers in such a way that they can support the facilities required in modern e-commerce systems. It is worth pointing out that one important component of this process is omitted: that of systems security. This is described in Chapter 11. Figure 7.1 shows a typical e-commerce application for a retailing company. Here customers employ browsers to access a stored database of details about products that the company sells via a Web server. The database would almost invariably be stored on the sort of database server described in Chapter 5.

The Open Source movement

Apache and the Open Source movement

Apache is the most popular server used within the World Wide Web. It is implemented on a variety of platforms, with UNIX being the most popular. Apache is remarkable for two reasons: first, it is free and, second, its source code is readily available. Apache is a manifestation of a movement known as Open Source. The philosophy behind this is that software has become so baroque and complex that no one company can reliably keep track of all the problems and errors. The only way that this can be done is via a large community of developers being exposed to the source code and being allowed to discover problems with it. In this way there would be a rapid dissemination of corrections and enhancements.

Apache

The Web server software, together with the business objects for an application, acts as the middle layer in a three-tier system, with the browser acting as a presentation layer and the database server acting as a database layer. Figure 7.1 is a simplification

Figure 7.1
A three-tier architecture

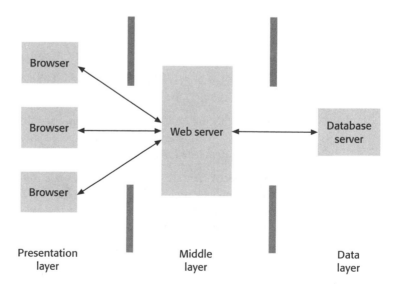

as it shows only one database server, there could be many more distributed around a network. This can complicate the programming considerably; nevertheless it does describe the essence of a modern e-commerce application.

Scour Net

Scour Net

This site is the most comprehensive site for locating multimedia files on the World Wide Web. It uses agent or bot technology to scour the net looking for video clips, audio clips, animations and broadcasts. This technology involves objects travelling around the Internet looking for information; it is briefly described in Chapter 8 and in more detail in Chapter 15. The site heavily relies on Web server programming in order to send back search results from its huge databases.

2   Servlets

The first technology that I shall examine is that of servlets. They are an example of the execution of some program when a resource is requested by a browser. Servlets are snippets of Java code which are loaded into a Web server and which are executed when an HTTP command is processed by the server. Servlets have a number of important features:

■ They are portable across a wide variety of servers.

■ Since servlets are written in Java they can access a huge variety of Java features including CORBA, RMI, Java security facilities and database connectivity facilities.

CGI programming

■ Servlets are resident in memory. With CGI programming in languages such as Perl every time a request comes in from a Web browser a new process has to be spawned and terminated when the connection ends. This means that there can be quite a heavy overhead on the Web server when it loads and unloads programs.

■ Since servlets are Java-based they will contain all the security and safety features that are built into the language.

■ Servlets can maintain state across requests, something that in the early days of the World Wide Web proved difficult. This means that a servlet can remember data and details from a previous request.

Perl

■ The object-oriented model within Java is a much cleaner model than is found with languages such as C and Perl. When you look at Perl CGI programs you often see huge, monolithic, difficult-to-understand programs. The object-oriented nature of Java also provides the potential for greater reuse.

■ Servlets, because they integrate well with the security technology associated with Java can be configured to be highly secure.

Before looking at servlets in some detail it is worth describing how Web servers process requests. A browser will issue a request in HTTP, for example to access a Web page. This is sent to a Web server which interprets the request and executes program code that returns an HTML page. The processing that is carried out by the server depends on the functionality implemented within the Web page. For example, the code that is executed could:

■   Return a Web page without modifying it.

■   Return a Web page and modify it, for example by inserting some dynamic content such as stock and share prices.

■   Process a form, access a database server to retrieve some data and then build a page based on these details.

2.1 Servlet mechanisms

A servlet does not contain a `main` method, but must implement an interface `javax.servlet.Servlet`. For a Web-based system that uses HTTP this is usually carried out via inheriting from a class `HttpServlet`: whenever a request is received by a Web server methods within this class are executed and in order to implement the functionality associated with a particular application the programmer has to provide code for these methods.

If the server uses another protocol then the class `GenericServlet` has to be subclassed. This topic is beyond the scope of this chapter

For a Web server the main method that is executed when an HTTP command is processed is called `service`. This calls a number of other methods depending on what HTTP command is received; for example, if a GET command is received then the method `doGet` is executed. Any processing associated with this command is thus inserted into this method. This is shown in Figure 7.2 which also details the `doPost` method which corresponds to the HTTP POST command. The GET command is communicated to the Web server by clicking a link with a URL of the form `http://server address/servlets/example`, where `servlets` would be a directory in which servlet code is stored; Exercise 7.1 provides further details of how this is achieved.

The GET command which forms part of HTTP was described in Chapter 6

As an example of a simple servlet consider the code shown below. What it does is to respond to a GET command by sending a very simple HTML page back to the browser that initiated the command. This page will just display a simple 'Hello there' message.

Figure 7.2
The servlet
mechanism

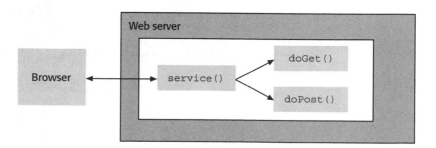

```
import java.io.*;
import javax.servlet.*;
import javax.servlet.http.*;
public class HelloThere extends HttpServlet{

public void doGet
    (HttpServletRequest rq, HttpServletResponse rp)
throws ServletException, IOException
{
    rp.setContentType("text/html");
    PrintWriter browserOut = rp.getWriter();
    browserOut.println("<HTML>");
    browserOut.println
       ("<HEAD><TITLE> Hello there </TITLE></HEAD>");
    browserOut.println("<BODY>");
    browserOut.println("<H3> Hello there</H3>");
    browserOut.println("</BODY></HTML>");
}

}
```

Exercise 7.1

Implementing the
simple example

The single class HttpServlet is subclassed and the code for doGet is provided. The method doGet has two arguments: the first is the request received from the browser, the second encapsulates the response that it sends back to the browser.

The first thing that the servlet does is to inform the rp response object that HTML is to be sent back in a textual format; this is part of the standard interchange between a browser and a Web server which was detailed in the previous chapter. The next line opens up a PrintWriter object attached to rp. After this, the lines of HTML associated with the page that is to be sent back is written to the PrintWriter object; this effectively sends this HTML back to the browser where a simple message is displayed using the <H3> format of the language.

In order to attach this code to a server it first has to be compiled and the class file that is produced placed in a directory nominated for servlets in the Web server. The servlet can then be accessed via its URL. The next example is slightly more complicated: this time I shall show the code for a hit counter.

The actual mechanics of deploying a servlet are detailed in Exercise 7.1 which asks you to implement a simple servlet

Hit counters

Hit counters are visual displays on a Web page which will show the number of visitors to a Web site. Experienced Web designers frown on them; they regard them as the electronic form of the furry dice that are often found hanging in the windows of cars. There are hundreds of different hit counters available, almost all of them being CGI scripts.

```
import java.io.*;
import javax.servlet.*;
import javax.servlet.http.*;
```

It is worth saying that this example has a defect: that every time the Web server is rebooted the hit counter is reset to zero – the hit counter is not persistent. A solution is presented later

```
public class HelloThere extends HttpServlet{
private int counter = 0;
public void doGet
    (HttpServletRequest rq, HttpServletResponse rp)
        throws ServletException, IOException
{

    counter++;
    rp.setContentType("text/html");
    PrintWriter browserOut = rp.getWriter();
    browserOut.println("<HTML>");
    browserOut.println
        ("<HEAD><TITLE> Counter </TITLE></HEAD>");
    browserOut.println("<BODY>");
    browserOut.println
        ("<P> This page has been accessed"+
        counter + " times</P>");
    browserOut.println("</BODY></HTML>");
}

}
```

Here the only change has been the inclusion of a private instance variable `counter` which is initialised to zero and then incremented every time the page is accessed.

It is worth reiterating that although the programming in the previous examples is fairly trivial, it is perfectly possible to write much more complicated code, for example code which processes a form containing some request, consults some stored database such as a catalogue of products and then writes back HTML pages which represent the results of the query.

2.2 The servlet lifecycle

A servlet has a lifecycle in which it finds itself in a number of states during the time that it interacts with a Web server. They are:

■   The servlet is initialised and is loaded into the Web server's memory.

■   The servlet resides in the memory waiting for requests from clients.

■   The servlet is destroyed.

Servlet programming

Servlets and link replacement: an application

One of the major problems with Web sites is that they often reference sites which have become obsolete. One technique to overcome this is to store the URL of any link in a page with one or more alternative links held in a separate database. When a page is referenced by a browser, a servlet will check each link to see if it references a live site; if it does not then the HTML page is sent back with one of the live alternative links embedded in the page.

I have already described the mechanisms whereby a servlet responds to commands generated by a browser: by executing methods such as doGet. For initialisation there is a corresponding method known as init. This is executed just after the servlet is loaded into memory. It would normally carry out any initialisations required by the servlet that is running. In order to do this it is able to access initialisation parameters. The method which accesses these parameters is getInitParameter. This has a string argument which represents the name of the parameter; for example the name of an initialisation file or the initial value of a variable. In order to function the method needs to access an object defined by the class ServletConfig, this object contains information about the current setup of the server which the servlet can access.

The argument to the init method is an object described by ServletConfig; init needs to set this object within its code. An example of the use of init and initialisation parameters is shown below: it represents the solution to the hit counter problem alluded to on page 185: that the servlet does not implement a persistent hit counter whose value survives an event such as the servlet being unloaded.

The solution is to place code in the init method which loads the value of the hit counter from its previous value when the servlet was closed down. This is shown below (the actual code for loading not shown):

```
public void init(ServletConfig cFig)
    throws ServletException
{
super.init(cFig);
String nameOfFile =
      cFig.getInitParameter("PersistentFile");
/*
    Code which connects to a file which is
    associated with the name PersistentFile and code which
    extracts out the value of counter from the file
    The code here should be enclosed with a
    try-catch construct which checks for
    a FileNotFoundException
*/
}
```

The method init first initialises the ServletConfig object which contains the initialisation data by calling the corresponding method in the class HttpServlet (the superclass of the class in which the init method is embedded).

Next, the code extracts out the name of the file in which the persistent count is contained. This is identified by the string argument "PersistentFile". This code, which is not shown, would create a stream to the file and extract out the value of the integer stored there.

It is worth pointing out that the values of the initialisation arguments are provided by the system administrator when configuring the Web server. This is done either by interacting with some graphical program that configures the server or by placing text inside a configuration file. So, for example, the administrator might assign the value

"Counter.txt" to the name PersistentFile, where Counter.txt would be the file which stored the persistent count.

Exercise 7.2

Implementing the persistent counter

The only problem left to solve is that of writing the value of the persistent counter to the file that holds it. Before looking at this it is worth looking at the final part of the lifecycle of the servlet: that of destruction. A servlet is destroyed when the Web server unloads it. The method destroy (again a method supplied by the superclass) should contain code which is executed when the life of the servlet comes to an end. Normally this code will release any resources that the servlet holds so that it can be garbage collected. It will also contain any code that needs to be executed to terminate the application that is being executed. In the case of the servlet which implements the persistent hit counter this would copy the value of the counter to the file that is used to store it in between activations of the servlet. The skeleton code is shown below:

It is worth pointing out that one problem remains with the persistent counter: that of concurrent access to a counter. Such concurrent access could lead to erroneous results

```
public void destroy()
{
//Code which writes counter to the file identified
//by the string PersistentFile
}
```

I have now detailed all the important servlet lifecycle methods associated with servlets. It is now worth describing, in more detail, the functionality of the methods which process commands such as POST and GET which are issued by forms within a Web browser and describe how servlets are embedded in Web forms.

Servlets are invoked from forms by specifying the directory they can be found in by the Web server within the HTML code for a form; for example, the header

```
<FORM METHOD = "POST" ACTION = "/servlets/formprocessor">
```

introduces a form which will be processed by the servlet found in the file *formprocessor* within the directory *servlets*. This file will be the class file produced by compiling the servlet. When the form's submit button is clicked this will result in some command such as POST or GET being issued to a Web server. For example, if a form contained the elements

If you have forgotten what this HTML means, Chapter 6 has a description

```
<INPUT TYPE = "text" NAME = "FirstName" SIZE = "40"
MAXLENGTH = "50">
```

```
<INPUT TYPE = "text" NAME = "SurName" SIZE = "40"
MAXLENGTH = "50">
```

then, when a submit button is clicked with the name 'Darrel' in the first box and the name 'Ince' in the second box, a POST command would be sent to the server with the string

```
FirstName=Darrel&SurName=Ince
```

When the servlet that contains a doPost method receives this message how does it proceed? The main action that needs to be taken is to extract the values for the form items. This is achieved by means of the method getParameter which is contained in the class HttpServletRequest. Some example code for processing the text boxes detailed above is shown below:

```
public void doPost (HttpServletRequest rq,
                    HttpServletResponse rp)
throws ServletException
{
..
String fName = rq.getParameter ("FirstName"),
       sName = rq.getParameter ("SurName");
if (fName = = null || sName = = null)
{
    //At least one of the text boxes is empty
    //Send an error page back to the user
}
else
    {
    ..
    PrintWriter out = rp.getWriter ();
    out.println
        ("Hello there <P>"+ fName+ " " + sName+ " <P>");
    ..
    }
}
```

Normally there would be a try–catch clause around the code in the else statement

Exercise 7.3

Implementing a catalogue browser for a retail site

Here the code picks up the values of the fields, checks if they are non-null (if they were null then the user has forgotten to type any text into a text box) and then displays the values of the first name and surname on a Web page which is sent back to the browser. Given the facilities described here you can develop some simple e-commerce applications which can access databases held on a database server: the method doPost, for example, can read data typed in by a user, for example the name of a product, and can then display a Web page containing details of the product – the product details having been retrieved from a database.

The code above contains statements which process a user error. The servlet API contains a number of methods which allow for HTTP errors and errors such as the one above to be communicated back to the client. For example, if the client asks for a resource that does not exist then it is relatively easy to program a servlet so that the standard 404 error message is returned.

You will remember from the previous chapter that a response from a Web server will consist of a header which provides the response together with a number of string pairs separated by colons which provide further information, for example the response

```
HTTP/1.1 200 OK
Date: Thu, 22 July 1998 18:40:55 GMT
Server: Apache 1.3.5 (Unix) PHP/3.0.6
Last-Modified: Mon, 19 July 1997 16:03:22 GMT
Content-Type: text/html
Content-Length: 12987

. .
```

indicates that a resource has been successfully retrieved (status code 200) with information about the resource and the server provided by the lines which contain string pairs separated by colons.

With all the examples that have been shown previously the servlet has defaulted automatically to sending a 200 code. However, this can be overridden by the use of a method sendError. This method, found in the class HttpServletResponse, can set the response to any error code. The method has two forms:

```
sendError(int)
sendError(int, String)
```

The first variant just returns an error code and the standard textual message associated with the error code is displayed; the second variant sends back the error code, but overrides the standard error message with one supplied by the programmer. The class HttpServletResponse contains a number of static final public constants which define the standard HTTP messages, for example

```
HttpServletResponse.SC_OK
```

is the constant that indicates that an HTTP command has been carried out successfully and

```
HttpServletResponse.SC_MOVED_PERMANENTLY
```

indicates that a resource has been permanently moved to another server. Thus the method invocation of setStatus shown below will send back a 404 message that a resource – usually a Web page – has not been found.

```
public void doPost(HttpServletRequest rq,
                   HttpServletResponse rp)
{
..
//At this point a resource has not been found
String niceMessage =
    "I'm sorry we can't find the resource, our apologies";
rp.sendError
    (HttpServletResponse.SC_NOT_FOUND,  niceMessage);
..
}
```

Exercise 7.4

Implementing a
redirection servlet

2.3 Persistence at the client

In Chapter 6 I indicated that a major problem with the HTTP protocol was that it did not establish a persistent state; for example, that there is no memory of previous interactions. Many e-commerce applications require there to be a memory; a standard example of this is the shopping cart which holds items that the visitor to a retail site has bought.

2.3.1 Some solutions

There have been a number of hacks which have overcome this problem within the context of e-commerce applications.

> **Hacks and shims**
>
> A **hack**, sometimes known as a **shim**, is a convoluted piece of programming that overcomes an organic limitation in a technology. The Internet has grown very quickly and, because of this, many of the applications and tools that have been developed have not been able to directly implement functions which have arisen almost overnight. However, most of the technologies that have been developed can be tweaked by means of programming tricks known as hacks or shims to behave as required. Probably the best example of a hack occurs in early versions of the HTML markup language. This language did not provide facilities for free form layout where blocks of text and pictures could be positioned precisely on a page; however, it did provide facilities for the display of tables. Many HTML designers used these tables to produce layouts where sections of text were displayed with a large amount of space separating them.

The first solution to this problem – which is often referred to as the **session tracking** problem – is to ask the user of a Web site to sign in with their name or some other identification. Every time the user carries out an action such as putting an item in a shopping cart then the form that is used to implement this appends the user identification to the data that is sent to the server when the form is executed. The main problem with this approach is that every time the user interacts with the Web site they will need to log in; this is one of the biggest reasons for users not returning to a Web site after they have initially visited it: they do not want to carry out a time-consuming action just to access some Web pages. They also do not want to remember lots of passwords.

A second way of overcoming the state limitations of HTTP is to pass back pages from the server which contain hidden fields such as hidden text boxes which, when the form is clicked, will respond with some unique identifier of the session. An example of some HTML which constructs a hidden text field is shown below:

```
<INPUT TYPE = "hidden" NAME = "itemsbought" VALUE =
"209087">
```

Initially the Web server will construct a form with no hidden elements; gradually however, as the customer interacts with the server, a series of hidden elements is built up which represents the interaction of the user with the server; for example, each element might contain some identity of the item concatenated with the time when it was bought (this is shown below as the number of seconds past some specific time). Gradually a form will start looking like

```
<INPUT TYPE = "hidden" NAME = "Hide1"
VALUE = "MickyBook236678990">
<INPUT TYPE = "hidden" NAME = "Hide2"
VALUE = "DumboDoll236679002">
<INPUT TYPE = "hidden" NAME = "Hide3"
VALUE = "DonaldCoffee236679107">
<INPUT TYPE = "hidden" NAME = "Hide4"
VALUE = "ArthurBook236679207">
```

Here a set of four hidden HTML form objects have been generated by the server in a page that is returned to the client. These will usually be followed by 'real' visual objects such as text boxes and radio buttons which prompt the user for the next choice. When the user makes a choice a message containing

```
Hide1=MickyBook236678990&Hide2=DumboDoll236679002&
Hide3=DonaldCoffee236679107&Hide4=ArthurBook236679207&
ItemSelected=BarbyDoll
```

would be returned by the form, where the text box named *ItemSelected* would be one of the real visual objects used to communicate the item bought. This is then processed by the Web server which then returns a page containing five invisible form items and so on. When the user checks out the names of the items are collected up, the cost calculated and a page with this amount sent back to the client to confirm the sale. This is a hack which is not satisfactory when large amounts of interaction have to be remembered.

URL rewriting

Another technique is to dynamically rewrite Uniform Resource Locators so that extra information which identifies a session with the server is included in the URL before it is sent to the server. The details of this are beyond the scope of this book; however, it is worth saying that it is another example of a hack.

2.3.2 A servlet solution

The servlet API supports an elegant and convenient solution to the problem of keeping track of persistent data. It provides a class `HttpSession` which is a form of associative store that keeps track of the data associated with a session, where a session is the series of interactions a browser makes with a Web site before departing. A servlet can create an object described by this class by means of the method `getSession` found in the class `HttpServletRequest`, for example

```
public void doPost(HttpServletRequest rq,
                   HttpServletResponse rp)
{
 . .
HttpSession htSess = rq.getSession(true);
 . .
}
```

will return with a session object for the session that is currently being carried out between a specific client running a browser and the Web server in which the servlet is embedded. The Boolean argument determines what happens if the user has no current session. If the argument is true then a session object is created; if the argument is false then `null` is returned.

An `HttpSession` object acts as an associative store in many ways like a `Hashtable` object does: it associates keys with values, although the key used has to be a string object. In order to write data and retrieve it two methods are used. The first is the method `putValue` found in the class `HttpSession`. This has two arguments: a string which represents a key and the object associated with the string, so, for example, the code

```
HttpSession htSess = rq.getSession(true);
 . .
htSess.putValue("Orders", orderVector);
```

will associate the `Vector` object `orderVector` containing shopping orders with the string `"Orders"`. The second method `getValue` returns the object associated with a particular key, for example the code shown below will return the `Vector` object associated with the string `"Credit Cards"`.

```
HttpSession sess = rq.getSession(true);
. .
sess.putValue("Credit  Cards", orderVector);
. .
Vector shopVect = (Vector) sess.getValue("Credit Cards");
```

Two further methods tend to be used quite frequently when programming persistence using servlets: the method `getValueNames` returns with a string array of all the names of the objects associated with an `HttpSession` and `removeValue` removes an object from a session with the string argument of the method identifying the object, for example the statement

```
htSess.removeValue("Credit  Cards");
```

will remove the object associated with credit cards from a session.

Given these facilities an application which requires persistence can be easily programmed, for example a shopping cart could be associated with a servlet which holds products bought, which added products and which calculated the total value of the order when the user checks out.

This has been a very brief look at sessions; however, it has provided you with most of the tools to enable you to develop sophisticated Web applications which require persistence. The references at the end of the chapter provide much more detail on aspects of servlets such as using servlets in conjunction with each other, the security of servlets and logging.

3 Java Server Pages

3.1 Introduction

JSP

So far in this chapter you have seen how servlets can be used to respond to Web browser interactions. Such servlets are stand-alone snippets of code which monitor an HTTP request and act on it. An allied technology which is becoming even more popular than servlets is Java Server Pages (JSP). This is a technology that allows the developer to include Java code within an HTML page, with the code carrying out Web-related actions. This is an example of server-side programming because the code for JSP is executed at the Web server. This is in contrast to client-side programming exemplified by applets and JavaScript where the software is executed at the client.

JSP is an example of a **dynamic page technology**. It is closely related to the servlet technology that was detailed in the previous section in that a special processor takes JSP-coded pages and converts them into servlets, executes them and then sends any HTML required by the programmer back to the browser that accessed the page.

An example of some JSP code is shown below:

```
<HEAD>
<TITLE>
   First JSP program
</TITLE>
</HEAD>
<BODY>
   <H1>
      Calculator example
   </H1>
   3-2 equals <%= 3-2 %>
</BODY>
</HTML>
```

It not only contains standard HTML code but also a very small snippet of Java code. The Java code (3-2) is enclosed in the brackets <%= and %>. When the code is executed by a Web server that recognises JSP coding, the code is stripped out, converted into a servlet, executed, the result of the execution placed in the page and the page sent back to the browser.

3.2 A forms processing program

An example of a page that contains a form that can be processed by JSP code is shown below:

```
<HTML>
   <HEAD>
   <TITLE>
      Second JSP program
   </TITLE>
   </HEAD>
   <BODY>
      <H1>
         Forms test
      </H1>
      <FORM ACTION = "calculate.jsp" METHOD="GET">
         <BR><BR>
         <INPUT TYPE = "TEXT" NAME = "Number">
         <BR><BR>
         <INPUT TYPE="SUBMIT" NAME="Getvalue">
      </FORM>
   </BODY>
</HTML>
```


 is HTML for a
line break

This consists of a single text field with the name Number and a submit button labelled Getvalue. The form described by the HTML is shown as Figure 7.3.

Figure 7.3
A form to be
processed by a
JSP page

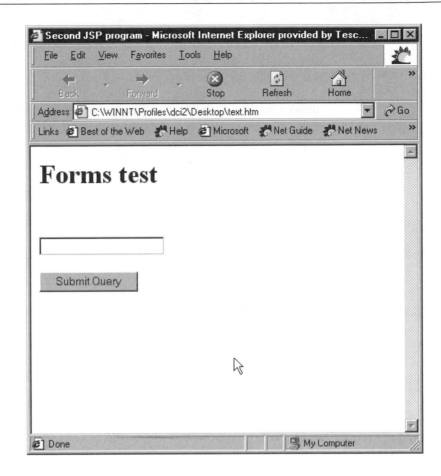

jsp is the file extension
for JSP programs

When the form is submitted, the JSP program `calculate.jsp` is executed. This
program is shown below:

```
<HTML>
    <HEAD>
    <TITLE>
        Third JSP program
    </TITLE>
    </HEAD>
    <BODY>
        <H1>
        One less than the value that you typed in is
        <%=Integer.parseInt(request.getParameter
            ("Number"))-1%>
        </H1>
    </BODY>
</HTML>
```

Here the main code is again shown enclosed by the `<%=` and `%>` brackets. All it does is to extract out the string which has been submitted in the text field, convert it to an integer and then subtract 1. The result is enclosed in the HTML code and then sent back to the browser. The program accesses an implicit object `request` which provides information about the form request that is processed. The method `getParameter` returns with the value of the string associated with the form element that is its argument. The object `request` is defined by the class `HttpServletRequest` detailed in the previous section on servlets.

Implicit means that you do not need to declare it

3.3 A page counter

The next program shows how Java code can be placed in a Web page in such a way that it is not sent back to the browser; typically this is code that carries out declarations or some form of intermediate processing. The code below represents a page counter which keeps details on the number of visitors to a Web page.

```
<%! int count =0; %>
<%! java.util.Date now = new java.util.Date(); %>
<HTML>
    <HEAD>
    <TITLE>
        Fourth JSP program
    </TITLE>
    </HEAD>
    <BODY>
        <H1>
            Welcome
        </H1>
        <%count++; %>
        You are visitor number <%= count %>.
        On <%= now.getHours() %>:<%= now.getMinutes() %>
        :<%= now.getSeconds()%>
    </BODY>
</HTML>
```

Every time that the page is accessed a count is incremented by 1. The page displays the number of visitors and the current time. In order to do this it employs the methods `getHours`, `getMinutes` and `getSeconds` found in the `Date` class packaged in `java.util`.

There are two things to notice about the code. The first is that the full declaration of the `Date` object is used whereby the object is designated as `java.util.Date`. Normally the programmer imports `java.util` and then refers to a `Date` object just using the class name `Date`. However, you are not allowed to import packages in servlets so you have to quote the names of classes in full.

The second thing to notice is the use of the `<%!` and `%>` which introduces Java declarations and the use of `<%` and `%>` to enclose Java code which does not issue any output to the Web page.

3.4 Using control structures

All sorts of Java code can be placed in a JSP page, including control constructs. The example below shows the HTML required to add two numbers together, with the numbers being provided by an HTML form.

```
<HTML>
<HEAD>
   <TITLE>
      Fifth JSP program
   </TITLE>
</HEAD>
   <BODY>
   <H1>
      Addition
   </H1>
   <% if
      (request.getParameter("first").
      equals("")||request.getParameter("second")
      .equals("")){   %>
      <BR>
      You have not provided two numbers
      <BR>
   <% } else { %>
      The result of the addition is
      <%=  Integer.parseInt(request.getParameter
      ("first"))+Integer.parseInt(request.
      getParameter("second"))  %>
   <% } %>
   </BODY>
</HTML>
```

The form that is processed would contain two text fields labelled `first` and `second`.

Here any code that is not required in the page that is sent back to the browser is enclosed within `<% %>` brackets. So, for example, the Java `if` statement that processes the contents of the text fields checking for whether the user has actually filled them in is contained in these brackets.

Dynamic page technology – both JSP and its Microsoft equivalent ASP – is a recent phenomenon. It is, however, rapidly taking over from technologies that were used for server-side programming such as Perl. However, these technologies are still quite important and, for the near future at least, will be fairly heavily used. It is for this reason that the next section describes the Perl programming language.

Active Server Pages

ASP and server side includes

JSP is not the only technology that can be used for the creation of dynamic Web pages. Even in the earliest days of the World Wide Web developers perceived a need for the generation of Web pages on-the-fly. Server side Includes were a form of primitive technology which allowed a developer to insert text into a place holder in an HTML page; it was a primitive technology which only really allowed the insertion of simple information such as the date when a page was last modified. Active Server Pages (ASP) is a recent, much more sophisticated technology developed by Microsoft. It allows the HTML developer to embed a wide variety of material in a Web page using the same delimiters as JSP: `<%` and `%>`. It allows the inclusion of Active X controls, scripts in programming languages such as VBScript and Java applets.

PHP and mod_perl

This section has been an introduction to one type of active page technology. It is worth pointing out that as well as JSP there are a number of other technologies that are used for generating pages on-the-fly. The two main ones are mod_perl and PHP. The latter is a software plug-in which when added to a Web server such as Apache enables dynamic pages to be displayed when Perl program scripts are executed. PHP is a server side scripting language which can be embedded in an HTML page. Its big advantage is the support that it offers for database connectivity. It has its roots in languages such as C, Perl and Java.

4   Perl

Perl resources

Perl has, until recently, been the language of choice for Web server programmers. It was originally developed by Larry Wall as a string processing language intended to produce reports from projects. The fact that you often require to do string processing when developing server code has meant that it has found use well outside its original domain. Perl stands for Practical Extraction and Report Language.

4.1 Data types

Perl contains three data types: scalars which can be integer, strings or floating point numbers, arrays which are collections of scalars that can be indexed, and hashes which correspond to Java Hashtable objects. Scalar variables are preceded by $, arrays by @ and hashes by %.

A very simple Perl program is shown below, it just sets the value of a variable and displays it; comments are introduced by the # symbol.

\n displays a new line as in Java

```
# First example program for book
$b = 3;
print "The value of the variable b is $b\n";
```

The program below sets the array `arr` to contain the scalar values 4, 5, 6 and 19 and then displays them:

```
# Second example for book
@arr = (4, 5, 6, 19);
print "The contents of the array arr are @arr\n"
```

The values are enclosed within brackets.

4.2 Control constructs

Perl contains the standard set of control constructs that you would expect in a higher-level language. An example of an if statement is shown below:

```
if($version eq "2")
{
    #Some processing code here
}
```

Here the string variable `version` is checked for equality to the string "2".

Perl also features a `foreach` construct which is similar to a for statement in Java. However, its action is slightly different. An example of this facility is shown below:

```
foreach $element(@users)
{
    #Some processing code here
}
```

Here the array `users` contains strings and the code iterates over the contents of the array setting the value of the scalar `element` to be each element of the array.

4.3 String processing

The power of Perl arises from the fact that it can carry out string processing. When Larry Wall developed Perl he was faced with the problem of processing large files of string data. Many of the languages which were in existence did not contain very sophisticated facilities for such processing and Wall had to carry out painstaking and error-prone coding to achieve his aims.

Perl contains the ability to match strings based on a wide variety of patterns and uses regular expressions to carry out this pattern matching. An example of a regular expression is shown below:

```
/Davis$/
```

This describes the string "Davis" which can be found at the end of a line, the $ character indicates the end of the line and the / characters indicate that the string is a regular expression. The Perl =~ operator provides the programmer with the ability to pattern match using regular expressions, for example in the code

```
if($programmer  =~  /Davis)
{
    # Code to be executed if Davis is
    # at the end of a line
}
```

Perl contains a very rich notation for specifying regular expressions. It enables the programmer to write if statements involving expressions such as:

Regular expressions

- The string contains one or more occurrences of the string "Williams".

- The string contains a string "ss" which is preceded by less than 2 occurrences of "dd" and occurs at the end of a line.

- The string is made up of five alternating sequences of the strings "22" and "uu".

- The string contains a substring which has at least five occurrences of the string "prog" inside it.

4.4 Perl and Web server programming

A language which can be used to program Web servers needs the following properties:

- It needs to be able to provide database facilities or be able to interface with other languages which provide these facilities.

Database access in Perl

- It needs to be able to access the environment variables of a Web server.

- It needs to be able to send Web pages back to a browser.

- It needs to be able to access the elements of a Web form.

The use of Perl within a database environment is out of the scope of this chapter. All that is necessary to say about the third property is that Perl has facilities whereby it can produce HTTP headers and HTML lines easily by treating the browser as file.

Environment variables and their values are held in a hash variable known as ENV. The code for accessing each variable and its value is shown below:

```
. .
foreach  $var(%ENV)
{
    print  <<PrintLabel
    <P>
    $var  $ENV($var))
    </P>
PrintLabel
. .
```

An entry in ENV is similar in concept to an entry in a Java hash table

Here each entry in ENV is extracted and is displayed together with its value (each entry consists of an identifier for the environment variable, for example HTTP_HOST, and its value). Each entry identifier and its corresponding value is displayed in an HTML paragraph with a space separating them.

The line

```
print  <<PrintLabel
```

informs the Perl interpreter that all the lines up to PrintLabel are to be output verbatim.

Perl also contains facilities for accessing forms. For example, the code

```
. .
$emailAddress  =  param("EmailAddress");
$name  =  param("UserName");
$address  =  param("UserAddress");
. .
```

accesses the strings which have been typed in by a user into three text fields in a Web page which are identified by the names EmailAddress, UserName, UserAddress.

This, then, is a brief introduction to Perl. The programs which Perl produces are known as scripts. If they are being used in a Web server then they are stored in a directory known as cgi-bin and are referred to in the HTML that is associated with a form. For example:

The file extension for Perl scripts is pl

The HTML for the submit button is not shown

```
<FORM METHOD "POST"
ACTION  =  "cgi-bin/formprocessor.pl">
    <INPUT TYPE = "TEXT" NAME = "UserName"><BR>
    <INPUT TYPE = "TEXT" NAME = "UserAddress"><BR>
    <INPUT TYPE = "TEXT" NAME = "EmailAddress"><BR>
    . .
</FORM>
```

will display the form defined within the <FORM></FORM> tags and when the user presses the submit button associated with the form the Perl script formprocessor associated with the form will be executed with the arguments being picked up by code such as

```
$emailAddress  =  param("EmailAddress");
```

5   Web services

5.1 Introduction

Before leaving this chapter it is worth looking at a type of service which has recently been thrust to the forefront by a messaging technology known as SOAP. This is the idea of a **Web service**.

A Web service is an interface to some application functionality which is achieved via Internet technology, usually Web technology. Typical examples of Web services are:

Web services have recently come into prominence by virtue of the fact that they form a central core of Microsoft's .Net strategy

- a request for a price of a particular stock or share;

- a request for available seats on a flight to a particular destination;

- a request for a book to be ordered and sent;

- a request for the best route from one town to another.

Such services are not new; however, with the increase in availability of technologies such as servlets, JSP and relational database APIs vendors such as Microsoft and Sun have started to position their software so that it can be readily integrated into a Web service framework.

5.2 Web service architecture

In the following chapter you will see the full code for a relatively simple Web service

A typical architecture for a Web service is shown as Figure 7.4. Here a browser issues requests to a Web server or a program that behaves like a Web server (in essence it understands HTTP). The request is decoded by the server and it then accesses application functionality. In Figure 7.4 this functionality is accessed by using business objects which front-end a relational database.

An architecture which provides a Web service will have two components: a platform-independent component represented by the parts of the architecture which use open Internet protocols such as HTTP and FTP, and a platform-specific component which employs technologies specific to a particular operating system such as LINUX or one of the Windows variants, for example object technologies such as COM and programming languages such as Visual Basic.

If you are hazy about the concept of a message then it might be worth your while re-reading the relevant section of Chapter 4

The key idea behind a Web service architecture is that it is message based, that is, standard protocols such as HTTP are used to send messages which invoke functionality on application code.

Figure 7.4
An example of a Web service architecture

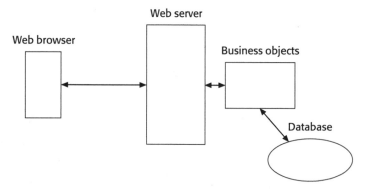

A Web services architecture is implemented using five types of layer. These are:

- ■ *Discovery.* This is a layer which enables the clients who call upon a Web service to fetch descriptions of the providers of the Web service. This will include a description of the interface to the service: what messages it can expect and its responses. There are a number of proposed standards for discovery including WDDI and WS-Inspection.

- ■ *Description.* This provides a description of the network, transport and packaging protocols that the service uses and can be used to communicate with it. There are a number of emerging and proposed standards for this layer including WDSL and the World Wide Web Consortium's RDF.

- ■ *Packaging.* This is a description of the format of the data that is to be moved to and from a Web service: what individual items will be contained in a request for a service and what items can be found in the response to a request. SOAP is used for this.

- ■ *Transport.* This includes the technologies that are used to send and receive messages. These include TCP, HTTP, POP3, SMTP and FTP.

- ■ *Network.* This layer corresponds to the network layer in the Internet layered model. It provides base facilities for error processing, sending messages, receiving messages, contacting hosts and routing.

5.3 The role of SOAP

SOAP is a recent technology which allows the messages to be sent from clients to servers, from servers to other servers and from servers back to clients, to be packaged up in such a way that all the entities involved in the message-passing process can understand the nature of the data that is being sent. SOAP has been implemented using the XML technology which will be described in the next chapter.

A SOAP message will contain enough data for the receiver to act upon it and provide the service that the client who sent the message requires.

SOAP messages consist of an envelope which contains an optional header and a mandatory body. An example of a SOAP message requesting that a customer buy a book from a book sales site is shown below, it is based on one found in [4]:

```
<s:Envelope
xmlns:s = "http//www.w3.org/2001/06/soap-envelope">
<s:header>
   <m:transaction xmlns:m = "soap-transaction"
                  s:mustUnderstand = "true">
      <transactionID>
         7788
      </transactionID>
   </m:transaction>
</s:header>
<s:body>
```

```
. .
<Bookpurchase><customer>
                Darrel Ince
    </customer>
    <CreditCard>
        Visa
    </CreditCard>
    <CardNumber>
        765433221256
    </CardNumber>
    <Address>
        23,The Laurels, Nottingham...
    </Address>
</Bookpurchase>
</s:body>
</s:Envelope>
```

As you will see in Chapter 8, XML allows us to define languages which use diamond brackets as tag delimiters

The message looks a little like HTML in that it uses diamond brackets as delimiters for tags.

The part of the message between the tag `<s:header>` and `</s:header>` defines the header of the message. It is preceded by a line which specifies which definition of SOAP the message is using (the one contained on the World Wide Web Consortium (W3) Web site). The header identifies the message as being a SOAP message, provides an identity for the message and tells the server providing the service that it must be capable of understanding the header. The body of a SOAP message must be understandable by the entity that receives the message; if not, an error message is sent back. However, this is not necessarily true of a header. The line

```
s:mustUnderstand = "true">
```

does, however, inform the recipient that it must understand the header.

The body of the message contains the payload. It specifies the transaction that is to be processed: a book order for a particular customer who possesses a Visa credit card.

The recipient of the message could be any type of software that recognises Internet protocols. It could be a Web server, a mail server, a server which communicates with other servers via sockets and server sockets or even an FTP server.

When the message is received it is processed for correctness, the application that the service calls on is executed and either data such as an acknowledgement sent back or a fault message generated, for example if the receiver of the message does not understand it.

6 An example of a Web service

This chapter concludes with an example of a Web service implemented using the forms facility of a Web page rather than SOAP. It brings together a number of topics which

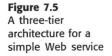

Figure 7.5
A three-tier
architecture for a
simple Web service

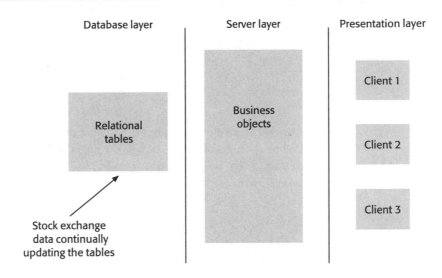

Database layer   Server layer   Presentation layer

Relational
tables

Business
objects

Client 1

Client 2

Client 3

Stock exchange
data continually
updating the tables

have been detailed in this and previous chapters: three-tier architectures, business objects, database processing, object to relational mapping, Web forms and servlets.

6.1 A stock exchange service

The example is that of a Web service which queries a database of stock or share prices which is continually updated from a stock market or stock exchange. Figure 7.5 shows the architecture of the system.

The Web service is very simple: all that it does is to respond to a query from a user about the current financial data for a particular company share. The data will be the current price of the share, its lowest value in the current financial year and its highest value in the financial year.

6.2 The presentation layer

The presentation layer is implemented as an HTML page. It is shown below:

```
<HTML>
<HEAD>
<TITLE>
Web service Servlet
</TITLE>
</HEAD>
<BODY>
<FORM  action  ="/servlet/webservice.ResponseServlet"
       method="post">
   <P> Insert the company name here
   <INPUT type="text" name="Stockname">
   </P>
```

```
< P >
    <INPUT  type="submit"  name="Submit"  value="Submit">
 </P>
</FORM>
</BODY>
</HTML>
```

All it consists of is a simple text box into which the name of a company can be typed and a submit button. When the Web server receives the form that has been sent it will execute the servlet `ResponseServlet` inside the package `webservice` stored in the directory `servlet`.

6.3 The business object

For such a simple service there is only one business object. For a more complicated service there would be many more. The object is a `StockQuote` object. It contains four instance variables: a string which holds the name of the company and three `int`s which hold the current price, highest price and lowest price. The class for this object is shown below. It gets its value by interacting with a relational table holding data which matches that in the class.

```
import  java.sql.*;

public class StockQuote {

private  int  currentPrice,  lowestPrice,  highestPrice;
private  String  stockName;

    // Business object for Web service example,
    // four instance variables representing the
    // stock name, lowest and highest daily price for
    // a stock or share and its current buy price.
    // The business object is formed by extracting data
    // from a simple relational table. The class contains
    // no facilities for changing a business object.
    // This would involve setter methods and code
    // which wrote back the object to the relational
    // table. In a real application this would
    // be required.

    // Note also no error processing is included, it is
    // assumed that the stock or share is in
    // the relational table

    public StockQuote(String stockName) {
        //Sets up all the parameters for connections etc
        this.stockName = stockName;
        String jdbcDriver =
            "sun.jdbc.odbc.JdbcOdbcDriver";
        String protocolHeader = "jdbc:odbc:";
        String dbName = "stocks";
```

```
        String user = "Darrel";
        String password = ""; //No password required
        try{
            // Load in the driver
            Class.forName(jdbcDriver);
            // Get a connection
            Connection cn =
                DriverManager.getConnection
                    (protocolHeader+dbName,  user,  password);
            // Create the query, it will only return
            // one row of the table since it uses the key
        Statement query = cn.createStatement();
        String stockQuery =
            "SELECT * from StocksTable WHERE StockName = '"
            + stockName+"'";
        ResultSet rSet = query.executeQuery(stockQuery);
        // Move to the single row
        rSet.next();
        // Query will only return with one row, set
        // the instance variable using its value
        currentPrice = rSet.getInt("CurrentPrice");
        lowestPrice  = rSet.getInt("LowPrice");
        highestPrice = rSet.getInt("HighPrice");
    }
catch (Exception e)
    {System.out.println
        ("Problem accessing the stock database "+e);}
    }

//Getter  methods

public  int  getCurrentPrice(){
    return  currentPrice;
}

public  int  getLowestPrice(){
    return  lowestPrice;
}

public  int  getHighestPrice(){
    return  highestPrice;
}

public  String  getStockName(){
    return  stockName;
}

}
```

The code here is fairly simple: the main complexity is in the constructor which sets the instance variables for the business object from values in the relational table.

6.4 The server component

As well as the business object the server layer will contain code that interacts with the client (remember the business object interacts with the database layer). The code for the servlet which resides on the Web server is shown below. All it does is to access the form data that is sent by a client, create a stock quote and returns the HTML that contains the result of the query. Only the code for the processing of the POST command is shown below:

```
public class ResponseServlet extends HttpServlet {

private StockQuote quote;
private static final String CONTENTTYPE =
                                    "text/html";

 ..

public void doPost(HttpServletRequest request,
                 HttpServletResponse   response)
                 throws  ServletException, IOException{
    response.setContentType(CONTENTTYPE);
    //Start up a print writer
    PrintWriter out = response.getWriter();
    // Get the stock name from the text field in the
    // Web form
    quote = new
       StockQuote(request.getParameter("Stockname"));
    //Send start of page
    out.println("<html>");
    out.println("<head>");
    out.println("<title>");
    out.println("Quote   service");
    out.println("</title>");
    out.println("</head>");
    out.println("<body>");
    //Send the information for the page
    out.println("The name of the stock is "
                +quote.getStockName()+"<BR>");
    out.println("The lowest price of the stock is "
                +quote.getLowestPrice()+"<BR>");
    out.println("The highest price of the stock is "
                +quote.getHighestPrice()+"<BR>");
    out.println("The current price of the stock is <B>"
                +quote.getCurrentPrice()+"</B><BR>");
    //Send the end of the page
    out.println("</body>");
    out.println("</html>");
}
```

Exercise 7.5

Implementing a
Web service

7   Further reading

An excellent introduction to servlets has been written by Jason Hunter and William Crawford [1]; it contains everything you need to know about servlets and how to program them. A good alternative is a book written by James Goodwill [2]. Deep and Holfelder have written a good, general book on CGI programming [3]; although the language used is Perl it contains a mass of information that would be useful to the Java programmer.

References

Internet book links

[1] J. Hunter and W. Crawford, *Java Servlet Programming*. Sebastopol, CA: O'Reilly, 1998.

[2] J. Goodwill, *Developing Java Servlets*. Indianapolis, IN: SAMS Publishing, 1999.

[3] J. Deep and P. Holfelder, *Developing CGI Applications with Perl*. New York: John Wiley, 1996.

[4] J. Snell, D. Tidwell and P. Kulchenko, *Programming Web Services with SOAP*. Sebastopol, CA: O'Reilly, 2002.

8

XML

Chapter contents

This chapter describes a markup technology known as XML. It is an attempt to overcome many of the problems associated with the HTML markup language. XML is a language for defining languages and the chapter first explores the essential difference between it and a language such as HTML. The history of XML is briefly outlined and a specific example of the language associated with dictionary markup described. The chapter looks at some of the linguistic elements of XML and details how it is parsed by an event-driven parser. An example of a simple language is presented and the processing of this language using the *Aelfred* non-validating parser is detailed. A number of approaches to processing XML documents are described, including DOM, SAX and XSLT. The chapter concludes with a description of three industrial examples of XML: a language used for defining vector graphics, a language used to define active Windows-based channels and a language for electronic business applications.

Aims

1. To describe the main elements of the XML language.
2. To detail how XML differs from conventional markup languages.
3. To describe the detailed operation of one XML parser.
4. To describe some industrial examples of XML in action.

Concepts

Attribute, Bit mapped graphic, Document type definition, DOM, FOP, Formatting object, Metalanguage, Mobile agent, Non-validating parser, Parser, SAX, SGML, Validating parser, Vector graphic, Web publishing system, XML, XSL, XSLT.

1   Introduction

This chapter introduces XML; you will see it fully used in the final chapter which describes a large-scale case study

The aim of this chapter is to describe a specific technology known as XML which promises to overcome a number of the problems found in distributed systems. It provides a portable description that describes what data means as well as the representation for data. The applications which XML can be applied to fall into four distinct groups:

- Those where a distributed program has to interact with two or more sources of data, where the sources are expressed in different formats. For example, data stored on a spreadsheet or in a relational database.

- Applications which attempt to move a large amount of processing onto client computers.

- Applications which require different users to have different views of the same data.

- Applications in which objects are allowed to wander around a network carrying out functions such as gathering information about commodities for sale, for example selecting the commodity with the cheapest price.

This introduction is based on a Web document 'XML, Java and the future of the Web', written by Jon Bosak of Sun Microsystems. It can be found in the first set of Web links below

As an example of the first application consider the travel industry; here travel packages are sold both by the companies themselves and by travel agents, and there has been a rise in the number of e-commerce companies who sell residual holidays – usually at short notice. Many of the companies who are involved in the travel agency industry have incompatible systems and incompatible databases. One of the predicted growth areas of the Internet is that of e-commerce travel agencies who deal with a large number of travel companies – both in their own country and also in other countries – and who trade in late or highly discounted holidays. The growth of such an industry will be slow when incompatibilities exist between the different data sets maintained by companies.

XML introductions

BizTalk

An area which is distinguished by large volumes of incompatible data is that of document interchange, where a document might be a conventional text-based document or a browser page. Here different companies have different standards for documents such as invoices, receipts and credit transfers. XML, the technology described in this chapter, is helping many companies overcome these problems. Microsoft has developed a software suite known as *BizTalk* which enables companies who use XML to exchange these documents. It consists of three components: a BizTalk server which enables the transfer of documents described by common formats, a BizTalk framework which contains descriptions of the messages which pass between companies who interchange documents and a *BizTalk* schema library which describes the various formats of the documents which can be interchanged.

BizTalk

The second type of application has features of some of the first, but with the added feature that it tries to push more processing onto client computers. Another embryonic e-commerce industry which suffers from incompatibility problems is that of electronic publishing. This book exists in two forms: as a set of HTML pages and a printed version. It took me a considerable amount of time to develop the HTML version from the printed version, even though I had planned for this in the first place: while there are a number of converters around which are capable of doing a rough bulk transfer of documents in MS Word (the processor I used) it still took a considerable amount of time to embed graphics such as the graphic I use for Web references. There is no standard interchange language which describes published documents and which requires the sort of precise markup that is required for modern texts. Such a standard would enable the development of markup tools which could be used by clients to lay out complicated texts such as the one found in this book, and would enable processors to be developed to convert documents written in this language to a variety of formats.

There is an excellent language known as SGML which you will meet later; however, it still falls a little short of the type of processing required for pinpoint layout

The third type of application is one where the user wants to examine or process a document in a variety of ways; for example, a collection of financial data might need to be displayed as a spreadsheet, in a word processing document or as an HTML page. A technology which stored this data in such a way that a client processor could take a document written in some markup language and display it in one of a number of ways would save storage space and, at the same time, simplify the development process.

The fourth type of application is one which contains the important element of mobility. Such applications involve mobile agents. A **mobile agent** is a collection of objects which travel over a network carrying out some function such as information gathering. There are a number of current retardants on mobile agent technology; these are so serious that, combined with a paucity of tools, it has meant that agent technology is still in its infancy.

Chapter 15 describes agents in more detail and Chapter 16 describes mobile computing

It is quite a difficult task to program a mobile agent: if you look at the HTML code for a variety of book retail sites you will see that a visiting agent would have difficulty discerning whether the site is a bookshop or whether it is a bibliographic site. Moreover, it would have difficulty discriminating the numbers on a page, for example does a number represent a quantity in stock, or is it part of the title of the book? The problem is even more critical when it comes to words, for example an agent might find it difficult to discover the author and title of a book *Marcel Proust* by David Enright. The same type of problem occurs with a client program running on one computer and referencing many sites.

The discussion here assumes that no form of artificial intelligence technology is employed and that the site has not used comments within the HTML to draw attention to specific chunks of data

What is lacking is semantics: some indication of what the elements of a page designate. There are some semantics built into HTML pages, for example the tag `<LI>` introduces an element of a list. However, these semantics are purely aimed at a browser; there are no application-specific semantics. As you will see later in this chapter the use of a parser adds semantics to a document expressed in a markup language.

2   What is XML?

XML resources

XML is not a markup language like HTML, it is a language used to describe a markup language. The technical term for such a language is **metalanguage**. Using XML a developer can define markup languages which describe electronic circuitry, information for electronic data interchange, the files produced by Web servers, mechanical parts of aircraft and so on. A developer defines a particular language using XML and a tool or utility then takes XML documents which contain text expressed in the language and carries out some process such as converting it to an MS Word document or into some form that can be displayed by a graphics program.

XML and browsers

XML documents can exist by themselves or can be embedded in HTML and then displayed by a browser. Internet Explorer 5 allows XML documents to be included in a Web page using the XML tag. An XML document that is found within an HTML page is known as a data island.

2.1 The history of XML

The browser wars

The roots of XML can be found in the explosive growth of the World Wide Web in the mid-1990s and in the browser wars that took place between the Microsoft Corporation and the Netscape Corporation, where each strived for dominance over the other with their respective browsers.

As the Web became larger and more and more users accessed it a number of problems were discovered by designers who used HTML:

■   The fact that a similar HTML source was displayed in different ways depending on what browser was used. This meant that designers of Web pages had at least to duplicate their efforts.

■   Some browser manufacturers developed HTML facilities which were not recognised by other browsers.

■   It was almost impossible to discern any semantics within a Web page: nowhere was this more apparent than in the use of search engines. Even in the mid-1990s many users were expressing disappointment with these programs because of the large number of retrieved documents that a search returned which were, at best, only marginally connected to the search. The reason for this poor performance was not the search engine technology – they are in fact highly sophisticated programs which are testament to the ingenuity of the human developer – but that the data they process, HTML pages, does not contain many clues about their content.

The World Wide Web Consortium

Because of these problems the World Wide Web Consortium, the group that controls the standardisation process for the Web, decided in 1996 to develop a markup language which would eventually supersede HTML. The major goals of the language are:

■   That it should be easy to use in the Internet.

■   That it should be capable of supporting a large number of applications ranging from browsers to search engine databases.

■   That it should be compatible with SGML, the text processing language which was the inspiration for HTML.

■   That it should not be a complicated process to develop processors for documents written in languages defined in XML, for example it should be easy to write a program to check that a source text reflects its definition.

■   That the number of optional facilities of the language should be very low.

■   That XML documents should be easy to read and understand.

■   That documents written using a language defined by XML should be easy to develop using simple editors.

SGML

In 1998 the language, XML, was presented to the world as a final recommendation of the World Wide Web Consortium; in effect it became an Internet standard. It was based on the SGML text processing language which provided the inspiration for HTML. The role of XML is encapsulated in Figure 8.1 which shows its relationship with other forms of storage and display.

Figure 8.1
The relationship between XML and storage media

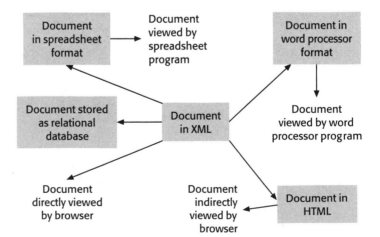

XSL

You will often see the acronym XSL used within the XML literature. XSL stands for eXtensible Style Language. This is a language which defines how the data within an XML-based document is displayed. It can also be used to define how an XML document can be converted into a document expressed in some other language such as HTML or a word processor format such as rtf.

2.2 An example of an XML-defined language

Before looking at XML in detail it is worth outlining some concepts and then describing an application that I was involved in developing. First the concepts.

2.2.1 Concepts

XML is used to define a markup language. The markup language will contain elements marked with tags. For example, the elements <PRODUCTNAME> and </PRODUCTNAME> might delineate a product name in an e-tailing catalogue. For example:

```
<PRODUCTNAME>  CoatBlueWool  </PRODUCTNAME>
```

Here there are two tags including an end tag </PRODUCTNAME> with the PRODUCTNAME element CoatBlueWool being enclosed by them. Each tag is normally associated with an end tag. Elements may be included within each other, for example

```
<PRODUCT>
<PRODUCTNAME>  CoatBlue</PRODUCTNAME>
<PRODUCTPRICE>  34000</PRODUCTPRICE>
. .
</PRODUCT>
```

shows product details being nested within PRODUCT tags.

An element can be associated with an attribute which is specified in its start tag. An attribute is data which provides information which slightly differentiates an element from another element described by the same tags. For example, an element associated with the tag <PRODUCT> might have an attribute which details its postage weight in order that when it is sent to a customer the total price of the order (product + postage) can be calculated. An example of an attribute is shown below:

```
<PRODUCT POSTAGE = "Heavy">
```

Here the PRODUCT element has an attribute "Heavy" which indicates that it is within the heavy postage range and differentiates it from a product which falls within another postage weight range. Attributes are written by preceding them with an equality sign and enclosing them within quotes.

2.2.2 An application

Before looking at XML in further detail it is worth looking at a simple example of the technology in action. In 1999–2000 I developed a dictionary of the Internet for Oxford University Press. One of the problems faced by anyone producing such a work is the fact that new terms are being invented on almost a daily basis, and that a printed version of a dictionary will soon become out of date. OUP and I decided that the only way to overcome this difficulty was to issue a paper-based version of the document together with an HTML version which the buyer could use on his or her computer. A Web site would then provide updates to the HTML version of the dictionary on a regular basis.

In this book I shall use the term 'XML document' to describe documents such as that shown here

I developed the entries using a simple markup language defined by XML. An example of one of the entries in the dictionary is shown below. I have edited it slightly, inserting white space to show its rough structure. The dictionary entry has to include the entry text, links to other entries in the dictionary and a list of external entries to Web sites which are relevant to the entry.

```
<ENTRY>
<ENTRYNAME>Cookie</ENTRYNAME>
<ENTRYTEXT>
    A cookie is a file that is stored on a client computer that is
    using a

    <INLINK filename = "Browser.htm"> BROWSER</INLINK>.

    It is initially deposited there by a

    <INLINK filename = "Server.htm">
    SERVER</INLINK>

    and is used to store information that might be required
    over one particular session with a browser or over a number of
    sessions. One use for cookies is to identify users and
    prepare customised Web pages for them. For example a cookie
    might be used to store the identity of someone who has
    used an

    <INLINK filename = "ECommerce.htm">ECOMMERCE</INLINK>

    site that sells some commodity by taking credit card details
    and the name of the user. This cookie can then be read by
    a server next time the buyer uses the browser in order to
    personalise a greeting and to relieve them of the repetitive
    effort of providing credit card details. Another use for a
    cookie is in

    <INLINK filename = "Etailing.htm">ETAILING</INLINK>

    sites where the cookie holds the contents of a

    <INLINK filename = "Shopping Cart.htm">
```

```
      SHOPPING  CART</INLINK>.

Cookies are used because

<INLINK filename = "HTTP.htm">HTTP</INLINK>

is a stateless protocol: each message sent by a browser in HTTP
has no knowledge of any previous message. The name cookie
derives from

<INLINK filename = "UNIX.htm">UNIX</INLINK>

entities called magic cookies. These are data that are
attached to a user or program and change depending on the
actions taken by the user of the program. Sometimes cookies
are referred to as

<INLINK filename = "Persistent  Cookie.htm">PERSISTENT
COOKIE</INLINK>s

because they stay in a computer for a long time rather than
staying just for a session. See also

<INLINK filename = "Applet.htm">APPLET</INLINK>
and

<INLINK filename = "Server API.htm">
SERVER API</INLINK>.
</ENTRYTEXT>

<LIST>

  <LISTITEM>
  An
  <EXLINK href =
  "http://www.cookiecentral.com/">excellent  magazine
  </EXLINK>
  devoted to cookies
  </LISTITEM>

  <LISTITEM>
  A
  <EXLINK href = "http://www.epic.org/privacy/
  Internet/cookies/">good set of links</EXLINK>
  on cookies.
  </LISTITEM>

  <LISTITEM>
  <EXLINK href  =  "http://www.webdeveloper.com/hotstuff/
  show_cookies.html">A  tool</EXLINK>
  which enables you to check what cookies are associated with a
  Web site.
  </LISTITEM>
```

```
<LISTITEM>
An article which looks at the
<EXLINK href = "http://ignitiondesign.com/journal
/cookies/">pros and cons of cookies
</EXLINK>.
</LISTITEM>

</LIST>

</ENTRY>
```

This corresponds to the entry shown below from the printed text of the dictionary. The terms that are capitalised have entries in the dictionary while the word LINKS at the end indicates that the Web version of the dictionary has a number of external links associated with this entry which are relevant to the entry.

> A cookie is a file that is stored on a client computer that is using a BROWSER. It is initially deposited there by a SERVER and is used to store information that might be required over one particular session with a browser or over a number of sessions. One use for cookies is to identify users and prepare customized Web pages for them. For example a cookie might be used to store the identity of someone who has used an ECOMMERCE site that sells some commodity by taking credit card details and the name of the user. This cookie can then be read by a server next time the buyer uses the browser in order to personalise a greeting and to relieve them of the repetitive effort of providing credit card details. Another use for a cookie is in ETAILING sites where the cookie holds the contents of a SHOPPING CART. Cookies are used because HTTP is a stateless protocol: each message sent by a browser in HTTP has no knowledge of any previous message. The name cookie derives from entities called magic cookies. These are data that are attached to a user or program and change depending on the actions taken by the user of the program. Sometimes cookies are referred to as PERSISTENT COOKIEs because they stay in a computer for a long time rather than staying just for a session. See also APPLET and SERVER API. LINKS.

The first thing to notice about this minimal markup language is that it has some of the features of HTML in that tags are enclosed within angle brackets and that each tag, for example <LIST>, has a corresponding end tag; in the case of <LIST> this is </LIST>. Another similarity to HTML is the fact that some of the elements are associated with attributes, for example the tag <EXLINK> is associated with an attribute which is a URL; in the case of <EXLINK> the name of the value is href. EXLINK represents an external link in the Web dictionary, where such a link is a pointer to an external site relevant to the entry.

This is where the similarity ends: some of the tags above are not part of the HTML tag set. The element identified by the tag <ENTRY> defines a dictionary entry, the element identified by the tag <ENTRYNAME> defines the dictionary name of an entry, the element identified by the tag <ENTRYTEXT> defines the text which describes the name, the element identified by the tag <INLINK> defines a hyperlink to another item in the dictionary with its single attribute *filename* holding the name of the file containing the entry, the element identified by the tag `<LIST>` introduces a number of list items which contain links to Web sites which are relevant to the entry and the element identified by the tag `<LISTITEM>` delineates each item in such a list with the attribute `href` pointing to the URL of the site.

This is a simple example of an XML-defined document. When preparing the dictionary I wrote a number of programs which accessed the file containing the entries: one program produced a MS Word document in which the name of the entry and the text were displayed together with an indication of whether there were any external links associated with the entry; another program produced a Web site in which each entry was contained in a file with anchors which cross-referenced other entries and also cross-referenced any external Web sites relevant to that entry and a further program checked that all the internal links actually referenced items in the dictionary.

It is worth pointing out at this stage that XML is much stricter than HTML, for example tags are case sensitive and end tags are compulsory.

Notice how the tags provide information about the document: any program which accesses the document will, for example, know that `<ENTRYNAME>` defines the name of a dictionary entry rather than the definition of the entry.

> The programs were pretty easy to develop because I used some of the software that is described later in the chapter, in particular a non-validating parser

MathML

MathML

One of the biggest problems that faced Web technologists was the inability of the World Wide Web to display maths and the fact that although some mathematics tags had been defined for HTML they had only been implemented in experimental browsers. The World Wide Web Consortium sponsored a project which has developed a mathematical markup language known as MathML. It was the first application of XML technology. It is beginning to be supported in mathematical packages such as *Mathematica* and *Maple*.

Examples of XML-based languages

3   Defining XML-based languages

The first thing that is needed when developing an XML application is to define the structure of the language that is to be processed: what the elements are, what tags are associated with the elements and what attributes can be associated with an element and the text which identifies a tag.

The definition is known as a **document type definition**, often abbreviated to DTD. An example of a simple document type definition is shown below:

> At this point all I am doing is defining symbols; the processing of such definitions is described later

```
<?xml version = "1.0" encoding ="UTF-8"?>
<!DOCTYPE   ENTRY[
<!ELEMENT   ENTRY  ENTRYPAIR*>
<!ELEMENT   ENTRYPAIR  (NAME,  DEFINITION)>
<!ELEMENT   NAME  (#PCDATA)>
<!ELEMENT   DEFINITION  (#PCDATA)>
]>
```

The first line specifies the version of XML used and the character encoding used, the second line specifies that the document type is named ENTRY. The third line which starts the body of the definition states that an ENTRY will consist of a sequence of zero or more ENTRYPAIR elements; the asterisk stands for repetition of zero or more times. The definition is enclosed by angle brackets and introduced by !ELEMENT. The next line states that an entry pair will consist of a name followed by a definition; the comma in this case marks a concatenation. The fifth line states that a name element will consist of parsed character data (PCDATA) (essentially non-tagged text) and the sixth line states that a definition element will again consist of character data. The final line terminates the definition.

This defines a simple XML-based language; an example of text expressed in the language is shown below:

The text here can be written in any format with any amount of white space; for example, it could all be written on the same line. XML is not a space-sensitive technology

```
<ENTRY>
    <ENTRYPAIR>
        <NAME>Dodo</NAME>
        <DEFINITION> A dead bird</DEFINITION>
    </ENTRYPAIR>
    <ENTRYPAIR>
        <NAME>Blackbird</NAME>
        <DEFINITION> A thieving bird</DEFINITION>
    </ENTRYPAIR>
    <ENTRYPAIR>
        <NAME>Peacock</NAME>
        <DEFINITION> An attractive bird</DEFINITION>
    </ENTRYPAIR>
</ENTRY>
```

Another example is the empty text

```
<ENTRY>
</ENTRY>
```

It is worth pointing out that the definition of XML-based notations bears some resemblance to that of the definition of programming languages, although in the case of the latter there are a number of restrictions placed on the structure of a language in order that it might be compiled efficiently

In both of these fragments the whole of the document is enclosed by <ENTRY> .. </ENTRY> tags, each of the pairs of entries are delineated by <ENTRYPAIR> .. </ENTRYPAIR> tags and each individual component is delineated by <NAME> .. </NAME> and <DEFINITION> .. </DEFINITION> tags, where each tag has the same name as its element description.

There are a number of characters which can be used to control repetition and positioning. You have already seen the comma used for concatenation and the asterisk character used for repetition for zero or more times. A question mark is used to indicate that an item can appear zero or one time and a plus sign indicates that an element can appear one or more times. If the previous document definition was written as

```
<!ELEMENT  ENTRY  ENTRYPAIR?>
<!ELEMENT  ENTRYPAIR  (NAME,  DEFINITION)>
<!ELEMENT  NAME  (#PCDATA)>
<!ELEMENT  DEFINITION  (#PCDATA)>
```

with the question mark in the first line replacing the asterisk, then the first extract above which contained three definitions of birds would not be a valid document which satisfies the definition since it contains three instances of an entry pair.

As well as tags XML provides facilities for defining attributes, or values which are associated with tags. The syntax is

Document type definitions

```
<!ATTLIST  elementname  attributename  attributetype
defaultdeclaration>
```

The attributetype part of such a line can contain a number of predefined values, for example CDATA stands for a string, ID stands for a string which must start with an alphabetic character and ENTITIES stands for multiple names separated by white space.

The value for the default declaration can be one of four options detailed below in Table 8.1.

An example of the definition of an attribute is shown below on the second line, where TOWN is the elementname, NAME is the attributename, CDATA is the attributetype and defaultdeclaration is #REQUIRED.

The definition of COUNTY and POPULATION is not shown here

```
<!ELEMENT  TOWN  (COUNTY,  POPULATION)>
<ATTLIST  TOWN  NAME  CDATA  #REQUIRED>
```

Here a TOWN element is defined; within TOWN there are two further elements, a COUNTY element and a POPULATION element, with the TOWN element having an attribute called NAME for which a value has to be supplied. For example, the fragment of text

Table 8.1
Defaults for XML attributes

Default	Meaning
#REQUIRED	A value must be provided for this attribute, it cannot be omitted
#IMPLIED	The value for the attribute is optional
"Character string"	The value for this attribute is optional; if it is omitted the string is assumed to be the value
#FIXED "Character string"	The value is permanently fixed to the string, i.e. constant

```
<TOWN NAME = "Towcester">
<COUNTY> Northamptonshire </COUNTY>
<POPULATION>  8300</POPULATION>
</TOWN>
```

adheres to the TOWN description above.

The only part of XML not yet defined in this section are entities. These are character strings which can be substituted into text. An example of an entity definition is

```
<!ENTITY Darrel "Darrel C Ince">
```

This means that when an XML-defined language document is processed and the entity line above forms part of the document type definition then whenever the string &Darrel is encountered it will be substituted by "Darrel C Ince".

To use XML you have to first define a markup language using a DTD. This will define elements, entities, attributes and tags. You will then need to write applications which process XML documents expressed in the language defined by the DTD. Such applications will read the DTD and then process the text of any XML document defined by the DTD in order to carry out its functions. More details of this are provided in the next section.

Exercise 8.1

Constructing a simple document type definition

This section has described the core of XML; there are a number of aspects of the technology which I have omitted, but they are just details. I have provided you with enough knowledge to enable you to develop some quite sophisticated applications.

4   Processing XML-based documents

4.1 Introduction

The aim of this section is to describe some of the types of processors that are available which take a file expressed in an XML-based language and the DTD for that language and do something to it, for example converting the elements described by the language into rows of a relational table.

The main tool that has been used by XML developers has been a parser. A **parser** is a program which takes the source of a language and checks that it correctly matches its definition. An XML parser will check an XML document against its DTD.

An XML parser can be a validating parser or a non-validating parser. A **validating parser** checks an XML document adheres to every rule in its DTD; a **non-validating parser** will make a smaller number of important checks such as the fact that a tag is matched by its end tag.

XML parsers

4.2 An example of a parser

In this section I shall describe a simple parser for XML known as *Aelfred*. It is a non-validating parser; this makes it small in size and fast. It is based on processing some

Aelfred is named after King Alfred of England (AD 871–899) who presided over a flourishing literary renewal of that country

source code and triggering a number of events associated with the tags found in an XML document.

The methods within the *Aelfred* parser are supplied by an interface called `XmlHandler`. The important methods are detailed below.

The method `startDocument` is executed when an XML document is first read by the Aelfred parser; similarly the method `endDocument` is executed when the end of the document is reached.

The method `startElement` which has a string argument is executed whenever the starting tag of an element is encountered and will have the name of the tag within it as a string argument. So, for example, the code

```
public void startElement(String tagName)
{
String currentTag = tagName;
. .
}
```

will set the local variable `currentTag` to be equal to the name of the tag that has just been processed.

The method `endElement` is executed when an end tag such as `</TOWN>` is executed; it has a single string argument which is given the value of the tag.

The method `charData` has three arguments: the first is an array of characters, the second and third are integers. This method will be executed when any character data is encountered, for example it will be executed when the string "Northamptonshire" within

```
<COUNTY>Northamptonshire</COUNTY>
```

is encountered. The first argument will hold the characters, the first integer argument will index the start of the characters and the last integer argument will index the end of the characters. Thus the code

The code uses a three-argument constructor of `String` which forms a string found in its first argument between the positions indexed by its second argument and its third argument

```
public void charData(char[] str, int first, int last)
{
String StrValue = new String(str, first, last);
. .
}
```

will extract out the string "Northamptonshire" and place it in `StrValue` when the fragment of source shown above is encountered.

The remaining important method is `attribute`. This has three arguments: the first is a string that is the name of the attribute, the second is a string that is the value of the attribute and the third is a Boolean which is true if the attribute is defined within the XML document and false if there is a default specified within the DTD which the second argument will be assigned to. For example, the code

```
public void attribute
    (String aName, String aValue, boolean found)
{
String attributeName = aName;
String attributeValue = aValue;
..
}
```

when it processes the line

```
<TOWN NAME = "Towcester">
```

will set `attributeName` to be the string `"NAME"` and `attributeValue` to be the string `"Towcester"`.

Aelfred is based on an event model which requires the programmer to carry out some programming that involves remembering the context in which particular XML elements are found. For example, the code for `attribute` above does not have an argument which identifies the element that the attribute belongs to: it would have to have been remembered from a previous invocation of `startElement`.

The code below shows an example of these methods in action; the code for any methods which I have not described above is omitted. I have also omitted the import statements required. The implementation is based on an applet.

If you are a little hazy over what event-based processing is Chapter 4 includes a discussion within the context of distributed development paradigms

```
public class XMLApplet extends Applet
        implements XmlHandler
{

public void init()
{
//Code here to declare visual objects within the applet
//I shall assume that there is a text area known as tArea

//Code to initialise and lay out the visual objects
//on the applet not shown

//Set up the parser
private XmlParser parser;
parser = new XmlParser();
//Applet is the event handler for the parser
parser.setHandler(this);
..
}

//
//Start of event methods
//
```

```
public void start()
{
    //Start the parser executing, the details are not shown
}

public void startDocument()
{
    tArea.appendText("Document started" +"\n");
}

public void endDocument()
{
    tArea.appendText("Document finished" +"\n");
}

public void startElement(String name)
{
    tArea.appendText
        ("Start Element " +name+"processed"+"\n");
}

public void endElement(String name)
{
    tArea.appendText
        ("End Element " +name+"processed"+"\n");
}

public void charData
    (char[] stringValue, int first, int last)
{
    String val = new String(stringValue, first, last);
    tArea.appendText
        ("Character string encountered "+val+"\n");
}

public void attribute
    (String aName, String aValue, boolean isSpecified)
{
    tArea.appendText
        ("Attribute name = "+aName+
        "Attribute value = "+aValue+"\n");
}

//Remainder of methods from XmlHandler

}
```

Exercise 8.2

Processing a DTD using a parser

If you feel a little confused by the concepts of events being trapped and methods being executed then it is worth saying that the model here is the same as that adopted in Java for handling events such as a button being pressed: that of implementing an interface registering a listener and then providing code for the methods in the interface

In this code the init method of the applet (the method that is first executed when the applet becomes visible in a browser) first creates an XML parser and then registers the applet as a listener to any parsing events that have occurred. Each of the events is then trapped within the methods that follow.

This will result in the text below being displayed in the `TextArea` object `tArea` for the XML fragment:

```
<COUNTY NAME = "Northampton" >
<POPULATION>
1356000
</POPULATION>
<TOWN SIZE = "556000">
Shoe industry
</TOWN>
</COUNTY>
```

The text displayed is

```
Document started
Start Element COUNTY processed
Attribute name = NAME Attribute value = Northampton
Start Element POPULATION processed
Character string encountered 1356000
End Element POPULATION processed
Start Element TOWN processed
Attribute name = SIZE Attribute value = 556000
Character string encountered Shoe industry
End Element TOWN processed
End Element COUNTY processed
Document  finished
```

Each occurrence of a tag, end tag, attribute or characters executes the corresponding method in the `XmlHandler` interface.

This is one example of an interface to an XML-defined document. There is one more type of interface that is worth outlining and that is where, instead of events being fired, a tree is built up which describes the document and which can then be traversed by methods which access the nodes of the tree. This is the idea behind the Document Object Model (DOM) which was recently standardised by the World Wide Web Consortium. An example of the sort of tree that is built up when an XML-based document is parsed is shown in Figure 8.2.

The DOM model

Exercise 8.3

Using a DOM API

The main difference between programming a DOM representation and the type of event programming detailed previously is that with the latter you have to keep track of where you are, for example you will need to keep track of the fact that you might be within one tag which is nested within another which, in turn, is nested within another. This requires some painstaking and error-prone programming. When accessing a tree representation this type of information is ready to hand.

In Figure 8.2 a COUNTRY element contains a number of COUNTY elements with the tree showing the hierarchic relationship between the two elements.

Figure 8.2
An internal XML tree

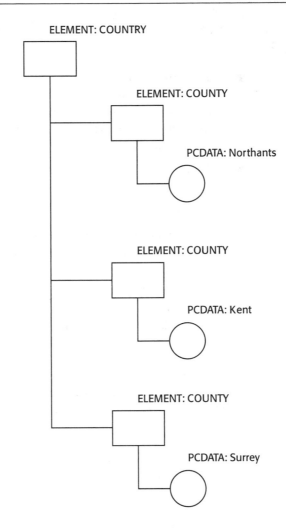

Exercise 8.4

Converting an
XML-based retail
catalogue to a
relational database

5   Approaches to XML processing

5.1 SAX

One of the problems with XML-based parsers is the fact that there has been no standardisation effort. There are a number of parsers each of which is implemented in different ways with different sets of methods. In order to overcome this problem an API has been developed which calls a parser and then processes an internal form of the XML source that has been built up by it. One such API known as SAX (Simple API for XML) had its origins in an XML mailing list. The developer Peter Murray-Rust who had developed a browser for XML known as JUMBO posted a message to the mailing list stating that he was fed up with maintaining JUMBO for three different parsers. This led to a number of XML developers collaborating on the API.

SAX

The SAX API contains a number of methods which are similar to those found in *Aelfred*:

- The method `characters` has three arguments: the first is an array containing characters, the second and third are integers. The first argument contains a string and the two integers delineate the string within the array. The second argument indexes its first character and the third argument indexes the last character. This method is the same as `charData` in *Aelfred*.

- The method `startDocument` is executed when a document is first read.

- The method `endDocument` is executed when the end of an XML document is encountered.

- The method `startElement` will be executed whenever a start tag is encountered. It has two arguments: the first is a string which holds the name of the tag and the second is an object defined by the SAX class `AtttributeList` which holds a sequence of name/value pairs for each attribute.

Exercise 8.5

Redoing Exercise 8.4 using SAX

- The method `endElement` will be executed whenever an end tag is encountered. It is associated with one argument which is a string that represents the name of the tag.

SAX is an example of event processing: the idea behind SAX is that lines of a language defined by some XML DTD are processed sequentially and every time that some event such as a start tag is encountered, the method associated with this event is executed.

An example of some SAX code is shown below. It processes the DTD shown below:

```
<?xml version = "1.0" standalone = "yes"?>
<!DOCTYPE BOOKLIST [
<!ELEMENT  BOOKLIST  (BOOK)*>
<!ELEMENT  BOOK
     (TITLE,  AUTHORS,  PRICE,  PUBLISHER)>
<!ELEMENT  TITLE  (#PCDATA)>
<!ELEMENT  AUTHORS  (#PCDATA)>
<!ELEMENT  PRICE  (#PCDATA)>
<!ELEMENT  PUBLISHER  (#PCDATA)>
<!ATTLIST  PRICE
     AMOUNTCURRENCY  CDATA  #REQUIRED
     DISCOUNT CDATA "0"
>
] >
```

It defines a sequence of book details. Each book is defined by its title, the author(s), the price and the publisher. Each of these entities is defined by a string. The price of the book is associated with an attribute which defines the currency used. The price is written as a string that is an integer. Each price is also associated with an optional discount. If the discount is absent then it is assumed to be zero (no discount).

Some source which is defined by the DTD is displayed below:

```
<BOOKLIST>
<BOOK>
<TITLE>The  Endless  Path</TITLE>
<AUTHORS>Jones</AUTHORS>
<PRICE  AMOUNTCURRENCY  =  "Pounds">200</PRICE>
<PUBLISHER>Pearson</PUBLISHER>
</BOOK>
<BOOK>
<TITLE>My   Story</TITLE>
<AUTHORS>Roberts</AUTHORS>
<PRICE  AMOUNTCURRENCY  =  "SW Francs">500</PRICE>
<PUBLISHER>McMillan</PUBLISHER>
</BOOK>
<BOOK>
<TITLE>XML  for  Beginners</TITLE>
<AUTHORS>Ince</AUTHORS>
<PRICE  AMOUNTCURRENCY  =  "Dollars"  DISCOUNT  =  "5">300</PRICE>
<PUBLISHER>Pearson</PUBLISHER>
</BOOK>
<BOOK>
<TITLE>Java  and  Nirvana</TITLE>
<AUTHORS>Rowlands</AUTHORS>
<PRICE  AMOUNTCURRENCY  =  "Pounds"> 400 </PRICE>
<PUBLISHER>Wiley</PUBLISHER>
</BOOK>
</BOOKLIST>
```

A program which processes the source is shown below:

```
//Imports for parser and SAX api
import  org.apache.xerces.parsers.*;
import  org.xml.sax.*;
import  org.xml.sax.helpers.DefaultHandler;

public  class  BookValues  extends  DefaultHandler{

public  static  void  main(String[]  args){
    BookValues  b  =  new  BookValues("catalogue.txt");
}

public  BookValues(String  file){
    try
    {
        //Sets up a parser
        SAXParser xParser = new SAXParser();
        xParser.setContentHandler(this);
```

DefaultHandler contains methods such as error, warning and startElement with empty code bodies. These need to be overridden

```
        try{
            xParser.parse(file);
        }catch(Exception  e)
            {System.out.println("Problem");}

    }
    catch(Exception  e)
        {System.out.println
        ("Problem starting XML processor "+
        e.getMessage());}
    }

public void error(SAXParseException se){
    //Executed when a serious error occurs
    //in processing the XML source
    System.out.println("Error: Problem with XML "
                    +se.getMessage());
}

public void warning(SAXParseException se){
    //Executed when a minor problem occurs
    //when processing the XML source
    System.out.println("Warning: Problem with XML "
                    +se.getMessage());
}

public void startDocument() throws SAXException{
    //Executed when the XML document is executed
    System.out.println("Document   started");
}

public void startElement
    (String elementName, Attributes al)
                        throws SAXException{
    //Executed when a start element such
    //as <TITLE> is encountered
    //elementName contains the name of
    //the element and al contains
    //a list of the attributes
    String attributeName, attributeValue;
    System.out.println("Start ELEMENT = "+ elementName);
    if(al.getLength()>0)
        //The element has a number of
        //attributes, for example PRICE
        System.out.println("Attributes are ");
        for(int j = 0;j<al.getLength();j++){
            //List the attributes the
            //method getLocalName returns the name of the attribute
            //for example AMOUNTCURRENCY and getValue
```

```
                    //returns with the value
                    //of the attribute, for example "Dollars"
                attributeName  =  al.getLocalName(j);
                attributeValue  =  al.getValue(j);
                System.out.println
                    ("Attribute name is " + attributeName+
                    " Attribute value is " + attributeValue);
            }
        }

    public void endElement(String elementName)
                                        throws  SAXException{
        //Executed when the end element is
        //encountered, for example </PUBLISHER>
        System.out.println("End ELEMENT = "+ elementName);
    }

    public void endDocument() throws SAXException{
        //Executed when the XML source has been
        //completely  processed
        System.out.println("Document  finished");
    }

    public void characters
            (char[] chars, int start, int length)
                                    throws  SAXException{
        //Executed when a string is encountered,
        //for example the name of an author
        System.out.println("String read is " +
                        new String(chars,  start,  length));
    }

    }
```

The code consists of a number of methods. The methods startDocument and endDocument are executed when the XML-defined source is first read and when it is terminated. The code also contains two methods – warning and error – which are executed if there is a serious problem or a minor problem with the XML source.

The remaining methods are triggered when events associated with the individual entities in the source occur. For example, the code

```
    public void endElement(String elementName)
                                        throws  SAXException{
        //Executed when the end element is
        //encountered, for example </PUBLISHER>
        System.out.println("End ELEMENT = "+ elementName);
    }
```

SAX

is executed when a terminating tag is encountered. Inside the code `startElement`, which is executed when a starting tag is encountered by the SAX processor, there is the code

```
if(al.getLength()>0)
    //The element has a number of
    //attributes, for example PRICE
    System.out.println("Attributes  are   ");
    for(int  j  =  0;j<al.getLength();j++){
        //List the attributes the
        //method getLocalName returns the name of the attribute
        //for example AMOUNTCURRENCY and amountValue
        //returns with the value
        //of the attribute, for example "Dollars"
    attributeName   =  al.getLocalName(j);
    attributeValue  =  al.getValue(j);
    System.out.println
        ("Attribute name is " + attributeName+
        " Attribute value is " + attributeValue);
}
```

This first checks whether there are any attributes which are associated with a particular element. If there are, then it iterates through these attributes indexing each by j and displaying them.

The constructor contains code which sets up a parser and starts the process of reading the lines in the XML-defined source. The file containing the source is passed as an argument to the parser.

The display text produced by the execution of the code is shown below:

```
Document  started
Start ELEMENT = BOOKLIST
Start ELEMENT = BOOK
Start ELEMENT = TITLE
String read is The Endless Path
End ELEMENT = TITLE
Start ELEMENT = AUTHORS
String read is Jones
End ELEMENT = AUTHORS
Start ELEMENT = PRICE
Attributes  are
Attribute name is AMOUNTCURRENCY Attribute value is Pounds
Attribute name is DISCOUNT Attribute value is 0
String read is 200
End ELEMENT = PRICE
Start ELEMENT = PUBLISHER
String read is Pearson
```

```
End ELEMENT = PUBLISHER
End ELEMENT = BOOK
Start ELEMENT = BOOK
Start ELEMENT = TITLE
String read is My Story
End ELEMENT = TITLE
Start ELEMENT = AUTHORS
String read is Roberts
End ELEMENT = AUTHORS
Start ELEMENT = PRICE
Attributes  are
Attribute name is AMOUNTCURRENCY Attribute value is SW Francs
Attribute name is DISCOUNT Attribute value is 0
String read is 500
End ELEMENT = PRICE
Start ELEMENT = PUBLISHER
String read is McMillan
End ELEMENT = PUBLISHER
End ELEMENT = BOOK
Start ELEMENT = BOOK
Start ELEMENT = TITLE
String read is XML for Beginners
End ELEMENT - TITLE
Start ELEMENT = AUTHORS
String read is Ince
End ELEMENT = AUTHORS
Start ELEMENT - PRICE
Attributes  are
Attribute name is AMOUNTCURRENCY Attribute value is Dollars
Attribute name is DISCOUNT Attribute value is 5
String read is 300
End ELEMENT = PRICE
Start ELEMENT = PUBLISHER
String read is Pearson
End ELEMENT = PUBLISHER
End ELEMENT = BOOK
Start ELEMENT = BOOK
Start ELEMENT = TITLE
String read is Java and Nirvana
End ELEMENT = TITLE
Start ELEMENT = AUTHORS
String read is Rowlands
End ELEMENT = AUTHORS
Start ELEMENT = PRICE
Attributes  are
Attribute name is AMOUNTCURRENCY Attribute value is Pounds
Attribute name is DISCOUNT Attribute value is 0
```

```
String read is 400
End ELEMENT = PRICE
Start ELEMENT = PUBLISHER
String read is Wiley
End ELEMENT = PUBLISHER
End ELEMENT = BOOK
End ELEMENT = BOOKLIST
Document  finished
```

Obviously some of the source needs to be stored in memory when using SAX; however, the essential difference between SAX and DOM is that with the latter the whole source is stored

5.2 DOM

The DOM model involves the storage of the XML source that is to be processed as a tree within memory. In this it differs from the SAX approach where the source is not stored but is processed sequentially.

A Java program based on DOM which processes the same source and DTD as detailed in the previous section is displayed below:

```java
import  org.w3c.dom.*;
import  com.ibm.xml.parser.Parser;
import  java.io.*;

public class DOMParser {

public static void displayXML(Node nd){
    short nodeVal  = nd.getNodeType();

    if(nd.DOCUMENT_NODE==nodeVal){
        //This is a document node apply displayXML again
        displayXML(((Document)  nd).getDocumentElement());
    }

    if(nd.ELEMENT_NODE==nodeVal)
    {
        //This is an element node get the
        //name of the node
        String nodeName  = nd.getNodeName();
        System.out.println("Name of Node = "+ nodeName);
        //Get the attributes
        NamedNodeMap nm  = nd.getAttributes();
        if  (nm!=null){
            //There are some attributes, display them
            for(int  k=0;  k<nm.getLength();k++)
            {
                //Iterate over the attributes,
                //getLength will have found them
                Node currAttribute = nm.item(k);
                //Get the name of an attribute
```

DOM

```
                              String attributeName =
                                    currAttribute.getNodeName();
                              //Get the value of the attribute
                              String attributeValue =
                                    currAttribute.getNodeValue();
                              System.out.println(
                                 " Attribute name = "+ attributeName +
                                 " Attribute value = "+ attributeValue);
                          }
                      }
```

The code contains
objects defined by
classes such as
Parser, Document
and Node which are
found in the packages
which are imported at
the beginning of the
code

```
                  //Get all the child nodes
                  NodeList nl = nd.getChildNodes();
                  //If there are any child nodes iterate over them
                  //executing  displayXML  again
                  if(nl!=null){
                      for(int j = 0; j<nl.getLength();j++)
                          displayXML(nl.item(j));
                  }
              }

          if(nd.TEXT_NODE==nodeVal){
          //Text   encountered
          if  (!nd.getNodeValue().equals("\n"))
              System.out.println(nd.getNodeValue());
          }
      }

      public static void main(String[] args){
          try{
              //Set up and start the parser
              String file = "catalogue.txt";
              InputStream inStream = new FileInputStream(file);
              Parser dp = new Parser(file);
              Document  doc = dp.readStream(inStream);
              //Execute displayXML to display the
              //source of the XML
              displayXML(doc);
              System.out.println("There were " +
                                 dp.getNumberOfErrors()+
                                 " Errors");

          }
          catch(Exception  e)
              {System.out.print(
                 "Problem with XML  processor"+e);}
      }

  }
```

DOM works by traversing the nodes of a document tree such as that shown in Figure 8.4. A node may be of a number of different types and the structure of the code that processes XML source will contain large collections of `if` statements which discover what type of node is being encountered when the tree is being traversed. This reflected in the code above.

The method `displayXML` carries out the processing of the tree with the first `if` statement retrieving the node that is being processed.

```
short nodeVal = nd.getNodeType();
```

The `getNodeType` method returns a short constant which designates what sort of node is being processed. The remaining code examines this node and carries out the processing depending on what type of node is being examined. First the node is checked to see if it is a document node:

```
if(nd.DOCUMENT_NODE==nodeVal){
    //This is a document node apply displayXML again
    displayXML(((Document)  nd).getDocumentElement());
}
```

This corresponds to source such as

```
<!DOCTYPE BOOKLIST SYSTEM "books.txt" >
```

which is the header in the source file which defines that a BOOKLIST element is to be processed and that the file of books defined by a BOOKSLIST element is found in the file *books.txt*.

What the code does is to recursively call `displayXML` with the argument being the node at the top of the tree. The constant `nd.DOCUMENT_NODE` contains the value that defines the fact that a document node is being processed.

The next `if` statement checks whether an element is encountered. For example the element `<BOOK>`.

```
if(nd.ELEMENT_NODE==nodeVal)
```

The first processing of the node

```
//This is an element node get the
//name of the node
String nodeName = nd.getNodeName();
System.out.println("Name of Node = "+ nodeName);
//Get the attributes
NamedNodeMap nm = nd.getAttributes();
```

finds the name of the node, for example BOOK or PUBLISHER and displays it. It then collects the attributes associated with the node into the NamedNodeMap object nm. The next chunk of code

```
if   (nm!=null){
    //There are some attributes, display them
    for(int   k=0;   k<nm.getLength();k++){
        //Iterate over the attributes,
        //getLength will have found them
        Node currAttribute = nm.item(k);
        //Get the name of an attribute
        String attributeName =
            currAttribute.getNodeName();
        //Get the value of the attribute
        String attributeValue =
            currAttribute.getNodeValue();
        System.out.println(
            " Attribute name = "+ attributeName +
            " Attribute value = "+ attributeValue);
    }
}
```

first checks whether there are any attributes, for example AMOUNTCURRENCY. It then iterates over all the attributes found in nm. Each attribute is placed in a Node variable and its name and its value extracted by means of getNodeName and getNodeValue, for example AMOUNTCURRENCY and Pounds. These are then displayed.

The next item of code then gets all the nodes which lie underneath the node currently being processed and applies displayXML to display the contents of these nodes. This uses recursion.

```
//Get all the child nodes
NodeList nl = nd.getChildNodes();
//If there are any child nodes iterate over them
//executing displayXML again
if(nl!=null)
{
    for(int j = 0; j<nl.getLength();j++)
        displayXML(nl.item(j));
}
```

This uses the method item to extract out each individual node that lies below the current node and then applies displayXML.

The final type of node that is processed checks if text has been encountered as for example the text Roberts in

```
<AUTHORS>Roberts</AUTHORS>
```

The code is

```
if(nd.TEXT_NODE==nodeVal){
   //Text   encountered
   if  (!nd.getNodeValue().equals("\n"))
      System.out.println(nd.getNodeValue());
}
```

The text returned could be a new line, so rather than display it this is ignored.

The final chunk of code sets up the parsing process:

```
public static void main(String[] args){
   try{
      //Set up and start the parser
      String file = "catalogue.txt";
      InputStream inStream = new FileInputStream(file);
      Parser dp = new Parser(file);
      Document doc = dp.readStream(inStream);
      //Execute displayXML to display the
      //source of the XML
      displayXML(doc);
      System.out.println("There were " +
                           dp.getNumberOfErrors()+
                           " Errors");
   }
   catch(Exception  e)
      {System.out.print(
         "Problem with XML processor"+e);}
   }

}
```

Here a parser is set up and the document object `doc` passed to the `displayXML` method.

Execution of the code will result in the following display:

```
Name of Node = BOOKLIST
Name of Node = BOOK
Name of Node = TITLE
The Endless Path
Name of Node = AUTHORS
Jones
Name of Node = PRICE
Attribute name = AMOUNTCURRENCY Attribute value = Pounds
Attribute name = DISCOUNT Attribute value = 0
```

```
200
Name of Node = PUBLISHER
Pearson
Name of Node = BOOK
Name of Node = TITLE
My Story
Name of Node = AUTHORS
Roberts
Name of Node = PRICE
Attribute name = AMOUNTCURRENCY Attribute value = SW Francs
Attribute name = DISCOUNT Attribute value = 0
500
Name of Node = PUBLISHER
McMillan
Name of Node = BOOK
Name of Node = TITLE
XML for Beginners
Name of Node = AUTHORS
Ince
Name of Node = PRICE
Attribute name = AMOUNTCURRENCY Attribute value = Dollars
Attribute name = DISCOUNT Attribute value = 5
300
Name of Node = PUBLISHER
Pearson
Name of Node = BOOK
Name of Node = TITLE
Java and Nirvana
Name of Node = AUTHORS
Rowlands
Name of Node = PRICE
Attribute name = AMOUNTCURRENCY Attribute value = Pounds
Attribute name = DISCOUNT Attribute value = 0
400
Name of Node = PUBLISHER
Wiley

There were 0 Errors
```

This, then, is DOM. If you are writing Java programs which access XML files you will be faced with the choice of what style of API to use: either the event-based SAX approach or the tree processing approach of DOM. There are a number of points to bear in mind when selecting which to use:

- SAX is a conceptually simple way to program an XML application. It is based on events occurring when some element in an XML-defined source is encountered.

- DOM is conceptually more difficult to program. It requires the programmer to develop code which traverses a tree made up of nodes and requires the use of recursion. Many programmers find recursion a difficult concept to understand and apply.

- When an XML document is defined by a complex DTD, for example with many elements nesting within other elements, then programs using SAX can be very complex and somewhat unreadable. For example, SAX programs often require information about what element is being processed when sub-elements are being processed and this is often implemented by variables known as flags which provide this information. For many levels of element nesting there will often be a number of flags which have to be defined, set and unset.

- DOM programs which access large DTDs are more readable and maintainable than SAX programs. This, of course, assumes that the programmer and the maintainer are happy with the concept of recursion.

- The memory demands of SAX are minimal.

- The memory demands of DOM can be very high when the XML source is textually large. This is because the whole of the tree representing the text has to be stored in memory. This can result in serious performance problems, for example starting up a DOM-based program will result in an initial processing hiatus while the DOM tree is constructed.

In this and the previous section I described two Java-based approaches to processing XML source. There is another popular way of processing source based on a concept known as XSL.

5.3 XSL

5.3.1 Introduction

XSL

XSL (eXtensible Style Language) is an XML-based language used for defining the type of processing that was discussed in the previous two sections. The language is often referred to as XSLT and was developed by the World Wide Web Consortium. Before looking in detail at how XSLT works it is first necessary to introduce the concept of a namespace.

A namespace is a way of prewriting some XML definitions which can be loaded into an existing definition. Let us assume that we want to define a user in XML and reuse this definition over a number of sources. As an example of this assume that we have the DTD for a user of a computer system stored at the location www.open.ac.uk/users/Ince/Departments. Let us assume that there are four elements EMPLOYEELIST, USER, NAME and EMAILADDRESS defined by the tag pairs <EMPLOYEELIST> </EMPLOYEELIST>, <USER> </USER>, <NAME> </NAME>, and

<EMAILADDRESS> </EMAILADDRESS>. These tags can then be used within an XML source. An example of such a use is shown below

```
<DEPARTMENT:EMPLOYEELIST   XMLNS:DEPARTMENT=
     "http://www.open.ac.uk/users/Ince/Departments"
<DEPARTMENT:USER>
   <DEPARTMENT:NAME>
   Darrel  Ince
   </DEPARTMENT:NAME>
   <DEPARTMENT:EMAILADDRESS>
   D.C.Ince@computing.ou.ac.uk
   </DEPARTMENT:EMAILADDRESS>
</DEPARTMENT: USER>

<DEPARTMENT:USER>
   <DEPARTMENT:NAME>
   Walter  Evans
   </DEPARTMENT:NAME>
   <DEPARTMENT:EMAILADDRESS>
   W.Evans@computing.ou.ac.uk
   </DEPARTMENT:EMAILADDRESS>
</DEPARTMENT: USER>

<DEPARTMENT:USER>
   <DEPARTMENT:NAME>
   Robert  Wilson
   </DEPARTMENT:NAME>
   <DEPARTMENT:EMAILADDRESS>
   R.S.Wilson@computing.ou.ac.uk
   </DEPARTMENT:EMAILADDRESS>
</DEPARTMENT: USER>
</DEPARTMENT: EMPLOYEELIST>
```

The attribute XMLNS marks this XML code above as a local namespace. This means that all the tags and attributes in the text have to be preceded by the name of the namespace (DEPARTMENT). The XMLNS attribute also specifies where the code can be found. The code above defines a **local namespace**.

Now, you might think that this is an unnecessary complication. If all that was done was to use tags and attributes from this namespace. However, by constructing our DTD in such a way we can use tags and attributes from other namespaces. For example, assume that we have a namespace that defines an element JOBTITLE and it is held at

```
www.open.ac.uk/users/Ince/UserDetails
```

The line opposite specifies a folder path in the computer www.open.ac.uk

The XML source below shows how this source can be inserted into the existing source.

```
<DEPARTMENT:EMPLOYEELIST  XMLNS:DEPARTMENT=
      "http://www.open.ac.uk/users/Ince/Departments"
   XMLNS:USERDETAILS=
      "http://www.open.ac.uk/users/Ince/UserDetails">
<DEPARTMENT:USER>
   <DEPARTMENT:NAME>
   Darrel Ince
   </DEPARTMENT:NAME>
   <USERDETAILS:JOBTITLE>
   Programmer
   </USERDETAILS:JOBTITLE>
   <DEPARTMENT:EMAILADDRESS>
   D.C.Ince@computing.ou.ac.uk
   </DEPARTMENT:EMAILADDRESS>
</DEPARTMENT: USER>

<DEPARTMENT: USER>
   <DEPARTMENT:NAME>
   Walter Evans
   </DEPARTMENT:NAME>
   <USERDETAILS:JOBTITLE>
   Project manager
   </USERDETAILS:JOBTITLE>
   <DEPARTMENT:EMAILADDRESS>
   W.Evans@computing.ou.ac.uk
   </DEPARTMENT:EMAILADDRESS>
</DEPARTMENT: USER>

<DEPARTMENT: USER>
   <DEPARTMENT:NAME>
   Robert Wilson
   </DEPARTMENT:NAME>
   <USERDETAILS:JOBTITLE>
   Project assistant
   </USERDETAILS:JOBTITLE>
   <DEPARTMENT:EMAILADDRESS>
   R.S.Wilson@computing.ou.ac.uk
   </DEPARTMENT:EMAILADDRESS>
</DEPARTMENT: USER>
</DEPARTMENT: EMPLOYEELIST>
```

The lines

```
XMLNS:USERDETAILS=
   "http://www.open.ac.uk/users/Ince/UserDetails">
```

introduce a remote namespace whose elements can be used within the XML; however, the elements all have to be prefaced with the name of the namespace, as in

```
<USERDETAILS:JOBTITLE>
Project  assistant
</USERDETAILS:JOBTITLE>
```

The origin of namespaces

Namespaces were originally developed by the World Wide Web Consortium because of the huge popularity of XML. Many users started defining their own XML DTDs and wanted to use DTDs externally. Unfortunately, some of the DTDs had element names which clashed with existing names. Namespaces were the solution. They are as much a mechanism for resolving name clashes as a mechanism for using external DTDs.

If the XMLNS attribute is just used by itself then there is no need to preface elements in the document which is to include other XML elements. For example, the XML source above could be written as

Notice that in the first reference XMLNS is not followed by a colon and a name

```
<DEPARTMENT:EMPLOYEELIST  XMLNS=
       "http://www.open.ac.uk/users/Ince/Departments"
    XMLNS:USERDETAILS=
       "http://www.open.ac.uk/users/Ince/Departments">
<USER>
   <NAME>
   Darrel  Ince
   </NAME>
   <USERDETAILS:JOBTITLE>
   Programmer
   </USERDETAILS:JOBTITLE>
   <EMAILADDRESS>
   D.C.Ince@computing.ou.ac.uk
   </EMAILADDRESS>
</USER>

<USER>
   <NAME>
   Walter  Evans
   </NAME>
   <USERDETAILS:JOBTITLE>
   Project  manager
   </USERDETAILS:JOBTITLE>
   <EMAILADDRESS>
   W.Evans@computing.ou.ac.uk
   </EMAILADDRESS>
</USER>
```

```
<USER>
  <NAME>
  Robert  Wilson
  </NAME>
  <USERDETAILS:JOBTITLE>
  Project  assistant
  </USERDETAILS:JOBTITLE>
  <EMAILADDRESS>
  R.S.Wilson@computing.ou.ac.uk
  </EMAILADDRESS>
</USER>
</EMPLOYEELIST>
```

5.3.2 Processing XML source using XSL

XSL is a type of primitive programming language which is expressed in terms of XML tags. It is best described using a small example. The example is that of a simple database of book details that a researcher might keep in a computer file.

An example of the source of such a file is shown below:

```
<?xml version = "1.0"?>
<?xml-stylesheet type = "text/xml"
                 href = "example.xsl" ?>
<BOOKLIST>
<BOOK>
   <TITLE>
   An introduction to the saxophone
   </TITLE>
   <AUTHORS>
   E.J Wilson and R.Vitre
   </AUTHORS>
   <COMMENT>
   Good introductory stuff but ignores recent history
   post 1955
   </COMMENT>
</BOOK>

<BOOK>
   <TITLE>
   The Selmer Factory
   </TITLE>
   <AUTHORS>
   R.Logier
   </AUTHORS>
   <COMMENT>
```

```
        The definitive work on the Selmer factory,
        a bit light on early saxophone production
        </COMMENT>
    </BOOK>

    <BOOK>
    <TITLE>
    New Orleans, Jazz and the rise of the Saxophone
    </TITLE>
    <AUTHORS>
    D Brindeck
    </AUTHORS>
    <COMMENT>
    A popular treatment
    </COMMENT>
    </BOOK>

    </BOOKLIST>
```

A style sheet which produces an HTML document for this source is shown below:

```
<?xml version = "1.0" ?>
<xsl:stylesheet version = "1.0" xmlns:xsl = "..">
<xsl:template match = "BOOKLIST">
    <HTML>
    <HEAD>
    <TITLE>
        Generated HTML for the book
    </TITLE>
    </HEAD>
    <BODY>
    <xsl:apply-templates/>
    </BODY>
    </HTML>
</xsl:template>

<xsl:template match = "BOOK">
    <P>
    <xsl: value-of select = "TITLE"/>
    </P>
</xsl:template>

<xsl:stylesheet>
```

Note that I am using lower case here for tags such as xsl:apply-templates. Upper and lower case are interchangeable in XML, also the location of the xsl file is not specified but replaced by two dots

The first two lines

```
<?xml version = "1.0" ?>
<xsl:stylesheet version = "1.0" xmlns:xsl = "..">
```

specify the version of XML that is used and the location of the style sheet standard that is used. In the inverted commas would be the URL of its location on the WWW Consortium Web site, another Web site or if a copy existed the location of the file on a local computer. Notice that the second line specifies a namespace with the name xsl; this means that all tags and attributes associated with that namespace will need to be prefaced with xsl.

The next lines

```
<xsl:template match = "BOOKLIST">
    <HTML>
    <HEAD>
    <TITLE>
        Generated HTML for the book
    </TITLE>
    </HEAD>
    <BODY>
    <xsl:apply-templates/>
    </BODY>
    </HTML>
</xsl:template>
```

This is very much like a recursive call in a conventional programming language

specify what happens when the tag BOOKLIST is encountered. The processing associated with this is that the header elements of an HTML document are emitted, the template processor applied to the remaining parts of the XML source and then the final elements of an HTML document emitted. Note that the line

```
<xsl:apply-templates/>
```

is a shorthand way of writing

```
<xsl:apply-templates>
</xsl:apply-templates>
```

which is an element which has no text associated with it. The next part of the XSL source is

```
<xsl:template match = "BOOK">
    <P>
    <xsl: value-of select = "TITLE"/>
    </P>
</xsl:template>
```

value-of-select gets this text

This defines the transformation that will occur when a BOOK element is encountered. What will happen is that a paragraph tag is emitted followed by the text associated with TITLE and terminated with the paragraph end tag.

The result of all this processing will be the production of the HTML document

```
<HTML>
<HEAD>
<TITLE>
    Generated HTML for the book
</TITLE>
</HEAD>
<BODY>
<P>
An introduction to the saxophone
</P>
<P>
The Selmer Factory
</P>
<P>
New Orleans, Jazz and the rise of the Saxophone
</P>
</BODY>
</HTML>
```

The code below shows the transformations needed to cope with the remaining elements of the XML. Each of the TITLE, ELEMENT, COMMENT elements are transformed into their value and separated by a break (
) element.

```
<?xml version = "1.0" ?>
<xsl:stylesheet version = "1.0" xmlns:xsl = "..">

<xsl:template match = "BOOKLIST">
   <HTML>
   <HEAD>
   <TITLE>
       Generated HTML for the book
   </TITLE>
   </HEAD>
   <BODY>
   <xsl:apply-templates/>
   </BODY>
   </HTML>
</xsl:template>

<xsl:template match = "BOOK">
   <P>
   <xsl: value-of select = "TITLE"/>
   </P>
</xsl:template>
```

The matching code
for TITLE written
previous to this code
and using value-of
could have been
implemented in the
same way by, for
example, matching on
BOOK/TITLE

```
<xsl:template match = "BOOK/AUTHORS">
    <xsl: value-of select = "."/>
    <BR>
</xsl:template>

<xsl:template match = "BOOK/COMMENT">
    <xsl: value-of select = "."/>
    <BR>
</xsl:template>

<xsl:stylesheet>
```

Here three matches are specified. They are all virtually the same so it is just worth concentrating on one:

```
<xsl:template match = "BOOK/COMMENT">
    <xsl: value-of select = "."/>
    <BR>
</xsl:template>
```

Here the match is on a COMMENT element within the element BOOK. When this match occurs the current value of the element matched (designated by the full stop) is emitted followed by a
 HTML tag.

The style sheet, when processed, will result in the HTML below being produced:

```
<HTML>
    <HEAD>
    <TITLE>
        Generated HTML for the book
    </TITLE>
    </HEAD>
    <BODY>
    <P>
    An introduction to the saxophone
    <BR>
    E.J Wilson and R.Vitre
    <BR>
    Good introductory stuff but ignores recent history
    post 1955
    <BR>
    </P>

    . . .
    </BODY>
    </HTML>
```

This section has been a brief introduction to XSL. However, it has described the main concepts which underpin the technology. XSL is a very large technology with facilities which are analogous to those found in standard procedural programming languages such as if statements and iterative statements.

XSL can be applied in a number of ways:

- *At the server.* A program in a server can transform a document, into a form which can then be sent to a client. For example, a program can convert text to some HTML and send it to a Web browser.

- *At the browser.* Internet Explorer can read a style sheet and transform text sent to it using the style sheet to direct the transformations.

- *Using a stand alone program.* You can write stand-alone programs in Java which take some XML source and a style sheet and carry out the transformation.

5.4 Formatting objects

Formatting objects

So far in this section I have concentrated on showing simple transformations from XML source to HTML. While this is an important transformation there will be more complex ones which will often be required, for example transformations into some printed form.

In order to support such transformation the WWW Consortium have defined formatting objects which support different print properties such as font-size and font-family.

An example of a formatting object being used to define some print functionality is shown below

fo is the name of the namespace

```
<fo:block font-family = "sans-serif"
          font-weight = "bold"
          font-size = "36pt"
          line-height = "48pt" >
 . .
</fo:block>
```

Here the code emitted within the block is defined as being bold, of 36 points in height, from the sans-serif collection of fonts and 48 points in line height.

PDF

To use formatting objects you insert formatting instructions such as the one above within the XSL transformations and then apply a processor known as FOP supplied by the World Wide Web Consortium which is able to carry out the conversion into PDF (Portable Document Format) which is the textual format recognised by the hugely popular Adobe Acrobat reader.

Formatting objects contain all the facilities that you would expect in a sophisticated print package, including:

- the formatting of pages including setting page size and margins;
- the formatting of text including the size, font and separation of text;
- the specification and formatting of tables;

- the inclusion of extra textual material such as graphics;

- the specification of text such as side matter and footnotes;

- the formatting of bulleted lists.

They are normally used in conjunction with XSL where the XSL processor references the formatting instructions when processing some XML-defined source.

5.5 Web publishing systems

A Web publishing system, often called a Web publishing framework, is software that is usually implemented as a set of APIs which enable a large corpus of XML documents to be maintained.

For example, a Web publishing system should enable the staff who are in charge of a large collection of documents to change the source of an XML-based document and then republish this document in a variety of ways, for example by downloading, by printing it in some format or by including it as a page in a Web site. The process whereby this occurs should be as automated as possible. For example, assume that the user of a Web publishing system is a software development company that keeps all base documents in a strict format, for example requirements specifications would be kept in such a way that each requirement would need to be included in a bulleted point. When a change is required to such a document the following actions should occur:

- The member of staff responsible for the maintenance – let me call them the document administrator – of a project's document database receives a request for a change, perhaps the customer has decided on a new software requirement.

- The administrator calls up the collection of XML-based documents that make up the project's collection of documents.

- The administrator is faced with a display of the file names of all the documents, including files holding requirements specifications, designs, test plans and even program code.

- The administrator selects the file to be changed and an editor is called into action. The administrator uses the editor to change the source and clicks a button labelled 'publish'.

- The publishing system then looks at how many versions of the document are in existence. Let us say that there are two: an HTML version which is published on the project's Web site and a pdf version which can be downloaded from the site.

- The publishing system then generates the two versions of the changed file and updates some version number. This generation could be carried out by XSL or via special-purpose programs which call on some API such as SAX.

- The publishing system then automatically notifies any staff whom the publishing system has been told need to be notified of the change. These would be notified via e-mail with the names of the staff and their e-mail addresses having been preloaded into the system when the project database was first set up.

Cocoon

There are a small number of Web publishing systems in existence. Probably the most well-known is Cocoon which is part of the Apache project. Cocoon is an Open Source project which is based on Java servlets. All the user does to employ it is to enter a URL to reference a document or generate either an HTML file or a pdf file.

6 XML in action

The previous sections have detailed the basics of XML and how it can be used to define markup languages. The aim of this section is to look at two particular applications based on XML.

6.1 Scalable vector graphics

Graphic formats

The vast majority of graphical images found on the World Wide Web are bit mapped graphics. This means that every pixel in the graphics is held in a file, where each pixel has information such as its colour and saturation stored. Two of the most popular formats used for images on the Internet, GIF and JPEG, are both bit mapped formats which describe fixed resolution graphics.

SVG

Bit mapped graphics suffer from two disadvantages: first, when you zoom into such a graphic or resize it quite a lot of detail can be lost; second, bit mapped graphics can occupy a large amount of storage. The competitor to bit-mapped graphics is vector graphics. Here, instead of every pixel detail being stored, what is stored are a series of drawing instructions; for example, instructions such as draw a line from one point to another point, draw a circle with its centre at a point and display some text of a specific height and font at a point.

There have been a small number of global standards, for example the standard for VRML, the virtual reality modelling language

A major problem with vector graphics on the Web has been the fact that there have been few global standards, only proprietary standards such as *Flash* and *QuickTime*. This prompted the World Wide Web Consortium to develop a standard known as the Scalable Vector Graphics Standard (SVG). This is a standard based on XML which has a number of advantages. It encompasses some very sophisticated requirements: high-quality printing, fast zooming and panning without reloading, ease of animation, and the ability to easily carry out filtering. Since the language is text based it holds out the prospect that a search engine can index graphics in the same way that it would index the text in a Web page. For example, a graphic containing an organisation chart for a company might have each of the functional areas in the company registered by a search engine.

Another advantage of using such a markup language is the fact that graphics can be created on-the-fly by programs. For example, animation on the Web is often carried out by drawing the same image a number of times with slight differences between the images and then displaying each image momentarily. This can consume a large amount of storage. An alternative would be to let a program (on the client side) process animation instructions in the graphic file to display the animations.

An example of a fragment from this language is shown below:

It is worth noticing that the `<CIRCLE>` tag has been defined as not being associated with any text; this means that a short version of the `<TAG>..</TAG>` construct is used where all that is required is a closing `/>` within the start tag

```
<SVG width = "3in" height = "2in">
<DESC>
This is a sample circle drawn for the book Distributed
Applications  and  E-Commerce
</DESC>
<G>
<CIRCLE style = "fill: red; stroke: black" cx = 100
cy = 100 r = 100/>
</G>
</SVG>
```

Exercise 8.6

Developing a simple XML-based graphics language

The `<SVG>` tag identifies the text as representing an SVG graphic. The `<DESC>` tags enclose descriptive text which summarises the graphic. The `<G>` tag introduces the graphic and the `<CIRCLE>` tag describes a drawn circle with a centre at point (100, 100) and a radius of 100. The circle is outlined in black and is filled with red.

SVG is currently under development. The next example of an XML-based technology is widely used.

6.2 The Channel Definition Format

The Channel Definition Format

The vast majority of technologies developed for the Internet are what are known as **pull technologies** where information is only transferred after an explicit request for it. The World Wide Web is a good example of this: users who employ browsers explicitly ask for a Web page when they click a hyperlink.

This is in contrast to **push technology** where material is broadcast at will to a subscriber. One of the most popular push technologies is known as **active channels**. It was developed by the Microsoft Corporation. It enables the user of a Windows operating system to subscribe to a particular channel. When a channel is subscribed to, a small Web page appears on a windows desktop which is updated on a regular basis by the company that owns the channel. Most channel companies are news or information providers such as CNN or the BBC.

The Channel Definition Format is an XML-based language which provides details about a channel, for example the Web pages associated with the channel and the frequency of update. A fragment of the language is displayed below; it describes channels and sub-channels.

```
<CHANNEL>
<TITLE>
News Headlines
</TITLE>
<SCHEDULE>
<INTERVALTIME HOUR = "1"/>
</SCHEDULE>
<CHANNEL>
    <TITLE> News </TITLE>
        <ITEM HREF = http://www.newsservice.com/british>
            <TITLE> British News </TITLE>
        </ITEM>
        <ITEM HREF = http://www.newsservice.com/american>
            <TITLE> American News </TITLE>
        </ITEM>
 . .
</CHANNEL>
 . .
</CHANNEL>
```

Here a news channel is defined with a number of different sub-channels dealing with different geographical news areas. Each sub-channel is associated with a URL from which news is downloaded. The tag <INTERVALTIME> specifies when each sub-channel is to be updated; the example specifies that this should occur each hour when new news is downloaded to a channel.

XHTML

XHTML

XHTML (the eXtensible Hypertext Markup Language) is an XML-related technology which is the current proposed successor to HTML. It includes HTML 4 as a subset and has been designed to represent complex data on the Internet. XHTML allows authors to create their own documents and enables browsers to make rigorous checks on the XHTML code developed by a Web designer. Thus it overcomes a major problem: current browsers react differently to poorly formed HTML and display it in different ways.

6.3 ebXML

ebXML

ebXML is an XML-based language used for implementing electronic business applications. When two companies interact via the Internet to carry out some business they need to carry out a number of processes. These are broadly:

- Discovering the products and services that are being offered or required by each party.

- Discovering what common information is required to carry out the business transactions.

- Establishing how communication is to be carried out: for example, who is to carry out the communication and the format of the messages that need to be sent.

- Agreeing on the contractual documents and contractual processes that are required.

ebXML provides mechanisms whereby a communication infrastructure can be set up between the parties to an electronic business transaction. This enables some form of transport mechanism to be agreed on, the provision of software which handles incoming and outgoing messages and the provision of software which interfaces to existing applications.

Chapter 3 described business objects in a little detail

The ebXML standard also provides facilities for a company to define business processes, for example receiving requests for services such as the purchase of some bulk commodity, responding to these requests and facilities for defining reusable business objects.

A major component of the ebXML standard is that it defines how an electronic marketplace can be set up. Such a marketplace will rely on centrally stored data which enables companies to register and discover information about each other, for example what services they offer. Such a marketplace relies heavily on some directory service.

A short extract of a business transaction expressed in XML is detailed below. It is taken from an overview of Web services maintained by Sun; it can be found in the collection of resource links associated with this topic.

Non-repudiation is the process whereby someone who sends a message can be confident that it has been received

```
<BusinessTransaction name = "Create Order">
<RequestingBusinessActivity   name  =""
    isNonRepudiationRequired   =  "true"
    timeToAcknowledgeReceipt   =  "P2D"
    timetoAcknowledgeAcceptance   =   "P3D"
>
<DocumentEnvelope
    BusinessDocument  =  "Purchase Order"/>
</RequestingBusinessActivity>
  . .
```

Here a purchase order is created which requires the user to acknowledge that it has been received (isNonRepudiationRequired = "true") and in which the limit on acknowledging receipt is 2 days (P2D), with the time to acknowledge acceptance of the order being 3 days (P3D).

The code above would be followed by more text which defined how the business responding to the transaction should act.

This, then is a very brief introduction to ebXML. The Web links associated with this section provide a much bigger introduction to this large and evolving standard.

7   XML in a retail environment

The examples in the previous section describe some applications which were important but a little peripheral to mainstream e-commerce. The aim of this brief section is to describe how XML is used by conventional retailers such as booksellers. At the heart of any retailing system will be a catalogue of items for sale. This catalogue will contain information which varies from retailer to retailer, for example a bookseller will have a catalogue which contains details such as a book title, authors, ISBN number and prices. There will be a number of forms this catalogue will need to be stored in. For example, it may be displayed on a Web site and need to be expressed in HTML, it might need to be printed as a conventional paper-based catalogue, it might need to be stored in a form which allowed mobile users to access it or it might need to be stored in a relational database. Equally importantly it may need to be stored in an indeterminate form in some forthcoming technology, for example the next five to ten years may see the advent of e-books: electronic devices with many of the characteristics of books including readability; almost invariably some markup technology will be required to be invented for this medium.

XML offers a way of centrally storing product details in such a way that a processor can be easily written to convert the XML into one of the forms detailed above: HTML, relational tables, some internal form for a word processor, a comma delimited form for a spreadsheet, a wireless markup language or any other markup language.

XML and relational databases

The main way that the vast majority of companies store their data is in a relational database. It is therefore not surprising that one of the fastest growing areas in terms of software support is for software that interfaces between XML-based documents and relational database systems. This software includes that for converting from an XML-based language to relational tables and back, software that mimics an object-oriented database with the XML-based data used as the source, software for converting from a DOM tree to a relational database, software for returning the results of a relational query in XML form, database systems which recognise XML entities as data types and XML servers.

8   Further reading

Internet book links

Much of what is happening to XML occurs on a day-to-day basis. Because of this books can become out of date very quickly. The books detailed below concentrate, in the main, on fundamentals. There are two books which approach XML in a non-dated way. The first has been written by St Laurent and Cerami [1]. It is a good general introduction to XML which is centred around Java. A very detailed treatment

If you are doing the
case study as you
progress through the
book, read Section 7.3
of Chapter 17

of XML has been published by Wrox and written by a large number of XML developers [2]; it should last for a couple of years. A book which deals with applying XML has been written by Leventhal [3].

References

[1] S. St Laurent and E. Cerami, *Building XML Applications*. New York: McGraw-Hill, 1999.

[2] R. Anderson, D. Baliles, *et al.*, *Professional XML*. Birmingham: Wrox, 2000.

[3] M. Leventhal, *Designing XML Internet Applications*. Old Tappan, NJ: Prentice Hall, 1998.

RMI and Distributed Objects

9

Chapter contents

This chapter is an introduction to distributed objects. It uses the Java RMI technology to detail the main facilities found in a distributed object package. RMI is a lightweight, efficient distributed object technology which is mainly suitable for distributed systems that contain only Java code. The first part of the chapter details how to develop a simple distributed object application and details the steps that need to be taken. The focus in the middle part of the chapter is on the RMI registry which provides a naming service for distributed objects. The chapter concludes with a description of one particular application of distributed objects: that of connecting to legacy software in an e-commerce application.

Aims

1. To describe some of the facilities found in a distributed object technology.
2. To describe one particular distributed object technology: RMI.
3. To show how distributed objects can be implemented using RMI.

Concepts

Bot, Distributed garbage collection, Distributed object, Distributed object middleware, Legacy software, Marshalling, Pattern, Proxy object, Remote procedure call, RMI compiler, RMI registry, Robot, Spoofing, Unmarshalling.

1 Introduction

As part of Chapter 2 you might have carried out some exercises which involved you writing a special-purpose, application-specific protocol which enabled a client and a server to communicate with each other. For example, when writing a name server you developed a protocol which had as part of its vocabulary commands such as F which found the address of a particular resource, for example

```
F*OldSite*
```

If you are still hazy about protocols then reread the message passing section in Chapter 4

sent a message to a server to find the IP address of the computer known as OldSite.

While such protocols give rise to fast and efficient applications there are a number of disadvantages:

Distributed objects

- When the functionality of an application changes, for example a new function is required, the amount of effort to develop new code which responds to a particular message in the protocol can be very heavy; moreover, this code has to be changed at both the client and server.

- The use of application-specific protocols encourages a monolithic form of coding which is difficult to maintain.

- It is difficult to fit such protocols into an object-oriented paradigm. Sending messages to a server using an application-specific protocol is, at its heart, just the sending of a string from a client over some communication line, with the server decoding the string, carrying out the functionality associated with the string and often sending a string back which requires decoding and acting upon by the client.

Internet developers speak in terms of a 'Web year' when they discuss technological advances and project duration; it is equivalent to seven calendar years

- The form of coding, because it is monolithic, does not encourage reuse. One of the problems that I discussed in Chapter 1 was the fact that the Internet economy moves so fast that forms of software development involving rapid application development and the reuse of components have almost become a necessity. Unfortunately, application-specific protocols and the program codes associated with them militate against such rapid development.

- Using an application-specific protocol means that the client code can be quite large: the code has to deal with the sending and processing of strings which represent individual commands in a protocol. This encourages the development of thick clients that contain a large amount of code and which require a major maintenance effort.

2 Distributed objects

The basic idea behind distributed object technology is that objects should be able to reside on any computer within a distributed system, and that programs can be written which enable code on other computers to send messages to them, just as if they were residing on the computer which hosts the message sending code. The ideal is that if you look at a fragment of code such as

```
oldUpdateProxy.adjust(oldVal, newVal);
```

As you will see later
in this chapter and in
Chapter 10 there will
always be a little code
which reveals an object
to be distributed;
however, it should be a
very small proportion of
the code

then, it should not be possible to discover from a reading of the code whether the object `oldUpdateProxy` resides on the same computer on which the code is executed or on another, remote computer.

In this and the next chapter we will look in detail at two distributed object technologies.

> ## Remote procedure call
>
> Distributed objects are not a new idea. The idea that you can execute program code on a computer from another computer has been around for a couple of decades. The original technology was known as remote procedure call; it has proved to be a valuable source of technological ideas which the implementers of distributed object technologies have freely drawn upon.

The RMI specification

The first is RMI which is a pure Java technology that is restricted to the development of distributed objects expressed only in Java; the second is CORBA which is a mixed language approach which can be used to develop systems containing distributed objects, where the objects can be implemented in a wide variety of programming languages.

3   Object-oriented middleware

In order for a distributed object scheme to function there is a requirement for software which implements the interface between a client sending messages and a server on which a distributed object is resident. There is a need to:

I use the term
'message' in its
object-oriented
context throughout
this section: that is,
as the invocation
of a method

- recognise when a distributed object is to be sent messages;
- locate the server on which a distributed object is held;
- resolve any differences in data format between the client and the server;
- package up the data that forms part of a message into a form that can be sent to the server containing the remote object; for example, the name of the method and the arguments of the method need to be packaged;
- package up any data sent back to the client from the object to which a message has been sent;
- communicate with the network layer that actually sends the raw data representing a method invocation.

In the remainder of this chapter and in the next I shall describe two implementations of distributed object schemes: RMI and CORBA. Both require middleware to carry out the processes detailed above. There are a number of components to this middleware:

- An interface definition language which defines the services that a distributed object provides. Such a language will define the structure of the methods that are available to the remote client and the structure of the instance variables that make up the state of the object. This interface definition language could be some special-purpose language such as that associated with CORBA or could just be a part of a programming language such as the Java interface associated with RMI.

- A layer, often known as a presentation layer, which maps data into a form that can be transported over some transmission technology. This is a process known as **marshalling**; the reverse process – that of converting the transmitted data into a form that an application can understand – is known as **unmarshalling**. The code that carries out this process is known as stub or skeleton code. This code is usually automatically generated by passing interface definition language code through a special processor and then linking that code into the client and server code.

- A layer, often known as the session layer, which implements connections between multiple objects. This layer carries out processes such as mapping the reference of an object to a host, activating a remote object, deactivating a remote object and carrying out the process of invoking a method on an object.

4   Developing object-oriented remote systems

Figure 9.1 shows the processes required to develop a system based on distributed object technology. It is taken from Emmerich [5].

The first step in the process is to design the system in terms of the classes that define the business objects that are employed. This step will be the same irrespective of whether the system is distributed or not.

The product of this first step will be a specification of the classes and the services associated with these classes written in terms of the methods found in each class. The next step is to define these classes in terms of some interface definition language.

The files containing the definitions of the interfaces will then be processed by some utility which generates helper code (stubs) that implements processes such as marshalling and unmarshalling data and sending raw data across some transmission medium. This code will eventually be merged with the application code.

The next step is to program the server. The server will make distributed objects available to clients. Objects will be created either statically – they are created just once

Figure 9.1
The process of
designing and
implementing a
distributed object
system

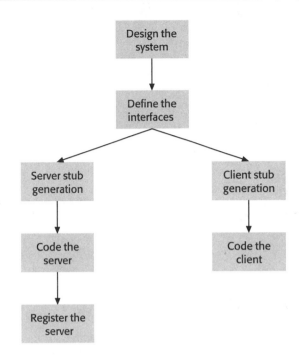

Nomenclature is
notoriously loose
in this area. The
figure shows stubs
being generated;
be aware, however,
that sometimes the
term 'stub' is solely
associated with the
client and the term
'skeleton' with the
server. This is true
for RMI

and remain on the server – or dynamically, where they are created on-the-fly according to demand and are deactivated when they are no longer needed. The server code will make use of the helper code.

The final server task is to register the objects with some naming service so that clients can find them. This usually involves registering the names of the objects with a name server associated with the distributed object scheme. The naming convention used will depend on which distributed technology is used: RMI has a simple naming scheme, but CORBA has a hierarchic naming scheme similar to that found in the Internet Domain Naming System.

The code for the client then needs to be developed. Again, this code will interface with the helper code that has been generated. The client code in effect refers to the remote objects via the naming service, invokes methods on the remote methods and processes any data that has been sent back as a result of this invocation.

This, then, is the process of developing distributed object code. There are a number of important points to be made about it:

■ The first stage is identical to any object development method, irrespective of whether the objects to be accessed are distributed or not.

■ A name service is always used.

■ The client and server code should contain very few references to the fact that a remote object is being accessed; the most that the reader of the code should see is the fact that a naming service is being consulted.

Figure 9.2
The three layers
of RMI

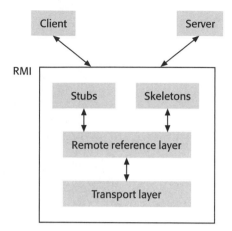

The RMI architecture

5 The RMI architecture

5.1 The three-layered architecture

The RMI system has a layered architecture, albeit a simple one. This architecture is shown in Figure 9.2. It consists of three layers:

■ *The stub/skeleton layer.* This is the layer that the remote objects on a client and a server communicate with. When, for example, a remote object on the server side is sent a message from the client end the first thing that happens is that any data required is sent to a stub which resides on the stub/skeleton layer. Both the stub and the skeleton act as proxies for the actual remote object that is being processed – all processing for the remote object passes through them. In effect the stub/skeleton layer implements local objects at the server and client which communicate with the remaining layers. The programmer communicates with any remote objects by sending messages to these local objects. Such objects are known as proxy objects. The stub is associated with a client and the skeleton is associated with the server.

If you are hazy about layered architectures then it might be worth revisiting Chapter 1

■ *The remote reference layer.* This layer is concerned with the protocol that is to be used for invoking remote methods, for example this layer might support a protocol which only results in a single object being sent messages (a unicast protocol) or it might support a protocol whereby a number of objects are sent messages (a multicast protocol).

When I use the term 'message' in this section I shall be referring to the invocation of a method not as in 'message passing'

■ *The transport layer.* This is the layer which is concerned with sending any data that is associated with sending a message to a remote object. This layer supports a number of transport mechanisms: the default is TCP/IP, but there is no reason why another protocol cannot be used.

In order to see how each of these layers work it is worth looking at the invocation of the method `remoteMethod` which has two arguments applied to a remote object `remoteObject`.

```
remoteObject.remoteMethod(arg1, arg2)
```

This object resides on a server and the client contains the code shown in the line above.

First, the remote method corresponding to `remoteObject` in the stub/skeleton layer is invoked, it collects up the arguments that are used for the method invocation, informs the remote reference layer that the code should be executed and sends any data required to this layer.

The remote reference layer will then determine whether the object that is referenced resides on the local computer or on a remote computer. If it resides on a remote computer it will pass to the transport layer any data that is required to invoke the method on the remote computer.

RMI resources

The transport layer will then set up a connection and carry out the physical sending of any data associated with the method invocation, for example the values of the method's arguments. When the remote object has had the message applied to it any data that is produced is sent back to the client that invoked the method using the three layers. When the invocation has completed the stub at the client end decodes any results which the method returns and passes them to the entity that caused the remote invocation.

5.2 Garbage collection

During the execution of a system which contains remote objects some of those objects will be de-referenced and will no longer be referenced by variables. RMI contains a distributed garbage collector which keeps track of remote objects; when it discovers any that are not referenced by any variables then it will destroy them and return the memory used to the free store of memory; this reclaimed memory can then be used by newly created remote objects. In order to do this the garbage collector keeps a count of the number of references to each object; when that count is zero the memory occupied by the object is reclaimed.

5.3 Security

Security and RMI

In its purest form RMI is an insecure way of communicating over a network; for example, when a remote object is invoked the data associated with the invocation is sent as character data which can be read by anyone who taps into the communication medium used. Also, there is no authentication: when a remote invocation of a method occurs at a server there is no guarantee that this invocation has come from the same client that carried out previous invocations; this means that someone can masquerade

I shall be looking at spoofing in more detail in Chapter 11

as a client and could potentially read and update any sensitive data that the remote object has access to – a process known as **spoofing**. In order to guard against this a security manager has to be used. There is a class known as RMISecurityManager which enables this to happen.

6 Developing remote object programs

The aim of this section is to show you in detail the processes that are involved when you program access to a remote object which resides on a server. The remote object that I shall implement has a limited functionality: all that it does is to return the current time in milliseconds since 1 January 1970.

6.1 Developing the server code

The first task that the programmer has to carry out when implementing a remote object in RMI is to define an interface that specifies the methods that the object is associated with. For our millisecond returning object the interface is shown below:

```
import java.rmi.*;

public interface SecondGenerator extends Remote
{
long getMilliSeconds() throws RemoteException;
}
```

Here the interface contains the single method getMilliSeconds; this is the method which will return the time in milliseconds.

There are a number of things to notice about this interface: the first is that the interface inherits from the class Remote which is found in the package java.rmi. This means that any object that is created using this interface will have facilities that enable it to have remote messages sent to it. The second is that the interface will need to be declared as public in order that clients can access objects which have been developed by implementing it. The third is that the method getMilliSeconds throws an exception known as a RemoteException. All methods that are called remotely must throw this exception. There are a number of things that could go wrong when a method is invoked on a remote object, for example the communication medium could be malfunctioning. If there is a problem then a RemoteException is created. This exception is created under the bonnet and is not programmed when the remote object is implemented.

There are many other things that can go wrong, for example the remote object may not have been found

The next step is to implement the remote interface and provide a distributed object stored on a server. The code for this is shown below:

```
import java.rmi.*;
import java.util.Date;
import java.rmi.server.UnicastRemoteObject;

public class SecondGeneratorImpl
    extends UnicastRemoteObject implements SecondGenerator
{
private String objName;

public SecondGeneratorImpl (String objName)
      throws RemoteException
{
super();
this.objName = objName;
}

public long getMilliSeconds() throws RemoteException
{
return(new Date().getTime()); //The method getTime
                              //returns the time in msecs
}

public static void main(String[] args)
{
String oName = "Dater";
System.out.println("Loading in security manager…");
RMISecurityManager sManager = new RMISecurityManager();
System.setSecurityManager(sManager);
try
    {
        SecondGeneratorImpl remote =
            new SecondGeneratorImpl (oName);
        Naming.rebind(oName, remote);
        System.out.println("Object bound to name");
    }
    catch(Exception e)
        {System.out.println("Error occurred at server"+e);}
}

}
```

It is a good practice to name a class which implements an interface by postfixing the string 'Impl' to the name of the interface

It is worth walking through the code as it contains many features which you will not have seen before.

The class `SecondGeneratorImpl` extends another class known as `UnicastRemoteObject`. This class implements a remote access protocol which enables communication between a client and a *single* object residing on a server. The class also implements the interface `SecondGenerator` which we defined earlier and which specified the services provided by the remote object.

Remember that in
Chapter 2 I stressed
that there were more
examples of a naming
service over and above
that of the Internet
domain naming
service. This is one
of them

The class contains a `String` instance variable `oname` which gives the name of the remote object. This string is used to identify the object within a distributed system.

The first method that can be found in the class is the constructor; this initialises the name of the remote object and also calls on the no-argument constructor of the superclass. What this does is to enable the remote object to listen for methods applied to it; again this is carried out under the bonnet and the programmer does not have to worry about this. It is worth pointing out that since this constructor represents a remote object it could throw a `RemoteException` object and hence this should be documented by a `throws` clause.

The next method is the implementation of the `getMilliSeconds` method found in the interface `SecondGenerator`. This just returns the time in milliseconds. Again since it is a method which can be invoked remotely it could throw a `RemoteException` object.

The final method is `main`; this carries out a number of important functions:

■ It loads in a security manager for the remote object. If this is not done then malicious code could be sent from the client.

■ It creates an object with a particular name (`"Dater"`) given by the constructor argument.

The alternative to
using reBind is to
use the method bind.
This carries out the
same naming process;
however, it generates
an AlreadyBound
Exception if the
object has already
been bound to a name

■ Finally, it informs the RMI naming service that the object that has been created (`remote`) is given the string name `oName`. The RMI naming service is a program which runs in the background, keeps track of all the distributed objects that are in existence and associates (or binds) a unique name with each of them. The method used for this binding is called `reBind`. Later I shall show how this naming service is invoked. At this point do not worry about it.

The server code is now complete: a remote object has been created, a security manager has been deployed and the RMI naming service has been told what the name of the object that has been created is. The remote object that we have created is now ready to be sent messages by client code. The next stage is to develop this code.

6.2 Developing the client code

Some example client code is shown below:

```
import java.rmi.*;

public class TimeClient
{
public static void main(String[] args)
{
try
{
    SecondGenerator sgen =(SecondGenerator)
                Naming.lookup("rmi://hostname/Dater");
```

```
        System.out.println("Milliseconds are   "
                            +sgen.getMilliSeconds());
    }
    catch(Exception e)
    {System.out.println
        ("Problem encountered accessing remote object "+e);}
    }

    }
```

The class just contains the entry point code in the method `main`. The code in `main` first looks up the object within the naming service which is running on the server. In order to do this it uses the static method `lookup`. This takes a string as an argument. Notice that the string has the same form as the URL that is used to identify documents stored in the World Wide Web, the only difference being the fact that the string is prefixed with *rmi* rather than *http*. The method `lookup` will obtain a reference to the object identified by the string `"Dater"` which is resident on the server that is identified by `"hostname"`; in order to do this it consults the naming service running on that server. Since lookup returns an `Object` the object returned should be cast to `SecondGenerator` before it is assigned (it could also be cast to `SecondGeneratorImpl`). All that remains in the code is for the method `getMilliSeconds` to be invoked on the `sgen` object.

The `sgen` object is a reference or proxy for the real object residing on the server, with `sgen` residing in the stub layer

There are two questions that need to be answered before I recap the processes involved in developing systems containing remote objects: the first is how are stubs and skeletons created; and the second is how do we start up the RMI registry?

The answer to both these questions is simple: the stubs and skeletons are created by running a utility known as the **RMI compiler**. In a Windows environment all you have to do is to execute the utility in an MSDOS line or by using the *start program* facility, for example the MSDOS line

```
C:\>rmic  SecondGeneratorImpl
```

will create the stubs and skeletons for the class which defines the very simple objects that we described above. This will generate the files

```
SecondGeneratorImpl_Skel.class  SecondGeneratorImpl_Stub.class
```

Running the naming service in the background in a Windows environment involves opening a separate MSDOS command window for it

The former is the skeleton class which must be deployed on the server and the latter is the stub class which must be deployed on the client. The RMIC utility will always postfix the argument that it receives with the strings `"_Skel"` and `"_Stub"`.

The naming service implemented by the RMI registry is started up on the server by typing

```
rmiregistry
```

This program can then be run in the background.

Exercise 9.1

Developing a
simple remote
object server which
implements a
simple naming
service

There are a number
of ways of distributing
the skeleton and stub
files; probably the
easiest is to take
advantage of RMI
facilities which allow
you to download the
files via a Web server

Developing remote objects with RMI

Developing a remote object system using RMI involves the following steps:

1.   Develop the interface that describes the services provided by the remote object(s).

2.   Implement the server code by developing a class which implements the remote interface. This class can contain the code which registers the object with the RMI registry as described here; however, the code can be placed in another class. Compile the code.

3.   Implement the code for the client which uses the RMI registry to connect to the remote object. Compile the code.

4.   Run the RMI compiler on the remote class in order to generate the stubs and skeletons and then make them available to the client and the server.

5.   Run the RMI registry on the server.

6.   Execute the class file associated with the server. The remote object that is associated with the server is now ready for receiving messages from code running on other computers.

7.   Execute the class file associated with any client. This will hook into the remote object that was made available and carry out the processing that was required.

6.3 The RMI registry

Before looking at some more advanced techniques associated with RMI it is worth looking at some of the programming that can be carried out on the RMI registry. Already you have seen two examples of this programming: when a server registered a particular object with the registry and when a client retrieved a reference to a remote object by employing the string name of the object in a lookup method. The two main classes which you will use to manipulate the content of the RMI registry are the interface `java.rmi.registry.Registry` and the main registry class `java.rmi.registry.LocateRegistry`. The former contains methods which allow you to associate and disassociate a string name with a particular remote object, while the latter contains methods which allow you to find and access an RMI registry which is either running on your local host or on a remote host. An example of the type of programming associated with the RMI registry is shown below. It finds all the objects associated with a particular RMI registry and displays their names on `System.out`; the `import` statement and much of the details of the class in which the code is embedded are not shown.

```
String  remoteObjectNames[]= null;
..
try
{
remoteObjectNames =
      Naming.list("rmi://onserver.open.ac.uk");
}
```

```
catch(RemoteException  re)
    {System.out.println("Problem with connection "+re);}
catch(MalformedURLException  murl)
    {System.out.println("Problem with URL "+murl);}
System.out.println
    ("** List of objects in the registry **");
for(int i = 0; i < remoteObjectNames.length; i++)
    System.out.println(remoteObjectNames[i]);
```

The RMI naming service defaults to using port 1099. If you have an application which uses this port you will need to specify a new port for the service, for example `rmi://hostname:1023` accesses the service via port 1023

The static method `Naming.list` extracts all the names of the objects whose details are currently stored in an RMI registry. It takes a single argument which is the name of the computer which is running the registry; in the case of the code above this is the computer `onserver.open.ac.uk`. Two exception objects could be generated: the first is a `RemoteException` which is generated if a connection with the host running the RMI registry fails; the second is generated if the URL presented to the method is malformed, for example the colon is missed out. `Naming.list` will return with a reference to a string array containing the names of the remote objects. This array is then traversed and the names displayed.

7   Two examples

To conclude this chapter it is worth looking at two uses of distributed objects within an e-commerce application. The first, discussed below, is also relevant to the CORBA distributed technology discussed in the next chapter.

7.1 Legacy software

Many commercial companies have a huge portfolio of software which has been in use for some time. Such **legacy software** cannot be instantly rewritten: often the software is the result of many tens of years of design and programming effort and many companies are keen to keep this software going – even when they migrate many of their applications to the Internet. A typical piece of legacy software used by a retailer would administer stocks of products in a warehouse, and would include functions which:

- keep track of deliveries of stock;
- provide information for staff concerned with selling the product;
- provide warnings when the stock of a product falls below a predetermined limit; when this happens the system would either inform staff concerned with reordering or automatically reorder the stock;
- provide marketing information about popular products;
- provide accounting information which is used for tax purposes.

Often this software will be hosted by a server at a location such as a warehouse.

A company that wishes to integrate such software with, say, a Web-based customer ordering facility faces a number of problems, for example the language used to develop the application would certainly not be Java.

One solution to this problem involves remote objects and a Java technology known as JNI.

JNI

At the server, the code is hidden by a layer of software written in Java and using facilities from JNI (Java Native Interface). This technology allows Java code to be interfaced with legacy code. This means that the functions of the stock control system can be invoked by calling Java methods. The interface of the stock control system can then be embedded in remote objects running on the computer used for stock control, for example an object described by a class `PopularLines` would contain data on which were the most popular products and when the peak demand for the product occurred. Code such as

```
popObj.getPopularProduct()
```

would be used to discover the most popular product.

A customer would use a browser to carry out functions such as ordering a product. The order would be processed by the middleware associated with a Web server and would result in one of the remote object methods being executed. This method, after interacting with the legacy software, would then return some data, even if it is just the confirmation of a correct order; the warehouse system would then take over, deducting the stock from the warehouse database and informing any software that handles the order – such as credit card payment software – that the order has been placed.

7.2 Agents

An agent is a chunk of software which carries out some useful process on the Internet. For example, an agent might wander travel sites on the Internet looking for holiday bargains or visit news sites looking for breaking news in which the agent owner might be interested. Agents are often called **bot**s which is short for **robot**.

The aim of this section is to show you how a simple agent is developed. Later, in Chapter 15, I shall look at distributed agent technology in a lot more detail. This section details how RMI might be used to develop an agent using a distributed object technology such as RMI.

RMI is a good medium for developing agents since, in contrast to CORBA, a wide variety of objects with built-in intelligence can be sent over some transmission medium.

An interface for an agent which can roam the Internet is shown below:

```
public interface DistAgent extends Remote
{
public void runIt();
}
```

Bots and agents

This defines a template for agents which have to implement the method `runIt`; within this method is found the code that needs to be executed when the agent visits some location on the Internet.

An object stored at the visited location can be defined using the interface `Destination` shown below:

```
public interface Destination extends Remote
{
public DistAgent receive (DistAgent da)
                              throws RemoteException;
}
```

This represents a remote object which can be created at a server and which can respond to the visit of an agent.

The code for an invocation of the agent is shown below. It would be placed within any class which implements `Destination`.

There is no reason why the agent could not be sent on to another server rather than return to the client; the code presented is simply for pedagogic purposes

```
public DistAgent receive(DistAgent da)
                              throws RemoteException;
{
da.runIt()
return da;
}
```

This code takes the agent that has arrived, executes its `execute` method and then returns it back to the client that sent it. Normally the agent will have been modified in order to contain useful information obtained from the visit.

This, then, is the simple architecture of an agent. The processes that the agent is to carry out are embedded in the code of the method `runIt`.

8 Summary

Exercise 9.2

Executing a simple agent

This chapter has been an introduction to one specific distributed object technology known as RMI. I choose to describe this technology first, rather than the CORBA technology detailed in the next chapter, though it is worth pointing out that there are a number of other distributed object technologies. Almost certainly the most popular of these is DCOM, a technology developed and marketed by the Microsoft Corporation. One of the aims of this book is to keep it platform neutral; hence I have not described it in detail.

RMI is very simple and enabled me to describe the main principle behind remote objects without being encumbered by lots of detail. RMI is a lightweight, fast, distributed technology which is ideal for a pure Java distributed application, for example an intranet which contains applications programmed in Java; however, for developing

You may remember from Chapter 1 that an intranet is a local network running TCP which is just used by the employees of a company

COM and DCOM

heterogeneous systems which contain software developed in a variety of languages it lacks functionality. The next chapter describes a much more heavyweight technology known as CORBA.

DCOM

DCOM is Microsoft's implementation of distributed object technology. It is built on top of COM which is the Microsoft object component model. Developers who produce DCOM objects first produce COM objects and then convert them for distributed working – usually a relatively trivial process. The COM object is developed by programming it using one of the Microsoft proprietary languages such as Visual C++. Hence, DCOM has some similarities with RMI in terms of implementation, although DCOM objects can only be developed using a variety of Microsoft compilers.

---

9 # Further reading

Exercise 9.3

Developing an object factory

If you are doing the case study as you progress through the book, read Section 7.4 of Chapter 14

This chapter has just been a brief introduction to the RMI technology. There are, however, a number of professional books which go into a large amount of detail. The book by Downing [2] is a solid introduction. George Reese has written a good introduction to database programming with Java which features RMI [3]. Jim Farley has developed a useful introduction to distributed computing using Java. This book covers a number of topics ranging from simple socket programming to CORBA, but does contain a good chunk of material on RMI [4].

Internet book links

References

[1] E. Gamma, R. Helm, R. Johnson and J. Vlissides, *Design Patterns*. Reading, MA: Addison-Wesley, 1995.

[2] T. Downing, *Java RMI: Remote Method Invocation*. Foster City, CA: IDG Books, 1998.

[3] G. Reese, *Database Programming with JDBC and Java*. Sebastopol, CA: O'Reilly, 1997.

[4] J. Farley, *Java Distributed Computing*. Sebastopol, CA: O'Reilly, 1997.

[5] W. Emmerich, *Engineering Distributed Objects*. Chichester: John Wiley, 2000.

CORBA

10

Chapter contents

CORBA is a distributed object technology which enables remote objects in a variety of languages to interact with each other. This chapter introduces the main concepts of CORBA, looks at the architectural components of the technology and details the services that CORBA offers. It describes the Interface Definition Language used to describe remote objects and how elements of the language are mapped into Java. The key role of the Object Request Broker is described and the development steps needed to implement CORBA code for the Java ORB are detailed. The chapter concludes with a description of CORBA within a three-tier architecture.

Aims

1. To describe the main features of the CORBA architecture.
2. To outline how Java can act as a medium for CORBA programming.
3. To detail the main steps required to develop and deploy CORBA remote objects.
4. To describe the role that CORBA distributed objects play in three-tier architectures.

Concepts

Attribute, Collection service, Concurrency control service, CORBA, Dynamic skeleton, Event service, Externalisation service, Interface, Interface Definition Language, Interface repository, Internet Inter ORB Protocol (IIOP), Licensing service, Lifecycle service, Module, Naming context, Naming service, Object adapter, Object Request Broker, Persistence service, Properties service, Query service, Relationship service, Security service, Skeleton, Stub, Time service, Trader service.

1 Introduction

There are ways in which RMI can be used within a mixed language environment: Java has a facility known as JNI (Java Native Interface) which is capable of interfacing with some languages written using certain compilers; however, the number of languages and compilers is restricted and the solution is often inelegant

The previous chapter described a distributed object technology known as RMI. This technology is a pure Java solution to the problem of distributing objects around a network. Because Java is still in its infancy it has not yet spread widely into non-Internet-based applications; consequently, many long-established companies who wish to develop applications that interface with their current software – often written in languages such as C, COBOL and C++ – do not consider RMI as an implementation medium.

One solution which has been in existence for many more years than Java is known as **CORBA** (Common Request Broker Architecture). It was developed by a group of over 700 companies known as the Object Management Group (OMG). CORBA is not an implementation medium as RMI is, but is a specification of the services provided by a system which can support distributed objects programmed in a wide variety of languages on a wide variety of operating systems. It is the fact that CORBA is multi-language that mainly distinguishes it from RMI and enables it to be used for legacy applications.

The architecture of CORBA is shown in Figure 10.1. This shows a client interacting with a CORBA object residing on a server. There are a number of components to the architecture:

The Object Management Group

- *Client IDL stubs.* This is code and data which is used by the client as a proxy for the real objects that reside on the server. These stubs are generated by a simple utility which is provided by a CORBA implementation. They carry out processes such as collecting data together ready for dispatch to a remote object.

- *The Interface Definition Language.* This is a language, usually abbreviated to IDL, which defines interfaces to CORBA distributed objects; as you will see later it looks a little like C. The IDL defines the instance variables of a distributed object

Figure 10.1
The CORBA architecture

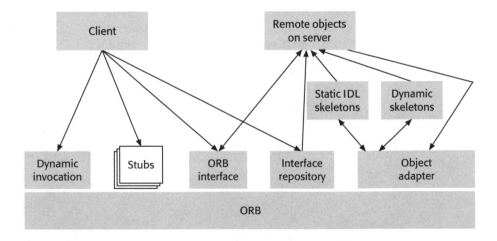

I shall be looking in detail at the IDL later in this chapter

together with the methods which the object can respond to. The IDL stubs are, as their name suggests, generated from files of IDL code.

- *Dynamic Invocation Interface.* Messages can be sent to distributed objects either statically where the objects are defined by IDL and where the type of the object is known at compile time, or dynamically where the CORBA run-time system is able to determine the type of an object. The part of the CORBA architecture which deals with this is known as the Dynamic Invocation Interface.

CORBA resources

- *Static IDL skeletons.* These are the server side equivalent of the client IDL stubs. It is code which carries out a number of functions such as extracting out the arguments from a remote method invocation and carrying out the actual process of sending a message to the remote object. These skeletons are implemented by the utility which creates the client IDL stubs.

- *Dynamic skeletons.* These are equivalent to the static IDL skeletons. However, they enable clients to access remote objects for which the clients do not have compile-time knowledge.

- *Interface repository.* This is a database of all the object descriptions expressed in IDL.

CORBA products

- *Object Request Broker.* The ORB is the part of the CORBA architecture which provides the plumbing between distributed CORBA objects and the clients that reference them. It is the ORB which carries out the process of communication between distributed objects and it is the ORB that communicates with the transport medium used to convey the raw data used in object communication. There are a number of different ORBs developed by software vendors. In the early days of CORBA these ORBs were not compatible with each other: you could not send a message from a client which had stubs generated by one ORB vendor to a server object which had skeletons generated by another ORB vendor. However, version 2.0 of the standard specifies that all ORBs should be able to communicate using an Internet Inter Orb Protocol, usually abbreviated to IIOP.

Even though version 2 of the CORBA standard specifies interoperability there are still a few problems with different products operating with each other

- *Object adapter.* This is a layer which enables a remote object to access the facilities of the ORB.

OHIO Department of Transport and CORBA

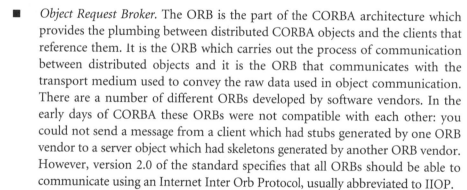

Ohio Department of Transport and CORBA

The Ohio Department of Transport (ODOT) is one of the services run by the state of Ohio in the United States. It is responsible for activities such as road building and maintenance. In the past ODOT had invested heavily in IT and had a number of systems for processes such as payroll, leave, warehousing and project accounting. One of the problems that they had encountered in the 1990s was that legislation and building practices forced a large number of changes to be made to their IT systems. Unfortunately ODOT found that these changes took more and more resources to implement. It was decided to redesign the architecture of the ODOT system so that it was based around a three-tier architecture. This architecture was designed so that change could be carried out easily. A major decision was made that as much of

> the old system should be used within the new system and so CORBA was chosen as one of the technologies. The use of CORBA enabled the developers to front-end existing packages (such as those which carried out payroll functions which did not change much) by an object interface. New components of the system were then able to communicate with these packages using standard object message passing.

2   CORBA services

CORBA provides a large number of services. Many of these services are transparent to the programmer, although some can be invoked programmatically. There are 14 services embedded in the CORBA 2.0 standard. They are:

■   *The Life Cycle Service*. This provides facilities for creating, copying, transporting and deleting objects.

■   *The Persistence Service*. This provides facilities whereby objects can be stored on some permanent medium including relational databases, object-oriented databases and flat files.

The event service is similar to the event registration that occurs when a Java object such as a `Frame` registers itself as a listener to IO events such as a mouse being clicked. However, it is much more complicated

■   *The Event Service*. This allows objects to register themselves as listeners to events and respond to events; for example, an object might register itself as a listener to an event which occurs when another object changes one of its instance variable values and carry out some processing when this occurs. This service also allows objects to de-register themselves from events.

■   *The Naming Service*. This allows objects to be given names and located by other objects which quote the name.

■   *The Concurrency Control Service*. This provides facilities which ensure that concurrent processes are not allowed to access an object in such a way that the object is left in an inconsistent state.

■   *The Relationship Service*. This allows relationships to be established between remote objects. For example, a book object can be specified to be related to an author object by virtue of the fact that the author has written the book.

■   *The Externalisation Service*. This enables data to be sent to or read from a remote object using a technique akin to Java streams.

Some of the services briefly outlined here, for example the naming service, are described in more detail in Chapter 13 which looks at transactions in distributed systems

■   *The Query Service*. This allows queries to be sent to remote objects or collections of remote objects using a syntax which is a superset of SQL.

■   *The Licensing Service*. This allows the use of an object to be monitored in order, for example, to ensure that the user is charged for the use.

■   *The Properties Service*. This allows properties to be associated with an object such as a creation date.

CORBA services

- *The Time Service.* One of the problems in a distributed system is managing time, for example a transaction may need to be applied in some temporal order, but the clocks of the servers involved in the transaction may be inaccurate. The time service manages transactions on objects within an environment where time may be out of synchronisation.

- *The Security Service.* This is a service which ensures that facilities such as authentication are provided.

- *The Trader Service.* This is a service which is very much like a yellow pages service in which distributed objects advertise what services they are capable of providing; for example, a distributed object may advertise the fact that it is capable of retrieving certain types of data from a database.

- *The Collection Service.* This enables collections of distributed objects to be associated together using standard collections such as queues and trees.

These, then, are the main CORBA services. Much of the detail of these services is beyond the scope of this book; however, some of the programs which are presented will use a small number of these services such as the naming service.

3 The Interface Definition Language

3.1 Interfaces and modules

You might be forgiven for asking why can't the IDL look like Java? The answer is that since CORBA is a multi-language approach the IDL has to be converted into any language. Thus, facilities such as `readonly`, which can be found in other languages, have to be included in the IDL

The Interface Definition Language (IDL) is used to define the instance variables and methods associated with the various distributed objects in a CORBA implemented system. The language itself looks very much like C. An example is shown below:

```
module  Tester{

interface  Single{
    attribute string exname;
    readonly attribute string location;
    string returnsVals(in string point);
}

}
```

Here a module `Tester` is defined which effectively defines a single class `Single`. This class is associated with two instance values (indicated by the keyword `attribute`) which are both strings. The first is a name which can be read or written to; the second can only be read (indicated by the keyword `readonly`). The method `returnsVals` takes a single argument which is a string with the keyword `in` designating the fact that it can only be read from.

CORBA tutorials

Two questions which are worth resolving are: how does the IDL such as the fragment shown above get converted into Java and what does the Java code look like?

The answer to the second question is shown below in terms of the Java code that is generated from the IDL above.

```
package  Tester;
public  interface  Single  extends  org.omg.CORBA.Object
{
String  exname();
void  exname(String  arg);
String  location();
String  returnsVals(String  point);
}

}
```

The class is embedded in a package which can be imported into a Java program. An interface is produced which contains methods to read and write to the attribute's name and location. Since the attribute location is read only a single method is specified which just returns the value of the attribute. The other attribute, exname, has two methods associated with it: the second sets the attribute and the first returns with the value of the attribute. Finally, the method returnsVals is specified.

There are two further points to make about the generated code: the first is that since it only involves an interface the code for each of the methods needs to be provided by a programmer; the second point is that by extending the class org.omg.CORBA.Object the objects defined by the Single interface inherit facilities which enable them to function as CORBA objects.

The first question posed above is: how does the IDL get converted to Java? The answer is that a file containing the IDL is processed by a utility which carries out the conversion; for example, if you were using the classes provided as part of the Java 2 package then you would use a utility known as idltojava. This is an example of a tool generally known as an IDL compiler.

When the conversion utility is executed there are a number of files generated; however, we leave consideration of these until later, after describing the main elements of the CORBA IDL.

The description here is in terms of the files generated by idltojava which is provided as part of the Java 2 system; different file names and even different numbers of files will be generated by other CORBA/Java products. Also the Java 3 release has a new compiler called idlj

3.2 Attributes

Attributes are basic types similar to scalar types in Java. You have already seen one example of attributes above when a string was declared. Attributes act as instance variables. Table 10.1 shows all the IDL data types and their mapping to Java. When CORBA fields are generated from fragments of IDL it is the scalar data types in the right-hand column which replace the data types in the left-hand column.

The IDL also contains facilities for naming data types: the keyword typedef associates a name with a data type, for example

Table 10.1
Attributes in CORBA

IDL type	Java type
double	double
float	float
unsigned long	int
long	int
long long	int
unsigned long long	long
char	char
wchar	char
boolean	boolean
octet	byte
string	java.lang.String
wstring	java.lang.String
struct	class
union	class
enum	class

I shall be dealing with enum later in the chapter

```
typedef  long  socSecurityNumber;
```

associates the name socSecurityNumber with the long integer IDL type. The typeDef facility is used in order to make IDL definitions a bit more readable.

3.3 The struct facility

The IDL also contains a facility for associating a number of IDL types together so that, for example, they can be passed as an argument in a method; a construct known as a struct. A definition of a struct is shown below:

// is used in IDL as in Java: as a comment

```
//Fragment of IDL
module  Tester{
..
struct  WorkPlace{
string  name;
```

```
boolean  mobile;
};
. .
};
```

3.4 The `sequence` facility

An IDL sequence is very much like a one-dimensional array. A sequence can be fixed or can grow. Two examples of sequence declarations are shown below:

```
typedef  sequence<Employee,  8>  employeeSeq;
typedef  sequence  <Employee>  varEmployeeSeq;
```

The first declares a sequence (known as a bounded sequence) `employeeSeq` which contains employees, is of a fixed size and contains a maximum of eight employees; the second line declares an expandable sequence of `Employee` objects called `varEmployeeSeq`. Sequences are mapped into Java single-dimensional arrays.

The fixed length nature of Java arrays provides something of a problem: a Java array is of fixed length, where the length is determined at compile time. This is not a problem when an IDL expandable sequence is *received* by the Java code: the CORBA run time converts it into a fixed length Java array. However, if the size of the sequence cannot be determined at compile time the programmer must use `Vector` object for any processing of the sequence and when the data contained in the `Vector` object needs to be passed to, say, a remote CORBA object, it must be copied into a fixed length array before being sent.

3.5 The `array` facility

The IDL also has an `array` facility: this is the same as the `array` facility in Java and is mapped directly into this type. There is a major difference between an `array` type and the bounded sequence type detailed in the previous section: this is that a bounded sequence can accept arrays which are smaller; the `array` type only accepts arrays which are the same length.

3.6 The `enum` facility

The `enum` facility in the IDL has no direct analogue in Java, but some programming languages such as Pascal, C and C++ implement it. An `enum` type describes variables which are allowed to contain one of a set of possible values. For example, the IDL declaration

```
//Example of enum
enum EmployeeStatus {employed, unemployed, transient}
```

declares an enumeration type whose variables will contain one of three values employed, unemployed or transient.

3.7 Using the facilities

Once the Java code that corresponds to the CORBA facilities described in this section has been generated by the idltojava utility the programmer is free to use it to produce both client and server code. Later in this chapter I shall describe this process in much more detail. Before doing this it is worth looking at the architecture of a CORBA/Java application.

4   Developing CORBA/Java code

4.1 An application architecture

Figure 10.2 shows an outline architecture for a CORBA-based application. The client code will usually have minimal references to the fact that a CORBA object is manipulated and will carry out the invocation of methods associated with the distributed object. On the server side a number of CORBA objects will have been created and made ready for receiving messages from clients.

The client code communicates with a local object which contains stub code: this code communicates with the Object Request Broker which carries out processes such as identifying what object is to be communicated with. The skeleton code is the analogue of the stub code on the server side; it carries out functions such as extracting the arguments from the method data passed to it by the Object Request Broker (ORB).

Remember that since CORBA 2 it has been possible for ORBs to communicate using an Internet Inter ORB Protocol (IIOP)

The ORB carries out processes such as identifying objects, converting data into a character stream for transmission and identifying the server that contains a particular remote object. There may be a number of ORBs which take part in accessing a distributed object: the client may be associated with one ORB from a particular

Figure 10.2
A CORBA application

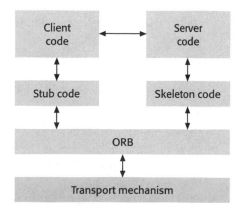

vendor, while the server may use another. The transport mechanism is the underlying set of protocols which actually carry out the transfer of method call data and return values from method calls. Usually the mechanism is TCP/IP.

These are the mechanisms used for distributed objects to be accessed. They are very similar to those found in RMI, although there are major differences between the two technologies, for example RMI is a pure Java solution while CORBA is a multi-language approach.

4.2 Files for remote code

Before looking at how CORBA objects are created, deployed and accessed it is worth returning to the `idltojava` utility in order to describe the files that are generated when it maps IDL statements to Java code. In order to describe these files I shall assume that the remote objects that will be generated will be defined by an IDL interface called `RemoteObject`. The files that are generated are:

■   A file containing a Java interface which has the same name as the CORBA interface. This class is used by a programmer to develop the functionality associated with the client and server code.

■   A helper class which contains some utility methods. The main utility method is called `narrow`; this has the function of casting a CORBA object to the Java interface type corresponding to the IDL interface. The name of the class is formed by postfixing the IDL interface name with the word `Helper`, for example `RemoteObjectHelper`.

■   A holder class. This class is created when objects in an interface are used as `out` or `inout` arguments in methods. This enables the methods to pass values out to these arguments. The name of this class is formed by appending `Holder` to the name of the IDL interface, for example `RemoteObjectHolder`.

■   A stub class. This is the class which communicates between the remote code at the client and the ORB. It implements the interface described in the first bullet point above. This class is used as the basis of the implementation of the client code. Inside it is code that communicates with the ORB and carries out the processes which eventually involve the sending of arguments and other data to a remote object. The class name is formed by prefacing the name of the IDL interface with an underscore character and postfixing it with the word `Stub`, for example `_RemoteObjectStub`.

An important point to be made about both the stub and skeleton classes is that the programmer does not have to know anything about what is contained in them

■   A skeleton class. This class is used as the basis of the implementation of the remote objects stored on a server. When the programmer writes code that sets up remote objects and makes them ready for receiving messages it is this class which needs to be inherited from. It is formed by prefixing the name of the IDL interface with an underscore character and postfixing it with `ImplBase`, for example `_RemoteObjectImplBase`.

Table 10.2
Files generated from
the IDL shown on
this page

File	Use
`DateGenerator.java`	The interface that describes the IDL interface
`DateGeneratorHelper.java`	The helper class primarily used for narrowing
`DateGeneratorHolder.java`	Used to cope with `inout` and `out` arguments in IDL methods
`_DateGeneratorImplBase`	The skeleton code for the server side
`_DateGeneratorStub`	The stub code for the client side

4.3 Developing a CORBA application

This example is very
loosely based on one
provided as part of the
SUN training course
*SL301 Distributed
Programming with
Java*

When developing code for accessing remote CORBA objects a number of steps need to be carried out. In describing these steps I shall use a very simple example of an object which has a method called `replyWithDate`; the method has a string argument and a string result. The result of the call is today's date if the string argument is "Date required" or an error indication if it isn't. The date is preceded by an argument, the string "This is the" and terminated by the current value of the attribute `namevalue`.

4.3.1 Developing the IDL

The first step is to obtain or develop the IDL description of the object(s) which you want to communicate with. The IDL used in the example is shown below:

The package part of the
code is not shown

```
module  DateApplication{
interface  DateGenerator
{
    string attribute namevalue; //Can read and write to this
    string replyWithDate (in string greeting);
};
```

Next process the IDL using the `idltojava` utility. This will create the files detailed in Table 10.2.

4.3.2 Developing the remote object class

The next step is to create the class that implements the functionality of the remote object that is to be found on the server. This means that in the example I use here the interface `DateGenerator` needs to be implemented. This is shown below:

A convention
often used by Java
programmers is to
append `Impl` at
the end of an
implementation

```
public  class  DateGeneratorImpl  implements  DateGenerator
{
private  String  nameval;
```

```
public String replyWithDate(String greeting)
{
    if(greeting.equals("Date   required"))
        return greeting +"This is the " +
        new Date()+"  "+nameval;
    else
        return("Error:  Argument  incorrect");
}
```

Both the namevalue methods will have been generated by the idltojava compiler

```
void  namevalue(String  argument)
{
    nameval = argument;
}

String  nameValue()
{
    return  nameval;
}

}
```

4.3.3 Developing the server code

The next step is to create a remote object at the server, give it a name and then make it available as a destination for messages. The code for this is shown below; an explanation follows.

```
public class Server
{
public static void main(String[] args)
{
try
{
    ORB orb = ORB.init();
    //Create a DateGeneratorImpl object
    System.out.println("Creating  a  remote  object...");
    DateGeneratorImpl dgi = new DateGeneratorImpl ();
    dgi.namevalue("Darrel");
    orb.connect(dgi);
    //Obtain the root name context
    org.omg.CORBA.Object oRef  =
        orb.resolve_initial_references("NameService");
    NamingContext nContext =
        NamingContextHelper.narrow(oRef);
    System.out.println
        ("Registering  object  with  naming  service...");
    //Register the object with the naming service
    NameComponent comp =
        new  NameComponent("RemoteDate","");
    NameComponent [] path = {comp};
```

```
        nContext.rebind(path, dgi);
        /*
        Suspend program in wait state, waiting for
        remote method calls, code not shown
        */
    }
    catch(Exception e)
    {
        System.out.println
            ("Error setting up the remote object");}
    }
}
```

This looks quite complicated code, and it is in a sense; however the functions that it carries out are quite simple. The code

```
ORB orb = ORB.init();
//Create a DateGeneratorImpl object
System.out.println("Creating a remote object...");
DateGeneratorImpl dgi = new DateGeneratorImpl();
dgi.nameValue("Darrel");
orb.connect(dgi);
```

first initialises the ORB. Then an instance of the remote object is created and linked to the ORB with the attribute associated with the object being given the value "Darrel". The next chunk of code is concerned with the naming of CORBA objects so it is worth outlining how this is done before looking at the code.

In computer science terms a leaf is part of a tree which has no descendants

CORBA keeps track of the names of remote objects by storing them in a tree structure. The internal parts of a tree represent a directory name and the leaves of the tree are the names of an object. Figure 10.3 shows an example of such a tree. In

Figure 10.3
A CORBA naming service

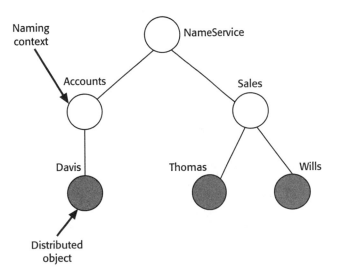

Figure 10.3 the name of the top node is `NameService`; this is the standard name for the first node in any CORBA naming structure.

Each internal node of the tree is known as a **naming context**; they are implemented in Java as the class `NamingContext`. For example, in Figure 10.3 the nodes labelled *Accounts* and *Sales* are naming contexts and the nodes labelled *Davis*, *Thomas* and *Wills* are remote objects.

This hierarchic form of naming allows objects with the same name to be stored since they can be distinguished by the path taken through the tree from the root of the tree. For example, if there was an employee *Wills* in the Accounts Department in Figure 10.3, then they would be identified as

```
NameService.Accounts.Wills
```

This is another example of the sort of naming service detailed in Chapter 2

while the employee *Wills* in the Sales Department would be identified as

```
NameService.Sales.Wills.
```

When you need to retrieve details of an object from such a tree it is a requirement to specify the naming context that you want to start the search at, where the search proceeds downwards from the specified naming context. The code for setting a naming context is

```
org.omg.CORBA.Object  oRef  =
    orb.resolve_initial_references("NameService");
NamingContext  nContext  =
    NamingContextHelper.narrow(oRef);
System.out.println
    ("Registering  object  with  naming  service...");
```

The first assignment provides a reference to the *top* of the naming tree; this returns with an object of type `org.omg.CORBA.Object`. The next assignment then converts this object into a `NamingContext` object.

The next lines of code are

```
//Register the object with the naming service
NameComponent comp =
    new  NameComponent("RemoteDate","");
NameComponent[] path = {comp};
nContext.rebind(path, dgi);
```

The first line establishes a `NameComponent` object. This corresponds to an entry in the naming tree. Each entry is associated with two items of data (this was not shown in Figure 10.3), an `id` and a `kind`, both of which are strings. The `id` is the name which is used for the object and the `kind` is used to distinguish between identical names; so, for example, an object with an `id` of "Williams" and a `kind` of "TemporaryStaff" would not conflict with an object which has an id of "Williams" and a kind of "PermanentStaff".

Remember from your initial learning of Java that you can set up the values of an array by enclosing them in curly brackets

The first assignment sets up a name with just an id component, the string "RemoteDate", but with no kind component (the second argument is the empty string). The next line places this object into an array of NameComponents. This is used in the next method rebind which carries out the process of associating the name established in the NameComponent with the remote object that has been constructed; effectively this places the object in the naming tree. The elements of the array are strings which represent the path to the object from the initial naming context, so, for example, if the array contained

```
{"Department", "Section", "Group", "DAVIS"}
```

then the object identified by the string "DAVIS" would be inserted into the tree underneath the three nodes labelled "Department", "Section" and "Group".

The final chunk of code which is not shown will suspend the program forever. The reason for suspending the program is that if we didn't it would stop executing and the remote object that we had set up would disappear.

Before looking at the code for the client it is worth saying that both java.lang and org.omg.CORBA have an Object class associated with them. Thus, when using any object described by either of these classes you will need to preface them with the full class path, for example as in

```
java.lang.Object dummyObject =
                        new java.lang.Object();
```

rather than

```
Object dummyObject = new Object();
```

4.3.4 Developing client code

The code for a client accessing the remote object that was set up using the code detailed in the previous section is shown below:

```
class DateClient

public static void main(String[] args)
{
try
{
    //Create and initialise the ORB
    System.out.println("Initialising the ORB...");
    ORB theORB = ORB.init();
    //Get the naming context for the remote object
    System.out.println("Getting naming context...");
```

```
        org.omg.CORBA.Object theObj =
                orb.resolve_initial_references("NameService");
        NamingContext nc =
                NamingContextHelper.narrow(theObj);
        //Get the name component
        System.out.println("Getting name component...");
        NameComponent nComp =
                new NameComponent("RemoteDate","");
        NameComponent[] pathToObject = {nComp};
        //Obtain a CORBA object
        System.out.println("Obtaining the remote object...");
        org.omg.CORBA.Object corbaObject =
                        nc.resolve(pathToObject);
        //Create a reference to the DateGeneratorImpl object
        System.out.println
            ("Creating a date generator object...");
        DateGeneratorImpl dgi =
                DataGeneratorHelper.narrow(corbaObject);
        //Send the message
        String reply = dgi.replyWithDate("Hello there ");
        //Display the reply, it will consist of the string
        //'Hello there This is the' followed by the date and
        //terminated by the string 'Darrel'
        //The string 'Darrel' has been set by
        //the server; there is no reason why the client could
        //not do this by sending a namevalue message before
        //sending the replyWithDate message
        System.out.println("Reply is "+reply);
    }
    catch (Exception e)
    {
        System.out.println
            ("Problems connecting to remote object");
    }
    }
    }

    }
```

The first fragment of code

```
//Create and initialise the ORB
System.out.println("Initialising the ORB...");
ORB theORB = ORB.init();
```

just initialises the object request broker and starts it running. The next fragment of
code

```
//Get the naming context for the remote object
System.out.println("Getting naming context...");
org.omg.CORBA.Object theObj =
        orb.resolve_initial_references("NameService");
NamingContext nc =
        NamingContextHelper.narrow(theObj);
```

is similar to that found on the server code: it establishes a naming context which is at
the top of the CORBA naming service tree.

The next fragment

```
System.out.println("Getting name component...");
NameComponent nComp =
        new NameComponent("RemoteDate","");
NameComponent[] pathToObject = {nComp};
```

carries out the process of specifying the path to the object; since the remote object just
lies below "NameService" in the tree then this is the only reference that is placed in
the array pathToObject.

The next fragment

```
//Obtain a CORBA object
System.out.println("Obtaining the remote object...");
org.omg.CORBA.Object corbaObject =
                    nc.resolve(pathToObject);
```

creates a CORBA object; this object is referenced by the contents of the array
pathToObject. The next fragment

```
//Create a DateGeneratorImpl object
System.out.println("Creating a date generator object...");
DateGeneratorImpl dgi =
                DataGeneratorHelper.narrow(corbaObject);
```

creates a reference to the remote object from the CORBA object that has been
referenced by consulting the CORBA naming service. In order to do this the method
narrow is used. This method can be found in the helper file which is created when the
IDL source for the remote object is processed by the idltojava utility.

All that is now required is for a method to be invoked on the remote object. The
code for this is shown below:

```
//Send the message
String reply = dgi.replyWithDate("Hello there");
//Display the reply
System.out.println("Reply is "+reply);
```

That completes the code. It is worth pointing out that the code above only works on a client and a server which are currently running on the same computer; in a short while I will describe the changes that need to be carried out in order to connect a client to a server which runs on a different computer.

4.3.5 Running the client and the server

The process of running the client and the server is straightforward. It only requires three steps. First you need to start the CORBA name server. This is the program that will communicate with the client and the server to identify a CORBA object from its name. The execution of the name server is usually done via a single line

```
tnameserv
```

The next step is to execute the server code. This will make the object created in this code ready as the destination of any messages that clients will send. The final step is to execute the client. The client will send the message to the remote object, display the string that it has received and then quit.

4.3.6 Communicating with a distant computer

The client code presented here communicates with a server that resides on the same computer as the client. Here the same ORB is accessed. If you want to access a server which is running on another computer then you will need to replace the constructor in the code

```
ORB theORB = ORB.init();
```

with the method

```
ORB.init(String[], Properties);
```

The CORBA name server uses port 900. If you are using UNIX then only someone with root privileges can access this port. The way to overcome this is to place

```
-ORBInitialPort
1050
```

after the command line shown on the right. This directs the name server to use another port, in this case port 1050

This method has two arguments: the first is a string array and the second is a `Properties` object which can be used to implement special-purpose ORBs. This two-argument method creates an ORB which is running on a remote computer identified by a set of arguments and argument values stored in the array which is the first argument to the method. These can be passed to the client code from the array `args` which is created when the command line execution of the code takes place. In order for this to happen the code needs to be modified to

A `Properties` object is like a hashtable stored on a file. What this object does in the context of this chapter is outside the scope of this book

```
ORB theORB = ORB.init(args, null);
```

where `args` is the array which is the argument to a main method. Then, after typing in the initial characters

```
java DateClient
```

The example shows the array `args` picking up values from the command line; there is no reason why they cannot be set within the program code

you will need to type in the name of the argument `-ORBInitialHost` and follow it with the name of the computer on which the ORB is running, for example

```
java DateClient  -ORBInitialHost  CORBAhost.co.uk
```

This will initialise the array `args` to contain `-ORBInitialHost` in element 0 of `args` and `CORBAhost.co.uk` within element 1 of `args`. This call on the ORB constructor will then connect the client to the host which contains the server that has set up the remote objects. The ORB constructor will interpret each pair of strings in its first argument as an argument name and an argument value. Another argument name that sometimes needs to be communicated to a client is the port on which the naming service is based. The argument name is `-ORBInitialPort` and will have a value which is an integer representing the port number which the naming service is using. For example, the command line

```
java Xate  -ORBInitialHost Ct.co.uk  -ORBInitialPort 1202
```

will execute the client code in `Xate` and communicate with the computer `Ct.co.uk` with its naming service using port 1202.

4.4 The code

You would be forgiven for thinking the coding presented here looked arcane. Part of the problem is that it is unfamiliar to you since it has not been the aim of the book to look in huge depth at the various technologies that it presents. The second reason is that CORBA is quite a baroque technology – it has to be since its aims are ambitious and work began on it when software engineering was less developed – and this is reflected in the ways in which programmers have to interact with CORBA objects. However, what is worth saying is that for any substantial CORBA application the CORBA-specific code is small in size with conventional Java code which sends messages to objects predominating, since the Java code makes use of large prewritten libraries.

The second thing worth saying about the code presented here is that it was developed for the Java ORB produced by Sun. There are a number of commercial ORBs which are on the market and the Java ORB is still in its infancy in terms of facilities.

The Java ORB

This ORB is still quite a primitive one. It lacks facilities: at the time of writing the only service it offers is a name service. It is only usable with the Java programming language and does not recover gracefully from a crash. It also does not contain an interface repository. No doubt, as time proceeds, it will improve. However, the main use for the Java ORB currently is for testing. If a developer has a requirement for an ORB in a production environment then they normally choose one of the more robust commercial ORBs.

Figure 10.4
A three-tier
architecture involving
distributed objects

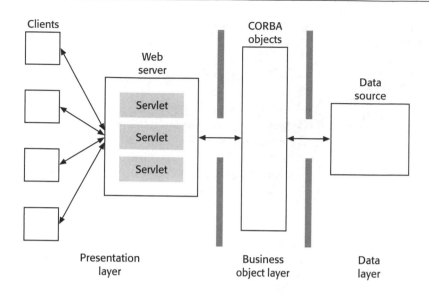

5   An application architecture

If you are hazy about what a business object is, Chapter 3 contains a description of this concept

Figure 10.4 shows a typical three-tier application architecture which might make use of CORBA objects. The presentation layer is implemented via applets or HTML forms which run on client computers and which communicate with a middle layer which is implemented as a series of business objects that reflect objects in the application domain, for example objects such as `catalogue`, `product` and `invoice` for an e-tailing application. This middle layer is implemented as a series of distributed objects which may reside on a server which is separate from the Web server which deals with client requests. These business objects will communicate with any number of potential sources of data: a relational database, an object-oriented database or legacy code which has been in existence for a long time. This architecture enables an application to be re-engineered as requirements change, for example an architecture such as the one shown in Figure 10.4 enables a current database to be replaced by another one: all that is required is for the business objects lying in the middle tier to be reprogrammed – usually a very straightforward process.

It is worth pointing out that the distributed objects could be implemented in RMI

6   Evaluating distributed object schemes

There are a number of criteria used to evaluate distributed object schemes:

∎   Speed. How fast the process of carrying out an action such as updating a remote object is.

- Programming complexity. How much extra programming is required in order to process a distributed object, over the programming that would be needed if the object was local.

- The degree of platform independence. Whether the technology can be used over a number of operating systems or is confined to one. For example, DCOM can only be used with Microsoft operating systems.

- The degree of language independence. Whether the technology can be used simply within a wide variety of programming languages, something which CORBA, for example, can do.

- The degree of complexity of objects created. Some technologies such as CORBA only allow simple objects made up from simple data types and disallow subclassing. Other technologies such as RMI allow object-oriented features such as subclassing.

7 Further reading

Much of what is happening to CORBA occurs on a day-to-day basis. Because of this books become out of date very quickly. The books detailed below concentrate, in the main, on fundamentals. A solid book on programming in Java for CORBA has been written by Vogel and Duddy [1]; a warning, though, the code was developed for a commercial ORB. Orfali and Harkey are very successful authors of books on distributed technologies. I find their books too acronym ridden with appalling cartoons and lots of meaningless diagrams; however, they do have a good writing style and keep their contents relatively free from being affected by minor changes in base technology. They have written an introduction to CORBA (with Edwards) [2] and a book which, although it purports to be about programming in Java for CORBA, is really a review of a number of distributed technologies [3]. If you really want to know about the details of CORBA programming then a book by McCaffery and Scott is one of the best; again, though, it uses a commercial ORB [4]. Slama has also written a good book on how to develop systems using CORBA although it is not Java-specific [5]. Ruh, Herron and Klinker have written a very good reference text which describes the IIOP protocol [6].

References

Internet book links

[1] A. Vogel and K. Duddy, *Java Programming with CORBA*. New York: John Wiley, 1998.

[2] R. Orfali, D. Harkey and J. Edwards, *Instant CORBA*. New York: John Wiley, 1997.

[3] R. Orfali and D. Harkey, *Client/server Programming with Java and CORBA*. New York: John Wiley, 1998.

[4] M. McCaffery and W. Scott, *Official Visibroker for Java Handbook*. Indianapolis, IN: SAMS Publishing, 1999.

[5] D. Slama, *Enterprise CORBA*. Old Tappan, NJ: Prentice Hall, 1999.

[6] W. Ruh, T. Herron and P. Klinker, *IIOP Complete*. Old Tappan, NJ: Addison-Wesley, 1999.

Internet Security

Chapter contents

This chapter examines the topic of network security. It first examines the reasons why the Internet is insecure. It then looks at some of the types of attack that have been carried out over the last decade and some of the techniques that have been used to guard against them. A major part of the chapter looks at cryptography: the process of modifying data and messages so that they cannot be read and understood by a third party. A number of different technologies based on cryptography are detailed and a case study presented. The case study is the Secure Sockets Layer, the most popular technology used to transfer secure data over the Internet. The chapter concludes with a description of some of the security facilities provided in Java security APIs.

Aims

1. To outline the security weaknesses of the Internet.
2. To examine how current security technology is able to counter many of the security threats that are current on the Internet.
3. To detail the base technology of cryptography.
4. To outline some of the Java facilities that can be used in computer security.

Concepts

ARP cache, ARP spoofing, Bastion host, Chosen plain text attack, Cipher text, Cryptography, Data virus, Decryption, Demilitarised zone, Device driver virus, Differential cryptanalysis attack, Differential fault analysis, Diffie–Hellman key exchange, Digest, Digital certificate, Digital Signature Algorithm, Digital Signature Standard, Directory server, DNS spoofing, E-card, ElGamel system, Encryption, Executable virus, Factoring attack, Family and friends virus, Firewall, Infection, IP spoofing, Key, Known plain text attack, Master secret, Message authentication code, Mutation, Plain text, Polymorphic virus, Premaster secret, Private key, Proxy server, Public key, RSA, Scanner, Screened host firewall, Screened subnet, Smart card, SSL handshake protocol, SSL record protocol, Startup file, Stealth virus, Substitution, Symmetric key, Transformation, Trojan horse, Virus, Warez.

1   Introduction

In September 1997 a number of crackers stopped the Coca-Cola Web site from operating. The crackers left behind a number of anti-Coca-Cola slogans. Earlier in that year two major credit card companies had their security compromised when a cracker stole a large number of credit card numbers and subscriber information and mailed the subscribers telling them that their company trusted their security to a third-party company that did not take security seriously. In the same year Carlos Salgado installed a program known as a **sniffer** at a credit card company; the sniffer monitored the use of a server and captured user identities and passwords for over 100 000 credit cards.

In 1996 Dan Farmer, a security consultant and programmer, used a tool known as SATAN to check out the security of a number of Internet sites. He examined 2200 sites and discovered that around 65 per cent of them were vulnerable to attack. This is quite a staggering statistic; however, what made it more staggering was that Farmer concentrated on sites which should have been very secure: those belonging to banks, insurance companies, credit card companies and government departments.

It is clear that security is a problem in the Internet. What are the reasons for it and how can security problems be solved using technological means? The aim of this chapter is to answer both of these questions. I first examine the reasons why networks are insecure, particularly TCP/IP-based networks; then I examine some of the common forms of attack that occur and describe one of the main techniques used in security: cryptography. I then examine some technologies based on encryption and some software tools that are used to secure a system. Finally I examine SSL as an example of an industrial strength technology and the Java Cryptographic Extension as an example of a facility for building secure systems. The chapter concludes with a description of electronic commerce payment protocols.

While this chapter concentrates on technological attacks it is worth making the point that many attacks on computer systems take advantage of flaws *outside* a computer system, for example 'dumpster diving' is the term used to describe the process of stealing discarded printouts from a skip (dumpster) or some other waste repository in order to find out information about a company or an individual

The Ernst & Young survey

In 1998 Ernst & Young carried out a survey of around 400 information managers in order to determine how seriously security was taken in the United States. Ernst & Young discovered that 35 per cent of all installations had no facility for detecting an intrusion into their computer system, 50 per cent did not monitor any Internet connections made to their system and 60 per cent did not have any formal policy for responding to an illegal intrusion.

2   Reasons for insecurity

There are a number of reasons why the Internet is insecure compared with other closed networks [1]:

Crime on the Internet

■ The standards used for basic Internet protocols are public. This means that intruders know much more about how the Internet works than a proprietary network. However, the flip side is that the open nature of the Internet is a boon to security, for example all weaknesses and attacks are immediately public and patches and modifications to cover attacks are realised very quickly.

■ The Internet is pervasive. It can be found in ordinary homes, in cybercafés, libraries and in many commercial premises. There is no need for complicated hardware or the burglar's tools of trade in order to carry out some intrusion: a PC and a browser will enable you to access the home page of a financial institution in a matter of seconds.

■ Web servers are extensible: they can be connected to all types of technologies, for example database management systems. Much of the software that carries out the interfacing to these technologies is complicated and transforms a Web server into something it was not intended to do. Consequently such software is vulnerable to attack.

■ The speed of development of the Internet has been huge. This means that much of the software that is used was developed with its main functionality in mind, with little thought being given to the security aspects. The most secure systems are those which have been designed from the start with security in mind; the Internet wasn't.

■ The Internet contains many interconnecting elements which require each other in order to carry out basic functions such as routing data to some destination computer.

■ Browsers originally had very little functionality. As originally envisaged they were no more than a program for downloading text files from a Web server. The speed of growth of the Internet has meant that they have had to be continually modified in order to respond to increasing demands on their functionality; often this has been achieved via insecure **plug-ins** which have had serious security flaws.

A myth about computer security

One of the enduring myths about computer security is that intrusions are carried out by software experts with huge technological skills. While this is partly true, there are a large number of network-based crimes which require very little skill to carry them out. For example, in an environment with few physical controls it can be quite easy to discover passwords. Next time you visit a company have a look at some whiteboards in the offices that you visit – you occasionally see a cryptic word which has been written in one corner to remind the user of the office what their password is.

Another aspect to security and the Internet is the fact that since communication is so fast – an e-mail from the United Kingdom can be sent to the United States and

Charles Ponzi

received in a matter of seconds – and can be automated, it means that criminals can automate processes which would have taken them days or months to carry out in the past. The Internet has given a fillip to scams and crimes which were gradually dying out. An example of this is the Ponzi scheme – named after the nineteenth-century fraudster Charles Ponzi – which involves promising investors a huge rate of interest as a result of some convoluted business scheme such as growing a little known crop in some third-world country. The perpetrator of the scheme takes a high proportion of the funds which have been entrusted to them and initially pays the first investors the promised returns. These investors are then used to reassure further investors of the financial probity of the scheme. Eventually the fraudster disappears with the bulk of the funds. Since mailing lists with thousands of e-mail addresses can be bought for as little as £50 and shareware bulk mailers can be purchased for as little as £15 the last five years have seen a resurgence of bogus pyramid selling schemes, credit repair schemes and Ponzi schemes.

Site stealing

Site stealing

Nowhere is the speed and openness of the Internet better exemplified than in the crime known as site stealing. This involves criminals copying some of the initial Web pages of a respectable site such as an online bank and then setting up a new site which is fronted by these pages. Visitors to this site looking for financial services are asked for financial details such as credit card numbers. These are then used criminally.

3   Forms of attack

This section looks at some of the ways that criminal acts are perpetrated on the Internet. These range from those which just take advantage of human frailty to those which require sophisticated technology and a deep knowledge of the Internet techno-logical infrastructure. However, before looking at these it is worth examining the types of threats that can occur in a Web site. Stallings [2] has categorised them as follows:

- *Integrity threats.* These include an intruder modifying stored data such as credit card details or modifying data in transit, for example adding a credit to the intruder's credit card account.

- *Confidentiality threats.* These include reading important stored data such as company secrets or credit card details.

- *Denial of service threats.* These include flooding a Web server with very large numbers of transactions which effectively make the server inoperable.

- *Authentication threats.* Here the intruder impersonates a legitimate user, for example a user in a B2B system who is allowed to make large financial transactions.

This leads to a series of requirements for secure commerce [2]:

- *Confidentiality.* This means that information stored on a system such as credit card details cannot be accessed by unauthorised parties.

- *Authentication.* This means that the origin of a message or transaction is correctly identified and the originator is who they claim to be. For example, someone who is able to access business information from an intelligence Web site and has paid a fee for it should be correctly identified.

- *Integrity.* This means that only authorised parties are able to change data, for example sales data or personal data.

- *Non-repudiation.* That neither the sender nor receiver of a transaction is able to deny that the transaction took place.

- *Access control.* This means that facilities in an e-commerce system are controlled so that users are only allowed to use resources that they require and which they are authorised to access.

- *Availability.* That the resources of a system are available to authorised users when they are needed by the users.

Before looking at some of the solutions to security problems it is worth looking at some concrete examples of attacks.

3.1 Non-technological attacks

These are attacks which either rely on some weakness in an organisation or require a minimal knowledge of computing in order to carry them out. An example of this is site stealing described on the previous page. Other examples are:

In the late 1970s there were a number of surveys carried out on the use of passwords. They indicated that in some installations as many as 60 per cent of the passwords which were employed could be easily guessed

- Guessing someone's password and then using this password to gain access to secure files. Often passwords are chosen which are memorable, for example the name of the password holder's wife, dog or one of their children.

- Stealing a password which is unsecured; for example, the password could have been written on a whiteboard, could be written inside a diary or stored on a sheet of paper in a drawer.

- Taking advantage of poor physical or clerical controls. There is a history of bank employees authorising credit cards or bank guarantee cards to non-existent customers, keeping the card themselves and using the card for their own purchases. This type of crime is the furthest away from the image of the technologically inspired criminal act: it just relies on internal weaknesses in some organisation.

- Writing a short script which pops up a window which, when a user browses a particular page, will prompt the user for some important information such as a

There are a number of guards against this; Java, for example, will display a prominent warning that an applet is untrusted when a frame is displayed when the applet executes. However, there are a number of instances when users have ignored this warning

Mail bomb incidents

credit card number or a password. A common window to pop up has been one which seems to indicate that their connection to a Web server has been severed and they need to log in again. Both the programming languages Java and JavaScript provide facilities for this type of interaction.

3.2 Destructive devices

These are the electronic equivalents of bombs: they require very little technical expertise but their consequences can be quite serious.

3.2.1 The e-mail bomb

This is an e-mail which either has a large amount of text pasted into it or has a large file attachment associated with it. Often such devices are sent to newsgroup participants who the sender has disagreed with. They are a nuisance: if you have a dial-up connection and someone sends you a substantial e-mail bomb then you could be waiting quite a long time before it is delivered. There are, however, examples of large quantities of e-mail bombs being sent to an organisation and disabling its mail server which becomes overwhelmed by the load.

Another more serious form of e-mail bombing is list linking. Here the recipient of a list linking attack is subscribed to a large number of mailing lists by the person who carries out the attack. Many mailing lists send attachments with the messages they transmit to the members of the list so that the recipient effectively gets e-mail bombed continually. Many e-mail providers will allocate a quota of e-mail space to their customers; when that space is full then no more e-mail will be accepted.

There is no quick and easy way to unsubscribe from hundreds, or even thousands, of mailing lists: you need to find out how to unsubscribe and then carry out the process of sending unsubscribe messages to the servers for each list. Often the only solution – a drastic one – is to get a new e-mail address. The moral is clear: treat your e-mail address carefully, for example do not put it on your Web pages

Newt Gingrich and list linking

One of the most famous examples of list linking occurred in 1996 when a senior editor of *Time Magazine* was subscribed to 1800 lists. At the same time the perpetrator linked the list to Newt Gingrich, a prominent American politician and House leader. Gingrich's computer had an auto-responder which replied to every e-mail message he received and appended a short reply. These were then sent to the mailing list server which appended them to more mailing list messages; in effect Gingrich's auto-responder made the problem much worse for him.

3.2.2 Denial of service attacks

A denial of service attack is one in which an intruder carries out some action which either prevents access to a service or degrades the quality of the service. For example, running a program on a computer which will spawn other programs which, in turn, spawn further programs is an example of a denial of service attack.

The Ping of Death and Teardrop

These are two infamous denial of service attacks which exploit insecurities in the TCP-IP protocol and the software that uses TCP-IP to send data over the Internet. The Ping of Death involves the perpetrator sending packets of data larger than the maximum of 65,536 bytes which are allowed in the TCP-IP specification. When a computer receives such a packet it will often crash. Happily, the major vendors have issued software patches which have made the Ping of Death obsolete. A more recent denial of service attack is the Teardrop attack. In the Internet, messages are sent in packets which are reassembled in the right order at the recipient computer. The Teardrop attack produces packets which contain contradictory information about the whole collection of packets. Faced with this contradictory information many computers crash when attempting to reassemble the packets into the original message.

One of the first denial of service attacks which affected the Internet was the infamous Morris Worm attack. Robert Morris, an American undergraduate, released a program onto the Internet in 1988. The worm was developed in such a way that it spawned other programs which themselves migrated to other computers on the Internet until many thousands were infected.

Denial of service attacks

One of the problems with denial of service attacks which affect Internet software is that since the software is implemented in roughly the same way an attack can affect virtually any operating system which has a TCP-IP implementation.

3.3 Viruses

Viruses are a form of malignant code (malcode) that subverts functionality; they can be used for a variety of attacks. They are separately detailed here because they often require a high degree of technical expertise to enter a system and then create chaos. Normal denial of service attacks are dirty and unsubtle, while viruses embody quite a high degree of technical sophistication.

A computer **virus** is a program that attaches itself to files which are resident on a computer – a process known as **infection**. Once a virus is established on a computer it can replicate itself, both inside the computer and on computers which are connected to its original host.

The rise of virus development

3.3.1 Categories of virus

There are three main types of virus: executable viruses, data viruses and device driver viruses. An **executable virus** is a virus which is attached to an executable file which, when executed, will result in the virus code being run. This code will then carry out some malicious act such as deleting important files. A **data virus** is a virus which infects a file containing data, rather than executable code. Often this data is associated with some program and which the program requires in order to carry out its functions. For example, many programs require a **startup file** which initialises the program and sets up basic parameters for its operation. A data virus could infect such a file and set the data in it to values such that the program will crash or its functions will be compromised; another type of data virus could add an entry to a password file that allows access to an intruder. Another example is that of a data virus for a word processor that can be easily written and which would corrupt every document opened by the word processor or, even worse, delete every document. A third class of virus is the **device driver virus**. This infects the device drivers of an operating system which are then used to piggy-back into other parts of a computer such as its file store. Happily this type of virus is usually associated with older operating systems such as MSDOS.

There is also a further classification of viruses which categorise the ways that they use to hide their presence on a computer. There are two types of virus which are categorised in this way, the **stealth virus** and the **polymorphic virus**.

Examples of anti-virus software

Before describing these two types of virus it is worth digressing a little in order to describe how the majority of anti-virus software works. Such software works by scanning the file store of a computer looking for known viruses or for changes in files, for example an operating system file suddenly becoming larger, even though no update to the operating system has taken place.

Stealth viruses hide their existence using a number of techniques, for example they may take over some of the operating system so that when anti-virus software checks that the sizes of files are the same as they were last time the software was employed, they will return with the old sizes of the files.

Polymorphic viruses are capable of frequently changing their characteristics – for example, their size – a process known as **mutation**. This means that it becomes much harder for anti-virus software based on the known characteristics of viruses to detect them.

Viruses in the wild and in the zoo

Virus researchers categorise viruses as either 'in the wild' or 'in the zoo'. The former means that the virus has been released into the public domain. 'In the zoo' means that a virus – usually artificially created by a virus researcher – has been confined to a single, well-secured computer (the zoo).

3.3.2 Constructing viruses

A warez site is a server which contains commercial software which is freely available. Such software is constructed by removing the security provisions which prevent anybody but the original buyer using it. Such sites are illegal. The programmers who maintain these sites are known as warez d00Dz (*sic*)

There are a number of ways of developing viruses. They can be constructed from scratch using a low-level programming language such as C or an assembler language. Such languages are used because it is in the virus writer's interest to make their products as small as possible in order to avoid detection; these languages also provide hooks into the low-level facilities of a computer such as the file store. There are, however, a number of virus developer kits which can be accessed via underground bulletin boards and pirated software sites known as **warez** sites.

3.3.3 A typical virus

To conclude this section of the chapter it is worth looking at the operation of one type of insidious virus, just to see how cunning virus writers can be. The virus is known as a **family and friends virus**. It uses file attachments in e-mails to propagate itself; however, it does it in a particularly devious way.

There have been a large number of viruses, both executable viruses and data viruses, which have been spread by e-mail. All the recipient has to do is to open a file attachment; this results in the execution of a program which would infect the recipient's computer. Often such an e-mail has a simple header such as 'Hello' or 'Just keeping in touch' which indicates that the sender is known to the recipient and can safely open any attachment. In these days of electronic greeting cards known as **e-card**s it is quite common for such attachments to masquerade as electronic greetings.

There has been a huge amount of publicity about viruses spread via e-mail and, as a consequence, many users of the Internet are reluctant to open attachments from other users whom they do not know. This is where the friends and family virus acts in such an insidious way. The virus infects a host computer using some other non-e-mail technology, for example it may infect the computer when the user downloads some free software from an ftp site. It will then look at the address book on the host computer and send e-mails to all the users who are stored in the address book on the host purporting to be from the user of the computer. The e-mail message which is sent will contain an attachment. The users who, after all the publicity about virus propagation via e-mail, would not normally open an attachment in a strange e-mail, readily open one from someone they know. The virus will then infect all the recipient's computers and send many more e-mails using the new address books that it has found. Often such e-mails are sent back to the original sender who might even have removed the virus.

3.4 Scanners

A scanner is a program which detects security weaknesses. There will be some controversy about placing this topic in a section devoted to attacks on a computer system, since scanners have been developed to help system administrators pinpoint security weaknesses in a system. However, some of the scanners that have been developed can be used outside a network in order to probe it for potential ways of intruding or crashing the computers on the network.

SATAN

Probably the most famous scanner is SATAN. When it was released in 1995 it generated uproar since it was the first scanner that could be used for detecting security problems from *outside* a network. There were two other reasons which can be ascribed to the controversy that arose: the first was that when it detected a weakness it provided an authoritative tutorial on the weakness and the second was the poor choice of name for the utility; it provided evidence to its detractors, albeit indirectly, of nefarious intent. SATAN was developed by two security consultants, Dan Farmer and Weitse Venema, for the UNIX operating system. SATAN stands for Security Administrator's Tool for Analyzing Networks.

A **scanner** is a software tool that looks at the various components of an operating system and checks whether they are secure, for example some scanners for the UNIX operating system are capable of checking whether the popular *sendmail* utility is secure enough to prevent intrusion; other scanners can check the robustness of the ftp facility at a site, for example by checking whether sending an overlong password will result in an ftp server crashing.

Scanners have usually been written for the UNIX platform, but the last year or so has seen a number marketed for other operating systems such as Windows NT.

3.5 Password crackers

Commercial password crackers

A password cracker is a program which attempts to find out a user's password or the identity of a number of passwords stored in the password file of a computer. Crackers were originally used by system administrators to check that the passwords that users of a system had chosen were not easily detectable. However, they have also been used for criminal purposes, for example to gain access to a computer system where the users have chosen easily detectable passwords such as 'system' or 'admin'.

Most password crackers either attempt to discover a password by consulting a large corpus of words which users habitually employ for passwords and check on characteristics of passwords which make them easy to detect such as a short password of a few alphabetic letters which could be detected by a brute force attack; or they may attempt a brute force attack on a password file.

Commercial sniffers

> ### l0phtCrack 2.0
> This is a password cracker for Windows NT. It works in two modes. It first checks passwords on an NT-supported network using a user-supplied file of passwords. The second mode involves the tool attempting to carry out a brute force search of all the passwords in an NT system using a limited set of characters: those drawn from alphabetic characters, both upper and lower case, and the digits 0 to 9.

3.6 Sniffers

Most sniffers are programmed to select only a small amount of data: usually the first few hundred bytes of a user session. These are the bytes containing passwords and account names; if they were programmed to capture everything they would soon be overwhelmed

These are devices which read the packets of data that travel around a network. They have a legitimate use for systems administrators since they can be used for determining the efficiencies and inefficiencies in a network, for example they can be used for detecting choke points: parts of a system where network traffic is heavy. They are also used by developers, for example, in order to judge the design of a distributed system in terms of the traffic it generates.

However, they have often been used for siphoning off sensitive data. An intruder might install a sniffer at a strategic point in a network such as a gateway and read the traffic that is passing through the gateway. A successful sniffer can detect hundreds, if not thousands, of passwords in a matter of hours and send them to a remote computer where they can be used for unauthorised intrusions.

Sniffer attacks are, surprisingly, not very prevalent; however, when they occur they can compromise a very large number of computers. For example, a recent sniffer attack on a number of computers resulted in 268 sites (not computers, but sites!) having their computers violated.

Trojan horses

3.7 Trojan horses

A Trojan horse is malcode which looks legitimate but attempts to do something which the user does not expect it to do. For example, a shareware program which provides a system administrator with information about file usage in a networked system but which, after a number of uses, destroys many of these files is an example of a Trojan horse.

Trojan horses can be used for financially criminal purposes such as discovering passwords and secure network information or they can be used to destroy resources or carry out a denial of service attack.

The major problem with Trojan horses is that they are very difficult to detect. They are difficult to detect for two reasons: the first is that they often masquerade as utilities which would normally be found stored on a computer or would require installing on a computer, for example in 1997 a Trojan horse was in circulation masquerading as the popular *Stuffit* file compression program used in Macintoshes. This particular Trojan horse deleted important files when it was installed on a host.

The second reason that they are difficult to detect is that they are stored in a computer in object code form and it can be difficult to detect whether they contain malicious code.

Spoofing attacks

3.8 Spoofing

This is a jargon term used to describe the fact that an intruder uses a computer to masquerade as another trusted computer in order to carry out operations that the users of the trusted computer are allowed to initiate. Spoofing does not require the in-depth knowledge of passwords and authentication that the previous intrusion methods do: it just relies on masquerading as a computer that a network trusts.

In order to understand what spoofing involves it is worth looking at one variety of this technique known as **IP spoofing**. This attack uses the TCP-IP protocol to subvert the normal authentication controls in a system by running a computer which purports to have an address that is trusted.

Cookies

Cookies and security

A cookie is a file which is placed on a client running a browser and which usually contains details of a particular transaction, for example the products which someone has bought from an e-tailing site. In this case the cookie will contain details of each item bought and is consulted when the user finishes the transaction in order to calculate the total cost. Such cookies are transient. Other cookies are permanent and can reside on the file store of a client. A typical use for this type of cookie is in keeping credit card details for a user so that they do not have to enter a large amount of data when a transaction is carried out. Cookies are a threat to privacy: it is relatively easy to build up a profile of someone's likes and preferences by depositing a permanent cookie on their computer. If you have objections to this form of privacy being compromised there is a relatively simple solution; this is to switch on a browser option which displays a box that allows you to choose whether a cookie is to be accepted or not. However, this can be a nuisance to the user!

When a computer establishes a connection using TCP-IP the client sends a TCP packet with an initial integer. The receiving computer (the server) sends back a packet which contains a unique integer known as a sequence number and an acknowledgement which is the client's sequence number plus one; the client then has to send back an acknowledgement which is the server's sequence number + 1. From this point the client and the server involve themselves in a dialogue in which the client sends packets of data and the server sends back packets which contain sequence numbers which the client has to return in order to validate the fact that it is the computer that it purports to be. The server sequence numbers are determined by an algorithm which is built into the TCP-IP software of the server.

The major problem in carrying out an IP spoofing attack is that the computer carrying out the spoofing will not know what the sequence numbers being generated by the receiving server are after the initial handshake has occurred: the server computer will be receiving packets of data which purport to be from a trusted computer and will be returning replies to the trusted computer; however, the network software will be routing them to the *real* trusted computer. Because the invading client has to reply with packets of data which contain the returned index in order to carry out a validated dialogue, any packet which does not contain the index will alert the TCP-IP software (and the system administrator) that there is a problem with the connection, possibly one involving an unauthorised intrusion.

In order to carry out an IP spoofing attack the intruder has to carry out a number of tasks:

- The trusted computer has to be put out of action. This is usually carried out by means of some denial of service attack.

- The intruding computer has to be assigned the IP address of the trusted computer.

- The intruding client must then connect to the computer and establish a handshake spoofing the server that it is a trusted computer.

Most IP spoofing attacks have been carried out on varieties of the UNIX operating system

- The client computer must then attempt to infer the sequence numbers that are generated by the server. This is the most difficult task of all for many systems, but not impossible. In some local area networks this can be carried out quite easily.

Often the sequence numbers that are generated by a vulnerable server are discovered by means of a trial and error process whereby the intruding client generates a series of attempted connections.

Usually after an intruder has entered a system they find a more convenient way of accessing the compromised server, for example by password guessing or altering parts of the TCP-IP software so that the intruding computer becomes trusted.

This is one type of spoofing; there are others. **ARP spoofing** is one example. ARP stands for Address Resolution Protocol: the part of the TCP-IP suite of protocols, which relates computer hardware addresses to IP addresses. The area of an operating system which relates hardware addresses to IP addresses is known as the **ARP cache**. An ARP spoofing attack involves rewriting this cache so that an intruding client can assume the IP address of a trusted computer.

Another form of spoofing is **DNS spoofing**. This is less serious than the previous two types of spoofing as it can easily be detected; however, this has not prevented a small number of such attacks over the last five years. It involves infiltrating a domain name server and rewriting the files of the server so that a computer which is outside a network can be given the same name as a trusted computer. This means that clients who request a service from the trusted computer using a symbolic name would be routed to the rogue computer which could then involve them in a dialogue in which important information such as credit card details is elicited.

3.9 Technology-based attacks

These are attacks which take cognisance of security flaws in new technologies. At present mobile and active code present the largest threat. There have been such a large number of flaws in many of the new technologies that are used for the Internet that if this section detailed all of them it would have a size out of proportion to its importance: while many defects have been discovered, many of them have been closed fairly quickly. In this section I shall concentrate on defects associated with two, Java and Active X, and use them as examples of technology-based attacks based on new technology.

Security problems with applets

3.9.1 Java

The fact that Java offered superb facilities for Internet system programming was initially ignored. The reverse now almost holds: Java is now seen as the language for enterprise systems while the importance of applets has been de-emphasised

When Java was announced it was one of the big events in Internet history and attention mainly focused on applets. These are Java programs which are embedded into HTML files and which are executed on the client.

Applets provided major enhancements to Web pages: they enabled animations, sophisticated image maps and client side forms processing. However, the downside was that they provided means whereby clever Java programmers could compromise the security of a client running an applet. Before describing this it is worth saying that many of the initial security problems associated with Java were eradicated quickly by means of software modifications from Sun Microsystems.

There were a number of initial problems with Java that came to the attention of researchers early in its history:

Later in this chapter, I describe methods based on cryptography which have reduced the risks associated with both Java and Active X

- Applets could be used for denial of service attacks with certain browsers.

- One browser was vulnerable to applets writing data to the system files used in Windows 95.

- An applet has been written which would automatically reboot Windows 95.

- On one version of the Netscape Navigator browser an applet can capture a Web page which acts as a form, read some data entered by the user and then send that data to a remote server.

- With some versions of the Netscape Navigator and Internet Explorer applets can capture the IP addresses of computers in a closed network.

Many of the initial problems with Java have been ironed out; however, the moral here is that in its initial stages any new technology will contain flaws which could seriously compromise security.

3.9.2 Active X

This is a technology from the Microsoft Corporation which is similar to applets. Because Active X, like Java applets, is an executable content technology which is embedded within a Web page it suffers from many of the same problems that have afflicted applets. For example, in January 1996 two German hackers demonstrated that they were able to develop an Active X component which was able to take funds from one bank account and place them in another account.

Browser insecurity

New technologies are not just susceptible to security flaws. There is a history of browsers from different companies having problems. In 1996 a small company called *InfoSpace* developed a program for search engines which were the default engines for the Internet Explorer 3 browser. It was written in such a way that anyone who uses it opens their computer to the possibility of malicious code being easily downloaded. The program bypasses a number of the security controls which were aimed at preventing illegal software entering a computer.

---

4 ▶ Cryptography and its products

In this section the main technology for security, cryptography, is described and a number of technologies outlined. Marginal notes will draw your attention to the threats and requirements for secure e-commerce detailed at the beginning of Section 3.

4.1 The basis of cryptography

The previous section looked at a number of miscellaneous technologies and techniques which can be used to secure a network. This section looks at core technology which has given rise to a large number of products which can greatly enhance the security of a network. The technology is **cryptography**.

The term 'cryptography' refers to a collection of techniques which are used to ensure that data cannot be read by anyone who is not a party to its creation or dissemination. It involves transforming a collection of data (often known as the **plain text**) into a scrambled form known as the **cipher text**. For example, scrambling the letters of the message 'I am here' so that it reads 'heIm a er' is an example of cryptography in action – albeit a very simple and easily cracked application.

ROT13

One very simple cryptographic transformation is ROT13. This involves taking an alphabetic message and replacing each character in the message with its equivalent character 13 positions along in the alphabet. If the letter lies in the lower half of the alphabet then it is replaced by its equivalent in the top half. This technique, while easily crackable, is used in newsgroups when submitting postings which, for example, the poster did not want children to read.

History of cryptography

Early cryptographic schemes used two forms of transformation on a plain text: **substitution** and **transformation**. The former involves individual chunks of a message being replaced by other data, while the latter involves the elements of a message being scrambled about. In the twentieth century a number of mechanical devices were developed which carried out substitution; probably the most infamous of these was the Enigma typewriter device which was used by German forces in the Second World War to send secret messages to forces in the field. It was cracked by the Allies, yet the German forces remained unaware that their most precious secrets had been decrypted. The methods employed by modern cryptographic technology rely on both transposition and substitution.

Modern cryptography relies on immensely complex, validated algorithms to transform a plain text into a cipher text, the transformation being known as **encryption**. The algorithm that is used will vary its action according to a **key**. This is a set of characters which change the action of the algorithm. A very simple, easily crackable, example of this is an algorithm which will replace every character in a plain text by its ASCII equivalent n positions ahead of it in a table of ASCII codes, where the algorithm is varied by providing it with different values of n. In this case n is the key – albeit a trivial one.

When the cipher text that has been produced by encryption is received, the recipient uses the algorithm and the key to unscramble the message. This is a process known as **decryption**. This is shown in Figure 11.1.

The last 20 years have seen a huge increase in the development and utilisation of cryptography. Before the 1970s the technology was associated with military

Figure 11.1
The essence of
cryptography

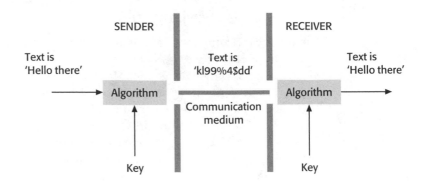

applications; however, the advent of network technology has meant that cryptography is now used much more in civilian applications.

4.2 Symmetric key cryptography

Public key
cryptography is often
known as asymmetric
cryptography

There are two forms of cryptography currently being employed in computer networks: **symmetric key cryptography** and **public key cryptography**. The former has been briefly described already and involves a number of steps:

*Cryptography
resources*

- The sender of secure data encrypts the data using an algorithm which depends for its operation on a key.

- The encrypted data is sent over some insecure medium such as the Internet.

- The key is conveyed to the recipient of the message using some secure method.

- The recipient receives the key and then uses it to decrypt the message that has been received.

Symmetric key encryption is very efficient in terms of resources; however, it suffers from one major problem: the fact that the key has to be conveyed via a secure medium and could potentially be captured and compromise the process of sending secure data. Furthermore it does not distinguish between sender and receiver. There are a number of symmetric key algorithms currently in use:

*Symmetric key
methods*

- *DES.* This is an American government standard that has been in use since 1977. The algorithm used transforms blocks of data rather than individual characters. It employs 56 bit keys and can be configured in a number of modes depending on the level of security that is required. DES is a reasonably strong cryptography scheme; however, a number of security experts have conjectured that it can be broken by anyone with around $750 000 to spend on a special-purpose code cracking computer. DES was decertified in 1998 and was replaced by a scheme known as 3DEA.

Mass distributed computing and the Internet

The cracking of DES

One of the competitions which are regularly posted on the Web is one which challenges users to crack a particular cryptography algorithm in record time. In 1999 a collection of researchers and computer hobbyists deciphered a DES encoded message in 22 hours using over 100 000 computers throughout the world. The processing required to crack the code was distributed over these computers and coordinated by a number of other computers. This form of mass distributed computing is becoming more and more prevalent on the Internet; for example, there is a project which uses slack time on computers to analyse radiation from outer space in order to determine whether it represents intelligent emanations from alien life and there is another project which is attempting to calculate pi to the highest number of decimal places.

Symmetric key encryption guards against integrity and confidentiality threats and helps ensure confidentiality, authentication and integrity requirements

- *Triple DES.* As its name suggests this is a variant of the DES scheme. It involves applying the DES algorithm three times to a plain text. Triple DES has been used by financial institutions such as banks as a more secure alternative to DES.

- *Blowfish.* This is an algorithm which is capable of using a 448 bit key. It is unpatented and is available for anyone to use.

- *IDEA.* This is an algorithm developed in Switzerland and published in 1990. It uses a 128 bit key and is patented.

- *RC2.* This is a cipher which was developed by the American security researcher Ronald Rivest. It transforms blocks of data and relies on a key which can range from 1 to 128 bits.

- *RC4.* This is a cipher which transforms data on a character by character basis. It was originally a trade secret; however, it was published on a Usenet newsgroup in 1994. It can employ a key which ranges between 1 and 2048 bits. The cipher was developed, like RC2, by the American researcher Ronald Rivest.

- *RC5.* This is a cipher which encrypts blocks of text and which was developed in 1994, again by Ronald Rivest.

4.3 Attacks on symmetric key schemes

Attacks on symmetric schemes

There are a number of ways in which a symmetric key scheme can be attacked. The most unsophisticated is a brute force approach in which every possible key is applied until a sensible looking plain text is retrieved. This looks quite a tough prospect. However, if the size of the key is small, then special-purpose computers can be built which can crack a cryptography schema relatively easily. However, when large keys are used, for example those of around 128 bits, this method becomes infeasible.

Cracking 40 bit keys and the cost of cracking adjustment

In 1994 it was possible to develop a computer from $20 000 worth of parts which could process 150 000 keys in a second, and in 1997 a 40 bit code was deciphered in a mere 3.5 hours [1]. The power of computers has increased since then to the point where larger keys can be cracked. This has lead cryptographers to coin the term **cost of cracking adjustment**. This describes the number of bits that need to be added to a key for a cryptographic algorithm in order to keep it as secure as it was in the previous year of its existence.

There are, however, better ways of cracking a symmetric key encryption scheme. One simple way has already been alluded to: stealing the key used for encryption. There are a number of other methods.

The first is a form of attack known as a **known plain text attack**. This technique relies on the intruder having an example of a plain text together with the cipher text that has been produced. From these two it is possible to infer the key used for encryption; once this key has been inferred further messages can be read. Obtaining a copy of a cipher text and the corresponding plain text is often quite easy since many computers send messages for which it is fairly simple to infer at least part of the message, for example e-mails will contain a standard set of headers.

The second form of attack is the **chosen plain text attack**. Here the attacker gets the computer which is carrying out the encryption process to transform specially created blocks of data that have been chosen with the property that the resulting cipher text provides large clues about the key.

The third form of attack is known as a **differential cryptanalysis attack**. Here the attacker generates a number of plain text messages which differ slightly. They then analyse the cipher texts that are produced in order to infer the key that was used.

The final form of attack is known as **differential fault analysis**. This is a hardware attack where an encryption device is subjected to stress such as heat in order to force the device into making mistakes. By closely examining the faults that are induced by this process an attacker can discover both the key and the algorithm used.

4.4 Public key cryptography

4.4.1 The concept

The secret key used to access pornographic sites is often referred to as a pubic key

This is a form of cryptography which does not require the use of the same key to encrypt and decrypt a plain text; rather it uses two keys: a **public key** and a **private key**. One key is held securely, while the other is distributed. They have the two properties:

- Keys must be generated in pairs and it must be computationally infeasible to obtain one key from the other key alone.

- Information that is encrypted by one key can be decrypted only by the other key of the key pair, and information decrypted by one of the keys could only have been encrypted by the other key of the key pair.

It was originally proposed in 1976 by two American researchers, Whitfield Diffie and Martin Hellman, as a means of eliminating the need for a key to be transmitted from one party to another party when using symmetric encryption. The details of the schema are complex and quite mathematical, so all that is worth saying about it is that it was originally based on the fact that finding the prime factors of large integers greater than say 10^{100} is so computationally difficult that it is effectively impossible to do.

The recipient of a message which uses public key encryption uses the two keys in the following way:

- They publish their public key, for example on their Web site.

- Anyone who wants to send a message to the recipient uses the public key to carry out encryption.

- The encrypted text is processed by the recipient who applies a decryption algorithm which employs the secret key.

A number of other alternative hard computational problems have been suggested for public key encryption. However, factoring a large number has stood the test of time and still is the underlying idea

Public key cryptography

In this way there is no need for the recipient to publish the key that is used for decryption. It is worth at this stage comparing the two methods of encryption before looking at some of the technologies and some of the attacks that have been carried out on public key systems.

- When they use sufficiently large keys both methods are secure.

- Public key encryption is easier to implement because there is no need to worry about transmitting keys over some insecure medium.

- The processing power required for symmetric key encryption is much lower than for public key encryption. This means that for the bulk transmission of data symmetric key encryption is normally preferred.

Sarah Flannery

Sarah Flannery and public key encryption

There have been a number of improvements to public key encryption. One of the most remarkable was devised in 1999 by a 16-year-old Irish schoolgirl, Sarah Flannery, who developed a technique which was almost 30 times faster than one of the existing, widely-used public key systems. However, while her achievement can be hailed as a major one, it still does not alter the processing imbalance between public and symmetric key methods.

4.4.2 Technologies

There are a number of technologies and different implementations of public key cryptography.

Smart cards

Smart cards, private keys and public keys

One of the most secure ways of ensuring privacy of a private key is to store it on a smart card. These are credit-card-sized pieces of plastic which can contain both the private and public keys. They can be plugged into a computer, with the private key being sent to the computer carrying out encryption. This means that the private key need never be stored on the computer and anyone who wants to find your private key has to steal the smart card. Even then it might be impossible to use the private key because smart cards can be programmed to demand a PIN number before they are used.

The first is **Diffie–Hellman key exchange**. This is a technique that is used to secure a key used in symmetric key encryption. With this the two parties who are going to exchange some information first negotiate and exchange a private key using public key technology.

RSA is almost certainly the most well-known public key cryptography system. It was developed by three professors at the Massachusetts Institute of Technology: Ronald Rivest, Adi Shamir and Leonard Adelman. RSA can be used for sending data over an insecure line and also used for constructing digital signatures: sequences of characters which provide evidence that the initiator of a transaction is who they claim they are.

The **ElGamel sytem** is a public key system based on the Diffie–Hellman key exchange idea. It can be used for digital signatures.

The **Digital Signature Standard**, often known as DSS, was developed by the American National Security Agency and has been enshrined as a standard by the American National Institute of Standards. In its original form it can only be used for digital signatures; however, it can be modified for normal data transfer. The technique relies on an algorithm known as the **Digital Signature Algorithm**.

Later in this chapter I shall look at digital signatures in more detail

4.4.3 Attacks on public key systems

There are two types of attack on public key systems. The first is the **factoring attack**. You will remember that early in this section I described the fact that popular public key encryption methods rely on the huge difficulty of solving inverse problems such as factoring very large numbers. Anyone who can factor very large numbers efficiently is capable of breaking a public key system based on factoring. This is not an unlikely occurrence: mathematicians working in the area known as number theory have been studying problems involving factoring for a very long time and have been partially successful with numbers which have special properties.

Some popular factoring challenges

The RSA-129 attack

Almost certainly the most famous factoring attack has been that on the RSA-129 number (129 digits). This large number was published in an issue of the American magazine *Popular Science* in 1977. It was eventually factored by a team of researchers coordinated by Arjen Lenstra who was then working at Bellcore.

The other technique used to crack a public key encryption is to find a flaw in the algorithm used. For example, one of the problems first posted as a candidate for a computationally hard problem to base public key encryption techniques on was one known as the knapsack problem. It has been found that it can be quite easy to derive a private key from a public key in a system which is based on this type of problem.

Elliptic curve cryptography

Elliptic curve cryptography

A very promising form of cryptography which threatens to overtake the use of factoring in public key systems is elliptic curve cryptography. It involves solving computationally very hard problems using a family of curves known as elliptic curves. Many public key systems uses RSA; however, the increasing power of computers has meant that bit lengths have had to be increased for this technique, which has led to greater and greater computational demands. Elliptic curve cryptography seems to be as secure as RSA; however, it requires smaller bit lengths and, as a consequence, requires less powerful processing. The Web reference at the side contains links for the mathematically brave reader.

5   Technologies based on encryption

The previous section looked at the mechanics of encryption. The role of this section is to look at how encryption plays a major part in securing a networked system from intrusion.

Message digest functions

5.1 Message digest functions

These are mathematical functions which, when applied to a file, return with some number known as a **digest** that somehow provides some near unique characterisation of the file. An example of an immensely poor message digest function would be one which took every character in the file, added their bit codes together and took the remainder when divided by a very large number. A message digest function should have a number of properties [1]:

■   All the input to a message digest function should influence the output.

■   If a bit in the message digest function's input is modified then every bit in the output has a probability of 0.5 of changing.

■   It should be computationally infeasible to find a file which has the same message digest function value as another file.

Message digest functions guard against integrity threats and help ensure authentication and integrity requirements

There are a number of uses for such functions; we shall be looking at one in particular, the digital signature, later in this chapter. However, one low-tech use is to discover whether any files have been modified in a system, either by an intruder or by a virus. In the early days of viruses you could detect this by means of looking at the size in bytes of the code; however, virus writers have managed to subvert this by deploying viruses which lop off code from existing programs and embed themselves in the code in such a way that the file size is unaffected or by subverting the file reading components of the operating system. One way of detecting file changes is to compare a digest of a file with its previous value; if they are the same then there is a very high probability that the file has not been modified, but if they are not the same then the file has been changed.

There are a number of message digest functions and technologies which have been devised:

- *HMAC*. This is a technique used to provide evidence that a particular message has not been altered. It uses both a message digest function and a private key. A message digest is calculated for the text, it is encrypted and sent with the text. The receiver decrypts the digest, calculates the digest of the text using a message digest function and compares it with the decrypted value; if they are the same then the message has not been tampered with.

- *The MD series*. This is a series of message digest functions developed by Ronald Rivest. They all use a 128 bit digest. They differ with regard to the speed with which they can be calculated and the strength of the digest function: how easy it can be to discover a file which has the same function value as another file.

- *The SHA series*. These are message digest functions developed by the American National Security Administration. They produce 160 bit digests.

There are a number of uses for message digest functions over and above that of checking files for tampering. They are used for **message authentication codes**. In this use a digest is calculated for a message that is sent between two parties and then appended to the end of the message. Each of the parties has knowledge of the message digest function used: the sender uses it to carry out the calculation of the digest while the recipient uses it to calculate the value of the digest from the received message. If the value calculated by the recipient is the same as the appended value then there is a very high probability that the message has not been tampered with during its traversal of the communication medium used.

This technique is used in the Pretty Good Privacy secure e-mail system

Another use for message digest functions is in producing a password from a series of words known as a **passphrase**. Passphrases have a long history in order to remember passwords, for example the password itbil#ptooway can be remembered by the passphrase 'In the beginning I liked hash potatoes, what about you'. Here initial letters and symbols are used to remember a hard-to-crack password. Message digest functions are also used in digital signatures; these are discussed in the next section.

5.2 Digital signatures

A digital signature is some data that uniquely identifies a person or an organisation. Digital signatures rely on message digest functions and public key cryptography. In

Digital signatures guard against authentication and confidentiality threats and help ensure confidentiality, authentication, non-repudiation, access control and integrity requirements

order to describe how they work consider the sending of a message from one agent (A) to another (B) where agent A publishes a public key. The steps below assume that B knows what message digest function is being used. The following steps occur:

■ Agent A calculates a message digest of the message to be sent.

■ The message digest is then encrypted using the private key. This is the digital signature.

■ The message, along with the digital signature, is sent to B.

■ B decrypts the digital signature using the public key to obtain the message digest.

■ B then calculates the message digest of the sent message using the message digest function that A used and compares it with the decrypted digest. If they match then the message has been sent by the owner of the private and public key.

An important point to make is that digital signatures can give irrefutable proof that content has been changed en-route. They ensure integrity but not privacy.

Digital certificates guard against authentication and confidentiality threats and help ensure confidentiality, authentication, non-repudiation and access control

5.3 Digital certificates

One of the problems with public key systems is that while they allow secure communication between individuals they do not easily allow more public communication: that is, there is no guarantee that the person who purports to issue a particular public key is that person.

Exercise 11.1

Examining a digital certificate

The x509.v3 standard

Probably the most popular standard for digital certificates is the x509.v3 standard. This contains all the information that has been detailed above; however, it also defines the ability of digital certificates to contain name/value pairs which help in authentication. For example, a certificate defined by this standard might embed details of which message digest function has been used to create the digital signature of the certificate.

In order to get over this problem **digital certificates** have been developed. A digital certificate is a document which is issued by a trusted third-party organisation such as a national post office which describes a particular user. The certificate will contain data such as the name of the user, a unique serial number and, of course, the public key used by the person who wishes to carry out communications. The certificate will carry a digital signature written by the organisation which issued the certificate. In order to verify the authenticity of a digital signature the recipient of any data will need to have access to the third party's public key. Often these are embedded in packaged software such as Web browsers.

Once a certificate has been established all a client has to do to convince itself that it is interacting with a particular entity such as a company, say via a browser, is to carry out the following processes:

■   Obtain the digital certificate.

■   Check that the signature that is provided by the certification authority is valid using the public key employed by the certification authority; often this will be embedded in the browser.

■   Use the public key specified in the digital certificate to decrypt any data sent by the organisation that is described by the digital certificate. Often this data might be a key used for symmetric encryption.

I shall be looking at SSL in more detail later in the chapter when I consider commercial cryptographic systems

As a practical example of this consider the digital certificate associated with a very popular security technology known as the Secure Sockets Layer (SSL), the details of which are presented later. This technology is used to send encrypted messages between a browser and a server, for example credit card details.

When a browser connects to a Web server which uses SSL the first thing that happens is for the server to send to the client a x509.v3 digital certificate which contains the server's public key. The browser then checks the certificate for integrity, for example checking that it contains the correct signature. If the check is successful the public key embedded in the certificate is then used by the client to decode the initial information that the server sends to establish the dialogue between itself and the browser. A product of this initial information is an agreement to interchange further data, for example financial transactions, using symmetric key encryption and the public key is used to convey all the data required to start up the data interchange process. The reason that SSL does not use public key encryption to transfer data is that the data can be bulky and public key encryption and decryption are very much slower than their symmetric key counterparts.

There are four types of digital certificates that are currently used on the Internet. All conform to the rules of x509.v3.

Digital certificates

■   *Certification authority certificates.* These are used to establish the identity of an authority such as the Canadian Post Office which issues digital certificates.

■   *Server certificates.* These identify a server and prove that a particular server is what it purports to be. Such certificates are used in conjunction with technologies such as SSL.

■   *Personal certificates.* These identify individuals.

■   *Software developer certificates.* These are used to sign software that is sold and distributed.

Commercial cryptography systems

5.4 Cryptographic systems

The aim of this section is to outline the details of some commercial products which employ cryptographic techniques. Some of these products are packages, while others are software entities which provide infrastructural facilities for sending coded data and are often hidden deep in system software. This section does not include details of SSL: the section that follows it treats this technology as a detailed case study.

PGP stands for Pretty Good Privacy

5.4.1 PGP

This is a publicly available system for encrypting files and e-mail messages. It was one of the first commercial products which used public key cryptography. It was developed by Phil Zimmermann while he was at the Massachusetts Institute of Technology. It uses the RSA scheme for the management of keys used in symmetric encryption, the IDEA algorithm for sending data using symmetric encryption and the MD5 scheme for ensuring that messages have not been tampered with.

PGP is available as a standalone mailing system or as file encryption package. The major weakness with the system is the management of public keys: if a public key is compromised then a revocation certificate has to be sent to everybody who is in communication with the person whose keys have been compromised.

In PGP a public key is either advertised on special public key servers or reproduced on a Web page.

5.4.2 PCT

This is a Microsoft product which is very similar to the SSL briefly described earlier in this section and described in more detail later. As SSL gains more and more adherents it is expected that this technology will be phased out.

5.4.3 SHTTP

This is a version of the HTTP protocol which enables secure transactions to be sent over the Web. However, since the browser developers have shown little interest in it, it has virtually died.

5.4.4 SET

This is not the only financial transaction technology based on this idea; there is another called *CyberCash*, details of which can be found in the Web references associated with this section

This is a protocol which is used for sending credit card information over the Internet. It has three components: an electronic wallet which resides on a client computer, an SET server which is the responsibility of some vendor or merchant and a payment server which is resident at the premises of a bank or a credit card company.

The first thing that the user has to do when employing SET is to enter their credit card details into the electronic wallet. This will be stored as an encrypted file on the customer's computer. At the same time the software associated with SET will produce a public and a private key.

When a purchase is made by an SET user the credit card details are encrypted using the private key; they are then sent to the merchant who is selling the goods or services that are to be paid for by the credit card. The merchant's server then attaches a digital signature to the credit card details to establish the identity of the merchant; the resulting transaction is then sent to the bank or credit card company's computer. This computer then validates the card and sends a receipt back to the merchant and to the customer. A major advantage of this technology is that the merchant's staff are not able to discover the details of the credit cards that are used and the bank is not aware of what the customer bought; this cuts down on a large amount of the fraud associated with credit cards.

5.4.5 DNSSEC

This is the Domain Name System Security Standard. It has been designed to prevent attacks such as domain name spoofing. Again this uses public key encryption, where each domain name server is associated with a public key/private key pair. Every domain in the Internet domain system is assigned a public key which is then used by computers connected to the Internet to validate a domain name.

5.4.6 Kerberos

Cerberus was the many-headed dog that guarded Hades and prevented any condemned souls from leaving

This is a network security system which was developed at the Massachusetts Institute of Technology. It uses symmetric key encryption to send data and messages to and from computers connected together in a network which is used for authentication purposes. Each user of Kerberos is assigned a password and this is used to send data to and from a user. There are Kerberos versions of a number of Internet protocols including POP3, Telnet and FTP.

5.5 Key exchange

One use for public key cryptography is in establishing a shared secret such as a key used in symmetric encryption even when there is an observer or an intruder. An example of this is **Diffie–Hellman key exchange**. This is a technique that is used to secure a key used in symmetric key encryption. With this the two parties who are going to exchange some information first negotiate and exchange a symmetric key using public key technology.

6 Techniques and software tools

The previous sections described a number of ways in which the security of a network can be compromised and looked at cryptography. The aim of this section is to look at a number of miscellaneous techniques and tools which can be used to minimise the risk. Before looking at these it is worth saying that much can be done about system security which does not involve high-tech methods and tools. For example, a major problem which I detailed in the previous section was the fact that users often choose passwords which are easy to crack, for example passwords which are their family's names or which are so short they can be cracked by a simple brute force attack. This problem can be partly solved by having passwords dispensed by the system administrator who would choose random sequences of letters and digits which, while being difficult to crack, would also be relatively memorable – passwords such as *Icee6Tepigkun*.

There are a number of built-in logging tools that are, for example, provided by Web server vendors and which analyse operating system log files and server log files. Unfortunately, most practised crackers have worked out the details of such tools and can, without too much difficulty, subvert them so that evidence of intrusions is not written to a log file

6.1 Logging tools

These are software tools which monitor the use of a computer or part of a computer and which log events that occur to a secure file or to some write-only medium such as a CD. Typical events that such tools monitor are a user logging in, transferring a Web page or trying to read a file.

There are a number of secure commercial logging tools which will, for example, check for unusual events such as:

■ A user logging on at an unusual time: for example, a user logging on after midnight when they usually log on during the working day.

■ A user logging on briefly and then logging out and then repeating this process a number of times. The user could be attempting to gather information for an IP spoofing attempt.

■ A user mistyping a password a number of times – certainly more times than would be expected if the user was a poor typist. Often this occurs when someone is trying to guess a password.

A good system administrator will install a third-party logging tool and produce daily reports of its results and should also arrange that immediate exception reporting occurs: that a very serious event such as the modification of a sensitive file such as a password file is immediately reported.

6.2 Virus scanners

These are software tools which look for unusual changes in the files stored in a computer and also look for file characteristics which are associated with known viruses. Many of the tools allow the user to download a database of current virus signatures; often these databases are only a matter of hours out of date so they will catch most viruses.

6.3 Network topology techniques

One major way of guarding against a number of forms of attack is to design the topology of your network in such a way that it is difficult for intrusion to occur. For example, it can be virtually impossible for a sniffer to be placed in a network if it is highly compartmentalised. One of the most effective ways of using network topology is by implementing a **firewall**.

A firewall is an extra layer of protection placed around a network or around a particular application. A firewall placed around a network will usually employ a router which can be programmed to deny access to a network, for example it can be programmed to deny access to any packets of data which have been sent to a particular dedicated port.

Figure 11.2 shows one very popular configuration which is used to protect a Web server and the internal computers connected to it from being compromised; it is

Figure 11.2
A simple firewall

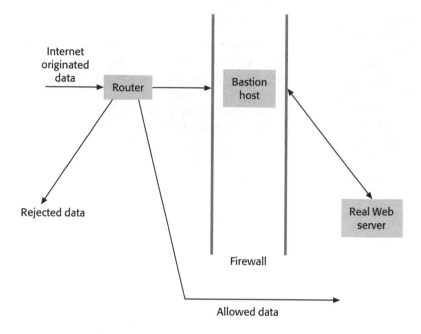

known as a **screened host firewall**. The configuration is intended to protect a Web server which dispenses pages to the public from being compromised and perhaps acting as a starting point for a more serious intrusion which affects other computers in the internal network. The configuration involves a programmable router which is able to monitor, re-route and reject packets of data and a Web server known as a **bastion host** or a **proxy server**. The bastion host acts as a temporary store or 'cache' of pages which have been dispensed by a real Web server which resides within a closed network.

Firewall products

When a packet of data is processed by the firewall router it will determine what to allow through to the internal network that it protects. Often the data allowed through will be a very small subset of the data which could be sent to it: for example, it might only allow through data which represents e-mails. If the router detects data which is intended for the Web server it will forward the data to the bastion host. Any other data is rejected.

When the bastion host receives data which accesses Web services it will satisfy that service. It will first check that the pages required by the request are contained in its cache of pages; if so, then it will send the pages to the computer that requested them. If the pages are not contained in the cache then it will request the real Web server, which resides within the firewall, to send it the pages so that it can satisfy the request.

The use of a bastion host secures Web services because any intruder has to compromise this computer before they can enter the network in which the real server resides. For example, a malicious attack on the bastion host which attempted to delete Web pages would only delete the temporary cached pages.

An even stronger use of a firewall is to employ two layers of protection: a router which is open to the Internet and a further router which guards the internal network.

Figure 11.3
A screened subnet

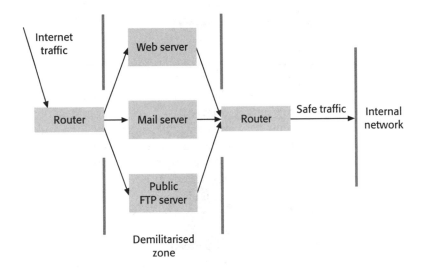

Demilitarised
zone

*Firewalls and
security*

In between these two routers there would be further bastion servers which offer services that outside users may need to access, services such as a mail service or an ftp service which enables customers to download company samples or brochures; again these bastion servers would communicate with the real servers which are located in an internal network. This form of organisation is known as a **screened subnet**; the area in which the public services are located is often known as a **demilitarised zone**. This security configuration is shown in Figure 11.3.

6.4 Security checking software

Already I have discussed a number of software tools and utilities which can be used to probe a network for weaknesses in the context of the dangers they pose to networks; however, in the hands of a skilful security administrator such tools can greatly reduce the probability of a network being compromised by an intruder. By running scanner and password cracker software regularly a security administrator is able to notify potential problems that could occur, associated with (amongst others):

- Denial of service attacks.

- Abuses involving mailing utilities such as *sendmail*.

- Attempts to crash a server by violating the rules of TCP/IP.

- Vulnerabilities associated with the File Transfer Protocol.

- Vulnerabilities associated with any naming services.

- Badly constructed passwords.

- The ability of an intruder to take over the identity of a trusted user such as a system administrator.

7   SSL: a case study

7.1 Functionality

The previous sections have described, in outline, a number of technologies based on cryptography. Nowhere have I described in detail how they work. The aim of this section is to examine in a little more detail one of the most popular – probably *the* most popular – technology that is based on cryptography: Secure Sockets Layer (SSL).

The Secure Sockets Layer

This technology was originally developed by the Netscape Corporation for its browser Netscape Navigator. It works as a layer which lies between protocols such as HTTP and FTP and underlying protocols embedded in the TCP/IP suite. There are a number of functions embedded in SSL:

- *SSL server authentication.* This enables a client to confirm the identity of a server. SSL uses public key cryptography to validate the digital certificate of a server and confirm that it has been issued by a valid certification authority.

Client validation is not commonly used

- *SSL client authentication.* In a similar way that servers are validated, clients are validated: an SSL-enabled server is able to check the digital certificates of clients in order to ensure that they are who they say they are before sending sensitive data.

- *SSL encryption.* SSL uses a variety of symmetric encryption techniques to send data to and from servers and clients. The mechanisms for doing this are detailed below.

SSL supports two sub-protocols. The first is the **SSL record protocol**. This is used for the transmission of bulk data. The second protocol is the **SSL handshake protocol**; this is used to establish the ciphers and algorithms which are to be used for data transfer. It is a form of handshake protocol which initialises the two computers involved in an SSL transfer to coordinate with each other.

7.2 Supported cipher suites

Until 2000 the American government prohibited the export of strong cryptographic software, thus preventing many other countries from using SSL in its strongest form. In 2000 this restriction was virtually lifted. At the time of writing, the effect of this on cryptographic technology has not been fully felt; however, by the time that you read this book it should be easy to buy strong encryption tools

The SSL protocol supports a number of ciphers and cryptographic algorithms; which ones it supports depend on a number of factors such as what version of SSL is being employed, the security policy of at least one of the organisations involved in the data transfer and the current American government restrictions on the use and deployment of cryptography technology.

There is a wide variety of technologies used by SSL. It includes: the DES (Data Encryption Standard); the DSA (Digital Signature Algorithm); KEA, an algorithm used by the American government for exchanging keys; the MD5 message digest algorithm; the RC2 and RC4 encryption methods; the RSA algorithm for public key encryption; the SHA-1 algorithm for constructing message digests; SKIPJACK, a classified symmetric encryption algorithm used by the American government; and Triple DES.

The range of encryption is from the strongest, Triple DES which is supported by the SHA-1 algorithm for message authentication, to the weakest, no encryption with message authentication provided by the MD5 algorithm.

7.3 The transfer process

The process of transferring data from a client such as a Web browser and a server such as a Web server using SSL is a two-stage process. The first stage involves the SSL handshake protocol, as shown in Figure 11.4.

- The client sends the server a number of items of data including the client's SSL version number, the cipher settings for the client and some randomly generated data.

- The server responds with a burst of similar data and also sends its digital certificate; if the interchange of data requires the client to provide a digital certificate then it will ask for this item.

- The client authenticates the server; if this fails the user of the client is informed.

- Using the data that has been generated in the handshake the client creates an item of data known as the **premaster secret**. This is used later in the handshake.

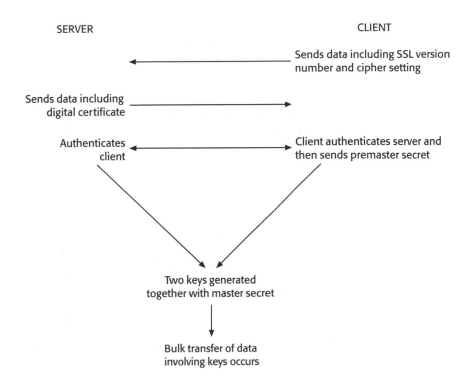

Figure 11.4
The SSL handshake
and bulk transfer

SERVER

CLIENT

Sends data including SSL version number and cipher setting

Sends data including digital certificate

Authenticates client

Client authenticates server and then sends premaster secret

Two keys generated together with master secret

Bulk transfer of data involving keys occurs

- The server authenticates the client. This only happens if the transaction requires both parties to be authenticated. SSL is capable of being used when only the server is authenticated and so this step could be omitted, and most of the time it is.

- If the client and the server have been successfully authenticated then both sides carry out the process of generating another item of data known as the **master secret**; this item is partly generated from the premaster secret. The master secret is a one-time 48 bit quantity that is used to create the keys used in the bulk transfer of data between the client and the server after the handshake has been completed.

- At this point the client and the server generate a pair of keys from the master secret. One key is used for encrypting and decrypting data from the client to the server; the other key is used for encrypting and decrypting data from the server to the client.

The handshake is complete and the client and the server can start exchanging encrypted data employing one of the algorithms which are built into the version of SSL that is used. Part of the handshake involves the parties to the transfer of data deciding on which algorithm to use. Once a session has been completed the connection is severed. If the two parties wish to communicate again then they have to carry out the handshake; each time that the handshake takes place a different pair of encryption keys are generated and a different master secret generated.

7.4 Server authentication

The server authentication alluded to briefly in the previous section is a five-part process. The client first checks whether the server's digital certificate is valid for the date of the transaction: the certificate could have expired. Next the server checks whether the certification authority that issued the digital certificate associated with the server is a trusted authority. Usually the client will have a list of trusted authorities and will consult these in order to carry out this validation.

Man-in-the-middle attacks

SSL is potentially susceptible to an attack known as the man-in-the-middle attack. Here an intruder interposes another computer or program between the client and the server. The rogue computer or program engages in a handshake with the client computer and develops a rogue master secret and hence two rogue session keys. These keys are then used to encrypt and decrypt information which should be travelling from the client to the real server; this information can then be read by an intruder.

The next step is to validate the digital signature of the certificate's issuer. The key which is used for this is found in the details of certificate issuers stored on the client.

If this process succeeds then the client can have a high confidence that the server certificate is valid.

The next step is to check that the domain name in the server's certificate matches the domain name of the server. This is done to ensure that a man-in-the-middle attack has not taken place. Once this step is complete the client can be authorised (this is an optional step).

7.5 Client authentication

If client authentication is required the client sends the server a digital certificate and a signed piece of digital data to identify itself. The digest of the data is then encrypted with the private key which is associated with the public key in the client's digital certificate. This acts as a digital signature. The server then authenticates the client in a number of steps.

The first step is to check that the user's public key validates the signature that has been sent. The next step is to check that today's date lies within the client certificate's time period. The third step is to check that the issuer of the digital certificate is a trusted issuer; in order to do this the server will carry out the same processes that the client carries out when authenticating the server certificate, which includes checking that the certificate issuer's public key validates the issuer's digital signature found on its own digital certificate.

An optional step is to check that the certificate is listed by a computer known as a **directory server**. This directory server keeps track of the resources and users of a distributed system. If the organisation that owns the client has revoked the certificate then the directory server will inform the server which is trying to authenticate the client and the server will not authorise the transaction between the client and itself.

Finally, the server checks that the client is authorised to carry out the transaction that it is attempting to make. If so, the transaction takes place. This transaction uses symmetric key cryptography with parameters such as keys generated by the initial handshake.

This, then, is SSL. Like most practical transmission schemes it uses public key cryptography to establish the cryptographic parameters of the data transfer – the keys used and the algorithms employed – and then employs symmetric key encryption and decryption for the bulk transfer of data.

8   Security facilities in Java

The Java Cryptography Extension

Java was designed with security in mind from its first implementation. The reason behind this was the potential insecurities that were introduced by applets. However, the designers of the language, having targeted Java at the Internet, realised that much stronger facilities than those associated with applets were needed in the language. As a consequence some of the earliest APIs that were released were concerned with security.

8.1 The Java security model

Before looking at the facilities found in the main Java security API it is worth outlining the security facilities of the language itself. Java is based on a **sandbox** model of security, where the sandbox is a restricted environment in which the program resides. A Java program running on a computer can access a number of resources associated with that computer: memory files, the cpu and any other computer connected to it. The sandbox model of security builds into Java a set of facilities which monitor access to these resources. What resources can be accessed is determined by a security policy which can range from the least restrictive (access anything) to the most restrictive (access only to cpu, keyboard, mouse and memory).

In Java there are two types of programs: applets which are programs loaded down from a Web server and applications, normal programs. Applets are potentially hugely damaging to a computer system as they could, in theory, carry out dangerous acts such as deleting files. When Java was announced its opponents often referred to it as the best way of creating viruses that had been developed.

This is not strictly true for applets: in later versions of the language digital signatures can be used to modify this harsh security policy

Applets have a very restrictive security policy in that any action which could cause damage to the client computer or the user is disallowed, for example they cannot delete a file or read the contents of a file on the client. Applications are more flexible in that from Java 1.2 it is possible to run an application within a sandbox whose security policy has been specified by a system administrator or even the user.

8.2 The Java Cryptography Extension

Exercise 11.2

Using the message digest facilities of the JCE

Many of the current Java security facilities are embedded in a collection of classes known as the Java Cryptography Extension (JCE). This section looks at some of the facilities and provides you with enough knowledge of the facilities of the API for you to carry out a programming exercise.

The JCE contains a number of facilities for the implementation of the technologies detailed in the previous sections, they include:

- Coding messages using a number of popular encryption algorithms such as DES.

- Producing message digests from a series of bytes.

- Generating digital signatures using the facilities for message digests.

- Generating keys for a wide variety of cryptographic algorithms.

- Managing a database of keys.

- Processing security certificates.

Many of the methods within the JCE process streams of data or arrays of data and transform them into some encrypted entity by means of a number of engines. For example, Figure 11.5 shows how Java would transform a text into a digital signature.

Figure 11.5
Java and digital
signatures

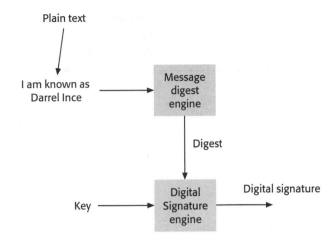

Here the plain text which forms the signature is transformed by a message digest engine to a digest which is then transformed into a digital signature using a private key. When this digital signature is received, together with the original message, the original message is processed by a message digest algorithm and the result compared with the result of decrypting the digital signature using the public key which corresponds to the private key that was used for the original encryption.

9 Payment systems

One area where security technology is extensively used is in payment systems where some Internet user (it could be a company) makes a payment over some transmission medium. Clearly, if data used for payments such as a credit card number was intercepted, then some criminal activity can occur such as buying goods using the number. In this section I shall look briefly at a number of payment systems, both those which occur between an individual retail customer and some business but also those which occur when businesses transfer financial information to other businesses.

9.1 Customer to business payments

9.1.1 Credit card schemes

The main medium for paying for goods on the Internet is the credit card. One of the most popular systems for administering this has been developed by a company known as CyberCash. Its *CashRegister* system works by connecting to the Web sites of any business which buys or licenses the *CashRegister* system. This connection is administered by a plug-in and HTML code which resides on a merchant's Web site.

CashRegister and other systems

When a customer fills in a form on the retailer's Web site buying some product and completes the transaction, the details of the credit card used to make the purchase are sent securely to the *CashRegister* system; it then validates the transaction, carrying out activities such as ensuring that the credit card number is valid, checking whether the credit card has been stolen and ensuring that the purchase limit of the card has not been breached. If the transaction is valid the *CashRegister* system will then debit the customer's account, credit the merchant's account and signal to the merchant that the goods bought can be safely sent to the customer. This is just one example of a credit card payment system; many others exist. Without exception they are heavily secured relying on technologies such as the SSL and firewalls to keep financial transactions secure.

9.1.2 E-wallets

E-wallets

The best place to find an example of this form of one-click processing is the Amazon Web site

An e-wallet is a continuation and progression of the core idea behind credit card schemes such as *CashRegister*. Such wallets keep track of your credit card payments, administer the use of a number of credit cards and automate much of the processing of the buying of goods on the Internet. For example, they remove the need to type in a large amount of detail about your credit card. Most of the developments within this area have been made by credit card companies such as Mastercard and Visa who have licensed the technology to individual banks. As with the credit card schemes outlined above security technology such as the SSL is used extensively.

9.1.3 Digital cash

Digital cash

The idea behind digital cash is simple: a customer buys an amount of credit from a digital cash vendor. The payment is made in a conventional way, even by the process of sending a cheque to the digital cash company; there is even one digital cash scheme *InternetCash* which sells cards at conventional retail outlets such as newsagents. The buyer of the digital cash can then use it at retail sites which accept this cash. A major advantage of this model is that the buyer does not have to own a credit card: payment for the digital cash can be made using other means such as sending a cheque.

9.1.4 Micropayment systems

Micropayment schemes

A large number of products on the Internet are sold for a relatively small amount: items such as fonts, small shareware products and graphics can be sold for a few dollars. Unfortunately monetary transactions below a certain limit are often financially unfeasible: the cost of a credit card transaction to a merchant will usually exceed any profit to be made from the transaction. Micropayment systems overcome this problem. A micropayment system accumulates the small payments that are made by a customer into a monthly or quarterly aggregate and then bills the customer. How the customer is billed depends on the micropayment scheme, for example the scheme could be organised in a similar way to a digital cash system where the user sets up an account which is debited when a purchase is made; other more popular options include adding purchase amounts to the monthly bill of the Internet service provider used by the customer or to a bill produced by one of the utilities companies used by the customer. Micropayments are characterised by the fact that the 'coins' are validated by the merchant without consulting a bank.

Business to business payment systems

9.2 Business to business payments

Customer to business payments are relatively small and involve a small amount of bureaucracy: after checking, an account (the customer's account) is debited and another account (the vendor's account) is credited. Business to business payments in contrast to this are usually large and involve a greater degree of procedural complication in that financial and bureaucratic standards and procedures used by both the buyer and vendor have to be adhered to.

A typical system which automates financial transactions between businesses is *Clareon*. A typical set of processes that occur when a *Clareon* transaction occurs is:

- A buyer and seller agree that a financial transaction will occur, for example the buyer might agree to some financial deal when hiring spare shipping capacity from a road haulier.

- The seller sends an invoice to the buyer over the Internet.

- The buyer sends an authorisation message to the *Clareon* system. This starts the process of financial settlement.

- The *Clareon* system debits and credits any accounts that require adjusting.

- The *Clareon* system sends data to both the buyer and seller in a form which is compatible with their standards and procedures.

The key to the functioning of this part of the Clareon system is its use of XML to store base financial data

Superficially this looks very much like the sort of processes that are involved in a credit card transaction. The main difference lies in the final step where *Clareon* sends data in a form which can be processed by both the seller's and vendor's computer systems. In the diverse world in which we exist this data will vary – often considerably – from vendor to vendor and from seller to seller.

As with any payment system *Clareon* makes extensive use of security technology, for example a digital signature is created when the buyer authorises the payment for the goods or services that have been received.

10   Web sites and security

You will remember that Stallings [2] has categorised a number of threats against Web sites:

Web sites,
webmasters
and security

- *Integrity threats.* These include an intruder modifying stored data such as credit card details or modifying data in transit, for example adding a credit to the intruder's credit card account.

- *Confidentiality threats.* These include reading important stored data such as company secrets or credit card details.

- *Denial of service threats.* These include flooding a Web server with very large numbers of transactions which effectively make the server inoperable.

- *Authentication threats.* Here the intruder impersonates a legitimate user, for example a user in a B2B system who is allowed to make large financial transactions.

Integrity threats result in a loss of important information and can make a Web server vulnerable to further threats, for example a common way of entering a server is to modify the password file so that the intruder is recognised as an authorised user. There are a number of ways of minimising such a threat:

- Use cryptographic methods to make sensitive files unreadable.

- Use message digests to check that sensitive files have not been modified.

- Back up sensitive files regularly.

- Use firewall technology to prevent access to the servers containing the data.

Confidentiality threats are not only concerned with reading stored application data but might also involve the theft of data which describes a network, for example data which describes the security policies adopted by the network administrator. Many of the techniques detailed above such as proxy servers and encryption will greatly minimise confidentiality threats.

Bandwidth theft

Bandwidth theft

This is a pretty invidious form of theft in which a Web site includes a link to an image on another Web site on one of its pages. Often the link is to some excellent graphic which has taken a long time to produce or has cost the webmaster a lot of money to commission. The law about linking is somewhat ambiguous and, strictly, no theft has occurred since all that has happened is that the offending Web site has taken advantage of one of the features of the Web: its interconnectivity. Bandwidth theft is universally detested on the Internet: it is after all a form of copyright violation and can slow down an innocent Web server if the offending server is frequently accessed.

Denial of service attacks are the most difficult to react to. They are disruptive and annoying and can put such a load on a Web server that it becomes inoperable. The main advice that is given to webmasters about this is to ensure that you use the latest version of the TCP/IP and HTTP software on your server; the latest versions of this software usually contain modifications which prevent many denial of service attacks.

However, there is no guarantee that up-to-date software prevents an attack method which has yet to be thought of.

Authentication threats can be countered by the use of digital signatures and heavily monitored password systems. For example, there is an active market in passwords to Web sites which offer some paid service. Such passwords are stolen by means of a technique known as war dialing, a brute force attack where a large number of passwords are tried out in the hope of accidentally discovering one. Two ways of minimising this threat is to install software which monitors users employing incorrect passwords and prevents the login process after a small number of password attempts. The other solution is to monitor the use by users of a particular password, for example if a particular password gives rise to a large number of page downloads or requests for the same service, then it is clear that the password is being used by a number of users who, almost invariably, have been sold the password illegally.

The term 'war dialing' is also used to describe the use of automatic diallers to discover modem banks

11   Further reading

An excellent practical introduction to e-commerce security has been written by Garfinkel and Spafford [1]; the two authors are UNIX experts and their book is driven and informed by their experiences in setting up as Internet service providers in the United States. The collection of articles edited by Denning and Denning [3] is an excellent introduction to topics such as spoofing and viruses; it is not too technocentric although one or two of the chapters are somewhat mathematical.

The definitive guide to Java security has been written by Scott Oaks [4]; it contains all that you want to know about using Java for security purposes and more. Without a doubt the best book on cryptography has been written by Bruce Schneier [5]; it contains descriptions of all the major algorithms together with the source code of many of them expressed in C.

A very good introduction to computer security has been written by Dieter Gollman [6]; this is a solid introduction to computer security which is relatively technology proof. A book [7] which is very detailed and technology driven has been written by an ex-hacker who signs himself 'Anonymous'; an excellent book which should be on every system administrator's book shelf. The book by Ghosh [8] is an excellent alternative to the Garfinkel and Spafford book; it describes many of the technologies described in this book, but in much greater detail.

There is very little written on digital certificates; however the book by Feghhi, Williams and Feghhi [9] is a good introduction. Martin Freiss has written a good introduction [10] to the SATAN tool and how to use it to protect your network. This tool is probably the most comprehensive of its type; no system administrator should be without it.

Finally, Sarah Flannery and her father have written a terrific book which describes her improvement to public key cryptography [11].

References

Internet book links

[1] S. Garfinkel and G. Spafford, *Web Security and Commerce*. Sebastopol, CA: O'Reilly, 1997.

[2] W. Stallings, *Cryptography and Network Security*. Old Tappan, NJ: Prentice Hall, 1999.

[3] D.E. Denning and P.J. Denning, *Internet Besieged*. Reading, MA: ACM Press, 1998.

[4] S. Oaks, *Java Security*. Sebastopol, CA: O'Reilly, 1998.

[5] B. Schneier, *Applied Cryptography*. New York: John Wiley, 1995.

[6] D. Gollman, *Computer Security*. Chichester: John Wiley, 1998.

[7] Anonymous, *Maximum Security: A Hacker's Guide to Protecting Your Internet Site and Network*. Indianapolis, IN: SAMS Publishing, 1998.

[8] A.K. Ghosh, *E-Commerce Security*. New York: John Wiley, 1998.

[9] J. Feghhi, P. Williams and J. Feghhi, *Digital Certificates*. Old Tappan, NJ: Addison-Wesley, 1998.

[10] M. Freiss, *Protecting Networks with SATAN*. Sebastopol, CA: O'Reilly, 1998.

[11] S. Flannery and D. Flannery, *In Code: a Mathematical Journey*. London: Profile Books, 2000.

Concurrency

12

Chapter contents

Concurrency involves the simultaneous execution of a number of sections of code. It is used in order to improve the efficiency of a system. The chapter first looks at how concurrency is implemented in Java using an object known as a thread. Many of the various methods associated with threads are detailed and the creation of threads described. The problem of shared data is detailed and the use of locks described. The second half of the chapter looks at concurrency in client–server systems and provides an introduction to lock management. The chapter concludes with a description of the more important concurrency features found in modern relational database management systems. Concurrency is taught at this point in the book in order to provide a background to Chapter 14 which deals with distributed system design.

Aims

1. To detail how threads can improve the efficiency of a distributed system.
2. To show how threads are implemented in Java.
3. To describe the main thread methods found in Java.
4. To show how the problems that arise from threads accessing shared data are overcome.
5. To detail how concurrency is managed in a client–server system.
6. To describe the role of a lock manager.
7. To outline the more important lock-based facilities found in modern relational database management systems.

Concepts

Circular buffer, Deadlock, Deadly embrace, Locking, Lock manager, Lock promotion, Many-reader single-writer scheme, Pre-emptive scheduling, Read lock, Scheduler, Thread, Wait-for graph, Write lock.

1 Introduction

You might be wondering why I deal with the topic of concurrency in a book on application development. The reason is that the way in which concurrency is designed in a system will have a great effect on its performance. Chapter 14 contains more details

In a distributed system there will be a number of activities being carried out at the same time. For example, a number of clients may be accessing the same server asking for a particular service to be provided. Such concurrent activities provide both opportunities for the developer to optimise a distributed system, but at the same time pose some sophisticated and tricky problems. This chapter looks at the topic of concurrency and how it affects a distributed system. It first looks at concurrency occurring at a single computer and examines the Java facilities for defining and controlling concurrent operations. It then looks at how a distributed system can be viewed as a set of concurrent processes running on a wide variety of computers.

2 Concurrency in Java

Threads in Java

Concurrency in Java is implemented via objects known as threads. A **thread** is an execution of a chunk of code which can be carried out in parallel with the execution of other chunks of code. On a computer with a number of processors the threads can be executed concurrently, with each instruction of each thread being executed at the same time. In a computer, with only one processor a program known as a **scheduler** will determine which thread will be currently executed.

The use of a single processor raises a major question: what is the point of running a number of threads if there is only one processor working away? The answer to this lies in the fact that when a program is executed there will come a time when it has to stop and wait for some event to happen. The duration of this event can be huge compared with the cycle time of the computer and so there may be large periods during which the processor is idle. Typical examples of events which can cause delays are:

- A request for some data from a computer resident on a wide area network such as the Internet.

- A request for some data from a local mass storage device such as a hard disk. Even the retrieval time for such a transfer is very large compared with the cycle time of a modern PC.

- The user of a client pausing to think or read some data on a screen before issuing a request for a service from a server.

During the time that such events hold up a thread another thread can make use of the processor that has been forced to be idle.

I will look at this concept of isolation in Chapter 14 which describes the design of distributed systems

A well-designed distributed system will consist of a large number of threads operating in as much isolation as possible, cooperating to provide a range of services.

2.1 Implementing threads in Java

There are two ways of implementing threads in Java. The first is to inherit from the class `Thread` found in the package `java.lang`. This class has one method `run` which needs to be overridden with the code for a thread. An implementation of a simple thread is shown below:

This is an artificial example as there is strictly no need for the instance variable name. The thread class maintains a name for each thread. I have introduced `name` as an example of an instance variable associated with a thread

```java
class ThreadDemo extends Thread
{

private String name;

public  ThreadDemo(String name)
{
this.name = name;
}

public void run()
{
int count = 100;
while (count>0)
{
    count--;
    . .
    Thread.sleep(100);
    System.out.println("Thread "+name);
    . .
}
}

}
```

The `Thread.sleep` method must be enclosed in a try–catch clause; this is not shown. The reason for this is detailed later

This is a simple class which just has a single constructor and a single instance variable which identifies the thread. The code for the thread can be found within the method `run`. This code is straightforward: it loops a hundred times; each time it moves through the loop it sleeps for 100 milliseconds (the static method `sleep` takes an `int` argument which is the number of milliseconds to sleep) and then displays a message identifying the thread. A thread can then be created by code such as

```java
ThreadDemo th = new ThreadDemo("Thread A");
```

An important point to make is that this thread creation code does not start the thread executing, it just creates the thread. In order to start a thread executing the method `start` is used. Thus the code

```java
ThreadDemo thA = new ThreadDemo("Thread A");
ThreadDemo thB = new ThreadDemo("Thread B");
ThreadDemo thC = new ThreadDemo("Thread C");
```

```
thA.start();
thB.start();
thC.start();
```

Exercise 12.1

Developing and running some threads

will create three threads and put them in a state for running. When the thread is run is a decision made by the scheduler. When they are executing you will see the individual messages from each of the threads displayed a hundred times and interspersed with each other and then the threads will disappear as they will have exited their run method.

This is a simple example of three threads being executed in total isolation from each other. Before I look at some more complicated examples it is worth looking at a second, more popular way of creating threads. This is via an interface called Runnable.

This interface has a single method called run. Creating a thread with the Runnable interface is a two-stage process: first a class which implements Runnable needs to be developed. The second stage is to use a Thread constructor which takes a Runnable object as one of its arguments. In order to see how this is done the code for the class which implements Runnable is shown below. It carries out the same function as the class ThreadDemo described earlier.

```
class ThreadDemoRunnable implements Runnable
{

private String name;

ThreadDemoRunnable(String  name)
{
this.name = name;
}

public void run()
{
int count = 100;
while (count>0)
{
    count--;
    try
    {
        Thread.sleep(100);
        System.out.println("Thread  "+name);
    }
    catch(InterruptedException  ie){
        System.out.println
            ("Problem with thread interrupting");
    };
}
}
}
```

The method sleep could throw an InterruptedException if another thread tried to interrupt it. Because of this the code is enclosed in a try–catch construct. I am assuming this is almost impossible so only display code is placed in the catch section

The `Thread` class has a constructor which takes a `Runnable` object as an argument and creates a thread. Thus the code

```
Thread thA = new Thread
        (new ThreadDemoRunnable("Thread A"));
```

creates a thread `thA` which can then be made ready for running using the method `start`.

There are a number of methods associated with threads. Already you have seen two: the method `start` which makes a thread ready for running and the static method `sleep` which suspends the operation of a thread for a number of milliseconds. Before looking at some of the complications associated with threads it is worth looking at some of the more important thread methods:

- `destroy`. This method destroys a thread.

- `setPriority`. This changes the priority of a thread. The priority of a thread will determine how much of the processor a thread will gain: the higher the priority of a thread the more cycles of a processor the thread will be given by the scheduler. There are three static constants associated with thread priorities: `MAX_PRIORITY` which is the maximum priority for a thread, `MIN_PRIORITY` which is the minimum priority and `NORM_PRIORITY` which is the normal priority of a thread, the one that it is given when it is created.

- `getName`. This returns a string which is the name of the thread. The name of a thread can be given when it is created as some of its constructors have a string argument which represents the name of the thread.

- `setName`. This method gives a thread a name. The name is the single string argument of the method.

These, then, are some of the methods which can be used to manipulate threads. There are a number of other methods which are concerned with solving some of the problems associated with threads; however, before dealing with them it is worth looking at a major problem that occurs with threads.

setName and getName will access an instance variable of a thread which provides an identification of the thread. You will remember that when I introduced the ThreadDemo class I mentioned the existence of this variable

Exercise 12.2

Changing the priority of threads

Thread scheduling

This is a difficult topic within Java since the Java specification does not force implementations of the Java thread model to implement scheduling in a predefined manner. As a result the programmer cannot guarantee the order in which threads are executed for different platforms; the consequence is that it is highly dangerous to make any assumption in your programs about thread execution sequences.

3 Threads and shared objects

3.1 Locking

Consider the class IntTest shown below:

```
class IntTest
{
private int value;
public IntTest(int value)
{
this.value = value;
}
public void increment()
{
value++;
}

public void decrement()
{
value--;
}

}
```

The class just has one instance variable which is an int and two methods, one of which increments the instance variable by one and one which decrements it by one.

Now assume that a program generates an IntTest object which is accessed by two threads (thread1, thread2) which call increment and decrement and that the following sequence of actions takes place:

thread1 increments the IntTest object

thread2 decrements the IntTest object

If this sequence of actions was repeatedly executed – say in a loop – then you might think that the value of the IntTest object remained unchanged. Unfortunately, this is not true. Depending on the operating system and the number of times the sequence of actions was carried out the value of the object will have drifted from its original value. Why is this?

The reason is that both threads will have unfettered access to the object. In order to see why this gives rise to erroneous values it is worth working our way through some executions of the threads.

First, thread1 starts executing and uses the increment method. The thread takes a local copy of the int value in order to increment it; let us assume that this value is 10. However, before this thread has completed its action it may have been suspended; this

The problem that is
discussed here is
known as interference

can happen when the operating system in which the thread is contained uses what is
known as **a pre-emptive scheduling** strategy where executing threads are suspended
when it is deemed that they have had a big enough share of the processor. When
thread1 is suspended thread2 starts executing and starts to decrement the value of
the int instance variable. To do this it takes a local copy of this variable (value 10)
and decrements it to 9 copying back the value that has been formed, the assumption
here is that it is allowed to complete the execution of the decrement method. Let us
assume again that this thread now finds itself in a suspended state and thread1
restarts executing; it finishes executing when it has processed a local copy of the int (the
value 10). This local copy is incremented and the resulting value of 11 is copied into
the int instance variable within the IntTest object. This means that an erroneous
value of 11 has been created when the object should have remained at the same value.

This can be a huge problem for many applications, for example think of what the
implications would be if the object that was being accessed were a bank account and
the methods increment and decrement credited or debited the account.

Watch out for the fact
that synchronised is
spelt with a 'z'

What is required is some means whereby a thread can access an object and not be
interrupted in the middle of its processing. In Java one way of doing this is to preface a
method with the keyword synchronized, for example as in

```
class  IntTest
{

private int value;

public  IntTest(int  value)
{
this.value - value;
}

public  synchronized  void  increment()
{
value++;
}

public  synchronized  void  decrement()
{
value--;
}

}
```

When a method is prefaced with this keyword it means that only one thread is allowed
to execute at a time to access an object defined by the class. For example, only one
IntTest object can be accessed at a time. This process, known as **locking**, prevents
any other synchronised method within a class from executing while one of the
synchronised methods is executing. Each object is associated with a lock which is set
when a synchronised method is started; every time another synchronised method
wants to start it examines whether the lock is on: if it is not, then the method can be
executed: if it is then the method waits until the lock has been released.

I will look at this issue
in Chapter 14 which
describes the design of
distributed systems

Exercise 12.3

Developing a
simple threaded
server

The use of locks is very effective; however, it does affect the run time: in a system where there are threads contending for resources and being queued waiting for a resource to be unlocked, the queued threads will be unable to proceed, thus slowing the system down. A better, more efficient method is described later. The major reason for describing locks in this chapter is the large effect that a poor locking strategy can have on the performance of a distributed system.

3.2 Using `wait` and `notify`

There are two important methods which I have not yet dealt with. Both these methods deal with synchronised access to a shared resource such as the `IntTest` object described in the previous section. In order to introduce them I shall look at a common piece of system software used in a distributed system: a **circular buffer**.

A circular buffer is a linear collection of objects to which items are added at their end and removed from the front. As objects are added and items are removed the front and the back of the buffer start creeping towards the end of the array usually used to implement the buffer. Eventually the end of the buffer is reached and the next item to be added is placed at the beginning of the array.

The requirements for such a buffer are:

■   When the buffer is full no items are added to it.

■   When the buffer is empty no items are removed from it.

■   When the buffer is partially full items can be both added and removed from it.

An implementation of a circular buffer is shown below:

The buffer contains
`int` values; if this was
industrial code then it
would contain
`Object` objects in
order to make it general

```
class CircBuffer {
private int front, end, noInBuffer, bufferLength;
private int [] buffer;

CircBuffer(int  length){
buffer = new int [length];
front = 0;
bufferLength  = length;
end = -1;
noInBuffer = 0;
}

CircBuffer(){
this(100);
}

public synchronized void addItemToBuffer(int i)
{
while (noInBuffer == bufferLength)
```

```
        try
        {
            Thread.sleep(20);
        }
        catch (InterruptedException  e){};
    if (end == bufferLength-1)
        end = 0;
    else
        end++;
    buffer[end] = i;
    noInBuffer++;
    }

    public synchronized int removeItemFromBuffer()
    {
    int value;
    while (noInBuffer == 0)
        try
        {
            Thread.sleep(20);
        }
        catch (InterruptedException  e){};
    value = buffer[front];
    if (front == bufferLength-1)
        front = 0;
    else
        front++;
    noInBuffer--;
    return value;
    }

    public int noInBuffer(){
    return noInBuffer;
    }
    }
```

The implementation consists of four instance variables:

- front indexes the front of the buffer; as items are removed it will start moving towards the end of the buffer and eventually start again with the value 0.

- end indexes the end of the buffer; as items are added it will start moving towards the end of the buffer and when it reaches the end it will be reset to zero.

- noInBuffer holds the number of items in the buffer.

- bufferLength contains the length of the buffer in terms of the maximum number of items that the buffer can contain.

There are also a number of constructors and methods. The two most important methods are `addItemToBuffer` and `removeItemFromBuffer`. The former adds an item to the buffer, while the latter removes one. Both these methods access a shared resource and so are synchronised; this means that access to any `CircBuffer` objects by threads is rationed.

Both the methods work in the same way. They wait in a loop until an event occurs which allows them to carry out their processing. For example, the method `addItemToBuffer` waits until there is a spare place in the buffer to add an object. Until that happens it repeatedly sleeps for 20 milliseconds. Similarly, the method `removeItemFromBuffer` will wait for the buffer to become non-empty.

The implementation suffers from a problem – a major one. In order to illustrate the problem consider what happens when the buffer is empty and a thread executes the method `removeItemFromBuffer`. The method will go into a loop repeatedly sleeping until the method `addItemToBuffer` is executed by another thread. Unfortunately, this will never happen: the method `removeItemFromBuffer` is synchronised and is currently being executed and no other synchronised method can be executed. This will result in the system hanging and being unable to proceed. What is required is some mechanism for the thread that is waiting for data to signal all the other threads that it will not be proceeding any further and allowing them to access the buffer.

The methods `notify` and `wait`, inherited from `Object`, carry out this process. When a thread executes a `wait` method what will happen is that the thread is deactivated and placed on a queue of threads waiting to execute. This allows any other thread to execute any synchronised method. The `wait` method has an analogue in the `notify` method. When this method is executed by a thread it tells the part of the Java run-time system dealing with threads that a thread being queued for access to the object can be activated and executed.

The code below shows the use of `notify` and `wait` in the code previously presented.

The choice of sleep time depends on how frequently operations such as `removeItem FromBuffer` are executed

```
class CircBuffer {
private int front, end, noInBuffer, bufferLength;
private int [] buffer;

CircBuffer(int  length){
buffer = new int [length];
front = 0;
bufferLength = length;
end = -1;
noInBuffer = 0;
}

CircBuffer(){
this(100);
}

public synchronized void addItemToBuffer(int i){
while (noInBuffer == bufferLength)
```

```
        try
        {
            wait();
        }
        catch (InterruptedException e){};
    if (end == bufferLength-1)
        end = 0;
    else
        end++;
    buffer[end] = i;
    noInBuffer++;
    notify();
    }

    public synchronized int removeItemFromBuffer(){
    int value;
    while (noInBuffer == 0)
        try
        {
            wait();
        }
        catch (InterruptedException e){};
    value = buffer[front];
    if (front == bufferLength-1)
        front = 0;
    else
        front++;
    noInBuffer--;
    notify();
    return value;
    }

    public int noInBuffer(){
    return noInBuffer;
    }
    }
```

Note that the wait method throws an Interrupted Exception which needs to be caught; in the artificial world of this example I have done nothing if this event occurs

As an addItemToBuffer or removeItemFromBuffer method is initially executed it checks whether it can proceed; if it can, then the code for the method is executed. However, if it cannot the wait method is executed and the thread that called the method is suspended and queued up. When either of the methods terminate they call the notify method; this notifies the run-time system that either an object has been added to the buffer (in the case of addItemToBuffer) or an object has been removed from the buffer (in the case of removeItemFromBuffer). This means that threads being queued up on the CircBuffer object can be given a chance to execute. The scheduler will then execute a thread which could very well be one of the threads

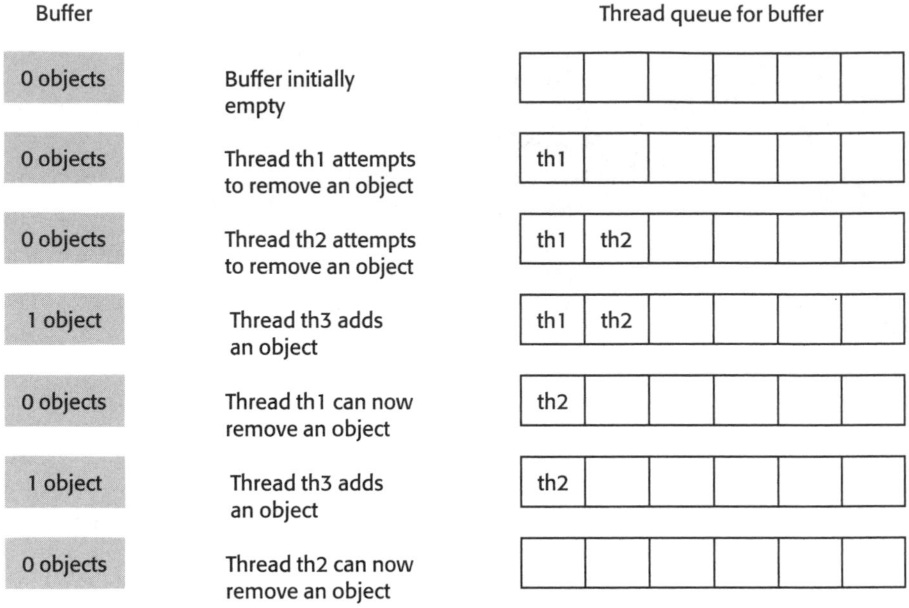

Figure 12.1
A thread queue and a circular buffer

Buffer		Thread queue for buffer

Buffer		
0 objects	Buffer initially empty	
0 objects	Thread th1 attempts to remove an object	th1
0 objects	Thread th2 attempts to remove an object	th1 th2
1 object	Thread th3 adds an object	th1 th2
0 objects	Thread th1 can now remove an object	th2
1 object	Thread th3 adds an object	th2
0 objects	Thread th2 can now remove an object	

queued up waiting to be executed, unless of course another thread has managed to gain control of the processor.

Figure 12.1 shows a `CircBuffer` object and a snapshot of the queue associated with it after a number of threads have executed the two synchronised methods `addItemToBuffer` and `RemoveItemFromBuffer`. The figure also shows the state of the buffer in terms of the number of objects it contains.

Figure 12.1 shows how threads are queued up and deactivated until another thread signals the fact that the deactivated threads can be activated and executed.

3.3 A threaded server

An example of threading in action is shown below. It describes the implementation of a simple server which implements a naming service that relates the names of employees in a company to their e-mail names. These are stored in a hash table: a Java data structure which allows one collection of data to be associated with another. In the case of the server shown here, the first collection is the name of users and the second collection is their e-mail names. The code for the server is shown below. It first sets up the database, then it sets up a socket on port 3000 and waits for a connection. When a connection comes in it creates a thread to process this connection by creating a `ConnectionThread` object. When the thread has been created, the server returns and keeps looping, waiting for the next connection to come in. In this way the server is functioning efficiently in that if the threads were not being created it would have to wait for the first connection to be processed before dealing with the next connection. If the processing required was lengthy, for example a database access, then there could be a large number of clients queuing up waiting for a service.

```
import java.io.*;
import java.util.Hashtable;
import java.net.*;

public class ThreadedServer {
    public static void main(String[] args){
        int connectionCount=0; //Count of clients
        String lineRead=""; //String read from client
        Thread   connThread=null;
        System.out.println("...Server  starting  up");
        //Set up name database
        Hashtable nameDatabase = new Hashtable();
        nameDatabase.put
            ("Darrel Ince",  "D.C.Ince");
        nameDatabase.put
            ("Robert  Thomas",  "R.Thomas");
        nameDatabase.put
            ("William  Wilson",  "W.Wilson");
        nameDatabase.put
            ("Anne  Dowland",  "A.P.Downland");
        nameDatabase.put
            ("Rowland  Phillips",  "R.Phillips");
        nameDatabase.put("Kirsten  Davis", "K.L.Davis");
        System.out.println("...Name  database  set  up");
        //Establish a Server socket, use a high
        //numbered  non-dedicated  port
        try{
            ServerSocket ss = new ServerSocket(3000);
            //Loop endlessly waiting for client connections
            while(true){
                //Block waiting for a connection
                Socket s = ss.accept();
                //Client has connected in
                connectionCount++;
                System.out.println("...connection"
                                +connectionCount+
                                " established");
                //Create and start connection thread
                connThread = new Thread
                    (new ConnectionThread(s,nameDatabase));
                connThread.start();
            }
        }
        catch(Exception  e)
            {System.out.println
                ("Trouble with a connection "+e);}
    }
}
```

The hash table is used for teaching purposes. Normally a more sophisticated form of storage, such as a relational database, would be used

The server needs to use a `ConnectionThread` object. This requires access to both the hash table containing the names and the socket that has been created and, hence, these are instance variables of the class. The code for this class is shown below:

```java
import  java.io.*;
import  java.net.*;
import  java.util.Hashtable;
public class ConnectionThread implements Runnable{
    private  Socket s;
    private  Hashtable  nameDatabase;

    public   ConnectionThread(
                Socket s, Hashtable nameDatabase) {
        this.s=s;
        this.nameDatabase=nameDatabase;
    }

    public void run(){ //Thread executable code
        Object o;
        String reply;
        PrintWriter  pw;
        BufferedReader  bf;
        InputStream  is;
        OutputStream  os;
        try{
            //Get streams for socket
            is = s.getInputStream();
            os = s.getOutputStream();
            System.out.println("...Streams  etc.  set  up");
            //Set up print writer and buffered reader
            //true below means that the print writer
            //is auto flushed
            pw=new  PrintWriter(os,  true);
            bf=new  BufferedReader(new
                        InputStreamReader(is));
            //Read and process user names until
            //the client informs the server that the
            //service is no longer required
            String lineRead ="";
            while(true){
                lineRead = bf.readLine();
                if(lineRead.equals("Exit"))
                    //Client has terminated
                    break;
                // Look up user in hash table
                o  =  nameDatabase.get(lineRead);
                if(o==null)
                    //User is not in the database
                    reply ="User not known";
```

```
                          else
                             reply = (String)o;
                             //Send reply to client, this is the
                             //email  address
                             pw.println(reply);
                     }
                     //Interaction with client is now complete,
                     //close down  connections
                     pw.close();
                     bf.close();
                     is.close();
                     os.close();
                     System.out.println
                                ("...Streams etc. closed down");
                }catch (Exception e)
                    {System.out.println
                               ("Trouble connecting to client "+e);}

             }

        }
```

What the thread does is to process two types of line of text from the client. The first line contains the string "Exit". This terminates the client's interaction with the server. The other type of line is the name of the user. The server looks up this name in the hash table; if the name is found then the e-mail address is returned, if it is not found then an error message is returned.

It is worth pointing out that the example here is a marginal one for a threaded server application since all it does is to consult an in-memory data structure; a process which is quite fast. However, if the processing was lengthy then the threaded code would come into its own.

4 Client and server locks

In a client–server system a number of clients will often access shared data stored on the server. Usually this data is stored in a relational database system rather than in fast memory. This does not eliminate the need for the form of control which removes the type of problems described in the previous section.

As you will see later in this chapter and in Chapter 14 locking has a major effect on performance. How you design a system in terms of locks can have a major performance impact

4.1 Locking

Normally having a single type of lock on a data item is too restrictive: it leads to a higher performance degradation than necessary. In order to optimise the locking process most server software employ two types of lock: a **read lock** and a **write lock**. The operation of these locks is dependent on the types of operations that transactions

Table 12.1
Operation conflicts
on shared data

Operation1	Operation2	Conflict
Read	Read	No
Write	Read	Yes
Write	Write	Yes

Table 12.2
Locking decisions

Type of lock set	Read lock requested	Write lock requested
None	Allowed	Allowed
Read	Allowed	Wait
Write	Wait	Wait

generate. In this section I shall be assuming that transactions will only generate read or write operations within their transactions. Table 12.1, taken from [1], shows the basis for making locking decisions in a client–server system. It shows that two transactions can simultaneously read a common data item and shows that a read by one transaction and a write by another transaction are in conflict because the effect of a read and write operation depends on the order that they are executed.

Looking at Table 12.1 it is clear that in order to minimise the holding of locks a suitable concurrency control scheme should take cognisance of the fact that a large number of transactions could be simultaneously reading data but that only one transaction would be able to write data.

A transaction is a set of operations which affect some stored data; Chapter 13 discusses the notion of transaction in more detail

Such a scheme implements what is known as the **many reader single writer scheme**. The most popular way of implementing this is via two types of lock: a read lock and a write lock.

When a transaction reads or writes a data item then it sets either a read or write lock or waits since, if a lock was granted, the data would become incompatible. Table 12.2 taken from [1] shows the lock decisions that are made when transactions request either read or write locks.

The process of monitoring transactions and ensuring data integrity is usually carried out using a scheme known as **strict two-phase locking**. The steps in this scheme are detailed below:

■   If an operation within a transaction accesses a data item and the item has not been locked then the item is locked and the operation proceeds; when a transaction accesses a data item and there is a conflicting lock, for example a write lock, then the transaction which contains the operation must wait.

■   If the operation accesses a data item which has a non-conflicting lock, for example the lock is a read lock and the operation is just going to retrieve the data, then the lock is shared and the transaction containing the operation proceeds.

- If the data item has been locked in the same transaction as the one containing the operation the lock can be promoted and the transaction proceeds. **Promotion** refers to the process of making a lock stronger, effectively promoting a read lock to a write lock. The rule for whether the lock is promoted depends on whether there are other transactions sharing the read lock. If there are none then the lock is promoted to a write lock; however, if there is at least one then the transaction is delayed until all the read locks have been released.

- When a transaction commits or aborts all the locks created by the transaction are released.

The process of locking and unlocking is carried out by a piece of software known as a **lock manager**. Such a program will maintain a table which contains an entry for the data items that are held at a server to which shared access is allowed. Each entry will contain data such as some form of identification of the transactions which created a lock, an identity for the data item which allows software at the server to access it and some description of the type of locks held for the data item. The lock manager will provide two methods, lock and unlock. The lock method will usually have three arguments: the name of the transaction asking for the lock, the data item that is to be locked and the type of lock requested. The unlock method will usually just have one argument: the name of the transaction that is requesting that lock to be relinquished.

4.2 Deadlock

The term *graph* is a mathematical one; it has nothing to do with graphs of data. Don't worry about the terminology; as long as you understand the idea behind the diagrams presented then you will be able to follow this subsection

One of the major problems that afflict concurrent systems is that of **deadlock**. This occurs when there is a contention between two transactions for two items of data. As an example of this consider a transaction (T_1) which requires access to an item of data (d_1), but which has already issued a write lock to an item of data (d_2). Also assume that another transaction (T_2) which currently has locked d_1 executes code which tries to access the item of data d_2. T_1 will be unable to proceed because T_2 has locked d_1, while T_2 will be unable to proceed because it requires d_2 which T_1 has locked. The two transactions are in a state of limbo waiting for each of them to proceed. This situation is also known as the **deadly embrace**. Deadlock occurs in all distributed systems where there is shared access; however, in those systems where there are a number of clients which hold data for a long time (the typical interactive system) it is a major occurrence. There are a number of ways of overcoming deadlock. This section will describe two.

4.2.1 Using a wait-for graph

A **wait-for graph** is a directed graph which shows the relationships between transactions and data. Figure 12.2 shows part of a very simple wait-for graph with data access omitted.

Here transactions are denoted by rectangular boxes labelled with the name of a transaction; the fact that a transaction is waiting for another transaction is indicated

Figure 12.2
An example of a
wait-for graph

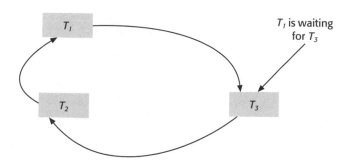

*T₁ is waiting
for T₃*

by an arrowed line from the transaction that is waiting to the transaction it is waiting
for. The wait normally occurs because the second transaction has a lock on a resource
that the first transaction wants to process.

Deadlock occurs when there is a path from a transaction which traverses other
transactions and ends up back at the first transaction. In Figure 12.2 there is a
deadlock since transaction T_1 is waiting for transaction T_3 which is waiting for
transaction T_2 which, in turn, is waiting for transaction T_1.

A wait-for graph will be built up by the lock manager every time a transaction asks
for a lock and will be reduced whenever a lock is released. Each time that a lock is
requested the lock manager will examine the graph to see whether a cycle is about to
be created. If so, then it will take action to ensure that a cycle does not occur, for
example by aborting another transaction in the loop.

There are two aspects to lock management based on a wait-for graph. First, there is
the detection of cycles and, second, there is the decision as to which lock to break when
a cycle is detected.

Detecting a cycle in a graph is a well-known problem and there are a number of
algorithms which are available for doing this. The second aspect is a little more tricky
and is based on factors such as how long a particular transaction has been waiting to
complete and how many cycles a particular transaction is involved in. The detailed
criteria for ensuring a cycle is not created are outside the scope of this book.

*In graph theory
such a path is known
as a cycle*

4.2.2 Using timeouts

The vast majority of database servers use timeouts to eliminate deadlock. Each lock
that is created is given a time period during which it can exist without being removed.
After this time if another transaction wants to use the data that is locked then the
transaction that holds the lock is aborted and the new transaction locks the data and
is allowed to access it.

Using timeouts is a rough and ready solution compared with processing a wait-for
graph. It suffers from a number of problems. The first is that transactions can often
be aborted even if they are not deadlocked. A second problem is that long-running
transactions can be penalised too heavily.

*In the commercial
database literature you
will often see a read
lock referred to as a
shared lock and a write
lock referred to as an
exclusive lock*

5   Locking and database servers

Most database systems obtain a read lock when they read data from a table and a write lock when they write to a table. Unfortunately the developer is unable to directly influence the locking strategy used for a particular database. It is managed by the database management system based on the following factors:

A dirty read is where a transaction can read data which has been updated but not yet committed

- The lock size chosen for the tables that make up the database – whether the lock is, for example, on a page, row or on a whole table.

- What sort of access is allowed, for example whether a dirty read is allowed on a table.

- The particular SQL statements involved.

- The number of items expected to be locked for a particular transaction.

- What mechanism is used to carry out an operation, for example whether an index is to be used.

Each database system will impose a locking strategy in its own way so the only thing to say in a technology-independent book such as this one is: experiment with a database management system in order to determine an optimal design of the databases that make up an application in order to minimise wasted locking time.

Most database management systems allow a number of lock levels. These include:

- Row locking, where a row of a relational table is locked.

- Page locking, where a page of file storage containing part of a table or table index is locked.

- Table locking, where a whole table is locked.

- Database locking, where the whole of a database (every table) is locked.

Most database products implement most or all of the above levels with row, page and table locking being the most common.

Most relational database systems handle deadlock via continual lock monitoring rather than preventing it via consulting a wait-for graph. The vast majority do this by periodically examining locks which have been in existence for some time and aborting the transactions that own these locks. A good database management system will allow the system administrator to set the time gap between these lock examinations.

Many database management systems also allow some form of data integrity which would have an effect on the locking strategy used and hence can reduce run time. The four main levels are:

Chapter 13 contains material on topics such as dirty reads

- *Dirty read*, where applications may read data which has been updated but has not yet been committed to a database.

- *Committed read*, where applications may not read dirty data.

- *Cursor stability*, where a row being read by a transaction is not allowed to be changed by another transaction.

- *Repeatable read*, where all data items read are locked until a transaction reaches a commit point.

6 Further reading

Almost certainly the best book on the internals of distributed systems has been written by Colouris, Dollimore and Kindberg [1], for example it describes other concurrency control management mechanisms over and above the locking scheme detailed here. However, it is definitely a book which looks under the bonnet of a distributed system.

Doug Lea has published a concurrency book [2] which relies heavily on the idea of a pattern. Opinions are divided on this book; many readers new to concurrency find it immensely difficult while experienced concurrent programmers elevate it to almost biblical status. If you want a theoretical introduction to concurrency which also delves into programming then I would recommend Magee and Kramer's book [3]; it is based on Java and the modelling notation UML. It contains a lot more detail than this chapter.

References

Internet book links

[1] G. Coulouris, J. Dollimore and T. Kindberg, *Distributed Systems Concepts and Design*. Harlow: Addison-Wesley, 2001.

[2] D. Lea, *Concurrent Programming in Java: Design Principles and Patterns*. Old Tappan, NJ: Addison-Wesley, 1996.

[3] J. Magee and J. Kramer, *Concurrency: State Models and Java Programs*. Chichester: John Wiley, 1999.

Transactions

13

Chapter contents

A transaction is set of operations which result in the state of a distributed system being accessed and often modified. The key idea behind a transaction is that all the operations that make up a transaction either succeed or fail. This chapter looks at the details of a transaction and the properties a transaction should have. The chapter looks at how software such as a transaction manager and a transaction monitor controls transactions and ensures that, for example, a system is not left in an inconsistent state by a series of concurrent transactions. The chapter concludes by looking at one example of a technology used to implement transactional control: Enterprise JavaBeans.

Aims

1. To detail the key ideas behind transactions.
2. To describe the main properties of transactions.
3. To outline how transactions are controlled in a modern distributed system.
4. To describe some of the algorithms used to control transactions.

Concepts

Application server, Atomic transaction, Atomicity, Consistency, Distributed deadlock, Durability, Edge chasing algorithm, Enterprise JavaBeans, Entity bean, Isolation, Lost update problem, One-phase atomic commit protocol, Probe, Serial equivalence, Session bean, TP monitor, Transaction.

1   Introduction

One of the major problems in a distributed system is the fact that servers provide access to shared resources, for example a naming service provides access to a database of names and locations which is accessed concurrently by a number of clients. As you will have seen in Chapter 12 access to shared resources on the same computer creates a number of problems; when the resources are spread around a number of servers which could very well be connected using wide area technology the problems become much more acute. Many e-commerce systems and distributed applications, particularly those associated with B2B applications, are large and complex and involve quite complex transactions. The potential quantity and complexity of the programming that needs to be done in order to overcome these problems can be overwhelming to the normal application programmer. Happily the vast majority of the problems are hidden behind system software. In this chapter I shall look at one example of such software: the Enterprise JavaBeans server and how the programmer interacts with it; however, before doing this it is worth looking at *some* of the problems involved and how they are solved.

Transactions

1.1 Transactions

Servers will execute sequences of operations known as transactions, where a **transaction** is a set of atomic operations which carry out some access to stored data. For example, a typical transaction which processes a database of stock for an online retailer is shown below:

- A customer orders an item.

- The system checks that the item is in stock.

- If the item is in stock then the customer is allocated the item and the stock total for the item is reduced by one.

- If the stock for the item is dangerously low then an order for new stock is placed.

An important property of each of the operations that make up a transaction is that it is **atomic**.

This means that when a client carries out an operation such as updating a database then this operation is free from interference by an operation which belongs to another transaction. In Chapter 12 I showed how, by using locks, this could be achieved.

Transactions can also be atomic. An **atomic transaction** is one which must either be totally carried out or not carried out at all. For example, a series of related credits and debits carried out on a bank account either must have all been carried out or, if some reason for aborting occurs, none of them must be carried out.

The acronym ACID is often given to the properties of a transaction. It stands for Atomicity, Consistency, Isolation and Durability. **Atomicity** means a transaction must be atomic as defined above. **Consistency** means that a transaction must leave stored data in a consistent state, for example the balance of a bank account must reflect the fact that credits have been added and debits subtracted. **Isolation** stands for the fact that a transaction must not be interfered with by other transactions. **Durability** stands for the fact that after a transaction has completed its operations the results are stored in permanent storage – usually some form of disk storage.

1.2 Serial equivalence

A major idea behind the design of transactional servers is that of **serial equivalence**. This arises from the fact that the vast majority of servers are concurrent in order to maximise the use of hardware resources. Serial equivalence, when applied to a transaction, means that when a number of transactions are applied concurrently the effect of these transactions will be the same as if they were applied one after the other. This, in effect, provides a hard requirement on a concurrent server that ensures that effects such as an inconsistent update should not occur. As an example of this consider one problem which occurs within concurrent systems: the **lost update problem**.

Chapter 12 detailed some of the problems associated with concurrency that occur within a single computer

Here a client takes a copy of some shared data and carries out a write operation on it; however, while the copy is being updated another client takes a further copy and then updates the data. The first client writes back the data followed by the second client doing the same. This means that the data written by the first client is lost. However, if the transactions were carried out in a serially equivalent way then the effect would be of the first client carrying out the update followed by the second client carrying out an update.

2   Distributed transactions

A transaction may consist of a number of sub-transactions. For example, a transaction which allocates a product sold to a customer may be structured as three further transactions: a transaction which associates the customer with the product that they have bought, a transaction which updates the stock details for the product and a transaction which creates accounting information such as a credit card debit. Distributed transactions are useful for two reasons [1]:

■ They allow more concurrency into a transaction and hence can potentially make the utilisation of hardware resources more efficient.

■ They allow more flexible policies for aborting a transaction. In a simple transaction if an operation fails then all the operations must be cancelled and the data which is affected rolled back to the state that it was in before the transaction was started. When transactions are organised hierarchically a sub-transaction can be allowed to fail and not affect other sub-transactions which have already been carried out; in such a case the sub-transaction that failed could be started again without any of the previous sub-transactions consuming hardware resources.

Figure 13.1
A distributed
transaction

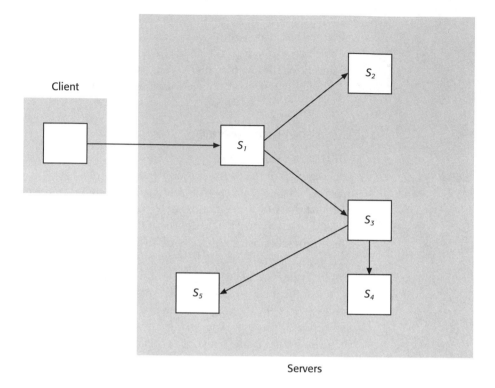

Figure 13.1 shows an example of a distributed transaction which is nested: here the client issues a transaction on server S_1; in order for S_1 to carry out this transaction it initiates transactions on servers S_2 and S_3; S_3 in turn issues a transaction on servers S_4 and S_5.

2.1 Atomic commit protocols

Because transactions should be atomic there is a requirement on a distributed transaction that either *all* the operations associated with it are carried out or *none at all*. In order for this to happen some form of protocol is needed. In order to describe an effective protocol known as a two-phase commit protocol I shall assume that one server is nominated as a coordinator for the distributed transaction; in a practical situation this is usually the first server that takes part in the distributed transaction. In Figure 13.1 this would be server S_1.

One particular strategy for ensuring that all or none of the operations in a distributed transaction either commit or abort is to keep sending a commit or abort message to the servers involved until they all have carried out the commit or the abort. This is known as a **one-phase atomic commit protocol**. Such a protocol is inadequate for practical purposes.

The reason that it is inadequate is that it prevents a server from making a decision unilaterally to abort a transaction, for example when a lock needs to be destroyed because of deadlock. A better solution is to use a two-phase commit atomic protocol. The description of the protocol is detailed below in steps 3.1 to 3.4. The general rule about aborting or committing a transaction is:

1. If the client requests that a transaction is aborted, for example the client is building up an order in a shopping cart and decides not to complete the order, then the coordinator will inform all the servers involved in the transaction that they should abort.

The description here assumes that there are no server failures

2. If one of the servers decides to abort a transaction, for example in order to release a lock, then the coordinator informs all the servers involved in the transaction; they will then all abort.

3. If the client asks for a transaction to be committed then the two-phase commit protocol starts and steps 3.1 to 3.4 are carried out.
   3.1 The coordinator asks each server whether they can commit.
   3.2 Each server decides whether it can commit or not and sends back a reply which indicates the result of its decision. If it cannot commit then it aborts its transaction.
   3.3 If all the servers have voted to commit their transactions then the coordinator informs all the servers that they can commit.
   3.4 If at least one server cannot commit then the coordinator decides to abort the transaction and sends an abort message to all the servers involved.

4. Those servers which have agreed to commit to a transaction wait for the final decision from the coordinator. This will be either a commit instruction or an abort instruction. They will then act on this.

2.2 Two-phase commit for nested transactions

The operation of a two-phase commit protocol for nested transactions is similar to that of simple distributed transactions. The only difference is that a server involved in a sub-transaction makes either a decision to abort or a provisional decision to commit to a transaction. A real commitment is made only when all the sub-transactions belonging to a transaction have had their state examined. They will wait until the whole transaction containing them is committed. Because sub-transactions are themselves transactions they can be aborted without causing their parent transaction to abort. The parent transaction may contain code which handles the abortion of any of its sub-transactions. For example, the transaction might be sent to another server holding replicated data.

Figure 13.2 makes this clear. This shows a transaction which contains three further sub-transactions which, in turn, are split up into further sub-transactions. This figure shows the state of each transaction at a point in time with each transaction being labelled with either *pc* (provisionally committed) or *a* (abort).The rule about committing is that a transaction will only commit if *each* of its sub-transactions which are provisionally committed can then commit.

Figure 13.2
Two-phase commit
for a distributed
nested transaction

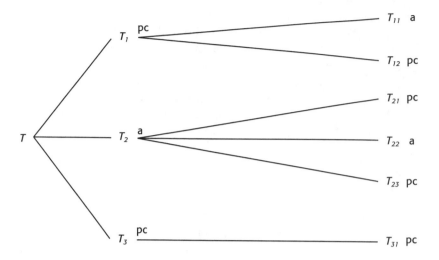

Commitment can occur even if some of the sub-transactions have been aborted. In Figure 13.2 the decision as to whether transaction T can commit is based on whether the transactions T_1 and T_3 can commit. If, for example, T_1 cannot commit then the transaction T will have to abort. This means that all the transactions belonging to transaction T will have to abort. If T_1 and T_3 are able to commit then the transactions T, T_1, T_3, T_{12} and T_{31} are committed and carried out. However, the transactions T_2, T_{21}, T_{22} and T_{23} will be aborted by virtue of the fact that transaction T_2 has aborted.

2.3 Concurrency control

As I have described earlier in Chapter 12 the most popular way of handling concurrency control is via locks. Each server in a distributed system will have a lock manager which will decide whether to grant a lock to a transaction; if it does not then the transaction has to be queued up to wait for the data that it is accessing to become free. When a transaction is committed or aborted it will release a lock. The rules for locking for a nested distributed transaction are as follows [1]:

■ Parent transactions are prevented from running at the same time as their children.

■ Children in a nested transaction will inherit their locks from their parent transaction.

■ If a nested transaction wants a read lock on a shared data item then all the holders of the write lock on the transaction must be its ancestors.

■ If a nested transaction wants a write lock on a shared data item then all the holders of both write and read locks must be its ancestors.

■ When a transaction commits then all its locks are inherited by its parent.

■ When a transaction aborts all its locks are removed.

Figure 13.3
Distributed deadlock

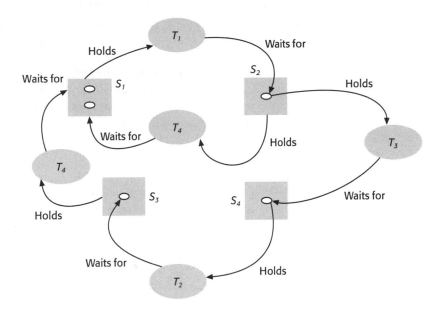

As with deadlocks in a single server there is always the possibility of deadlocks occurring between servers in a distributed system; such a deadlock is known as a **distributed deadlock**. Figure 13.3 shows an example of this. Here transactions labelled from T_1 to T_3 access shared data on servers labelled from S_1 to S_4. The line labelled *Waits for* indicates that a transaction is waiting for a lock to be released, while a line labelled *Holds* indicates that a lock is being held on a particular data item.

It can be seen from Figure 13.3 that there are two cycles indicating deadlock. The first just involves servers S_1 and S_2; the second involves the servers S_1, S_2, S_3 and S_4. In Chapter 12 I detailed two ways in which deadlocks can be eliminated: either by timing out a transaction involved in a deadlock cycle such as transaction T_1 in Figure 13.3, or by ensuring that just before a transaction attempts to access a particular data item a cycle is not created. In that chapter I described a graph known as a wait-for graph which allowed deadlocks to be detected before they occur. There is no theoretical reason why such a graph cannot be constructed for a number of servers participating in distributed transactions with one of the servers taking on the role of checking for cycles in the wait-for graph.

There are two major problems with using a central server. The first is that if only one server were used and that server malfunctioned then the system would be in great trouble and deadlocks would build up to the point where performance would greatly degrade. The second problem is that scalability cannot be achieved: as a system grows, more and more pressure would be built up on the server carrying out deadlock detection to the point where its performance would suffer; this degradation of performance would affect other servers which contain deadlocked transactions and hence the system itself, since the remaining servers would rely on an overloaded server to enable them to remove deadlocks and proceed. You will remember that earlier in

Scaling and distributed systems are discussed in Chapter 2

the book I described one of the major advantages of distributed computing being the fact that a task can be split up to be executed on a number of servers, thus leading to some degree of scalability. It is clearly an advantage for the deadlock detection process to be made distributed and not centralised on one particular server.

One popular way of distributing deadlock detection is for each server to send messages to other servers initiating transactions to indicate that they are waiting for another transaction. Such a distributed algorithm is known as an **edge chasing algorithm**. It has three phases [1]: initiation, detection and resolution.

- When a server detects that a transaction T_1 has started waiting for another transaction T_2 it sends an item of data $T_1 \rightarrow T_2$, known as a **probe**, to the server which contains the data item which is blocking T_2. If there are a number of transactions sharing the lock then the probe is also sent to them.

- When a server receives a probe $T_1 \rightarrow T_2$ it checks whether T_2 is waiting for another transaction, say T_3. If it is then the probe is augmented to be $T_1 \rightarrow T_2 \rightarrow T_3$ and if T_3 is waiting it is forwarded on to the server which holds the data that it is waiting for.

- When a server receives a probe and attempts to augment it, it will check for cycles. For example, if a probe is $T_1 \rightarrow T_2 \rightarrow T_3 \rightarrow T_4$ and an attempt is made to augment the probe with T_2 to form $T_1 \rightarrow T_2 \rightarrow T_3 \rightarrow T_4 \rightarrow T_2$ and form a cycle then a potential deadlock can be detected.

- When the deadlock is detected one of the transactions in the probe is aborted.

The Java Transaction API

Java Transaction API

Sun has developed an API which allows the programmer to create transactions, delineate the boundaries between transactions and control the action of transactions such as carrying out the roll back processing required when a transaction is aborted. For example, in the API there are methods such as `commit` which commits a transaction, `rollback` which returns a system state to the position it was in before a transaction started and `getStatus` which discovers the current status of a transaction. Although this API is normally used by the developers of system software such as transaction monitors it is occasionally used by programmers when they want to get some fine-grained control over transactions.

The only time that a designer needs to worry about what goes on under the bonnet is when designing a distributed system for performance. This is discussed in Chapter 14

This, then, is a very simple explanation of what can be a complicated algorithm. It concludes my description of some of the problems found in a distributed system. The good news is that for most of the time the programmer and designer of distributed systems will not meet these problems: they will be hidden under the bonnet. My aim in the text up to now has been to discuss problems with transactions and their solutions. I have done this in order to provide a background to the remainder of the chapter. The aim of the next section is to look at the technologies involved in transaction processing and, in one case, see how the programmer interacts with it.

3   TP monitors

Transaction processing monitors

A TP (Transaction Processing) monitor is a complex program which manages the execution of a transaction starting with the client executing the transaction; it will normally employ a number of servers and then return any results to the client. TP monitors carry out two important processes: they manage the concurrent execution of the threads and processes that make up a transaction and ensure that the ACID properties detailed earlier in the chapter are enforced; for example, a TP monitor ensures that when a transaction updates a shared item of data when other transactions wish to access the data then the result of the updating is consistent.

Originally TP monitors were associated with large mainframe computers and used in areas such as airline ticketing and banking. However, the technology has migrated to client–server systems.

The effective problem that TP monitors have to solve is that of potentially hundreds or even thousands of users wanting to access shared databases concurrently over a period of time. If these users were all statically allocated enough memory, file connections and threads to carry out their functions then there would be a massive degradation of any system which supported them.

What enables transaction monitors to function efficiently is that the vast majority of users only require the processor for very short bursts in between comparatively long periods of inactivity. For example, the user of a banking system which provides data on standing orders and balances of accounts will spend a long time typing in a query and an equally long time reading it. Even though the users of an interactive system will require a fast response when they have initiated a transaction, there will be a considerable longeur in between; it is this longeur which enables the TP monitor to provide an adequate service to clients.

The term 'long' is comparative: it is long in comparison with processor speeds

A TP monitor carries out a number of functions. The most complex, for example the CICS monitor marketed by IBM, will:

- Initiate and destroy threads to carry out transactional operations. Many transaction monitors will access a pool of threads which have been set up when the monitor was started.

- Manage the resources that are being accessed, for example ensuring that updates are carried out in such a way that the resource does not find itself in an inconsistent state.

- Ensure that if a transaction fails then suitable action is taken; this action can be provided by a programmer as code to be executed. In order to do this most TP monitors will use a two-phase atomic commit protocol.

- Schedule threads so that low-priority transactions, for example batch transactions, are allocated a smaller share of resources than high-priority transactions such as online transactions.

- Enable the processing load on a distributed system to be shared between a number of servers.

■ Enable a distributed system to function – even in the presence of the failure of one or more servers.

In order to carry out the functions detailed above TP monitors will draw upon basic functions provided by the operating system, for example facilities to create and destroy threads.

4   A simple example of a TP monitor

Enterprise JavaBeans

4.1 Introduction

This substantial section concludes the chapter. In it I look at one particular example of TP monitor technology: Enterprise JavaBeans.

> ### Enterprise JavaBeans and JavaBeans
>
> You will often see the term *JavaBeans* used within the Java community. It refers to a technology used to develop reusable components using the Java programming language. Fairly soon after the release of the initial Java system Sun Microsystems released an application programmer interface (API) which enabled developers to produce components – usually visual components – which could, for example, be added to an integrated development environment and be treated in a similar way to normal Java widgets using the visual designer part of the environment. Such components are known as JavaBeans. They only have a small similarity to Enterprise JavaBeans: the fact that they are reusable. As you will see in this section Enterprise JavaBeans can be moved easily from one server to another developed by a different company.

Enterprise JavaBeans technology forms one part of a package of middleware software developed by Java and known as the Java 2 Platform Enterprise Edition. You have already seen some of the components of this package in earlier chapters including Remote Method Invocation, the Java Database Connection (JDBC) and servlets. Other components of the package include JavaMail which enables a programmer to easily connect to some mailing protocol such as POP3, the Java messaging service which enables developers to produce message-oriented middleware and the Java Transaction Service which provides the programmer with facilities to manage transactions.

Chapter 2 described message-oriented middleware

Enterprise JavaBeans is a component technology. The model envisaged is that large-scale components which encompass some business logic are developed by a component manufacturer. For example, one component that might be developed for an airline would be one which allocates staff to flights according to a set of criteria such as the fact that pilots need certain times for resting.

These components, known as business components, will often need heavy transactional services in order to support them. These are provided by means of a TP monitor known as an **application server**. The business components which reside within an application server provide facilities which, for example, ensure that ACID properties are maintained.

When a system is developed the components are purchased and combined together by a systems integrator. During this process the integrator will not worry about transactional issues such as concurrency control but would concentrate on the logic involved in combining the business components.

Once the system has been developed the components and software glue that connects them together are deployed across one or more application servers.

An important point to make about Enterprise JavaBeans is that it recognises no differences between servers: that Enterprise JavaBeans is capable of being deployed to any server that supports the Enterprise JavaBeans technology. This is in contrast to very recent practice where software written for one TP monitor, for example CICS, could not be easily moved to another server.

This model of development recognises six parties to the development process:

- *The bean developer.* This is a company that has expertise in some domain such as ticket reservation or airline staff scheduling. This company would produce the Enterprise JavaBeans that implemented some application-specific logic.

The container provider and the server provider are usually the same company

- *The container provider.* This is a company that supplies low-level software which implements a run-time environment in which Enterprise JavaBeans can execute.

- *The server provider.* A company that sells an Enterprise JavaBeans-compliant server which provides transactional services. At present the container provider and the server provider are the same company.

Often the application assembler, the deployer and the system administrator are associated with some customer company

- *The application assembler.* This is the company that joins Enterprise JavaBeans together.

- *The deployer.* This is some organisation which, given the code for the beans and the glue code, will deploy the code across a number of servers. A number of criteria determine how they are deployed; these include performance, security and reliability.

- *The system administrator.* This is an individual or collection of individuals who are responsible for ensuring the maintenance of the bean, for example they will be responsible for tuning the bean for performance if requirements change such that the original tuning assumptions do not hold.

Enterprise JavaBeans servers

The architecture of the Enterprise JavaBeans technology is shown in Figure 13.4. An Enterprise JavaBeans-compliant server can contain a number of containers which themselves will contain a number of Enterprise JavaBeans. Clients are allowed to access the Enterprise JavaBeans via a number of method invocations found within the API for the Enterprise JavaBeans package.

The details of each proprietary server that supports the standard vary enormously; however, they should provide the following broad functions without any programming being required from developers who wish to make use of the beans:

- *Distributed transaction management.* The server should administer transactions and ensure that phenomena such as phantom updates and inconsistent retrievals do not occur.

Figure 13.4
The Enterprise
JavaBeans
architecture

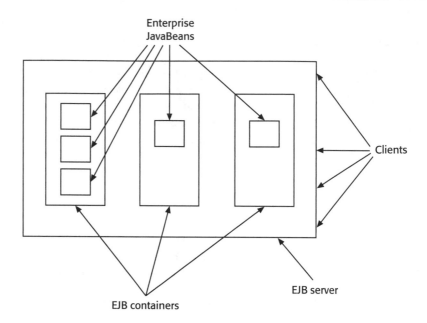

■ *Security.* The server should provide facilities which prevent unauthorised access to Enterprise JavaBeans.

■ *Resource management.* The server should provide resource management, for example it should oversee the creation and deletion of threads and file connections.

■ *Persistence.* Many Enterprise JavaBeans require to be held in some permanent storage medium. An Enterprise JavaBeans server should manage this process ensuring that all changes to transient data intended for permanent storage are carried out.

■ *Multiclient support.* The server should manage the process of clients connecting to Enterprise JavaBeans and mediate their interaction with the beans.

■ *Location transparency.* The server should operate in such a way that clients should have no knowledge of the physical location of Enterprise JavaBeans.

4.2 Entity and session beans

There are two types of Enterprise JavaBeans: **session beans** and **entity beans**.

4.2.1 Entity beans

An entity bean represents some stored entity that is used in an application and which requires permanent storage. Examples include: bank accounts, warehouses, stock containers, flight plans, stock portfolios, insurance policies and hotel bookings.

In the early days of Enterprise JavaBeans the developer had to provide the code which carried out the mapping of a bean to permanent storage. However, with version 1.1 of the Enterprise JavaBeans standard this can be virtually done automatically

An entity bean will normally be mapped into data stored in a relational database system, although it is quite possible for them to be mapped into data in an object-oriented database.

An important point to make about entity beans is that since they model long-lived data an application server will provide facilities whereby, if the server crashes or some other disastrous event occurs, the state of the bean will not be destroyed.

4.2.2 Session beans

A session bean is a bean which performs some business logic; they do not model some stored entity such as a bank account. Typical examples of the type of work that a session bean carries out are:

■   Processing a debit on a bank account.

■   Processing an order for some e-commerce product.

■   Making a trade for some stock or share.

■   Querying a warehouse for information about stock which requires replenishing.

A session bean will only last for the period during which a client interacts with the bean, for example if a client connects to a bean server to retrieve some information then, when the client relinquishes the connection, the bean will be destroyed. Session beans are used by one client at a time: this is in contrast to entity beans, where a number of clients can update and read an entity bean with the disciplined access to the bean being mediated by the server.

There are two types of session bean: stateful session beans and stateless session beans. The former maintain a state across a number of method calls; the best example of such a bean is one which maintains a shopping cart as an e-tailing customer builds up their order. The latter carries out some burst of processing and then finishes; an example of such a bean might be one which carries out some filtering on an image.

Instinet and Enterprise JavaBeans

Instinet and Enterprise JavaBeans

Instinet is a company which provides systems which help financial brokers to carry out their work. In 2000 they developed a real-time broker system which is based on both session and entity JavaBeans. The system is installed at this time of writing at 50 IT departments in major financial institutions in America and Europe. There were a number of reasons why Instinet chose the JavaBeans architecture. First, it provided a component model which encouraged reuse; second, portability – in the future if Instinet wanted to move beans to another server platform this could be done easily using an Enterprise JavaBeans-compliant server; third, speed – Enterprise JavaBeans servers are now quite mature and offer fast transaction times compared with other solutions; and fourth, the architecture and Enterprise JavaBeans server chosen were capable of being scaled up when growth took place.

4.3 Bean classes

In the remainder of the chapter I shall describe the coding that is required for Enterprise JavaBeans. There is much detail that I will omit about actually deploying beans, for example how to package the bean up so that it can be placed in a container. Before looking at detailed code it is worth looking at the classes and interfaces involved.

4.3.1 The remote interface

The vast majority of programmers will not have to do any programming concerned with these classes: they will usually be constructed by bean developers and system administrators

The first is the remote interface. This is an interface which specifies the methods associated with a bean, for example if the bean was a banking account then methods such as `credit` and `debit` would be specified in this interface. This remote interface should extend the class `javax.ejb.EJBObject`.

4.3.2 The home interface

This interface defines the methods for a bean's lifecycle. For example, it specifies methods for creating a bean, destroying a bean and locating a bean in a distributed system.

4.3.3 The bean class

This is the class which implements the methods for the bean. It does not implement the remote interface but must contain methods which actually match the methods defined in that interface and must have some methods corresponding to the methods which are in the home interface. This class and the remote interface are connected together via the server which contains the bean.

4.3.4 The primary key class

This is the class which provides a key into the database that is used for the beans. This is normally a very simple class which contains a small number of instance variables (often one) used to index the bean.

4.4 Developing bean code

In describing some detailed code I shall use an example of a simple entity bean: that of a banking account which contains instance variables that represent the name of the account holder, the unique number which identifies the account and a current balance expressed as an `int` which represents the number of pence (or cents) for which the account is in balance.

The first code is that for the remote interface, which is shown below: it just contains `set` and `get` methods; in a commercial environment there would be many more methods.

```
public interface Account extends javax.ejb.EJBObject

{

public String getHolder() throws RemoteException;
public void setHolder(String holder)
     throws RemoteException;
public int getIdentityNo() throws RemoteException;
public void setIdentityNo(int identityNo)
     throws RemoteException;
public int getBalance() throws RemoteException;
public void setBalance(int balance)
     throws RemoteException;

}
```

The interface extends the class javax.ejb.EJBObject which contains a number of methods which are usually provided by the server, for example it contains a method which checks whether a particular bean is equal to another bean. Often default implementations are used for these. All methods defined in this interface must throw a RemoteException.

The next part of the code is the home interface. The code for this is shown below:

AccKey is defined later in this section; it is an example of the primary key class

```
public interface AccountHome extends javax.ejb.EJBHome
{
public Account create(int no)
     throws CreateException, RemoteException;
public Account findByPrimaryKey(AccKey key)
     throws FinderException, RemoteException;
}
```

Here two methods are defined: a method which creates a bean and a method which finds a bean via its primary key. There is no reason why other methods cannot be defined, for example a method which retrieves an account based on another criterion other than the primary key.

The next piece of code is the bean class. This implements the interface javax.ejb.EntityBean.

```
public class AccountBean implements javax.ejb.EntityBean
{
public String holder;
public int identityNo;
public int balance;

public void ejbCreate(int identityNo)
{
this.identityNo = identityNo;
}
```

```
public void ejBPostCreate(int no)
{
//Do nothing
}

public String getHolder()
{
return holder;
}

public void setHolder(String holder)
{
this.holder = holder;
}

public int getIdentityNo()
{
return identityNo;
}

public void setIdentityNo(int identityNo)
{
this.identityNo = identityNo;
}

public int getBalance()
{
return balance;
}

public void setBalance(int balance)
{
this.balance = balance;
}

public void setEntityContext(EntityContext ec)
{
//Code for setEntityContext
}

public void unsetEntityContext()
{
//Code for unsetEntityContext
}

public ejbActivate()
{
//Code for ejbActivate
}

public ejbPassivate()
{
```

```
//Code  for  ejbPassivate
}

public  void  ejbLoad()
{
//Code  for  ejbLoad
}

public  void  ejbStore()
{
//Code  for  ejbStore
}

public  void  ejbRemove()
{
//Code  for  ejbRemove
}

}
```

The code for the class consists of methods which set and get the instance variables for the bean and also a number of methods which are inherited from `javax.ejb.EntityBean`. A description of some of them follows.

The method `ejbLoad` takes data from some permanent location such as a relational database and updates the bean with the data required, for example in the banking example the bean would be written to by removing data from an `Account` row in an accounts table.

The method `ejbStore` stores data from the bean to a relational database, for example when the bean has been updated by a transaction.

The method `ejbRemove` destroys the permanent data associated with the bean. This method and the previous two methods are concerned with keeping permanent data associated with the bean up to date.

The methods `ejbActivate` and `ejbPassivate` are concerned with moving a bean into and out of memory. When an Enterprise JavaBeans server needs to save resources it can evict the state of an object from a server.

The method `setEntityContext` provides the bean with an interface to the server in which it is held and `unsetEntityContext` is called by the server to notify the bean that it is about to be garbage collected.

Finally the method `ejbCreate` is executed when a new bean is created; the method `ejbPostCreate` is again an initialisation method which is called just prior to any of the normal methods being called, for example the method `getHolder`. It acts as a form of initialisation.

All the methods described above are examples of callback methods: these are methods which are called by the server when an event such as a bean being created occurs.

In the next version of Enterprise JavaBeans XML is used to describe the deployment of a bean

The final code required for the bean is that of the key class; remember that the key uniquely identifies a bean.

```
class AccKey implements Serializable
{
public int bankId;
}
```

As well as the classes described above there are a number of deployment descriptor classes associated with beans. These classes describe how a bean is to be managed at run time. For example, the class `ControlDescriptor` describes how transactions are handled, for example whether the server should handle all the problems associated with accessing shared data.

Normally with commercial Enterprise JavaBeans servers these classes are not programmed but objects based on them are created using a deployment wizard which takes the user through a set of questions and prompts about the run-time behaviour of the bean. When such a wizard concludes its actions a series of deployment classes are produced.

The final stage of developing Enterprise JavaBeans is deploying it in the server. Currently this is usually a straightforward but tedious process in which the classes are packaged into a JAR file and added to the server. At this point programmers are able to access the bean.

A JAR file is the Java version of a zip file

The only remaining code that needs to be examined is that used by a client. This is shown below; note that the imports are not included.

```
class  EJBTestclass
{
public static void main (String[] args)
{
try
{
    Properties  prop  =  System.getProperties();
    Context  ct = new  InitialContext(prop);
    AccountHome  ah  =  (AccountHome)ct.lookup("TheAccounts");
    Account  acc = ah.create(2000);
    acc.setHolder("D.Ince");
    String  holderName  =  acc.getHolder();
    System.out.println
        ("The name of the holder is "+ holderName);
    . . .
}
catch(Exception  e)
    {System.out.println("Problem  with  EJB  access");}
}
}
```

The first two lines interrogate a data structure which keeps details of properties of the system on which the code is executing and produce a `Context` data structure which provides a connection to the Enterprise JavaBeans server. A home object is then created by retrieving the home object identified by the string "TheAccounts". The association between a home object and its string identifier is established within the deployment classes. The code

```
Account acc = ah.create(2000);
acc.setHolder("D.Ince");
```

then creates an account with an account number of 2000 and an account holder name of "D.Ince". The final code just confirms that the Account object has had its holder instance variable set properly.

It is important to point out that for any programmer accessing an object stored on an application server the only code that betrays this fact is a very small amount of code, for example in the code above it is just two lines. It is also worth pointing out that beneath any object that is stored on an application server there is a huge amount of transactional functionality operating which, for example, maintains the ACID properties of the objects stored in the server. This functionality is all but invisible to the ordinary application programmer.

Enterprise JavaBeans programming

5 Further reading

Currently the best book which delves into the innards of distributed systems has been published by Colouris, Dollimore and Kindberg [1]. If you are interested in distributed algorithms then I would recommend Lynch's excellent and comprehensive book on the topic; it is regarded as the bible [2]; a warning, however: it is a long read (over 800 pages) and expensive. Magee and Kramer's book [3] on concurrency contains excellent material on distributed algorithms placed invisibly within a sound theoretical framework. There are a number of books written on Enterprise JavaBeans; all of them are oriented towards the developer of beans rather than the user. In fact there is no reason for writing a book on how to use them since as I have stressed in the previous section the application programmer requires little knowledge. However, if you want a recommendation then the book by Roman [4] is worth looking at.

Internet book links

References

[1] G. Coulouris, J. Dollimore and T. Kindberg, *Distributed Systems Concepts and Design*. Harlow: Addison-Wesley, 2001.
[2] N. Lynch, *Distributed Algorithms*. New York: Morgan Kauffman, 1996.
[3] J. Magee and J. Kramer, *Concurrency: State Models and Java Programs*. Chichester: John Wiley, 1999.
[4] E. Roman, *Mastering Enterprise JavaBeans*. New York: John Wiley, 1999.

14

Designing Distributed Systems

Chapter contents

This chapter is an introduction to the topic of design. It first looks at the process of performance prediction and continues by examining some of the main principles that are used for the design of a distributed system; in particular it looks at how locality, sharing and parallelism can be used to increase performance. Distributed system design is similar to any design process in that one design decision has to be traded off with another one. A number of examples of this are detailed. The chapter concludes with a brief outline of some of the design issues which are important when designing for reliability.

Aims

1. To outline some approaches to performance prediction and examine their advantages and disadvantages.
2. To show how locality can be used as a design principle for distributed systems.
3. To show how sharing can be used as a design principle for distributed systems.
4. To show how parallelism can be used as a design principle for distributed systems.
5. To briefly describe some ways of building reliability into a distributed system.

Concepts

Application resource usage matrix, Benchmarking, Caching, Data replication, Database lock, Isolation level, Least frequently used strategy, Least recently used strategy, Load balancing, Locality, Page lock, Parallel running, Parallelism, RAID, Recovery file, Recovery manager, Replicated data, Row lock, Sharing, Table lock, Write-back cache, Write-through cache.

1   Introduction

*Distributed system
disaster stories*

This chapter marks a further step in the transition from examining individual items of technology such as CORBA and XML to a more global concern: the development and design of distributed systems. Chapters 12 and 13 looked at some of the issues concerned with transactions and took – for this book at least – a rare look underneath the bonnet of a distributed system. The aim, in this case, was to look at some of the mechanisms involved in areas such as concurrency control in order to give you an idea of how they could affect performance.

For simple e-commerce systems design is a relatively straightforward process: if, for example, a retail site just consisted of a Web front end and number of relational databases stored on the same local area network then it would be an incompetent developer who built a system which, as a minimum, could not be easily optimised for performance after implementation. Larger systems, for example complex retail systems where the data is spread over a large geographic area, or B2B systems where a number of different networks need to interact, require very careful design. The aim of this chapter is to provide an introduction to the design processes involved in developing distributed systems.

This chapter looks mainly at the design of a distributed system for performance; however, I shall also look at some of the issues involved in ensuring that reliable services can be maintained in the presence of hardware failure. At this point it is worth stressing that many of the design decisions that are made do not have a *direct* effect on factors such as performance, but an indirect effect. As an example of this consider **data replication**. This is where a database in a distributed system is copied a number of times and located at a number of points in a network. There are a number of reasons for replicating data; a major one is that it enables data to be close to users. If a database is stored on a local area network rather than a location which requires a wide area network access, the amount of time for the wide area network to provide the data is often orders of magnitude higher than if it were provided over the local area network.

*Data replication
products*

Oracle and data replication

Nobody writes software from scratch for data replication: there are a number of mature tools available; mainly these are associated with particular database products. One of the most popular is the tool set associated with the Oracle line of database products. One concept on which the replication is based is known as a snapshot: a section of table which needs to be replicated. Oracle software allows replication over a time interval, for example every five minutes or on demand. The software allows the designer to designate a master table, usually the table which is the main repository of live data, and a number of slave tables to which replication messages can be sent.

You might think that many of the problems associated with low-speed access to databases across a network would be solved, at a stroke, by just carrying out large-scale replication; unfortunately this is not the case: replicated databases will need to coordinate with each other as each is updated. After a replicated database has been written to it has to send messages to all the other replicated databases in order that they reflect the changes that have occurred. This gives rise to two factors which reduce the performance of a distributed system. The first is that extra traffic is generated in the system; this is often high-priority traffic and will delay any traffic which has originated from application transactions. The second is that updates to a replicated database will delay transactions to that database until it matches the state of the database which they have originally been applied to.

In the remainder of this chapter I shall look at some of the design decisions that are associated with distributed systems. A major point that is worth making is that unless a system is an immensely mission-critical application, where response time leads to major losses, then a developer will not have a lot of resource available to predict performance. The consequence of this is that any performance figure produced will have a degree of inaccuracy associated with it. Because of this a distributed system should be designed for change. For example, sections of such a system should be designed using the three-layer principle described in Chapter 2. This architecture isolates critical performance elements to a particular layer and ensures that if the developer makes a change, for example replacing a particular database with another database or reorganising a set of relational tables, then the change can take place relatively painlessly.

In a highly competitive environment the developer may not even have much time to carry out an accurate performance prediction with competitors threatening to be the first on the block

Before looking at the topic of distributed system design it is worth stating the starting point that I shall adopt for this chapter and also what I will not be discussing. I shall be ignoring the topic of analysis; I will not be describing the process whereby entities are recognised and structured nor will I be looking at how system functionality is derived. These will be assumed to be a given. I shall assume, for example, that relational tables in third normal form have been derived, but not assume how such tables are split up and replicated in a distributed system.

Systems analysis for object-oriented systems

One of the first problems that a designer will face when developing a distributed system is that of performance prediction. Before looking at some design principles it is worth briefly looking at how performance prediction can be achieved.

2   Performance prediction

The remainder of this chapter draws heavily from [1], an excellent book on client–server development. This chapter will only be an introduction. If you want a really thorough treatment then this book is well worth buying

There are a number of techniques used to predict the performance of a distributed system. These are: using published vendor measurements, employing rules of thumb, projecting from measurements, carrying out analytical modelling using mathematical methods, simulation modelling and benchmarking [1].

2.1 Using vendor measurements

Many server vendors publish performance data on how their servers perform against a number of benchmarks. This type of data is moderately useful when making rough comparisons between servers in a search for the most powerful server. However, as the sole means of predicting performance in a distributed system it is almost useless. There are two reasons for this: first, server vendors will often choose a mix of transactions which make their servers perform well and, second, these benchmarks are often highly specialised and atypical and do not match the specific transaction mix of any particular application.

2.2 Rules of thumb

A developer who has implemented a number of small, similar distributed systems will often use sensible rules of thumb to roughly predict the performance of a new distributed system. For example, they might have discovered that certain queueing algorithms or caching strategies work well and give a certain percentage response time increase for particular clients. Often such rules of thumb will work to the point where certain hardware optimisations such as using a faster disk or cache memory will enable the developer to meet performance criteria. However, it is not a recommended method for systems which are either novel in terms of functionality, architecture, the technology that is to be employed or large in size and rich in functionality.

Simulation technology

2.3 Simulation modelling

This is the process of building an executable model of a system and executing it with a particular predefined mix of transactions. The simulation is usually based on some model of queueing where transactions which cannot be immediately serviced by a server are queued up waiting for the server to become free. There are a number of general-purpose modelling languages and technologies that can be used for simulation, together with one or two special-purpose tools which are oriented towards computer system simulation. In general, simulation modelling offers a none too expensive approach to performance prediction which is relatively accurate. However, it does require special expertise which, in small to medium companies, is often not available and has to be bought in via consultancy.

2.4 Analytical modelling

Analytical modelling uses applied mathematics – usually statistics and probability theory – to develop a model of a distributed system. The model is developed in terms of equations that relate entities in a system such as processors, I/O devices and servers to equations that describe the arrival rate and spread of transactions in a system. Analytical modelling is similar to simulation modelling in terms of cost and effectiveness: it is relatively good at prediction and the cost is not prohibitive. However, expertise in this area can be very thin on the ground: even large companies might find it difficult to discover someone who has the degree of expertise – both computing and mathematical – to carry this process out.

2.5 Projecting from measurements

This is often referred to as **benchmarking**. There are two types of projection that can be made. The first is to measure critical results such as internal wait times and the time taken for results to be processed and appear at a client for just *one* client–server relationship with no other competing work. This is an excellent way of predicting performance in small systems, particularly when it is augmented by a little simulation modelling or analytical modelling in order to cope with the added complexity of multi-threaded working.

The second type of projection is that made from data gathered by running a number of representative processes. In order for this to happen the following steps need to be taken [1]:

- Produce a working distributed system in terms of hardware elements.

- Find some programs which replicate the workload that will be experienced by the servers in the system.

- Find and load representative test data.

- Run the system with users who will generate a meaningful profile of transactions.

- Monitor key parameters of the system such as wait time.

- Analyse the data.

- Vary the workload and see how this affects critical parameters.

Once these processes have been carried out the developer will have gained a very good idea about how a target system will perform. Unfortunately there is a major problem: a large amount of resource needs to be committed for the process, often making it uneconomic. Only systems which are immensely performance-critical and mission-critical can be analysed in such a way.

3   Design principles

There are a number of design principles which should be applied or respected when developing a distributed system [1]:

- *The principle of locality.* This means that parts of a system which are associated with each other should be in close proximity. For example, programs which exchange large amounts of data should, ideally, be on the same computer or, less ideally, the same local area network.

- *The principle of sharing.* This means that ideally resources (memory, file space, processor power) should be carefully shared in order to minimise the load on some of the elements of a distributed system.

■   *The parallelism principle.* This means that maximum use should be made of the main rationale behind distributed systems: the fact that a heavy degree of scaling up can be achieved by means of the careful deployment of servers sharing processing load.

3.1 The locality principle

This is the principle that entities which comprise a distributed system should be located close together, ideally on the same server or client. These entities can be files, programs, objects or hardware.

As an example of this principle consider a distributed system whose clients issue a query which results in large amounts of data being retrieved from two tables located on two separate servers connected via a wide area network such as the Internet. An example of this would be a query which involved an SQL join. Let us also assume that a third server carries out the joining process and the construction of the resulting table. If the two tables are large then there will be a considerable delay while data is retrieved from the two servers and sent to the third server. If these two tables were situated on the same server then, theoretically, a considerable performance improvement can be achieved.

This decision looks very straightforward and one which should automatically be taken by the designer of a distributed system. However, trade offs also have to be considered. For example, as you will see later, an excellent way of improving the performance of a distributed system is to locate data close to the users: usually on the same local area network that they are situated. One of the tables that takes part in the joining process might have been specifically located at a distance from the other table for this very reason.

In order to make a decision about whether to combine the two tables the designer thus has to look at the transactions that are being generated against the tables. For example, if there are a hundred transactions generated against one of the tables to every joining transaction that is generated against both tables, then the degradation of service might be too high to consider bringing the tables together. If the balance was much more even then the designer might consider another strategy: that of bringing both the tables together at the same server but keeping a replicated version of one of the tables which would be updated every time its copy is changed.

There are many more examples of trade-offs which the distributed system designer is faced with: the important two points worth making here are that, first, almost invariably trade-offs will occur apart from when some incompetent design decision needs to be rectified. The second point is that in order to evaluate trade-offs the workload of the system needs to be carefully gauged, for example a good distributed system designer will estimate the number, frequency and originating location of every transaction and then estimate the response time and resource demands that each transaction might make. It is worth keeping this in mind as I describe a number of the design decisions that have to be taken in the remainder of this chapter.

3.1.1 Keeping data together

Probably the best known example of the locality principle is that data that is related to each other should be grouped together. Already in the introduction to this section I have described one example of this where two tables which were related by virtue of the fact that they were often accessed together were moved onto the same server. This whole principle applies to all sorts of groupings of data: rows in a relational table, columns in a relational table, tables themselves and attributes of objects. For example, the analysis of an object-oriented system will produce a series of documents which will describe information such as the functionality of the system, the classes involved in the implementation of the functionality and the relationship between the classes. If analysis has been carried out competently, then there should be little, if any, design information produced, apart from perhaps specification performance constraints.

The decision whether to composite is a serious one since it makes the system much less easy to maintain

The role of design is to take the analysis product and turn it into some form which is heavily adorned with physical detail. One application of the principle of keeping data together is to form composite classes which are constructed from two or more classes identified during the analysis phase. The decision as to whether classes should be composited is a serious one. It is based on an appraisal of the workload of a system and the transactions that objects derived from the classes take part in. If the developer used an object-oriented database system to store objects then such a compositing decision would have a significant impact on performance if the objects which were composited were frequently retrieved together.

3.1.2 Keeping code together

The idea behind this is that if two programs communicate with each other in a distributed system then, ideally, they should be located on the same computer or, at worst, they should be located on the same local area network. The worst case is where programs communicate by passing data over the slow communication media used in wide area networks. There are a number of ways of implementing this design decision, the most obvious being to statically store programs which communicate together on the same server; an alternative would be to dynamically load these programs at run time. However, a word of warning is necessary: many programs that are found on separate servers will be there because they are communicating with some local database. Thus, the decision to bring together two programs will often require data to be moved with an effect on performance ensuing.

Caching

3.1.3 Bringing users and data close together

There are two popular ways of implementing this principle. The first is the use of **replicated data** and the second is **caching**.

Replicated data is data that is duplicated at various locations in a distributed system. The rationale for replicating a file, database, part of a file or part of a database is simple. By replicating data which is stored on a wide area network and placing it on a local area network major improvements in performance can be obtained as local area technology can be orders of magnitude faster than wide area technology in delivering data.

Data replication can be a very easy decision to make when the data that is replicated is subject to regular predictable change. For example, British banks update their customer accounts on a daily basis and download copies of that part of a central database relevant to a branch to the branch server every day.

Unfortunately, design decisions about replication are often much more difficult to make. When a database is subject to updates and it is replicated then the traffic that is generated in order to keep the databases in synchronisation can be a heavy load on a distributed system. While replication in general does lead to increased performance the amount of replication to employ can only be gauged by a thorough analysis of the frequency and size of update transactions.

It is also worth pointing out that there are half-way positions between the real-time updating of replicated databases and very infrequent updating such as that encountered in a banking application. In applications where some degree of lack of synchronisation can be tolerated, replicated databases can be updated on a periodic basis, such as every hour. For example, an application which retrieved summary data on business performance such as the number of customers buying goods per hour on a particular day would be an excellent candidate for having replicated databases which are updated relatively infrequently.

The other method ensuring that users are close to data is caching. Caching is the storing of frequently used data in a fast memory, either at a client or at a server which is connected to clients via a local area network. Huge increases in performance can be obtained by storing frequently used data in a local file of memory – data which would normally be accessed over a slow wide area network connection or from some slow file device.

Every user of the Web encounters caching. The browser that you use to read Web pages will store a number of the pages that you have recently viewed in fast access storage so that if you return to them then they will appear quickly, rather than having to be transferred over the Internet. Caching is also used in Web servers. Here, frequently required pages, for example a home page, are held in some fast memory medium such as main memory. When a request for a page is received by the Web server it first checks whether the page required is in the fast memory: if it is then it is delivered quickly; if it isn't it is retrieved from file storage.

Static caching

Many distributed systems contain data which is much more frequently accessed than other data. For example, a travel agency may deal with the same holiday company for 60 per cent of the time. One startling way of increasing performance is to keep that data in main memory or a fast file medium in a local area network; for example, the main booking pages from the holiday company. I was once involved in a project which cried out such a simple optimisation: it increased the response of clients by a factor of 30 and took 20 minutes to program.

Many utilities such as Web browsers have the ability to alter cache parameters without any programming taking place, for example the size of the cache

Caching is an excellent way of speeding up a system for data which is not subject to much change such as simple Web pages which do not contain dynamic data. For data that does change performance gains can still be achieved; however, the maintenance of the pages in the fast area of memory devoted to storage – known as the **cache** – reduces the gains and sometimes requires quite a degree of extra programming.

Caches which deal with dynamically updated data are known as **write-back caches** or **write-through caches**. For such caches when a transaction updates some stored data which appears in a cache at a client computer the following must occur:

■ The data that is stored at the client's cache must be updated to reflect the change.

■ The stored data corresponding to the cached data must also be updated at its server.

■ All other caches at other clients must be changed to reflect the changed data.

You might be asking: why shouldn't all data be cached? The answer is that if it was, clients would run out of memory. In this case the operating system would kick in and start moving data to and from system files, thus removing the advantage of caching

All this will create further traffic whose effect must be judged before making a decision about caching; again this is another example of the trade-offs that need to be looked at when making design decisions about a distributed system.

When designing a caching mechanism there are a number of factors which should be considered. The most important are:

■ The pattern of access to the stored data that is to be cached.

■ The relative size of the cached data as against the size of the full set of data that the cache forms a part of.

■ How the cache is to be managed.

For example, one critical decision that has to be made by the designer is what strategy is to be used in a dynamic cache – where a dynamic cache is one in which the data stored changes over time, in contrast to a static cache where the data is pre-loaded and stays in the cache memory permanently. Most caching strategies employ a **least recently used strategy**, often abbreviated to LRU, where the data which has been longest in the cache is evicted by data which has been requested by a client. However, there are other strategies such as **the least frequently used strategy** where the data which has been least used over a particular time period is evicted from the cache.

Caching occurs at a number of levels in a distributed system [1]:

Exercise 14.1

Running a simple cached client

■ Programs on the client side, either shrink wrapped or specially written, will use caching to minimise data transfer requests on the server.

■ Major software sub-systems such as database management systems will use caching to minimise disk requests. The more sophisticated the DBMS the more caching options are open to the database administrator.

■ The operating system underneath the DBMS will carry out caching in order to efficiently utilise the file facilities used by the DBMS.

■ There will be various levels of hardware caching on both the servers and clients.

3.1.4 Keeping programs and data together

Details on stored procedures can be found in Chapter 5

A good precept to be used when designing a distributed system is that programs and the data that they operate on should be as close together as possible. An excellent example of this is the use of stored procedures. You will remember that such procedures are collections of code stored on a database server which are triggered by simple one-line SQL statements. Using these procedures takes the processing load off the client and ensures that a server tuned for database access carries out the tasks which it is designed for.

3.2 The principle of sharing

This principle is concerned with the sharing of resources – memory, software, processor – the best example of this being the sharing of a server's processor by a number of clients which take advantage of spare processor resource in order to improve the response time of transactions. This takes advantage of the slack resources that are generated when a lengthy external process such as accessing stored data on a file occurs.

3.2.1 Sharing amongst servers

A major decision to be made about the design of a distributed system is how the servers in a system are going to have the work performed by the system partitioned among them. The main rationale for sharing work amongst servers is to avoid bottlenecks where servers are overloaded with work which could be reallocated to other servers.

An **application resource usage matrix** [1] can be used in order to aid the process of allocating servers to applications. An example of this matrix is shown in Figure 14.1.

Each column in the matrix represents some system resource, for example a relational table, an object, a processor or a server. Each row represents a particular application. The entries in the matrix represent the utilisation made of the resource. At the initial stages of development these entries might just be binary.

In Figure 14.1 the fact that resource is used by an application is indicated by a *U* and the fact that it isn't is represented by a blank entry.

Figure 14.1
An application resource usage matrix

	R1	R2	R3	R4	R5	R6
A1				*U*	*U*	*U*
A2	*U*		*U*			
A3		*U*	*U*			
A4			*U*			*U*
A5			*U*	*U*	*U*	
A6					*U*	
A7			*U*		*U*	

As the process of analysis proceeds the entries might be replaced by more detailed figures such as quantitative estimates of the usage made of a particular resource. The process of designing the sharing part of distributed systems involves ensuring that each column has an even spread of utilisation at the same time respecting a number of heuristics that have emerged over the last decade or so, for example ensuring that small and large units of work are separated: one server should deal mainly with small transactions, while another server should deal with longer transactions.

3.2.2 Sharing data

Since a distributed system will have, as a given, the fact that data should be shared between users the decision to share an entity such as a relational table is not a decision that is taken by the designer. However, underneath the fact that data is shared are a number of design decisions which can have a major effect on performance. The two main decisions are where to situate the tables that make up a relational application and what locking strategy to adopt. The first has, to a certain extent, been dealt with in the previous section; it is worth looking at the second in a little detail.

Most of the decisions about locking will be made with respect to the database management system that is used. In general such systems allow locking at one or more sizes: **page locks**, **table locks**, **database locks** and **row locks**.

A row lock prevents a number of programs accessing the row of a relational table, a page lock will lock the area of file memory which a table or part of a table will be stored in, a table lock restricts access to the whole of a relational table and a database lock will control access to the whole collection of tables which make up a database.

Some SQL products allow the programmer to change a locking strategy on-the-fly

Locks are defined as a property of a table or database when the database designer defines the structure of the database. Many of the decisions about what sort of locking to adopt are common sense ones, for example when a table is going to be the target of a bulk update it is better for efficiency reasons to use a table lock and when data is just being read by online transactions and updated by batch processes to use the largest lock size in order to minimise the amount of locking that occurs.

Although many locking decisions are straightforward, some locking issues are much more subtle. For instance, the relationship between deadlock occurrence, the locking strategy adopted and performance can be a subtle one, where trade-offs have to be considered. For example, locking at the row level will enable more concurrency to take place at the cost of increased deadlocking where resources have to be expended in order to monitor and release deadlocks; conversely locking at the table level can lead to a major reduction in deadlock occurrence, but at the expense of efficient concurrent operations.

There are a number of ways of designing a system to minimise the effect of deadlocks. The first is to monitor where the deadlocks are occurring and then modify any database code which creates this situation. For example, you may find that changing the order in which tables are accessed will remove some deadlock occurrences. The second is to spread the occurrence of database locks more evenly across the tables.

The maths here is somewhat unsubtle, but it provides some sort of rationale for my statement

Another way of minimising distributed deadlocks is to carry out data replication. Already I have detailed how this technique can be used to locate data close to users; it is also quite a powerful technique for minimising locks since, if there are n clients accessing a replicated set of d databases, then the probability that a lock will occur will be the order of n/d of the single database example.

Another strategy which is applied post-design is to experiment with the deadlock break interval. Many database systems do not employ devices such as wait-for graphs in order to detect deadlocks before they happen. What they do is regularly examine locks which have been around for some time and release those which have been in existence for a period exceeding the deadlock break interval. Many database systems allow this interval to be set by the database administrator when the database is specified; in my experience varying the deadlock break interval can have a drastic effect on performance for many database designs.

Another factor which many database systems allow to be varied is the **isolation level** of a program. There can be as many as four isolation levels which a DBMS will allow the database administrator to choose. They are:

- *Dirty read*. This is where a transaction can read data which has been modified but the changes that have occurred have not been committed.

- *Committed read*. Here a transaction is not allowed to read dirty data and overwrite another transaction's dirty data.

- *Cursor stability*. Here a row being read by one transaction cannot be changed by another transaction.

- *Repeatable read*. All items are locked until a commit has been executed.

As you proceed down the list of bullet points above the strength of the isolation increases; this will increase the number of locks and hence the greater the chance of deadlock occurring and performance dropping. The design principle here should be that the isolation level chosen should be the weakest consistent with the application data integrity and the demands of the application.

For example, if you have an application which reports on data in a stored database and where 100 per cent accuracy in the data is not required, for example a transaction which reported on some averaged amount such as sales over the past n months, then such an application can be specified as having a dirty read isolation level.

3.3 The parallelism principle

In Chapter 3 I detailed one of the advantages of client–server systems: the fact that they exhibit some degree of scalability; that in the past, when mainframes were the main hardware base, it proved very difficult and often enormously expensive to adapt them to increasing workloads. Distributed client–server systems are capable of being scaled up with the addition of an extra server carrying out tasks in parallel. However, the designer should be aware of automatically assuming that increasing the number of servers providing a service by a power n will lead to a strict increase of n in the performance. The only type of applications where this is true – and only true for the first few servers – are those applications which are heavily computation bound, for example applications which are carrying out the numerical simulation of some large-scale structure such as a nuclear reactor. When parallelism is introduced there are a number of factors which reduce the gain from that which is theoretically possible:

- The cost of splitting the workload into a number of separate units.

- The locking that occurs when shared data is accessed.

- A reduction in the efficiency of hardware caching.

- Delays when transactions have to synchronise with each other.

- The extra work required by the operating system in maintaining and coordinating the underlying processes or threads which have to be created to carry out the application tasks.

All these factors get worse as more and more parallelism is introduced into a distributed system; in a poorly designed distributed system their effect can almost be exponential.

The key idea behind the parallel principle is that of **load balancing**: ensuring that a resource, be it a database, processor, relational table, memory or object, is subdivided without incurring too many of the overheads listed above.

For example, one decision that the designer of a distributed system has to make is what to do about very large programs which could theoretically execute on the same processor. Should this program be split up into different threads which execute in parallel, either on a single server or on a number of distributed servers? The designer here has to make a decision which is driven by a consideration of the amount of synchronisation and communication which occurs between the threads. If threads could spend a large amount of time working away at a particular algorithm with little access to shared data and with only small amounts of data required for communication, then splitting the program into a number of component programs would be a good decision, even over a number of servers. Unhappily things are never so clear cut as this: very few programs can be cleanly partitioned and a careful consideration of the operating system overhead and resources consumed by the various threads involved has to be carried out before making a partitioning decision.

Another ideal which designers try and aim for is to partition a database into tables and files in order that the transactions are evenly spread around the file storage devices that are found on a distributed system. Again, to achieve the ideal where the same density of retrievals and updates is spread over the same devices is impossible. There are a number of reasons for this: the first is that other design decisions might dominate this decision, for example the designer may decide that it is more important to keep two tables together on the same mass storage device because quite a high proportion of transactions involve these tables (the locality principle). However, on every distributed system designer's checklist there should be an injunction to consider data sharing.

Another area where parallelism can increase the performance of a distributed system is I/O parallelism. Usually design decisions which are made in this category involve the use of special software or hardware, for example the use of **RAID** devices or parallel database packages.

RAID

RAID stands for Redundant Array of Inexpensive Disks or Redundant Array of Independent Disks. This hardware technology involves using a technique known as **striping** in order to speed up access. Striping involves spreading data which might be retrieved by a transaction across the disks so that if the data is required it can be retrieved very quickly using a parallel read rather than sequentially.

Data mining

Parallel database packages carry out reads and updates in parallel, sometimes against a number of separate databases held on separate servers. Such technology can be highly effective, particularly in applications which carry out a large amount of disk read access combined with a large amount of mathematical processing, for example data mining where sophisticated statistical processing is applied to large collections of structured and unstructured data.

An important point to make about parallelism, particularly with respect to applying the principle of using partitioned databases and separate servers, is that the pattern of transactions in many distributed systems varies from hour to hour. For example, a retail sales system will often have peaks of demand in the evening when potential customers (increasingly disallowed from using their company computers for such activities) have come home and start browsing the Web.

This means that employing parallelism, together with many of the techniques described in this chapter, is always a compromise; a solution which is optimal for a particular system workload will often be less good for another workload.

This, then, marks the end of a brief discussion of some of the more important principles which underpin distributed system design. The references at the end of the chapter provide much more depth than this introductory chapter. Before leaving this chapter it is worth saying that in many practical situations designing for a particular set of performance figures is not a science: that a good designer will come relatively close to a target, but that quite a bit of optimisation will often need to be carried out during and after implementation. The point worth making about this is that only by employing a good set of design notations and adhering to software engineering principles will the designer enable the inevitable change that is required to be carried out.

4   Reliability

The previous sections of this chapter have outlined some techniques and principles for designing a distributed system so that it has an acceptable performance. The other major worry that a designer has is that of reliability. With the advent of distributed systems and the increasing incidence of systems which interact with the general public this has become a much more important design factor than it once was: for example, in the old days of mainframe computers and minicomputers when, say, customers phoned in their orders, companies could cope fairly easily with incidents which caused computers to malfunction: normally such companies would switch over to some manual form of ordering where order staff would consult printouts which were generated on a periodic basis, say every two or three hours.

System reliability

The advent of client–server computing and the World Wide Web, where customers can inspect stocks of products and order them online, has not only changed the importance of reliability where a malfunctioning server could effectively shut down a retailer for a period, but also, at the same time, provided many of the tools that can ensure that a system will always be running – albeit at a lower performance level.

The first aspect of dealing with failures is that of recovery: that when some failure occurs such as a server malfunctioning the data stored on that server can be quickly recovered and reconstituted at a working server. In order to do this many systems use some form of **recovery file**. This is a file which contains a list of changes that have been applied but have not yet been committed; if there is a malfunction then a program known as a **recovery manager** will carry out the process of restoring any files which are in limbo when the malfunction occurred.

Another technique for achieving reliability, and which has a faster response to failure than techniques which use a recovery file, is **parallel running**. Here a number of servers with replicated databases process the same transaction. Each time that a transaction is received by the distributed system in which the servers are located they will all apply that transaction to their databases. In this way, if a fault occurs, recovery from the fault would be virtually instantaneous.

This is an expensive way of implementing reliability and is only really suited to systems where a very high degree of reliability is required. There are intermediate solutions. For example, a server could be designated a primary server and a collection of other servers designated secondary servers. These servers would lag behind the primary server in terms of updates to their databases; however, if the primary server malfunctions one of the secondary servers would catch up by applying the transactions which distinguished the difference between the primary server and itself. These transactions would normally have been written to some recovery file.

It is worth stating before leaving this section that much of the implementation and design of reliability functionality is taken out of the hands of the designer: much of the software used in a distributed system such as database management systems comes with options which allow processes such as data mirroring to take place. The role of the designer is usually relegated to choosing the options.

5 Further reading

The book by Joel Crichlow [2] is an excellent overview of the architecture and design of distributed systems. Ozsu [3] has written a good introduction to many of the underlying issues associated with distributed databases. Maria Buretta has written an excellent book [4] on the design and use of distributed, replicated data – it is pretty comprehensive. There is a major shortage of books on distributed application design; the best is currently the book written by Loosley and Douglas [1], aimed at the developer of database-centric systems; it is very comprehensive and at the same time steers well away from looking at product-specific heuristics.

References

Internet book links

[1] C. Loosley and F. Douglas, *High Performance Client/Server*. New York: John Wiley, 1998.

[2] J. Crichlow, *The Essence of Distributed Systems*. Old Tappan, NJ: Prentice Hall, 1999.

[3] S. Ozsu, *The Principles of Distributed Databases*. Old Tappan, NJ: Prentice Hall, 1998.

[4] M. Buretta, *Data Replication: Tools and Techniques for Managing Distributed Information*. New York: John Wiley, 1997.

15 Bots, Agents and Spiders

Chapter contents

There is a large subset of e-commerce applications which have the function of accessing sites on the World Wide Web. These applications are known as agents. This chapter describes the main uses of agents, provides a taxonomy and looks at the software technology necessary to develop an agent. It concludes by looking at mobile agents: agents which can travel around a network.

Aims

1. To detail the main categories of agents.
2. To outline the architecture of simple static agents.
3. To outline the architecture of mobile agents.
4. To describe some uses of agents.
5. To look at how agents are structured in terms of their software architecture.

Concepts

Bot, Chatterbot, Commerce agent, Data management agent, Government agent, Mobile agent, News agent, Newsgroup agent, Robot, Robot exclusion, Shopping agent, Software agent, Spider, Stock agent, Update agent, Web development agent.

1 Introduction

This chapter looks at one advanced use of Internet technology which is increasingly becoming important in e-commerce. This is the use of computer programs to access Web sites in order to carry out some well-defined task, for example accessing auction sites in order to see whether a particular item is for sale and discover which site currently has the item at the lowest bid prices. The chapter looks at the different categories of application, describes some typical architectures and details some examples of products.

1.1 Terminology

There are a number of terms which are used for programs which visit Web sites. The common ones are **robot** (often shortened to bot), **agent** and **spider**. The first two terms are used interchangeably in the literature, while the term *spider* is normally used to describe software which harvests information for search engines and other allied sites, the image here being of a program which wanders around the strands of the World Wide Web. In this book I shall normally use the term *agent*.

The vast majority of agents carry out searching or information gathering. For example, one category of agent alerts users when a particular event such as a Web site being changed occurs.

Address harvesters

One execrable use of agent technology is for e-mail address harvesting. Here, an agent accesses pages on the Web and spots patterns which suggest an e-mail address is being displayed; these e-mail addresses are stored within a database and are then sold to other users of the Internet who will then use them for sending bulk e-mails advertising a product or a service, a process known as spamming. Such harvesters are surprisingly frequent visitors to Web sites: once I inadvertently published my e-mail address on my wife's Web site and within four days the spam came rolling in.

In Chapter 9 there was an exercise that asked you to develop a very simple mobile object

The only other piece of vocabulary that is necessary to know when accessing the agent literature is the term **mobile agent**. This is an agent whose code and data actually move to another computer. Most agents are not mobile: they establish a connection to a site on the Internet and request data from that computer. This can give rise to major bandwidth problems since a lot of intermediate data can flow down a communication medium which, in the end, is not needed for the process that the agent is carrying out. Mobile agents travel to another computer, carry out their task on the computer they visit, send any information to the user who started the agent off and then either destroy themselves or move on to another computer.

1.2 A taxonomy

There are a number of ways of characterising an agent. I have partly adopted a taxonomy presented by two American researchers, Franklin and Graesser [1]. The descriptors that can be used to characterise an agent are:

- *Reactive.* It responds to changes in its environment. It does not, for example, visit a site, gather some information and then stop.

- *Autonomous.* It exercises control over its environment with little or no intervention from the user.

- *Goal-oriented.* It carries out a well-defined set of tasks.

- *Continuous.* It is continually executed; it does not, for example, suspend itself for long periods and periodically wake up to carry out some task.

- *Collaborative.* It communicates with other agents.

- *Learning.* It modifies its behaviour based on previous experience.

- *Mobile.* It is able to move from one computer to another transporting both data and program code.

- *Flexible.* Its functions can be easily modified in a dynamic way.

2 The roots of agents

Agents, surprisingly, have a long history. Primitive agents were used in the first few years of the Internet as spiders and are still the most prevalent example of agent technology.

2.1 Search engines and spiders

When the owner of a Web site wishes to advertise that site with a search engine they will access a registration page at the search engine site. This page will usually contain a form which asks for details of the site such as its home page, the name and e-mail address of the person submitting the site and some brief description of the purpose of the site. Some time later the search engine will use a spider to look at the site and index it. This is a multi-step process:

Developing spiders

- The robot establishes a connection with the Web server and retrieves the home page.

- The home page is textually processed. How this is done depends on the search engine: some search engines just look at the meta tags in the HTML of the Web

Meta tags are HTML tags which provide information about a Web page

Exercise 15.1

Running a very simple spider

page, others look at the words which are displayed in the home page and others do both.

■ Some robots will then extract the links in the home page and identify which of them belong to the site being accessed; they will then visit these pages and process the HTML which was used to build them.

■ The keywords which have been extracted from the visited pages are then stored in the databases used by the search engine and associated with the URL of the site.

Once the spider has done its work the site can then be referenced by queries which are issued by the user of the search engine.

Other uses for spiders

Spiders are not just used for search engine indexing. There are also spiders which gather Web statistics, for example they can determine which sites are popular by examining links to them or count the number of Web pages in selected sites in order to calculate growth rates of the World Wide Web. Others spiders can be used to check for links in Web pages which reference resources that no longer exist.

One problem worth outlining here and which is at its worst with search engine spiders is that of bandwidth overload. In the early days of the Internet, when communication media were slow and computers were primitive, there was an acrimonious debate about whether spiders were a 'good thing' since the early spiders were developed in such a way that they would slow down the performance of the early Web servers by, for example, visiting the servers for too long a time or revisiting them at very frequent intervals. At one point those who thought they were a nuisance seemed to be in the ascendancy; however, as lessons were learned and the Web got larger, those who regarded them as an important technology have been to the fore.

The Robot Exclusion Standard

2.2 Exclusion technology

One of the problems that I alluded to above is the fact that robots can consume bandwidth. In 1994 a group of users concerned with this problem developed a standard known as the Robot Exclusion Standard which provided guidance to visiting robots about the site. The standard defines a very simple language which contains information about what pages can be accessed by a robot. An example of this language is shown below:

```
# Simple example for Book
User-agent: *
Disallow: /main/temp/dayfiles
```

It is worth pointing out that some webmasters place exclusion text within metatags of the home page of their site

The first line is a comment, the second line states that any robot can visit the site (the asterisk is used as a wild card) and the final line specifies any directories that the robot should not visit.

Text such as that shown above is stored in a file which is consulted by any robot that visits the site and is used mainly to:

- Restrict access to pages which have been dynamically generated using technologies such as Java Server Pages.

- Restrict access to pages which are not yet complete and which are under construction.

Spiders, agents and robots

- Restrict access to core pages of a site which contain the main information. This is done to ensure that a robot does not consume too much bandwidth by reading pages with no useful information on them.

It is worth pointing out that the onus on whether to consult the robot exclusion text is on the developer of the robot or spider; he or she can develop the robot in such a way that it can ignore the exclusion text.

3 Types of agent

BotSpot

There are a number of types of agent that have been developed. The aim of this section is to look at the various types and detail their application areas. The categorisation that I have used is based on one employed in the *BotSpot* Web site.

3.1 Chatterbots

A chatterbot is an agent which converses with the user in some restricted form of natural language. For example, such an agent might provide a front end to a retrieval Web site which retrieves documents in response to natural language questions. Chatterbots can also be malicious: for example, one popular form of chatterbot intrudes into a chat room and attempts to mimic a human user: issuing obscenities, trying to persuade participants in the chat room to move to another chat room where it claims the conversation is livelier or insulting participants.

Examples of agents

3.2 Commerce agents

These carry out large-scale, e-commerce functions as distinct from the more specialised agents such as electronic shopping agents described later. A typical example of such an agent is one which mediates between two companies who have a business relationship. Such an agent would visit the Web sites of the companies carrying out processes such as reconciling invoices, checking that material for some production process has arrived, notifying product arrival and generating financial statements based on financial data held by any of the participants.

3.3 Data management agents

These are agents which carry out tasks associated with corpora of data. For example, processing the text on a Web site and providing a summary of that text with associated keywords and keyphrases.

Prosum

NetSumm

One of the best known data management agents was known as NetSumm. It could be pointed at a particular Web page and would then extract the sentences that it considered were the key ones which characterised the page content. It was also capable of abridging the page and recognising the language that the page was written in. It has now morphed into a product known as Prosum which, for example, can summarise Word pages.

3.4 Government agents

These are agents which carry out some activity related to government such as searching for government regulations or extracting government statistics. Most of these agents are American. Agents exist which:

- Help researchers extract summary data from American census returns and population reports.

- Provide a form of directory service to government data such as federal regulations, legal documents and bills.

- Provide economic information from a number of federal Web sites.

- Enable researchers to carry out text searches on House of Representative and Senate bills.

3.5 News agents

A news agent is concerned with tasks that are associated with Web-based news services. Typical agents which fall into this category will:

- Display breaking news on your desktop as it is notified to the Web site which contains the news.

- Scan news sites for articles of interest to the user; the user will inform the agent which articles are of interest by providing a list of keywords.

- ∎ Send an e-mail when a news story on a particular topic is published.

- ∎ Develop a personalised newspaper which contains only stories of interest to the user, with the newspaper being delivered at some frequent interval.

3.6 Newsgroup agents

These are agents which carry out some task associated with Internet newsgroups. Typical tasks which such agents carry out are:

- ∎ Filtering out postings to particular newsgroups so that only those which match a set of keywords provided by the user will be displayed.

- ∎ Searching FAQ lists for relevant answers to a particular question with many lists being searched.

- ∎ Scanning and prioritising postings to newsgroups based on some criteria involving keywords, who carried out the posting and what the topic is.

- ∎ Notifying the user of any new URLs which have been discussed in a newsgroup.

- ∎ Searching newsgroups for pictures and displaying them to the user.

3.7 Shopping agents

These are currently the most popular agents used in the Internet. They are used to carry out tasks associated with the accessing of retail sites. Agents exist which, for example, access CD sites to find the cheapest quote for a particular compact disc, shop for books and shop for computer equipment. Agents have also been developed which scan online auction sites and keep you informed about the current bid prices of items that you are interested in and will signal to you when a particular auction is near to finishing.

Bidder's Edge

Bidder's Edge

Bidder's Edge is one of the most sophisticated auction agents. It scans auction sites on the Web and continuously updates its catalogue of products. There are two ways that you can access the Bidder's Edge Web site: first by scanning the various categories that are listed; second by personalising the Web site to your own interests, for example you can inform the site that all you are interested in is bidding for computer equipment and it will then only display items which fall under this category.

3.8 Software agents

These are agents which carry out tasks associated with software. For example, notifying the user of any new updates to an existing system, downloading updates and even applying an update when it is received.

3.9 Stock agents

These are agents which are associated with the purchasing and selling of stocks and shares. These include agents that:

- Send you e-mails when a certain condition occurs such as a stock falling below a specified price or a stock moving above a specified price.

- Provide technical analyses of collections of stocks and shares downloaded in some format such as those used for spreadsheets.

- Managing a portfolio of stocks and providing warning indicators when the portfolio is under-performing.

3.10 Update agents

These are agents which notify the user when a change has occurred which is of significance to the user. Typical agents in this category will:

- Alert the user when some news has been issued on a Web site about a company.

- Alert a user when a book published by a particular author becomes available.

- Report when a particular Web page has changed.

- Inform the user when a job has been announced in a series of situations vacant sites.

Morning Paper

Morning Paper

The agent that I use most is known as Morning Paper. It visits a number of Web sites that you designate and checks what has changed. It will then deliver a 'newspaper' which is expressed in HTML and which can be displayed using a browser. The HTML will contain hyperlinks to the resources that have changed. This agent will keep you up to date on any changes that occurred on topics which you are interested in. I tend to use my version of Morning Paper to keep track of news and items of interest connected with Java, saxophone playing and rugby.

3.11 Web developer agents

In Chapter 17 you will develop a simple link checking site based on such an agent

These are agents which are used by webmasters to carry out their job. The most popular Web developer agent checks links on Web sites; if a link references a resource that no longer exists then a report is sent back to the user of the agent, often via e-mail or sometimes via a pager.

Other typical agents in this category:

- Keep versions of Web sites on a local hard disk so that they can be accessed quickly; they do this by checking the site periodically and copying down the pages from the site that have recently changed.

- Track user hits on a number of Web sites.

- Track visits to a Web site in order to check if anyone is trying to enter the site illegally.

4   Development issues

The aim of this section is to look at how agents are developed and the issues that you need to be aware of when carrying out such development. As with previous chapters Java is used as the focus.

4.1 Base software

If you are going to develop a Web-based agent in Java then the main class that you will employ is URLConnect. This is a class which establishes a connection with any resource that can be identified using a Uniform Resource Locator. It is created by sending the message

```
openConnection();
```

to an object defined by the URL class. The URL class represents Uniform Resource Locators and can be found in the java.net package; it has a constructor which accepts a string as an argument, the string being the URL.

There are a large number of methods in URLConnect; many of them extract information about the resource identified by the URL. A selection is shown below:

- getDate() returns the creation date of the resource.

- getLastModified() returns with the date when the resource was last modified.

- getContentType() returns with a string which identifies the content type, for example "text/html".

- getExpiration() returns the expiration date for the resource.

Another set of methods return connections to the resource in terms of streams, for example the method getInputStream returns an input stream which can be used to read the content of the resources.

An example of the use of the URLConnection class is shown below:

```
import  java.net.*;
import  java.io.*;
public class URLRead
{
    public static void main(String[] args)
    {
    //Set up the string representing the URL
    // of the site to be accessed
    String  urlName  =  "http://www.open.ac.uk";
    DataInputStream  dstr;
    URLConnection urlConnect = null;
    BufferedReader bf = null;
    URL ur = null;
    String lineRead ="";
    try
    {
        // Create URL object from string
        ur = new URL(urlName);
        try
        {
            urlConnect  =  ur.openConnection();
            //
            // Get some information about the resource
            //
            System.out.println
                ("**Connecting  to  "+urlName);
            System.out.println
                ("**Last changed = "
                  +urlConnect.getLastModified());
            System.out.println
                ("**Length = "
                  +urlConnect.getContentLength());
            System.out.println
                ("**Content Type = "
                  +urlConnect.getContentType());
            //
            // Get an input stream to the resource
            //
            dstr = new DataInputStream
                         (urlConnect.getInputStream());
            //
            // Set up a reader
            //
            bf = new BufferedReader
                         (new InputStreamReader(dstr));
```

```
        try
        {
            // Loop until the last line has been read
            while(true)
            {
                lineRead = bf.readLine();
                if(lineRead !=null)
                    System.out.println(lineRead);
                else
                    break;
            }
        }
        catch(Exception  e)
            // Reading failed
            {System.out.println
                ("**Problem in reading stream");}
    }catch(Exception  e)
        // Can't establish connection
        {System.out.println
            ("**Problem setting up connection");}
    }
    catch(MalformedURLException  me)
        // URL was badly formed
        {System.out.println("**URL  Malformed");}
    }
}
```

The programming here is straightforward. First a URL object is created from the string that represents the URL. Then an openConnection message is sent to this object to obtain a URLConnection object urlConnect. This object is then used to obtain basic information about the resource such as the date when it was last modified, the length of the resource in bytes and the type of the content.

After the content information has been displayed on the console a DataInputStream is obtained from the connection by sending the message getInputStream to the URLConnection object urlConnect. The DataInputStream object is then used to obtain a BufferedReader object which is read continuously until the end of the resource is encountered; each line of the resource is displayed on the console as HTML. There are a number of problems which could occur within this program:

The end occurs when null is encountered

■   An incorrectly formed URL could have been provided.

■   There may be a problem with reading from the resource.

■   The resource may not exist, for example the domain may not exist or the resource within the domain may not exist.

Each of these will result in an exception being thrown and caught.

The code above encapsulates all the processing that would be needed for a simple non-mobile agent. Once a connection has been established and data (in the form of HTML source) read from a Web site then this data can be processed, for example if the agent was checking whether a page had been updated it would extract the last modified data from the resource and compare it with the data that was extracted the last time it accessed the resource.

In practice the code for agents that visit a large number of sites is usually threaded: accessing a remote site can take time and hence there will be longeurs when the processor of the computer which launched the agent will be idle; in this idle time other sites can be visited and their data processed.

4.2 Principles

The aim of this section and the next is to detail some general principles that you should adhere to when developing agents. The first section details identification issues; the next section looks at development issues.

4.2.1 Agent existence

The first principle – and one which will save you a lot of time – is to consult the catalogues of agents that are held on the World Wide Web. An idea which you might think excellent has often been implemented by someone else; most of the agents that I have come across are either free or are very cheap to buy.

4.2.2 Agent identification

When you develop an agent that is going to wander around the World Wide Web and visit other people's sites it is a good idea to provide identification for the agent. Even on the basis of politeness this is worth doing; however, you should automatically assume that there might be a finite chance that your agent will provide some problems to a visiting site and the webmaster of that site might want to contact you. The `URLConnection` class has facilities for identifying your agent via HTTP headers, for example the header *User-agent* can be used to give a name to the agent. In general you should use HTTP headers to provide: your e-mail address, the URL of any Web page which contains information on the agent, the name of the agent and what it does. You should also advertise your agent to the world by sending a posting to one of the newsgroups which are concerned with announcements, for example *comp.infosystems.www.providers*. If your agent only accesses a small number of sites, for example those which are maintained by major American newspapers, then inform the webmasters of those sites that the agent will be visiting them periodically.

How this is done is outside the scope of the book

4.3 Agent development

Agents can consume a lot of the bandwidth of a target Web server; because of this it is a good idea to test your agent locally by continually running it against a number of local servers and monitor the resources used. A number of principles which should improve the performance of an agent and limit the bandwidth use of an agent are detailed below.

4.3.1 Load minimisation

Developing robots and agents

Try not to hog the resources of a particular server, for example issuing a large number of Web page fetches in a few seconds. The best strategy for an agent that is to access a number of servers is to create a series of threads, one per server, and then execute them in a round-robin fashion delaying each fetch by some arbitrary time, say a few minutes. The time will depend on the number of pages that are to be fetched from a particular site.

4.3.2 Material acceptance

The `URLConnection` class allows you to set an HTTP header `accept` which specifies which type of media you want to accept; if you are just processing text then you should set this header to indicate this, it will save the server a lot of extra work in sending you material that you are not interested in.

4.3.3 Visiting time

There will be times when a server will be under-utilised; normally this will be in the period between 9pm and 6am local time. If your agent only visits a small number of fixed sites then it is worth finding out their rough physical location and program the agent only to visit them at night.

   If you have an agent which visits a large number of arbitrary sites then often the country in which the server is located can be found from its domain name and the site can then be placed in some queue and only accessed during the night time zones for that country. Even an unsubtle policy of assuming that domains containing com will reside in the United States will provide surprising speed gains.

4.3.4 The use of `robots.txt`

Dynamic page technology is described in Chapter 7

A conscientious webmaster will maintain a file `robots.txt` which will contain statements written in the Robots Exclusion Standard which will specify which parts of a Web site can be visited and which cannot be visited. Whether an agent takes notice of this file is optional; however, it often contains information which can save the agent time, for example it might contain the names of directories which contain temporary pages created by dynamic page technologies such as Java Server Pages, programs or parts of the Web site which are still undergoing considerable development. Such pages are often not required for many agent applications.

4.3.5 Tracking visits

Such a link checking agent is detailed in Chapter 17

An agent will usually visit a large number of pages over a short time; often many of these pages are unchanged since the last visit. It can save a large amount of your time and server bandwidth if you stored details of each page and its date of last modification. For example, if you have written an agent which tracks the growth of the World Wide Web in terms of the number of external links per page in a large sample of Web documents, then one strategy is to maintain a local database on the computer which starts the agent which relates the number of links to the page URL. If you store the date of last modification of each page in that database and write your agent so that it checks whether the page has been modified since its last visit, you can save a large amount of bandwidth by not reading the page.

It is also worth keeping data on which sites have been visited during the current traversal of an agent. Some sites are very popular and are referenced by many other sites and so the agent could repeat its processing a number of times when only one visit is necessary.

4.3.6 URL checking

Always assume that if you are processing a URL from a Web page that there is a good chance of it being incorrect or dead and include code that copes with this: the owner of a Web site does not want an agent looping continuously and affecting the site's response time because of poor programming.

4.3.7 Provide logging facilities

Make sure that the agent logs as much information as possible consistent with ensuring an adequate response time. For example, an agent should keep data on which server's access has been refused and which URLs are dead. Such information can be consulted before a time-consuming connection is established. Another collection of data which you will find useful is the frequency with which a page changes; based on this data you can modify your agent execution frequency.

4.3.8 Modification of search strategy

Depth here means depth of hyperlinking

It is always a good idea to ensure that the search strategy of an agent can be easily modified via parameters. Typical parameters which can be altered include the time interval between which pages at the same server are accessed, the maximum number of threads that can be created which fetch a Web page and the maximum depth to which you want to visit a Web site.

4.3.9 Agent execution

One of the largest nuisances in the World Wide Web is of agents which are executed far too frequently; agent and bot newsgroups often contain complaints about a particular agent which has revisited a site three or four times in a day and retrieved hundreds of pages which have not changed. In a previous section I detailed the fact that it is a good idea to log as much information from an agent's execution as possible so that you can determine when to execute an agent and how much you can restrict its visits.

Figure 15.1
Two agent
architectures

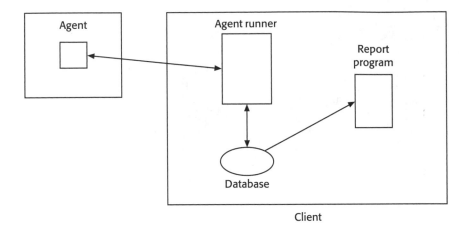

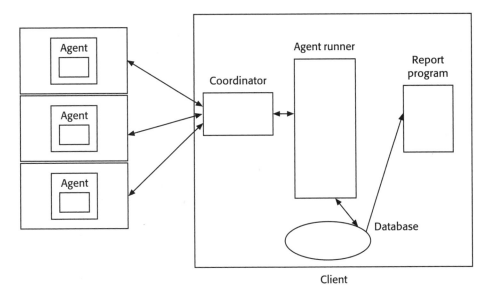

5 Agent architectures

5.1 Non-mobile agents

Although a single agent
is shown in the top
diagram there will
usually be a number
of identical, threaded
copies of the same
agent being executed

Such agents are programs which are executed on a client and access a remote site
with intermediate results from the agent's execution being passed back to the client.
The architecture of non-mobile agents is relatively simple. A schematic is shown in
Figure 15.1.

The top diagram is that of a single agent system where a single, non-cooperative
agent has been implemented. The architecture consists of an agent runner which
has the task of creating and deleting agents, sending commands and creating and
maintaining a database which contains data that has been retrieved by the agent. A

report program, often situated within a Web document, presents that data in a user-friendly way.

The lower part of Figure 15.1 shows a multi-agent system where agents communicate with each other in carrying out a specific task. Here a program known as the coordinator acts as the point of contact for the agents. The coordinator program normally acts as a whiteboard containing information from each agent and a list of tasks which need to be carried out.

5.2 Mobile agents

Article by Todd Sundsted

A mobile agent travels from computer to computer on a network carrying out its tasks. The main advantage of mobile agents is that they conserve bandwidth: there is no need to send intermediate results to the client computer for processing; they can all be processed on the computer that hosts the agent. A typical architecture for a distributed agent system is shown in Figure 15.2. It shows the classes involved. It is based on an article written by Todd Sundsted on developing mobile agents in Java.

It consists of four main classes:

- The `Agent` class defines the functionality of the agent. This is the class that is used when an agent is created.

Exercise 15.2

Running a very simple mobile agent

- The `AgentHost` class defines the software facilities offered by the computer which is acting as a host to the agent. It carries out a number of activities including terminating the execution of the agent, modifying its execution and passing data to the agent.

- The `AgentInterface` class defines a standard interface to the agent through which the host can communicate with the agent. Having a standard publishable interface means that a large number of developers can provide host facilities for the agent.

- The `AgentIdentity` class provides information about the identity of an agent, for example what facilities it offers and what interfaces it can work through.

Figure 15.2
A mobile agent architecture

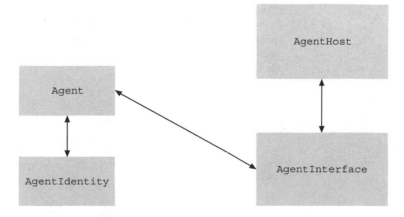

The Aglet development kit and other products

Aglets

It is quite a time-consuming process to develop agents. Because of this a number of companies have produced agent development kits for processing both static and mobile agents. One of the best known kits has been developed within IBM Japan. The Aglet development kit is a set of Java classes which enable the programmer to easily construct agents called aglets which can reside on a base computer and when circumstances dictate move to another computer. The Aglet development kit is both freely available and open-sourced. It represents the state of the art in agent development software.

6 Further reading

There has not been a lot published on agent technology. A good book which details the technologies and techniques necessary for developing mobile agents has been written by Nelson [2]. Microsoft has a very professional package for developing agents – the book by Cole [3] fully describes it. If you are interested in future technologies and applications of agents then the conference proceedings edited by Kotz and Mattern [4] is currently the best source; a warning, though, some of the articles are a very tough read.

References

Internet book links

[1] S. Franklin and A. Graesser, 'Is it an Agent, or just a Program? A Taxonomy for Autonomous Agents', in *Proceedings of the 3rd International Workshop on Agent Theories, Architectures, and Languages.* Berlin: Springer Verlag, 1996.

[2] J. Nelson, *Programming Mobile Objects in Java.* New York: John Wiley, 1999.

[3] M. Cole, *Programming Microsoft Agent Applications Using Visual Basic 6.0.* Redmond, WA: Microsoft Press, 1998.

[4] D. Kotz and F. Mattern, 'Agent Systems, Mobile Agents and Applications', *Proceedings of the Fourth International Symposium on Mobile Agents*, Zurich, 2000.

Ubiquitous and Mobile Computing

Chapter contents

Increasingly more and more applications of networked computing involve the use of mobile clients and non-standard clients such as vital-function wristbands and intelligent security alarms. This chapter, in many ways, looks at the future of the Internet in terms of its evolution towards supporting a wide diversity of computing uses and applications based on mobility.

Aims

1. To detail the main problems that occur with mobile computing.
2. To look at some applications of mobile and ubiquitous computing.
3. To look at the system demands that mobile and ubiquitous computing place on the distributed system developer.
4. To examine briefly the use of a particular technology known as JINI in integrating non-standard clients into a distributed system.

Concepts

Active badge, JINI, M-commerce, Mobile computing, Mobile middleware, Ubiquitous computing, Wireless Application Protocol, Wireless Markup Language.

1   Introduction

I am driving down a road in Wales. There's a short beep from the onboard computer and a sheet of A4 paper emerges from the mini-printer that is integrated into the dashboard. I pull into a layby. The paper gives me the agenda for a meeting that I am having later in the day with the staff of the computing department of a Welsh university. I'm late and start to get stressed. My electronic wristband starts beeping to alert me that my blood pressure is rising; I take a deep breath and do some breathing exercises and it falls. My navigation computer tells me that the traffic in Wales is light and I should get to my destination on time. I look at the wristband and notice that the data transfer light is flashing. This means that it is downloading data on my vital functions to a server which my doctor will consult next time that I log in for a consultation. As I pull away, I remember that I should have ordered the proceedings of a conference on distance education using the Web and speak to the onboard computer asking it to remind me to do this when I next stop.

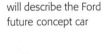

Later in the chapter I will describe the Ford future concept car

Science fiction, perhaps. In some cases yes; however, most of the technology that is described above is feasible and has been tested out in the field. The aim of this chapter is to look into the future somewhat and examine some of the changes that might occur in the Internet over the next decade.

Currently the popular view of the Internet is of a network mainly connected by conventional communications media with office-based PCs being used for communication. This chapter examines the evolution of the Internet to the point where significant numbers of users employ mobile devices such as PDAs or portable computers, or special-purpose devices such as badge readers or the wearable computing hardware described in the first paragraph above.

M-commerce

The main driver behind the evolution of the Internet is **mobile computing**: the use of cellular phones and small, lightweight computers to act as clients and servers within the Internet. It has given rise to the term **m-commerce** to describe e-commerce activities which are carried out on the move. Before looking at some applications it is worth looking at some of the problems with this type of computing.

2   Problems with mobile computing

There are a number of problems which beset mobile computing:

■   Mobile devices are at present less powerful than the type of computer found in an office, while portable computers are quite powerful, but PDAs and small hand-held devices lag behind in power. This means that the amount of client code that can be embedded in such devices can be very limited.

■   Bandwidth can be a problem. In some buildings a mobile device may have access to reliable local area network connections; in other buildings the access may be through modems or via ISDN connections. Outdoors the user may have to rely on low-bandwidth wireless connections. Any mobile system has to take account of the wide variation of bandwidth that this implies.

■ Reliability is a concern. Mobile computing is inherently more unreliable than fixed computing. A mobile device using wireless connections can be subject to interruptions in service which, if they occurred during an important activity such as a data download, can cause havoc in an application.

■ Many mobile applications are such that interaction with a network is intermittent. For example, a salesperson who is taking orders from a customer may talk to that customer for a few minutes, make an order via a mobile device, talk again for a few minutes and again make an order. This is a higher degree of intermittence than that experienced in many e-commerce systems.

Mobile system research

The problems that have been detailed above have prompted a large number of research projects aimed at providing the system software infrastructure that can support mobile computing over a network.

Coda

Coda is a research project at Carnegie Mellon University that is attempting to develop a file system which offers clients access to data for applications where the access is both intermittent and unreliable: mainly for mobile applications. The main idea behind this research is of a replicated file store which looks like a single file store supplemented by caches at each client, each of which stores data when the client is out of contact with any server holding a replicated file store. When a client is disconnected, either through events such as radio interference or when the user temporarily disconnects, all the data which is intended for a server is automatically written to a cache; when the connection is re-established the data in the cache is written to the server. This process is carried out in a transparent way: the user does not know where their data is destined and is unaware whether the data is written directly to a server or to the cache. The concept of Coda is simple; however, the implementation is very complex and requires some very sophisticated design and programming technologies to implement it

Coda

Since this book is not about the innards of the system software of a distributed system and also because much of the technology under development is new I shall not be looking at this technology in detail in the rest of the chapter. The chapter will be concentrating on applications and briefly examining some of the technologies used to implement ubiquitous and mobile computing. However, before leaving this section it is worth looking at some problems which are not systems problems but application and people problems which will slow down the adoption of new forms of network.

■ Customers are unconvinced by the utility of the Internet for mobile applications. In a survey carried out by the company International Data Corporation in 2000, only 9 per cent of current mobile phone users accessed the Internet using mobile phones and only 6 per cent of net users have access to a wireless device. There have been a number of reasons posited for this: the main one is the fact that mobile devices offer poor graphical interfaces to the Internet ranging from very poor (four lines of text on a mobile phone) to just about acceptable (the screen on a portable PC).

There are, however, some exceptions to this, for example the Japanese DoCoMu project

- Because of the limited nature of many mobile devices Web sites have to be limited both in terms of content and in terms of design values.

- In the United States the mobile phone pricing structure is different to that in Europe in that users of a mobile phone are charged for both the calls that they originate and the calls that they receive. This means that users can receive direct marketing calls which will cost money and which, if they were communicated via e-mail, would be a nuisance.

- In the United States the wireless telecommunications industry lags behind that in Europe. The main reason for this is that the land-based telephony systems in the United States have been very reliable and technologically superior to their European counterparts.

- In the United States wireless coverage is poor. This is a consequence of the large size of the United States and the lack of development of wireless technology and standards. This means that mobile users in the US are more prone to disconnections and stalls than their counterparts in Europe and Japan.

All these problems mean that development of ubiquitous computing will be slow over the next five to ten years with, for once, the United States lagging behind Europe and Japan.

3 Applications

The aim of this section is to look at some of the applications of ubiquitous and mobile computing. They range from the well-established to the speculative via the experimental and prototypic.

The Cambridge Active Badge System

3.1 Active badges

In the late 1980s and early 1990s, researchers within the AT&T Laboratories at the University of Cambridge developed a system whereby staff could be tracked within a building or set of buildings. A member of staff wore a badge which had a small microprocessor in it. The microprocessor was programmed to periodically emit a 48 bit code which is transmitted as an infrared signal to sensors which are situated within a building. Each sensor is situated in such a way that it can identify the location of the badge and, based on the signal emitted by the badge, can identify the wearer. The sensors send this information to a server which maintains a database of badge

Figure 16.1
Web page in an
active badge system

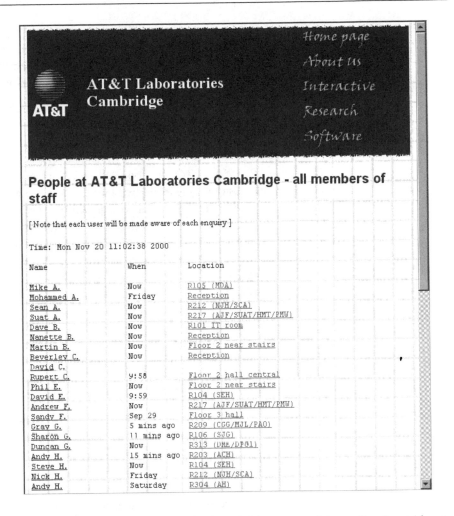

wearers and their locations. At Cambridge a Web server enables staff and outsiders to determine the position of a badge wearer. Figure 16.1 shows a snapshot of the Web page that provides this information.

This is one of the earliest examples of ubiquitous computing. The reason for this is that the functionality of the system is very simple and the environment straightforward:

■ Badge wearers usually stay in the same building.

■ An interruption in service, say when someone temporarily moves into a black spot such as a cupboard, is not a catastrophic event.

■ The functions that are required are simple. All the system does is to emit signals which are picked up by a sensor.

Such active badge systems can be employed within a wide variety of environments. One of the most valuable applications is in a hospital. Currently when a member of the medical staff is required to handle an emergency they are paged. Active badges enable the hospital to determine who to call based on their proximity to the point of emergency. Active badge systems can also be used for tagging valuable equipment where the movement of the equipment within a building would set off an immediate alarm.

3.2 Hand-held devices for nurses

Nurses from the Visiting Nurse Service of New York now use a simple hand-held computer when visiting patients in their homes and use this for gathering data about a patient. The device used is a Fujitsu Stylistic pen-based computer with 8 Mb of RAM and 170 MB of hard disk. The data that is gathered is sent to a hospital server via a mobile phone link. A typical application which is run on the computer is that of pre-admission screening, where the nurse will enter data about the patient which will be necessary when they enter or visit the hospital to start some treatment. This is a relatively low-level application of mobile computing, but a very typical one; applications similar to this can be found in stock control, railway track maintenance, water pipe maintenance, building site administration and traffic monitoring. The experience of the nurses on this project has been typical of many of the early applications: poor battery performance and some interruptions in service in some physical locations such as basements preventing 100 per cent operation; the latter problem is usually solved by carrying out an offline data capture and downloading the data later when better signal conditions ensue.

3.3 Keeping track of cows

Later in this chapter I shall be discussing a technology known as WAP which is an early Web-based access technology that allows mobile phone users to carry out primitive browsing of the Web. A recent application of this technology has been provided for British farmers in order to cope with the extra paperwork that has arisen over the BSE outbreak in the 1990s.

BSE is a form of neurological degradation which affects the brains of cattle. An outbreak of cases of CJD in humans in Europe is linked to the consumption of BSE-infected beef

In order to eradicate BSE, farmers have to inform health officials whenever a cow or calf is born, dies, is imported or exported. Normally they use a specially provided postcard to do this. A farmer can now use a WAP-enabled mobile phone to fill in a form which provides the details of the cow and this is validated by the company that provides the service (Bridgrove.com) before being added to a government database. This service was developed because farmers are very busy, have ten- to twelve-hour days and virtually live on the move.

3.4 Tracking stolen cars in the Netherlands

Over the past five years the Netherlands National Police Agency has installed a mobile query system which has dramatically increased the conviction rate for car-related offences. This is due to the installation of a mobile car tracking system which was installed for them by IBM. Patrol cars in the Netherlands are now equipped with a computer which accesses six law enforcement databases.

Officers type in a car registration number and within something like five or six seconds they receive information on the vehicle registration, driver's licence, car tax payments and whether the car is stolen. In the cars, radio modems are used to link with a mainframe computer with messages being sent using TCP/IP. The middleware that is used is a special software product from IBM which optimises the transport of radio messages and provides a high degree of security against eavesdropping.

3.5 The mobile computer engineer

IBM has developed a system which enables field engineers, the people who trouble-shoot hardware problems, to log into a customer computer that is experiencing problems and attempt to diagnose what has happened. The engineer can log into the system wherever he or she can find a radio connection, analogue phone connection or digital phone connection. This application is quite a simple one and is a form of mobile Telnet. However, it is highly effective: it has reduced the response time for IBM engineers from hours to minutes.

3.6 Relaxing with ClubNation

I look at WAP in some detail later in this chapter

A typical mobile application involves the user retrieving information about a particular leisure activity or topic. The ClubNation WAP site provides information about clubs and music venues around the United Kingdom. It can be accessed both via conventional Web browsers and also via WAP-enabled mobile phones. The site is designed in such a way that output does not stress the limited text display facilities of such phones. There are a variety of similar sites to this one, for example, listing sporting events, providing latest sport scores, reviewing restaurants, providing links to travel agents and providing travel information.

3.7 Multi-messaging services

Examples of mobile applications

These are semi-mobile services which integrate a number of messaging technologies including FAX, e-mail, pager and WAP. These services allow the user to sign up and register a FAX number, pager number and e-mail address and allow transfer of messages between these different media. For example, you may be a webmaster who runs link checking software on a continual basis. When the software discovers a problem with one of the links on your site it could have been programmed to send an e-mail message; if you use a multi-messaging service then the e-mail could be sent direct to your pager. Again this is a relatively simple application which just involves the sending of short messages and which makes use of an existing communications infrastructure.

Figure 16.2
Components for
mobile computing

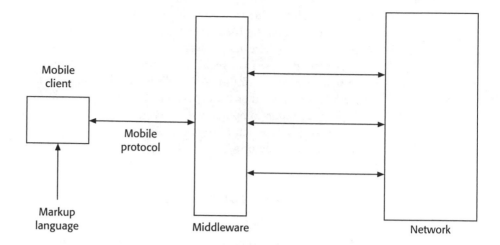

4 System aspects

In order to develop a mobile computing system a number of components need to be deployed by the developer. These are shown in Figure 16.2. This figure assumes a mobile client which can be anything from an active badge to a client issuing transactions as complex as those which are issued by a static client connected by some normal computer.

The first component that is required is some protocol which conveys functionality between a mobile client and the rest of the system to which it is connected. Because of the intermittent nature of mobile communication this protocol must have a high degree of error checking built into it.

The next component is some markup language; such a language would be used for those applications where a Web-like access is required. However, the nature of many mobile devices is such that the markup language used must be relatively simple and restricted to simple elements such as small monochrome pictures.

The third component is the middleware that connects between mobile clients and the network that they communicate with.

4.1 Mobile middleware

The current state of mobile middleware is such that most products do not perform well across the full spectrum of disconnection

There are huge demands placed on mobile clients and servers by mobile computing applications. The major demand is that they should be capable of reliably supporting intermittent connection. This intermittent operation ranges from clients which are connected for the vast majority of time but become disconnected when some unforeseen event occurs such as the user encountering a dark wireless area, to clients where disconnection is the norm, for example a salesperson who while travelling is not using their computer but uses it when they visit a customer. A middleware product which has to respond to intermittent connection has to have the capability to:

You will find a
description of the
ACID properties
of transactions in
Chapter 13

- Enforce the ACID properties of a transaction even when one of the transactions is interrupted, for example if a conflict occurs because multiple clients all try to change the same record in a database when they are disconnected then, when reconnection occurs and some integration process happens, the middleware must be able to mediate the effect of this.

- Keep transactions and transaction results even when the client has become disconnected. For example, mobile middleware often uses message-oriented middleware techniques to store queues of transactions and outputs from clients.

- Ensure that if the client was generating data, anything ranging from a simple form to data generated from a local client database, then that data is not lost when disconnection occurs. This is usually achieved in commercial mobile middleware by writing data to a local cache which, when a connection is re-established, is written to the server connected to the mobile client.

*Nettech mobile
middleware*

Nettech mobile middleware

A typical piece of mobile middleware is marketed by the American company Nettech. This middleware will carry out automatic connection to a server over a variety of communication media, will reconnect when a connection fails and will recover any data that could be potentially lost. The software is aimed at users who employ wireless connection and is based on a variant of IP known as Smart IP. The software is typical of a mobile middleware product which uses a proprietary protocol to implement reliability.

WAP

At the time of writing
(June 2002) the future
of WAP is not clear:
the take-up of WAP-
enabled devices has
not been large. One
future that has been
posited for WAP is that
it will be overtaken
and made defunct by
more sophisticated
technologies such
as UMTS and its
predecessors

4.2 Special protocols

A mobile communication system requires the use of a protocol which mediates between the protocols used by devices such as mobile phones and the IP protocol used within the Internet. There are a number of experimental protocols in existence with very few of them currently being employed in anger. The one protocol which has been successfully employed commercially is the Wireless Application Protocol (WAP).

4.2.1 The WAP protocol stack

Figure 16.3 shows the layered model for this protocol. At the top of the stack resides the presentation layer. This is represented by three components of a mobile system. The Wireless Markup Language (WML) is a markup language that has been defined using XML. This is used in the same way that HTML is used: to define pages which are displayed on a WAP-enabled device such as a WAP mobile phone. WMLScript is a scripting language which is used in a similar way to languages such as JavaScript and supports basic screen painting and text processing functions. WBMP is the WAP BitMap format which supports the interchange of graphics in WAP applications.

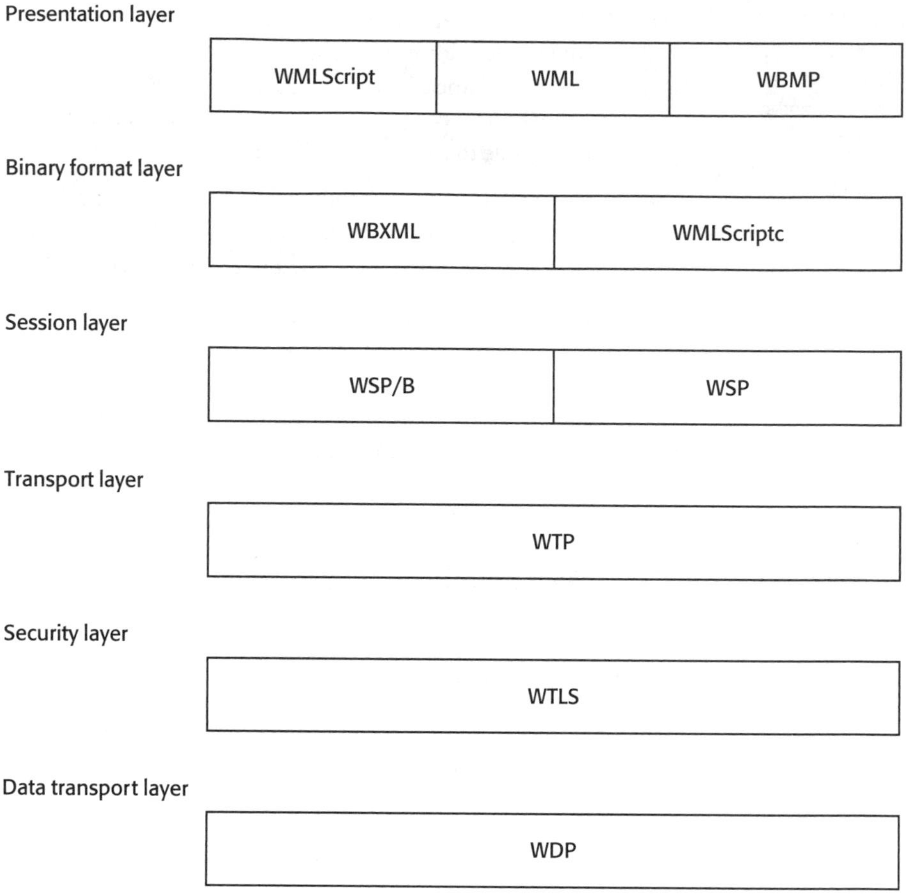

Figure 16.3
The WAP
protocol stack

Presentation layer

WMLScript	WML	WBMP

Binary format layer

WBXML	WMLScriptc

Session layer

WSP/B	WSP

Transport layer

WTP

Security layer

WTLS

Data transport layer

WDP

The binary format layer represents encoded binary forms of the WML languages WML and WMLScript. WBXML is the 'compiled' version of WML and WMLScriptc is the 'compiled' version of code expressed in WMLScript.

The session layer consists of two components, the WAP Session Protocol/B (WSP/B) and the WAP Session Protocol (WSP). The former carries out the same function as the HTTP Web protocol, while the latter carries out functions associated with the initiation, suspension and resumption of WAP sessions between a mobile user and a WAP server.

The transport layer consists of the WAP Transaction Protocol (WTP). This protocol carries out the function of sending data from a client to a server and contains facilities for the acknowledgement of data received by a server.

The security layer contains the WAP Transaction Layer Security facility (WTLS). This is similar to the Secure Session Layers protocol (SSL) and supports both cryptography and digital certificates.

The final layer is the data transport layer implemented via the WAP Datagram Protocol (WDP). This is a protocol which has been modelled on the User Datagram

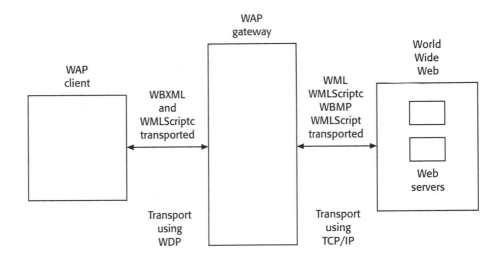

Figure 16.4
The WAP communication model

Protocol (UDP) found within TCP/IP. It is this protocol which carries out the bulk transfer of data.

4.2.2 The WAP communications model

Figure 16.4 shows how the user of a WAP-enabled device communicates with some service such as an information service that provides data on restaurants.

WML, WMLScript and WBMP source reside on Web servers resident on the Internet. A gateway receives data expressed in binary form such as WBXML from a client, translates it into text, for example WML, and then passes it on to the World Wide Web. The data required by the client is retrieved, sent to a gateway which then compiles it into a binary form, for example WBXML, and then sends it forward to the client for display.

4.3 Markup languages

Mobile applications which make use of small hand-held devices such as PDAs and mobile phones have to assume rudimentary display facilities: often a small screen with a monochrome display. This means that markup languages such as HTML contain too many facilities for such devices.

Almost certainly the most used current markup language employed for mobile communications is the Wireless Markup Language (WML) associated with WAP.

I discussed XML in some detail in Chapter 8

WML is conceptually similar to HTML in that it consists of a number of tags which convey the display of visual elements. It was developed using XML and the document data type definition is publicly available. The markup language is used to define the content of screens known as cards.

WML is much less sophisticated than HTML in that, of necessity, the type of content that it offers is limited by the target device's screen. The facilities of WML can be grouped into a number of categories:

- Facilities for defining a screen (a card) and a set of screens (a deck).

- Facilities for defining actions to be taken when an event occurs.

- Facilities for carrying out tasks such as refreshing a screen.

- Facilities for displaying and processing user input.

- Facilities for hyperlinking.

- Facilities for the display of images.

- Facilities for text formatting.

An example of some WML is shown below:

```
<wml>
<card id = "InitialCard" title "Initial">
<do type = "accept" label = "Password">
<go  href ="#InPassWord"/>
</do>
<p>
User Name
<select name = "name" title = "Name of User">
<option value = "Darrel Ince"> Darrel Ince </option>
<option value = "Alys Ince"> Alys Ince </option>
<option value = "Caitlin Ince"> Caitlin Ince </option>
</select>
<p>
</card>
..
</wml>
```

This defines a simple screen which is presented to the user in order that they can select which option they require (three options are presented).

The card (or screen) displays a title string "Initial" and is given a label "InitialCard"; it can then be referred to by this name from other screens. When the user indicates that they have finished their interaction with the screen the next screen labelled "Password" is displayed. The <p> tag, just as in HTML, displays a paragraph break and the text "Name of User" is displayed with three options presented, each with their values which will be communicated to a WAP server. Each option includes text that is displayed for the option, for example "Darrel Ince".

5 Integrating novel devices

One of the features of ubiquitous computing is the fact that many of the devices that might be destined to interact with a network such as the Internet will have novel interfaces and characteristics quite different to those found in a typical computer. In the past, when such devices have had to be connected into a network, it has meant quite a lot of complicated device-level programming. In this section I briefly look at a particular technology that attempts to make the integration of ubiquitous devices as smooth as it possibly can be.

The technology is known as JINI; it is a Java technology which provides a set of APIs that enable the programmer to seamlessly add devices such as active badges, smart cards, patient monitoring equipment, card readers, security products and wearable heart monitors to the Internet.

JINI is a return to the original roots of Java: it was originally developed as a language for controlling intelligent television sets

The JINI idea was developed in response to a number of requirements for networks containing novel devices:

- The software infrastructure for these devices must be robust; an intelligent TV set should not fail with some arcane error message being displayed by it.

- Devices should be capable of being easily added to a system in the same way that devices are currently added to computers via plug and play techniques.

- The technology should support evolution within devices: that, for example, a television could easily be replaced by another television with enhanced functionality.

- New modes of programming and technologies should not be necessary to integrate a novel device into a distributed system. Technologies such as TCP/IP and techniques such as multicasting should be used.

- Devices should be capable of creating spontaneous communities: for example, a voice-activated message communicated by a mobile phone to a home answering machine requesting a VCR to record a program should result in the phone communicating with the VCR without the user carrying out any extra functions over and above the transmittal of the recording information.

The main concepts which underpin the JINI model are:

- Discovery.
- Lookup.
- Leasing.
- Remote events.
- Transactions.

JINI

Discovery is the process whereby a device in a JINI-enabled network discovers communities of devices that it is required to join. For example, a security firm may administer the security of a number of offices on a business park via a series of consoles. During certain times of the day, for example night time, more staff might be needed to man the consoles; at six o'clock a console may switch itself on and join a number of communities each of which represents the security devices associated with a building or set of buildings.

Lookup is similar to the type of lookup that a directory service implements. However, the lookup functionality of JINI is more sophisticated as it is based on object technology and involves inheritance. This means that, for example, when a JINI-enabled network looks for a mobile telephone then it might be faced with the choice of a normal mobile phone, a monochrome WAP phone or a colour WAP phone, where each of these devices are subclassed from a mobile phone class.

Leasing is used to develop robust services. Leasing involves the allocation of a resource to a system, for example a digital camera, for a finite amount of time with the allocation being confirmed periodically. This means that, for example, if a resource physically disappears from the network then all trace of the resource will disappear after a period of time and requests for it might be diverted to other available resources.

Remote events are those events that are initiated by resources in a JINI system. Typical examples of these might be:

- The wearer of an active badge moving from one room to another.

- A video recorder switching off.

- The wearer of a heartbeat wristband taking it off.

- The motor of a curtain drawing system starting up.

- A still camera taking a picture of an intruder.

These events can be attached to processing code within a JINI-based system, for example the movement of the active badge wearer would initiate code which displayed the new location of the wearer on a Web page.

This is similar to the transaction processing detailed in Chapter 13

Transactions are used in JINI to ensure that when a process fails the system returns to a stable state. Transactions are used to guard against partial failures when the members of the JINI community communicate with each other.

This, then, is an introduction to a technology which will become very important over the next decade. The references at the end of the chapter provide further reading, as does the Web reference on the previous page.

The Ford future car and JINI

Ford's car of the future and JINI

Ford has been developing what it calls the 24*7 car, a model of what they think will be the car of the future. The current prototype offers a series of facilities whereby voice activation is used to access information such as e-mail, route assistance, weather reports and stock details and also provides a voice configurable display of facilities such as speedometer, oil, compact disc and clock time. Ford is currently using JINI to implement new devices on this concept car since it offers a fairly seamless way of integrating a large number of small, novel devices together with facilities which enable upgrading to take place easily. One of the major advantages of the JINI architecture that Ford found was that it enabled Ford to employ very small devices which were not big enough to support a software environment such as an operating system.

6 Further reading

There is not very much written on mobile computing or ubiquitous computing beyond some very expensive conference proceedings. Two very good books have been written on JINI by Oaks and Wong [1] and by Li [2]. The former is a concentrated treatment only suitable for the very experienced Java programmer; the latter is a more leisurely treatment full of technical details but still a hard read if you are unfamiliar with Java. A good book of edited readings has been produced by Milojicic and others [3] on mobile computing. If you are interested in using the TCP/IP protocols for mobile systems then the book by Perkins [4] is a good introduction.

References

Internet book links

[1] S. Oaks and H. Wong, *JINI in a Nutshell.* Sebastopol, CA: O'Reilly, 2000.

[2] S. Li, *Professional JINI.* Birmingham: Wrox, 2000.

[3] D.S. Milojicic, F. Douglis and R. Wheeler, *Mobility: Processes, Computers and Agents.* Old Tappan, NJ: Addison-Wesley, 1999.

[4] C.E. Perkins, *Mobile IP.* Old Tappan, NJ: Addison-Wesley, 1998.

17

Case Study

Chapter contents

So far in this book you will have seen small snippets of code and the ideas described in each chapter applied in the small. The aim of this chapter is to detail a large-scale case study which illustrates the use of many of the ideas described in previous chapters, including remote objects, server programming, three-tier architectures, database programming and XML. The case study is that of a company that decides to sell a link checking agent via a Web site. The chapter first discusses the rationale behind the venture, outlines the architecture of the Web site and then details the programming that occurs. The final part of the chapter deals with the processes that were carried out in order to get the Web site noticed. Throughout the chapter there are a number of exercises which are larger than those found in the previous chapters of the book and which take you through the development of a large part of the case study. These exercises draw on many of the technologies detailed in previous chapters.

Aims

1. To show many of the technologies detailed in previous chapters in action in a large case study.
2. To show some large examples of a three-tier architecture.
3. To describe the processes involved in promoting a Web site.

Concepts

No new concepts are introduced.

1 Introduction

This chapter describes an e-commerce application: one which sells a piece of software that checks the hyperlinks found in Web pages. The chapter details the application and links to a number of large exercises which are concerned with the development of code for parts of the application. Each exercise involves concepts that were described in previous chapters of the book. Figure 17.1 shows the links between each exercise and the technologies.

Figure 17.1
The relationship between the exercises in this chapter and the main topics of the book

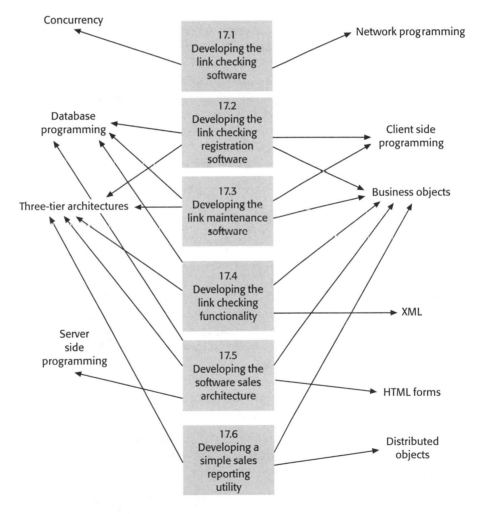

2 Links

One of the disappointments of using the World Wide Web is that links often do not work: you click on a link only to find some error message informing you that the server cannot find the Web page that you requested. I have used search engines which fail to return as many as 25 per cent of their hits to resources. There are a number of reasons why a Web page may not exist; the two main ones are that the page may have been deleted, or the user who set up the site may have moved on from the ISP whose server you are contacting.

Whatever the reason for it, dead links are a nuisance. In 2000 I wrote a dictionary of the Internet for Oxford University Press. One of the novel features of the dictionary is that it is accompanied by a CD in which the dictionary is stored as a series of Web documents. Each entry in the dictionary is stored on its own Web page and many of the pages contained links to external sites that contained material relevant to that entry.

I anticipated that a number of these links would become dead during the lifetime of the dictionary and so arranged with the publisher that new links would be supplied via a download site. In order to facilitate this process I developed a small but powerful piece of software which checked a collection of links and informed me when any of them became dead.

I felt that the software could easily be adapted for a number of uses:

- As a back end to a Web site which carried out link checking.

- As a personal piece of software which could either continually execute as a background process or be executed once as a stand-alone program.

- As a front end to a search engine which rejected any sites which no longer existed.

It is worth pointing out that this is a fictional site

The aim of this chapter is to describe the development of the Web site which supports the retailing of the link software. The Web site supports two broad functions: hosting a simple, restricted link checking service which is offered free to users and selling link checking software. It uses a number of the ideas and technologies described in this book:

- Database technology is used to store links and customer details and implements business objects.

rtf is a sort of markup language which describes MS Word documents

- XML is used to provide a base document for messages to users when links become dead. The document might be processed to produce Web pages, rtf documents or e-mail messages.

- Applets are used for the client-side programming which implement the free link checking.

- Servlets are used for the code which implement the retailing functions of the Web site.

- A three-tier architecture is adopted for the main components of the Web site.

- HTML is used to implement the Web pages.

- Business objects representing entities such as customers and sales are stored in the middle layer of a number of three-tiered architectures and are mapped onto relational tables.

The case study code is not shown in this chapter; exercises provide you with the bulk of the code.

3   The business model

The model adopted for the site was a tiered one. Such a model is fairly common on the Internet and involves a site offering a service or a product at a number of levels: the lowest level is usually free, while the highest level attracts a premium sales rate. The model I adopted had two tiers. The lowest level offered visitors to the site the service of registering up to a hundred links, with the site checking these links daily. The highest level offered for sale a program which can be resident on a computer and either check links continuously, or burst into action at pre-determined times. Such a business model relics on users checking out software at no cost, eventually outgrowing the software and then purchasing the powerful version of the software.

4   The base software

The software that drives the Web site and the standalone software has at its heart a class URLTest shown below which describes a URL.

```java
import java.net.*;
import java.util.Date;
import java.io.IOException;

public class URLTest
{

// Static constants

// Domain not recognised
public static final int siteNotFound =0;

// Domain recognised, resource not found
public static final int resourceNotFound = 1;

// Everything OK
public static final int resourceFound = 2;
```

URL and
URLConnection
are classes found in
java.net

```
//Instance  variables

private  URL  urlString;
private  URLConnection  connect;

public  URLTest(String  urlVal)throws  MalformedURLException
{
urlString = new URL(urlVal);
}

public int testURL()
{
int resCode =0;
HttpURLConnection ht= null;
try
{
    connect = urlString.openConnection();
    ht = (HttpURLConnection) connect;
    resCode = ht.getResponseCode();
}
catch (IOException e){
    // Domain not found -- takes time to get here
    return  siteNotFound;
}
if(resCode  ==  HttpURLConnection.HTTP_OK)
    //Server has  responded  positively
    return  resourceFound;
else
    // Server cannot find resource
    return  resourceNotFound;
}

public String getFile()
{
// Return with the file name of the URL
return  urlString.getFile();
}

public  String  getProtocol()
{
// Returns with the protocol of the URL, for example http
return   urlString.getProtocol();
}

public  String  getHost()
{
// Return with the host, for example www.open.ac
return  urlString.getHost();
}
```

```
public int getPort()
{
// Return with the port, for example 80
return  urlString.getPort();
}

public String getLastModified()
{
// Return with the date that the resource
// was last modified
long  lastMod = connect.getLastModified();
return  new  Date(lastMod)+"";
}

}
```

The class has two instance variables: the URL of the link that is to be checked and a URLConnection object which is used to check if a resource referred to by the URL link is available. Most of the methods in the class return with some part of the URL or information about the resource, for example getFile will return with the name of the file so, for example, if the URL was

```
http://www.open.ac/main/subsid/
```

then this method would return the string:

```
/main/subsid/
```

The method which carries out the checking of a link is testURL. The core of this method is the code

ht is an object defined by the HttpURLConnection class; this represents a connection to a Web resource

```
connect  = urlString.openConnection();
ht = (HttpURLConnection) connect;
resCode = ht.getResponseCode();
```

Here an HttpURLConnection is established by means of the method openConnection and a response code received from the server which could signal that the resource either is live or cannot be found. This is tested by means of the code

HttpURLConnection. HTTP_OK corresponds to the corresponding HTTP_OK status code discussed in Chapter 7

```
if(resCode  ==  HttpURLConnection.HTTP_OK)
    //Server has responded positively
    return resourceFound;
else
    // Server cannot find resource
    return resourceNotFound;
```

where `resourceFound` and `resourceNotFound` are static constants defined in the class. The static constant `HttpURLConnection.HTTP_OK` is returned if the resource has been found.

If the domain is not recognised an `IOException` is thrown; this is caught in the code

```
catch (IOException e){
    // Domain not found -- takes time to get here
    return  siteNotFound;
}
```

Exercise 17.1

Developing the link checking software. Relevant concepts: network programming and concurrency

The catch code is executed and the static constant `siteNotFound` is returned. Usually the processing of a domain which does not exist will take a long time as the Domain Name Service will keep searching for the domain a number of times.

The class `URLTest` is used in the link checking software as part of a thread: the software generates a large number of threads since accessing the Internet is slow and other threads can carry out their search for the state of a link while one thread is suspended waiting for the result of a search.

5   The Web site

5.1 The structure of the Web site

The linking service and the sale of the software are carried out via a Web site. The structure of the site is shown in Figure 17.2.

Figure 17.2
The structure of the Web site

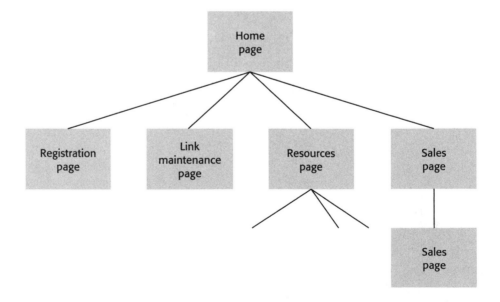

At the top of the hierarchy is a home page which introduces the services that are available to the user. Underneath this home page is a registration page which contains a form that the user of the site has to fill in: the user has to provide details such as their name and their e-mail address. Once they have done this they can use the link maintenance page which allows them to add or remove links from the collection of links administered by the site. There is also a sales page which administers the sale of the software and consists of a form which the user has to fill in; this page references another page which allows the user to download the software. The remaining page is a resource page which points at other resource pages that contain external links to HTML and Webmaster resources on the Web. The functionality of the site can be partitioned into four areas:

- Registration of customers who just want to use the link checking service.

- Maintenance of the database used to hold the links which are to be checked.

- The process of checking the links to ensure that they are alive and the e-mailing of warnings to users when a link goes dead.

- Sales of the link checking software.

The next section describes this functionality in more detail.

6   Functions of the Web site

6.1 Link checking site registration

Users of the link checking site register using a Web page. They provide their name, a chosen password and e-mail address. This is all that is required since notification of any links being broken is carried out by e-mailing the customer. The password allows the user to access the links database with the confidence that nobody else can access it. The form for this is shown in Figure 17.3.

6.2 Link checking database maintenance

Once a user has registered they are allowed to enter up to 100 URLs which define the pages they want checked. They access this page via the password they chose when registering themselves. They are allowed to:

- Add a link.

- Delete an existing link.

- Delete themselves as a registered user; in this case the whole collection of links that they have entered will be deleted. Their details, for example their password, will no longer be recognised.

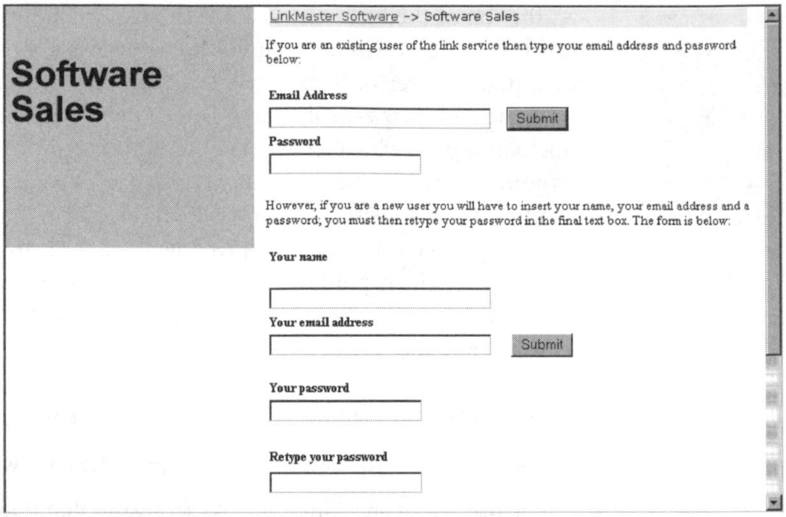

Figure 17.3
User registration

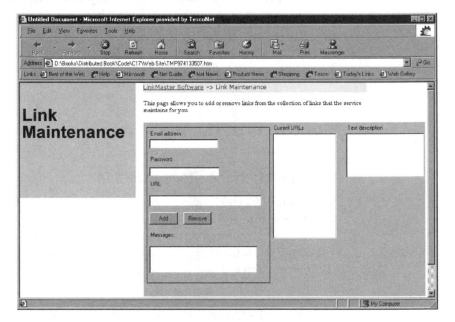

Figure 17.4
Link maintenance

A link is also associated with a textual description: links cannot tell the reader very much about the content that they describe and so, when a user wants to carry out an operation such as deleting a link, the textual description of the link is almost a necessity. The form for link maintenance is shown in Figure 17.4.

6.3 Link checking

This part of the system consists of a program which periodically checks the links that have been entered into the links database by users of the site. When it discovers a link which is dead it will e-mail the user who is associated with the link. The software is developed in such a way that the frequency with which it executes can be varied by the webmaster. Currently it checks links once per day. As you will see in the next section a large amount of flexibility is built into this program, much of which is enabled through the use of XML.

6.4 Link software sales

This is implemented via a form which asks the user for the same details that were asked for of users who just use the link checking service and, indeed, it places them into the database of users of this service even though they may not want to use the service. The sale is carried out via credit card with the system mailing the user a six-digit PIN number which allows them to download the link checking software.

7 The software architecture

Each of the three main components of the system are designed as a three-layer architecture with a relational database as the data layer.

7.1 The link checking service architecture

The architecture of the link checking service registration is shown as Figure 17.5.

It consists of an applet which provides the interface to the user, a middle layer in which the business objects reside and a database layer which consists of relational tables that store user information and link information.

Figure 17.5
A three-layer architecture for the user registration functions

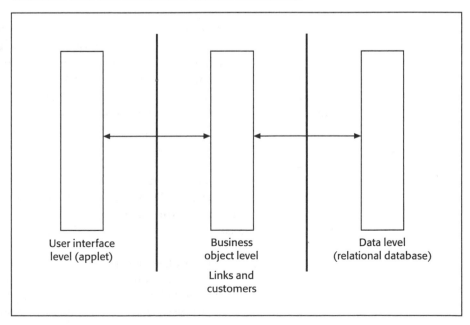

User interface	Business	Data level
level (applet)	object level	(relational database)
	Links and	
	customers	

There are two main business objects, Customer and Link. The instance variables and method headers for the first class are shown below:

```
class Customer
{
private  String  customerName;
private  String  password;
private  String  emailAddress;

//Constructor
public  Customer
     (String  customerName,  String  password,
      String  emailAddress);

// Get and set methods
public  String  getCustomerName();
public  void  setCustomerName(String customerName);
public  String  getPassword();
public  void  setPassword(String  password);
public  String  getEmailAddress();
public  void  setEmailAddress(String  emailAddress);

// Link manipulation methods
public  Enumeration  getLinks();
public  void  addLink(URL  link)throws  TooManyLinksException;
public  void  deleteLink(URL  link);
public  void  deleteUser();
}
```

Here the customer is identified by three instance variables which define their name, password and e-mail address. There is a single constructor and a number of get and set methods which retrieve or set the values of the instance variables. There are also four methods associated with the links that a user has notified for checking. The method getLinks returns with an Enumeration object which enables the programmer to traverse the links associated with a particular user. The method addLinks adds a link to those associated with a particular user. The method deleteLink deletes the link entry which is associated with the URL that is its argument. Finally, the method deleteUser deletes all data associated with the user including the links that are associated with them and personal data such as the user's password.

The code for these methods will include code which interacts with the relational database tables which implement customers and links which, for example, will traverse the relational tables returning link details when the method getLinks is executed.

A link is distinguished by its URL and also by data which describes its history, for example the number of times it has been found to be dead and the last two dates when an e-mail was sent to the link owner. This data is used to delete the link from the database with an e-mail message being sent to the user who added the link when this

The policy which
decides which links
are to be deleted is
delegated to the
software that checks
links for liveness

happens. The reason for deletion is that over time the database might get overloaded with dead links and users frustrated when they receive continual messages telling them a link no longer functions. The final data required is the e-mail address of the user who added the links to the database and a textual description of the link. The address is needed as a common index between Customer objects and Link objects so the relationship of customer being associated with links can be implemented.

The code for the instance variables and method headers for the Link class is shown below:

```
class Link
{
private  URL  linkAddress;
private  String  textDescription;
private  int  noOfDeadReferences;
private  Date  lastEmailButOneSent;
private Date lastEmail;
private  String  emailAddress;

//  Constructor
public  Link(URL  linkAddress, String  textDescription,
             String  emailAddress);

// Get and set methods
public  URL  getLinkAddress();
public  void  setlinkAddress(URL  linkAddress);
public  String  getTextDescription();
public  void  setTextDescription(String  textDescription);
public  int  getNoOfDeadReferences();
public  void  setNoOfDeadReferences(int  noOfDeadReferences);
public  Date  getLastEmailButOneSent();
public  void  setLastEmailButOneSent
                      (Date  lastEmailButOneSent);
public  Date  getLastEmail();
public  void  setLastEmail(Date  lastEmail);
public  String  getEmailAddress();
public  void  setEmailAddress(String  emailAddress);

//Other  methods
public  void  incrementDeadReferences();
public  void  deleteLink();

}
```

Most of the methods are self-explanatory, apart from the final two. The method incrementDeadReferences increments the number of times the link has been detected as being dead. The method deleteLink will delete a link from the relational database table holding links.

Exercise 17.2

Developing the link checking registration software. Relevant concepts: client side programming, database programming, business objects and three-tier architectures

Exercise 17.3

Developing the link maintenance software. Relevant concepts: client side programming, database programming, business objects and three-tier architectures

Again, like the Customer class, this class will contain code which interacts with the relational table that stores the links.

The applet which implements the human–computer interface which is used to interact with a user of the link checking site directly references the business objects and does not make any references to the relational database supporting customers and links. In this way the first layer is isolated from any changes that I might want to make in the future to the way that the data is stored and structured.

7.2 The link maintenance architecture

The architecture of the link maintenance part of the Web site is again a three-tier architecture. The first tier is implemented by an applet, a screenshot of which is shown in Figure 17.4. The middle tier contains Link and Customer objects and the final tier contains the relational database tables that store the data defined in these classes. There is little new coding to describe in this part of the system since the business objects code has already been described. The only new code is that associated with the applet.

7.3 The link checking software

This is the software which runs independently of the Web site and which periodically checks the links which have been added to the links database. It is based on the software that you developed in Exercise 17.1. The main function of this program is to e-mail users with details of any links which have broken. The program accesses a further business object known as LinkCollection. This represents the whole collection of links stored by users and contains the methods startAtFirstLink, getLink, moveToNextLink and noMoreLinks.

The method startAtFirstLink sets up a pointer to the first stored link in the relational table holding link data. The method moveToNextLink moves the pointer to the next link in the table. The method getLink returns the link referred to by the pointer and moreLinks returns a boolean false if there are no more links to process and true otherwise.

The processing that this software carries out is to sequentially examine each link in the collection of links and produce some XML text which describes any link which is dead. This XML text could, theoretically, be used in a number of ways:

- To generate the text of an e-mail message detailing the link breakage to the user who is associated with the link.

- To generate a message to the user with an attached word processor file detailing the link breakage.

- To generate a message to the user with an attached HTML file detailing the link breakage.

- To generate a personal Web page for the user with data about all their broken links.

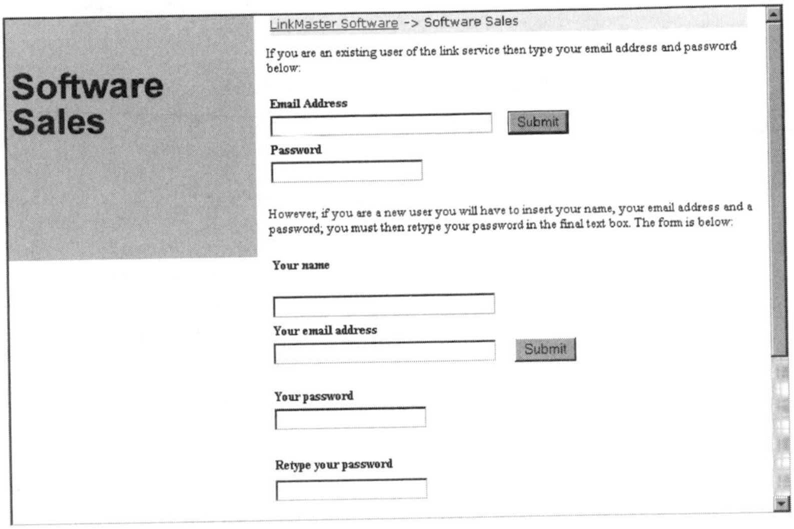

Figure 17.6
Software sales

In the first version of the site the XML was processed and a raw text e-mail message was sent to each user. An extract from the XML source describing a single broken link is shown below:

```
<LINKBREAK>
<URL> //http://www.htresource.com/links/ </URL>
<DESCRIPTION> Lots of links to HTML editors </DESCRIPTION>
<DATE>22/10/00</DATE>
<TIME>17:10:30 </TIME>
<USER>Dave Jones </USER>
<EMAIL>d.jones@hotmail.com </EMAIL>
</LINKBREAK>
```

Exercise 17.4

Developing the link checking functionality. Relevant concepts: database programming, business objects, XML and three-tier architectures

It describes the URL, the textual description of the page whose link was broken, the user who added the link to the link database and his or her e-mail address. The time and date components detail when the broken link was detected. The document type definition for this simple language is straightforward.

7.4 The software sales architecture

The final component of the system is concerned with the sales of the link checking software. Again this is structured as a three-tier architecture with the screen shown in Figure 17.6 providing the HCI layer. The middle layer consists of business objects described by the class PayingCustomer and the class Sale. The class PayingCustomer is similar to Customer since, as well as selling software, we are allowing this customer access to the link checking service. Hence it inherits from Customer. The code for the class PayingCustomer including instance variables and method headers is shown below:

```
class PayingCustomer extends Customer
{
private String sixDigitCode;

// Constructor
public PayingCustomer
          (String customerName, String password,
           String emailAddress);

// Methods to set and get instance variables
public String getSixDigitCode();
public void setSixDigitCode(String sixDigitCode);

// Other methods
public Sale getPaymentDetail();

}
```

It contains one instance variable which is the six-digit password which would be used by the customer when accessing the download page. It also contains one method which is used to retrieve the sale associated with the customer.

The code for the class Sale is shown below. It describes a sale made of one unit of the software. There are a number of instance variables associated with the class: the first is the e-mail address of the user who bought the software (this is used throughout the system to identify both users of the link checking service and purchasers of the software), the second is the version number of the software purchased, the date the purchase was made and a boolean which specifies whether the payment for the software has been received so that the user can download it. The code for the class showing the instance variables and the method headers is shown below:

```
class Sale
{
private  String  emailAddressOfBuyer;
private  String  versionNo;
private  Date  dateOfSale;
private  boolean  activated;

// Constructor
public  Sale(String  versionNo,  String  emailAddressOfBuyer);

// Get and set methods
public  String  getVersionNo();
public  void  setVersionNo(String  versionNo);
public  Date  getDateOfSale();
public  void  setDateOfSale(Date  dateOfSale);
public  String  getEmailAddressOfBuyer();
public  void  setEmailAddressOfBuyer
                        (String  emailAddressOfBuyer);
public  boolean  getActivated();
public  void  setActivated(boolean  activated);

}
```

Exercise 17.5

Developing the software sales architecture. Relevant concepts: server side programming, database programming, business objects, servlets, HTML forms and three-tier architectures

Exercise 17.6

Developing a
simple sales
reporting utility.
Relevant concepts:
database
programming,
business objects,
distributed objects
and three-tier
architectures

Both `Sale` and `PayingCustomer` contain code which reads from and writes to the relational tables implementing customer and payment data.

These business objects reside in the middle layer. The implementation of this part of the system uses a servlet: an HTML form communicates with a Web server which contains a servlet that reads and interprets the forms data that has been sent. The code in the servlet reads the data, updates the relational tables to reflect the sale and e-mails the user with the six-digit registration number which will be activated when payment is received.

The final component of the application is a simple utility which reports on sales made from the site. This is a simple Java application structured, yet again, as a three-tier architecture with the middle tier implemented by a distributed object technology RMI.

8   Promoting the site

The final part of the process of producing the case study was that of promoting the site. This section looks at the steps that I took.

8.1 Search engine notification

The description is of
a search engine
automatically indexing a
site; some use human
indexers, most notably
Yahoo

When the search
engine visits your site
will vary: sometimes it
is days, other times it is
weeks after you have
notified it

One of the most important means of promoting a site is by notifying search engines of its existence. The vast majority of search engines provide a very simple interface for notifying them. It usually consists of a form which asks for details about yourself and the site to be registered: what it is about, who it is aimed at and what keywords would describe it.

Once the form is filled in the search engine will visit your site and catalogue it in a database that it keeps in order to respond to search queries. The mechanism whereby it catalogues your site will differ from search engine to search engine. Some search engines will look at significant words on your home page and others will look at the keywords that you have inserted into special HTML tags known as meta tags. An example of two meta tags is shown below:

```
<META NAME = "KEYWORDS" CONTENT = "Java Links Resources Advice
Tutorials">

<META NAME = "DESCRIPTION" CONTENT = "This is a resources site for
programmers new to the Java language .. ">
```

Here the first tag specifies the list of keywords which describe the site and the second tag provides a description (not all the description is shown).

Once a search engine has visited your site it will add a listing of your site to its database and associate the site with a series of keywords. When anyone types in a selection of these keywords your site will become one of those retrieved.

*Search engines and
site submission*

*Multiple
submission sites*

There are other ways of submitting a site to a search engine. The first is to use a multiple submission service. This is a Web site which will automatically submit your site to a large number of search engines using the same form. These sites use a variety of revenue earning methods ranging from full charging to encouraging you to use the service of the banner advertisers found on the site.

Another option is to use companies who will do the submission for you; not only will they carry out the submission process but they will also try and ensure that your site will come close to the top of the list of sites retrieved by a search engine query. They will do this by carefully constructing the contents of the metatags and also rewriting the home page. Usually such companies charge for this service.

> ### Developing key words
>
> One very simple way of deciding on the keywords which describe a site is to type in a number of queries which you think users might use for finding the site. Then, count up the occurrence of each word and try to ensure that each word appears on your home page and in the meta tags. You will find it quite difficult placing *all* the words onto the home page, so ensure that, as a minimum, those which are the most popular are placed.

8.2 Best of the Web listings

Best of the Web sites

There are a number of Web sites which have titles such as 'Best of the Web', 'Hot Links', 'Cool Site', 'Hot Site of the Day'. These feature Web sites which are superior in either content and/or design. You should always try and submit your site to such showcase sites.

8.3 Links from other sites

Another way of attracting visitors is to ask the owners of other sites to include a link to your site in their site. It is surprisingly easy to do this: one of the reasons for visiting a site is to obtain information, and the more links a site has the more visits to the site will occur. Sometimes the site which you ask to link to your site will ask for some reciprocal link to be included in your site. It is important that you only contact sites which are relevant: it was no good my contacting the owners of sites which concern themselves with the works of William Shakespeare to ask them to include a link to my link checking site.

8.4 Using specialised indexes

Throughout the Web there are a number of sites which are devoted to a particular topic and which contain thousands of links to resources relevant to that topic. They are often known as specialised search engines; since the quantity of material they refer to is so large they provide special search engine facilities for visitors to the site. Since

Specialised search engines

such sites live or die by the quality and quantity of the resources they link to, you will almost invariably get a positive response when asking the owners of the site to include a link to your site.

8.5 Using newsgroups

There are a number of newsgroups which are devoted to commercial announcements such as a new Web site becoming live. It is worth sending a message to any of the newsgroups relevant to your Web site. A word of warning though: sending a commercial announcement to the vast majority of newsgroups is frowned upon by the members of those groups. If you do send an inappropriate message to a newsgroup, particularly if it contains some commercial content, then, at the very least, you will receive some nasty e-mails.

Sending a message not relevant to a particular newsgroup is known as 'going off topic'

8.6 Using the print media

Users of the Web often forget that magazines and newspapers are the main media whereby people obtain information and news, even those who use the Web. It is well worth writing to magazines in the area of interest that your Web site addresses in order to advertise it. For example, the Internet magazines often mention Web sites which are relevant to webmasters and history magazines, say, often contain mini-reviews of Web sites which are devoted to a particular historical topic.

9 Summary

This chapter concludes the book. In it you will have developed all the program code for a largish example of an e-commerce application. By now, after reading this book, you should be able to access deeper treatments of many of the technologies that have been described, be able to develop a simple e-commerce site using both client and server side programming, be able to participate in the design processes required to develop a distributed system, be able to design a tiered architecture for an e-commerce system, be aware of the threats that face networked applications and know how to respond to them and write moderately complex Java programs which achieve some distributed functionality.

10 Further reading

In this section I shall detail the further reading that you may like to do in order to build on the foundations provided by this book. Technologies such as servlets, XML and CORBA have a number of very detailed books written about them. The two best

Wrox and O'Reilly

publishers for a detailed professional treatment of such technologies are the British publisher, Wrox, and the American publisher, O'Reilly. For example, McLaughlin's book [1] is an excellent treatment of Java and XML and the book by Francis *et al.* [2] is a good treatment of Active Server Pages. Nielsen's book [3] is an excellent treatment of Web design from someone who has an academic background in usability. Stallings' book [4] on security is a good academic treatment based on cryptography; if you really want an in-depth knowledge of cryptography then Schneier's book [5] is widely regarded as the best. There are not many books on the design of distributed systems, but one of the best has been written by Wu [6]; if you want one of the best treatments of building reliable distributed systems then the book by Marcus and Stern [7] is excellent. If you are interested in the design of distributed systems then the book by Coad [8] gives a comprehensive treatment. A good introduction to agents has been written by Murch and Johnson [9].

Internet book links

References

[1] B. McLaughlin, *Java and XML*. Sebastopol, CA: O'Reilly, 2000.

[2] B. Francis *et al.*, *Professional Active Server Pages 2.0*. Birmingham: Wrox, 1998.

[3] J. Nielsen, *Designing Web Usability*. Indianapolis, IN: Red Riders, 1999.

[4] W. Stallings, *Cryptography and Network Security*. Old Tappan, NJ: Prentice Hall, 1998.

[5] B. Schneier, *Applied Cryptography*. New York, NY: John Wiley, 1995.

[6] J. Wu, *Distributed System Design*. Boca Raton, FL: CRC Press, 1998.

[7] E. Marcus and M. Stern, *Blueprint for High Availability: Designing Resilient Distributed Systems*. New York: John Wiley, 2000.

[8] P. Coad, *Distributed Java Design*. Harlow: Longman, 2000.

[9] R. Murch and T. Johnson, *Intelligent Software Agents*. Old Tappan, NJ: Prentice Hall, 1998.

Glossary

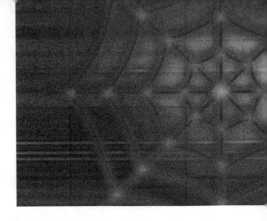

Active badge. A small hardware device used for tracking staff in a building or small geographical area.

Adaptive protocol. A protocol which changes over time.

Agent. A program that carries out some Internet-based function for a user.

Anchor. Part of a Web page that designates a hyperlink.

Anonymous remailer. A Web site which enables users to e-mail others without divulging their identity.

Applet. A Java program that can be embedded in a Web page.

Application resource usage matrix. A table which is used for performance prediction which relates workload to transactions.

Application server. A server which is dedicated to the running of a particular application.

ARP cache. An area of an operating system which associates hardware addresses with IP addresses.

ARP spoofing. An attack on a computer system which is achieved by accessing the ARP cache and enabling a computer to masquerade as a trusted computer.

ASPA. Microsoft technology used for developing dynamic Web pages.

Asynchronous message passing. Communication which does not have to occur in a fixed, predefined order.

Atomic transaction. A transaction which is free from interference from other transactions.

Atomicity. A property of a transaction that means it is free from interference.

Attribute. A property of an XML element.

Autocommit state. A state in which a database server automatically carries out transactions that have been applied to a database.

Backplane. A common connection within a computer.

Bastion host. Another name for a proxy server.

Benchmarking. Comparing the performance of a number of systems by executing them with a standard mix of transactions.

Bit mapped graphic. A graphic format where individual elements of a picture are represented as dots.

Bot. Short for robot.

Browser. A program which enables the user to read documents held on the World Wide Web.

Bus network. A computer network organised around a common connection known as a bus.

Caching. The process of storing frequently used data in a fast memory medium.

Callable statement. A collection of SQL statements which can be invoked by one call statement. Analogous to a subroutine.

Cascading Style Sheets. A HTML facility which allows users to define the general look and feel of a Web page.

CGI. See Common Gateway Interface.

Chatterbot. A bot which intrudes into a newsgroup trying to imitate a human user.

Checkout page. A page in a retailing site which carries out processes associated with finishing a commercial transaction, for example totalling the sales made and calculating the overall cost of a purchase.

Chosen plain text attack. An attack on a cryptographic scheme which relies on the fact that the attacker uses blocks of text with the property that the resulting cipher text provides large clues about the key used.

Cipher text. The text that is created when cryptographic methods are applied to a plain text.

Circular buffer. A storage medium where the last slot in the medium precedes the first slot.

Client. A computer or program which requires a service from a server.

Collaboration platform. A Web site or number of Web sites which allows companies and organisations to collaborate with each other.

Collection service. A service associated with CORBA which is concerned with the management of collections of distributed objects.

Commerce agent. An agent which carries out some task associated with commerce, for example buying and selling shares.

Common Gateway Interface. An interface to a Web server which contains useful information that can be used by server programs such as servlets. Usually abbreviated to CGI.

Common Object Request Broker Architecture (CORBA). A set of standards for maintaining distributed objects in a multi-language environment.

Concurrency control service. A service which coordinates the large number of concurrent processes which occur in a distributed system.

Consistency. A property of a transaction that means that it leaves a database in a consistent state.

Cookie. Data held on a Web client which enables state to be maintained across requests.

CORBA. See Common Object Request Broker Architecture.

Cryptography. The process of disguising a message so that it cannot be read by unauthorised users.

Data layer. The final layer in a three-layer architecture. It contains the data used in an application.

Data management agent. An agent which carries out some database-related task such as rearranging tables.

Data replication. The process of replicating a database in a distributed system in order to improve performance.

Data virus. A virus which works by infecting a file of data.

Database lock. A lock applied to a whole relational database.

Database server. A server which is used to access a database, usually a relational database.

Day trading. The use of the Web to buy and sell shares, normally shares are bought and sold over short periods.

Deadlock. Where two threads cannot proceed because each is holding resources required by the other.

Deadly embrace. Another name for deadlock.

Decryption. The process of making readable a message that has been transformed by some cryptographic method.

Demilitarised zone. The area within a firewall.

Denial of service attack. An attack on a computer or network which prevents making effective use of the services provided.

Device driver virus. A virus which works by attacking the code associated with the peripherals of a computer.

Differential cryptanalysis attack. An attack on a cryptographic scheme which uses text fragments which differ only slightly from each other.

Differential fault analysis. An attack on a cryptographic system which involves inducing hardware faults.

Diffie–Hellman key exchange. A public-key-based technique which allows participants using symmetric encryption to exchange keys.

Digest. Some number which is used to provide a near unique characterisation of some data.

Digital certificate. A digital document which provides authentication for someone involved in a transaction.

Digital signature. Data which provides evidence that someone associated with a particular document is who they claim they are.

Directory server. A computer used for validating digital certificates.

Directory service. A service which associates names and attributes with some resource.

Disintermediation. The process of removing middlemen such as an insurance broker from a commercial transaction.

Distributed database. A database which is held on a number of computers which are networked together.

Distributed deadlock. A deadlock that occurs when a number of distributed programs access shared resources.

Distributed event. An event which occurs in one part of a distributed system which activates some process in another part of the system.

Distributed garbage collection.   The process of reclaiming unused and useless memory in a distributed system.

Distributed object.   An object held on a remote computer to which messages can be sent from an object on another computer.

Distributed object middleware.   The software that allows distributed computers to access objects stored on other computers.

Distributed system.   A collection of computers which communicate by means of some networked media.

DNS spoofing.   An attempt to illegally access a computer system by pretending to be a trusted computer.

Document type definition.   A description of the structure of an XML document. Usually abbreviated to DTD.

Domain name system.   A service which enables clients to locate computers on the Internet given their symbolic name.

Dotted quad notation.   A way of writing the address of a computer on the Internet using integers separated by dots.

Downloading.   The process of copying a file to a computer.

DTD.   See Document Type Definition.

Durability.   A property of a transaction which means that its results are stored in some permanent medium.

Dynamic page.   A Web page which is changed before it is sent to a browser.

Dynamic pricing.   The process whereby Internet users determine the price of an item that is to be sold.

Dynamic skeleton.   Support code generated by a CORBA system.

E-auction.   An online auction found on the Internet. Sometimes the auction is in real-time, sometimes it is based on a deadline for bids.

ebXML.   An XML-based language for business transactions.

Edge chasing algorithm.   An algorithm used to ensure that deadlock does not occur.

E-learning.   The process of providing educational services using the Internet.

ElGamel system.   A public key cryptography system.

E-mail server.   A computer or program which sends and receives electronic mail.

Encryption.   The process of transforming a text so that it cannot be read by any unauthorised user.

Enterprise framework.   A collection of software which enables a programmer to develop distributed systems which implement some application.

Enterprise JavaBeans.   Distributed components which can be moved from one server to another different server.

Entity beans.   Enterprise JavaBeans which require permanent storage.

Environment variable.   A variable which holds important information about Web entities.

E-procurement.   The buying of company materials using the Internet, for example the purchase of stationary items.

E-shop.   An online shop found on the Internet.

E-tailing.   The use of the Internet, primarily the World Wide Web, for retailing services or products.

Event service.   A service associated with CORBA which allows objects to register as listeners to events.

Executable virus.   A virus which is attached to an executable file which when executed will carry out some malicious act.

Extensible Markup Language (XML).   A language used for describing the format of documents.

External service.   A service provided to the users of a distributed application.

Externalisation service.   A service associated with CORBA which allows objects to be converted into a form such that they can be sent over communication media.

Factoring attack.   An attack on a public key system which involves the factoring of very large numbers.

Family and friends virus.   A virus which infects the address books of users. Such address books are normally associated with mailing programs.

Fat client.   A client which contains a large amount of program code.

Fat server.   A server in a three-tier system which contains the bulk of the program code in the system.

File service.   An internal service that makes distributed files available to the user.

File Transfer Protocol.   A protocol which enables files to be sent from one computer to another. Often abbreviated to FTP.

Firewall. A protective layer of hardware and software placed around a computer installation which prevents unauthorised access.

Fixed protocol. A protocol whose elements are constant: the protocol does not change over time.

Form. A collection of visual objects such as text areas which are used to communicate data to a server.

Formatting object. An object that is used to generate some display instruction for an XML tag.

FTP. See File Transfer Protocol.

Gateway. A computer which acts as an entry point into a sub-network of computers.

Government agent. An agent which carries out some task related to government, for example finding relevant laws associated with some application area.

Groupware. Software which is used to administer a team of people, for example by providing appointment book and diary functions.

Hack. A technique which enables some technology to be used for a purpose which it was not intended for.

Hidden field. A field in a Web document which is used to contain state information.

Hit counter. A visual object which displays the number of visitors who have accessed a particular Web page.

Horizontal fragmentation. Where a table in a relational database is split into a number of smaller tables by partitioning the rows.

Host. A computer connected to the Internet.

Host processing. A form of processing where the vast majority of processing was carried out using a large central computer.

HTML. See Hypertext Markup Language.

HTTP. See Hypertext Transfer Protocol.

Hub network. A network based on a circular hub of communications media.

Hub and spoke architecture. A software architecture in which an entity (the hub) broadcasts messages to other entities on the spoke.

Hyperlink. An address in a Web page. It will point to an entity on the World Wide Web such as another Web page. Also known as a link.

Hypertext. The name given to a textual document which contains hyperlinks.

Hypertext mailer. A Web-based system which allows the user to send e-mails to other users.

Hypertext Markup Language. A markup language used to prepare documents for the World Wide Web.

Hypertext Transfer Protocol. The protocol which enables clients running browsers to communicate with a Web server.

IDL. See Interface Definition Language.

IIOP. See Internet Inter ORB Protocol.

Infection. The process whereby a virus is inserted into a computer or computer system.

Information brokerage. The provision of information services using the Internet.

Interface Definition Language. A language used to define the state and facilities of CORBA-based objects.

Interface repository. A collection of definitions of CORBA-based objects.

Internal service. A service provided by a distributed operating system or by network system software.

Internet. The collection of networks which are connected using the TCP/IP suite of protocols.

Internet Domain Name System. The collection of programs which keeps track of the location and names of computers on the Internet.

Internet Inter ORB Protocol (IIOP). A protocol which enables object request brokers from different vendors to communicate with each other.

Internet Protocol (IP). One of a suite of protocols used for communication within the Internet.

IP. See Internet Protocol.

IP address. The unique address of a computer on the Internet.

Isolation. A property of a transaction that means that it should not be interfered with by other transactions.

Java. A programming language which has extensive facilities for developing Internet-based applications.

Java Server Pages. Also known as JSP, a technology for dynamic page processing based on Java.

JavaScript. A scripting language used to add functionality to a Web page.

JSP. See Java Server Pages.

Key. Unique data used to identify an entity in a collection of entities. Usually used in connection with relational databases. It is also the text used in cryptographic schemes.

Known plain text attack.   An attack on a cryptographic scheme which involves using text for which the encrypted version is known.

Least frequently used strategy.   A strategy used for evicting data from a cache. The data that is used less frequently is removed.

Least recently used strategy.   A strategy used for evicting data from a cache. The data that is used less recently is evicted.

Legacy software.   Software which has been developed using past technology and which is ageing.

Licensing service.   A CORBA service which allows the use of objects to be monitored so that, for example, their use can be charged for.

Lifecycle method.   A method which is executed when an event occurs with an applet.

Lifecycle service.   A CORBA service for creating, modifying and deleting CORBA-based objects.

Link.   Another name for a hyperlink.

Load balancing.   The process of sharing the processing load in a distributed system equally among the servers in the system.

Locality.   A distributed system design principle in which resources required by users are kept as close to the users as possible.

Lock manager.   Part of an operating system which administers a locking strategy.

Locking.   The process of ensuring that only one thread at a time is given access to a resource.

Loopback address.   The IP address 127.0.0.1 used for the local testing of distributed systems.

Lost update problem.   What occurs when transactions interfere with each other. It results in the data change associated with one transaction not being applied.

Mailer.   A client program which can send and receive electronic mail.

Mail server.   A computer which is used to store and forward electronic mail messages.

Many-reader single-writer scheme.   A locking scheme whereby many threads are allowed to read the contents of a resource, but only one thread is allowed to write to the resource.

Markup language.   A language which is used to provide display instructions for a document. Elements of the language are embedded within the document.

Marshalling.   The process of converting data into a form in which it can be sent to another computer on the Internet.

Master secret.   Text used within the Secure Sockets Layer technology.

M-commerce.   Electronic commerce associated with mobile computing.

Message authentication code.   A code that is used to provide evidence that transmitted text has not been tampered with.

Message passing.   A form of communication in which textual messages are passed to and from entities in a network.

Metadata.   Data which describes other data, for example the names of the columns of a table stored in a relational database.

Metalanguage.   A language used to describe other languages. XML is an example of a metalanguage.

Middleware.   The software that lies between clients and servers.

Mobile agent.   A program which transports itself and its associated data from one computer to another in a network.

Mobile computing.   Computing using devices such as remote sensors or portable computers which physically move.

Mobile middleware.   The software which allows mobile computers to communicate with other computers on the Internet.

Multicast address.   A special address used to identify computers which are sent multicast messages.

Multicasting.   The broadcasting of a message to a number of computers within the Internet.

Multicasting protocol.   A protocol used for the broadcasting of multicast messages to a number of receivers.

Mutation.   The process whereby a virus changes its form in order to resist detection.

Name server.   A server which provides a naming service which given a symbolic name will return with the physical address of a resource such as a computer.

Namespace.   A library mechanism for XML.

Naming context.   An identification of a CORBA-based object in a tree of such objects.

Naming service.   An internal service that associates a resource with a name.

News agent. An agent which carries out some processing associated with news, for example notifying the user when a particular topic appears in an online newspaper.

Newsgroup agent. An agent which carries out some task associated with a newsgroup, for example notifying the user when a particular topic appears in a newsgroup.

Non-validating parser. An XML parser which only carries out rudimentary checks on some source expressed in an XML-defined language.

Object adapter. A layer in the CORBA model which allows objects to access the facilities of an ORB.

Object Request Broker. Software which provides the facilities whereby CORBA-based objects can communicate with each other.

Object server. A server in which remote objects reside.

Online trading. The process of selling and buying stocks and shares on the Internet.

Open system. A system whose source code is public.

OSI reference model. A layered architecture for networks which preceded the Internet architecture.

Page cache. An area of fast memory in which Web pages are held so that they can be accessed very quickly.

Page lock. A lock applied to an individual page in a relational database.

Parallel running. The process of running a number of programs at the same time.

Parser. A program which checks some source document or text against its definition.

Perl. A scripting language used for server-side processing.

Persistence. The ability of data to be stored for considerable periods of time and not disappear when the program that created it completes its execution.

Persistence service. A CORBA service which provides for the permanent storage of CORBA-based objects.

Plain text. The text that is transformed by some cryptographic scheme.

Polymorphic virus. A virus which changes its form in order to avoid detection.

POP3. See Post Office Protocol.

Port. A conduit attached to a computer on the Internet into which data flows.

Portal. A Web site which catalogues and characterises a large amount of information.

Post Office Protocol. A very simple protocol used for sending and receiving e-mail. The most popular version is POP3.

Posting. A message sent to a newsgroup.

Pre-emptive scheduling. Where a thread is suspended before it has completed its task or before it engages in a task which will result in it being suspended.

Premaster secret. An item of data used by the Secure Sockets Layer technology.

Prepared statement. An SQL statement consisting of a number of other SQL statements which have been pre-compiled.

Presentation and logic layer. The front layer in a three-tier architecture. It provides the human–computer interface.

Private key. The key that is secret in public key cryptography.

Probe. Data used to ensure that deadlock does not occur in a distributed system.

Processing layer. The middle layer in a three-tier architecture.

Procurement. The process of buying raw supplies for some commercial enterprise.

Properties service. A CORBA service which enables properties to be associated with CORBA-based objects.

Protocol. A series of rules which govern the communication between two or more entities in a network.

Protocol stack. The collection of protocols which implement some functionality. The term stack is used to describe the fact that each layer draws on facilities in the next layer down.

Proxy object. An object which acts as a stand-in for another object; often the second object resides on another computer from the proxy.

Proxy server. A computer which is associated with a firewall.

Public key. The key that is published in public key cryptography.

Pull technology. A general term used for any technology used for requesting data and information by clients from a server.

Push technology. A general term used for any technology used to send data and information to clients.

Query. A command which results in the retrieval of information from some database.

Query service. A CORBA service which allows queries to be generated against collections of CORBA-based objects.

RAID. See Redundant Array of Independent Disks.

Rapid application development. A generic term which describes the software engineering processes used to develop a system quickly.

Recovery file. A file which is created by a database management system which is used to recover a database if some catastrophic error occurs.

Recovery manager. A piece of system software which is used to return a database to the state that it was in prior to some major error such as a hardware fault.

Redundant Array of Inexpensive Disks. A hardware technique used for speeding up access to a storage disk.

Relational database. A database which is organised as a series of tables.

Relationship service. A CORBA service which provides facilities whereby one CORBA-based object can be associated with another CORBA-based object using a relation.

Remote Method Invocation. A Java-based distributed objects technology.

Remote procedure call. The process of executing code on a remote computer by invoking it from another computer. Often known as RPC.

Replicated data. Data which is duplicated throughout a network.

Replication service. An internal service which co-ordinates the changes to a number of identical databases in a distributed system.

Ring network. A network which is organised as a circular ring of computers.

RMI. See Remote Method Invocation.

RMI compiler. A tool which generates support code necessary for the development of RMI objects.

RMI registry. A naming service maintained by the RMI system.

Robot. Another name for an agent.

Robot Exclusion Standard. A standard which is used to specify text files which inform robots visiting a Web site which parts they should not visit.

Row lock. A lock on a row of a relational table.

RSA. One of the most well-known public key cryptography systems.

Scanner. A software tool that is used to check out the security of a computer network.

Scheduler. System software which shares out a processor among a number of competing threads.

Screened host firewall. A popular firewall configuration which is implemented by a computer known as the screened host having two levels of protection.

Search engine. A program which is used to retrieve information from the World Wide Web or from a single site on the Web.

Secure Sockets Layer. A software layer which enables communication across the Internet to be secret.

Security service. An internal service which provides security facilities for a distributed system, for example providing cryptographic transformations of data.

Serial equivalence. A property of a transaction which is made up of sub-transactions. It is that when the sub-transactions are applied in parallel the effect is the same as if they were applied one after the other.

Server. A computer or program which provides some service to clients.

Server Side Includes. An early technology for implementing dynamic pages.

Servlet. A Java technology which enables developers to program snippets of code which are executed when a Web server is accessed.

Session. A series of interactions with a Web page or Web site.

Session beans. Enterprise JavaBeans that embody some business logic.

Session tracking. The process of keeping track of data generated during a session with a Web site.

Shim. Another name for a hack.

Shopping agent. An agent that carries out some shopping task such as finding the cheapest price for a book.

Shopping cart. An area of memory used to contain items bought when accessing an e-tailing Web site.

Simple Mail Transfer Protocol. A protocol which is used for the delivery of e-mail across the Internet.

Skeleton. Code generated by a distributed object technology which is used to support access to server-based objects.

Smart card. A plastic card in which some magnetic media or processor is embedded and which can be used to contain security data.

SMTP. See Simple Mail Transfer Protocol.

SOAP. An XML-based standard used for communication between commuters.

Socket. The combination of IP address and port number which is used in the transfer of Internet data.

Software agent. An agent which carries out some software-related task such as informing a user when a software update has occurred.

Space. A collection of tuples maintained by a JavaSpaces-based system.

Spam. Unsolicited e-mail which is sent to large numbers of Internet users.

Spider. An agent which traverses the Internet gathering information used by search engines.

Spoofing. Used to describe the process whereby a computer or a user pretends to be another trusted computer or user in order to gain unauthorised access to a network.

SQL. See Structured Query Language.

SSL. See Secure Sockets Layer.

Startup file. A file which is read and whose elements are executed when a computer starts up. Often these files are the target for viruses.

Stateless server. A server which does not keep track of data generated by a transaction.

Status line. The line at the bottom of a browser window which contains text messages.

Stealth virus. A virus which hides itself by modifying operating system utilities which could be used to detect it.

Stored procedure. The SQL version of a subroutine.

Structured Query Language. A simple language used to access a relational database.

Stub. Code generated by a distributed object technology which is used to support client access to remote objects.

Supply chain. The set of links which join together a number of enterprises who engage in some commercial activity such as producing some manufactured good.

Symmetric key. A key used by both parties in a cryptographic scheme.

Synchronous message passing. Communication which has to occur in a predefined order.

Table lock. A lock applied to a table of a relational database.

Tag. Text which encloses some information in a document expressed using a markup language.

TCP. See Transfer Control Protocol.

TCP/IP. The collective name for the suite of protocols which the Internet is based on.

TFTP. See Trivial File Transfer Protocol.

Thin client. A client which contains a small amount of code.

Thread. An independent execution of some program code.

Threaded server. A server that processes a number of concurrent requests from users.

Three-tier architecture. An architecture which is used for distributed applications; one tier is used for the human-computer interface, a second tier for business objects and a third tier for database access.

Time service. An internal service which coordinates the clocks of a number of computers in a distributed system.

TP monitor. Software which manages the concurrent access to stored data.

Trader service. A yellow pages service found within CORBA which provides facilities for objects to advertise their services.

Transaction. A number of operations which when applied to a database transform the database into another state.

Transaction service. An internal service which ensures that transactions are correctly applied to stored data.

Transfer Control Protocol. A protocol which forms part of the Internet protocol suite.

Trigger. Processing that is invoked when a particular event associated with a relational database occurs.

Trivial File Transfer Protocol. A rudimentary protocol used for the transfer of files in the Internet.

Trojan horse. A virus which masquerades as some other program or is embedded in another program.

Trust brokerage. The provision of some security service using the Internet.

Tuple. A single item of data maintained by a JavaSpaces-based system.

Two-tier architecture. An architecture which is used for distributed applications. One tier is used for processing and human–computer interaction and the other for database access.

Ubiquitous computing. A future vision of distributed computing where computers can be found anywhere including being embedded in bodies and being sewn into clothes.

Uniform Resource Locator.   A string which uniquely identifies a resource, for example a Web page, on the World Wide Web.

Unmarshalling.   The process of converting data sent over the Internet to a form which can be used by the computer to which it has been sent.

Update agent.   An agent which informs the user when some change occurs, for example the content of a Web page changing.

URL.   See Uniform Resource Locator.

URL rewriting.   A technique used to implement state in a Web server. It involves augmenting a URL with extra information which details previous interactions with the server.

Validating parser.   A parser which carries out an extensive set of checks on a document defined in XML.

Vector graphic.   A picture which is expressed in a form which involves defining drawing instructions.

Vertical fragmentation.   Where a table in a relational database is split up by partitioning it over columns.

Virus.   A program which carries out some malicious act such as deleting important files.

Wait-for graph.   A data structure which is used to detect deadlocks.

WAP.   See Wireless Application Protocol.

Warez.   Pirated software for which the security functions have been disabled.

Web browser.   A program which allows a user to examine Web documents.

Web development agent.   An agent which carries out some task associated with the development of a Web site, for example notifying a webmaster when a link is dead.

Web page.   A file containing HTML code.

Web publishing system.   A Web-based system that administers the publication of a number of documents in a number of formats.

Web server.   A computer or program which dispenses Web pages to clients running browsers.

Web site.   A collection of Web pages devoted to some common purpose such as e-tailing a collection of products.

Webmaster.   The member of staff responsible for the maintenance of a Web site.

Wide Area Information System.   A now defunct information service that was found on the Internet.

Wireless Application Protocol.   A protocol used for communicating between mobile devices such as portable phones and Web servers.

Wireless Markup Language.   A markup language associated with the Wireless Application Protocol.

WML.   See Wireless Markup Language.

World Wide Web.   The total collection of Web sites hosted by the Internet.

Write-back cache.   Another name for a write-forward cache.

Write-forward cache.   A cache which contains dynamically changing data.

XML.   See Extensible Markup Language.

XSL.   A language for specifying the transformations that will occur on some XML source.

Index

IMPORTANT: READ CAREFULLY

WARNING: BY OPENING THE PACKAGE YOU AGREE TO BE BOUND BY THE TERMS OF THE LICENCE AGREEMENT BELOW.

This is a legally binding agreement between You (the user or purchaser) and Pearson Education Limited. By retaining this licence, any software media or accompanying written materials or carrying out any of the permitted activities You agree to be bound by the terms of the licence agreement below.

If You do not agree to these terms then promptly return the entire publication (this licence and all software, written materials, packaging and any other components received with it) with Your sales receipt to Your supplier for a full refund.

SINGLE USER LICENCE AGREEMENT

❏ YOU ARE PERMITTED TO:

- Use (load into temporary memory or permanent storage) a single copy of the software on only one computer at a time. If this computer is linked to a network then the software may only be installed in a manner such that it is not accessible to other machines on the network.

- Make one copy of the software solely for backup purposes or copy it to a single hard disk, provided you keep the original solely for back up purposes.

- Transfer the software from one computer to another provided that you only use it on one computer at a time.

❏ YOU MAY NOT:

- Rent or lease the software or any part of the publication.

- Copy any part of the documentation, except where specifically indicated otherwise.

- Make copies of the software, other than for backup purposes.

- Reverse engineer, decompile or disassemble the software.

- Use the software on more than one computer at a time.

- Install the software on any networked computer in a way that could allow access to it from more than one machine on the network.

- Use the software in any way not specified above without the prior written consent of Pearson Education Limited.

ONE COPY ONLY

This licence is for a single user copy of the software

PEARSON EDUCATION LIMITED RESERVES THE RIGHT TO TERMINATE THIS LICENCE BY WRITTEN NOTICE AND TO TAKE ACTION TO RECOVER ANY DAMAGES SUFFERED BY PEARSON EDUCATION LIMITED IF YOU BREACH ANY PROVISION OF THIS AGREEMENT.

Pearson Education Limited owns the software You only own the disk on which the software is supplied.

LIMITED WARRANTY

Pearson Education Limited warrants that the diskette or CD rom on which the software is supplied are free from defects in materials and workmanship under normal use for ninety (90) days from the date You receive them. This warranty is limited to You and is not transferable. Pearson Education Limited does not warrant that the functions of the software meet Your requirements or that the media is compatible with any computer system on which it is used or that the operation of the software will be unlimited or error free.

You assume responsibility for selecting the software to achieve Your intended results and for the installation of, the use of and the results obtained from the software. The entire liability of Pearson Education Limited and its suppliers and your only remedy shall be replacement of the components that do not meet this warranty free of charge.

This limited warranty is void if any damage has resulted from accident, abuse, misapplication, service or modification by someone other than Pearson Education Limited. In no event shall Pearson Education Limited or its suppliers be liable for any damages whatsoever arising out of installation of the software, even if advised of the possibility of such damages. Pearson Education Limited will not be liable for any loss or damage of any nature suffered by any party as a result of reliance upon or reproduction of or any errors in the content of the publication.

Pearson Education Limited does not limit its liability for death or personal injury caused by its negligence.

This licence agreement shall be governed by and interpreted and construed in accordance with English law.